Seven Decisions when

Teaching Students

Donald Bligh
David Jaques
David Warren Piper

A EUTS Production
Exeter University Teaching Services
Devon, England

Exeter University Teaching Services:

One of the functions of EUTS is to provide information about teaching in Higher Education. One way to do this is by publications with a research emphasis.

The publications may also serve to arouse debate, and for this reason they may be controversial. Opinions expressed in its publications do not necessarily reflect the policies of EUTS nor the opinions of its members.

ISBN 0 905314 04 2

First Edition, 1975
Second Edition, Revised 1981

Printed and bound in Great Britain by
A. Wheaton & Co. Ltd., Exeter

PREFACE

This book was written in response to a need for a reference book on research into teaching "students". Particularly in the third world, there is no ready source of information on research and ideas relating to the wide range of educational decisions teachers have to take. Even in western countries research reports are widely scattered, not ready to hand. There is no way the average teacher can bring together the plethora of studies that have been published.

This book aims to provide information, to encourage academic discussion of teaching, to contribute to rational and informed educational decisions, to assist in professional and personal development, and to widen horizons. It is an attempt to provide a summary of research and ideas relevant to seven groups of decisions that often have to be taken by teachers. It is principally about methods, but it is *not* a "how to do it" book. It does not give advice; on the contrary, it presents information and assumes the freedom and ability of the academic to make up his own mind and to apply the information and ideas to his own circumstances. For example when an issue is known to be coming up at a staff meeting, academics could at least get an entrée to the relevant research by referring to this book and possibly then follow it up in greater detail elsewhere.

It is intended to complement the reader's own experience. Of course, all books require interpretation in the light of personal experience and consequently say different things to different people; but education is a field in which expertise varies widely. Where there are contrasting interpretations or a mismatch in experience, there is a place for further enquiry.

The need for experience before knowing how to apply the research findings and general principles in this book, means that it is not a book for beginners. Nonetheless senior staff could use it as a spring-board for informal discussion of educational issues with those newer to teaching. If so, a page and a half will often be as much as should be considered at a time. It is not intended as a book to be read in large chunks.

This book has an international aspect. I make no apology, first because it has had an international readership (the first edition sold in over 40 countries); and secondly because the pursuit of learning, is, and ought to be, an international activity. Furthermore the similarities in the ways students are taught in different countries are very great. Consequently the relevance of educational research crosses international boundaries more easily at the post-secondary level than is often supposed.

In my opinion the most important decisions in post-secondary education today are not being taken in the west, but in the world's developing nations. Their minds are the most powerful emergent resources in the world, and unlike oil, they are regenerative. If, as seems possible, the nations of Asia will soon be the most influential, the attitudes towards authority, enquiry and criticism encouraged by their pattern of education may have far reaching effects on human history. For this reason I have tried to include research from developing countries when appropriate but, perhaps inevitably, there is an emphasis upon British and American sources.

Since the first edition there has been a shift away from the psychometric tradition towards detailed participant observation and description. The approach in this book is neither. It is a contribution to picture building (see pages 107 and 232). That is to say, it attempts to give a picture by summarising, or giving representative samples of evidence, knowledge and ideas on a topic. Consequently, although most chapters have been updated since the first edition, I have not substituted new research for old where my interpretation of the overall picture remains the same. In education the latest research is not necessarily the best, because much of it does not, like science, build upon previous findings.

While the contrasting styles of the authors partly reflect the topics considered, they may reflect different approaches to the study of education which may also be worth discussion. David Jaques has been chiefly responsible for Chapter 4 and David Warren Piper has contributed Chapter 6 from his experience in organising courses for senior academic and administrative university staff.

In normal print this book would be well over 700 pages. In the readers' interests we have attempted to produce it cheaply and in a compact form. We must beg some tolerance if, in consequence, some readers find the style of presentation displeasing.

Its production would have been impossible without secretarial help from Angela Cooper, June Clark and Ros Webber. A particular word of thanks goes to Alan Wakelam who designed the front cover and has given much valuable advice.

Donald Bligh
December 1981

CONTENTS

CHAPTER 1: Justifying Decisions in Teaching

CHAPTER 2: Assessment of Students

CHAPTER 3: Selection methods and students' circumstances

CHAPTER 4: Organising the content of the curriculum

CHAPTER 5: Teaching methods

CHAPTER 6: The Management of a Course. Some Analytic Models

CHAPTER 7: Evaluation and the Development of Teaching

CHAPTER 1

I. What is the place of objectives?

II. Constraints & Limitations of the model

III. How are objectives specified?

IV. Attempts to justify aims

CHAPTER 1: Justifying Decisions in Teaching

I What is the place of objectives?

Teaching consists of taking, and acting upon, decisions. By "decisions" I include not only the big decisions of policy, planning courses and preparation of teaching, but the almost unconscious immediate practical decisions that are taken from moment to moment in the classroom itself.

Methods and techniques are tools. Like other tools they should be used for specific purposes, or to achieve specific objectives. Imagine a surgeon who chooses a tool, say a 'swab', only then decides that he needs to make an incision, and continues to use the swab for this purpose for his entire career. It is doubtful whether he would achieve very much.

Yet this is the *logic* used by some of the most intelligent people in the world, not about matters with which they are unfamiliar, but about their everyday job. Their methods are decided before their objectives. For example, university professors frequently decide the methods to assess student achievement before deciding what achievement is to be assessed. In the same way teaching methods are often controlled by architects who build inflexible lecture theatres, administrators who make timetables and the professors who decide the size of the classes, before knowing what is to be achieved within these constraints.

Thus there is a logical precedence in which certain kinds of decisions need to be taken. This is developed further in an extremely simplified form in Figure 1.1. Although the reader will have no difficulty in seeing the many limitations of this model, it draws attention to some neglected principles and partially reflects the plan of this book.

(1) Is the first step to specify objectives?

(a) Arguments in favour
Objectives are statements of intended achievements. Normally they describe what students should be able to do at the end of the course that they could not do at the beginning. Because students can only be assessed by what they do, one school of thought (Bloom 1954) has argued that objectives should be expressed in behavioural terms. It is doubtful whether this is always possible. This controversy will be considered in a moment, but there are five logical reasons (their denial results in self-contradiction) why the method of first specifying objectives should be accepted. Unless we know what we want the students to achieve:

(i) we cannot assess whether they have achieved it, (Design of Assessment),

(ii) we cannot select students most likely to achieve it, (Student Selection Criteria),

Figure 1.1: Simplified model of the decision order in course planning.

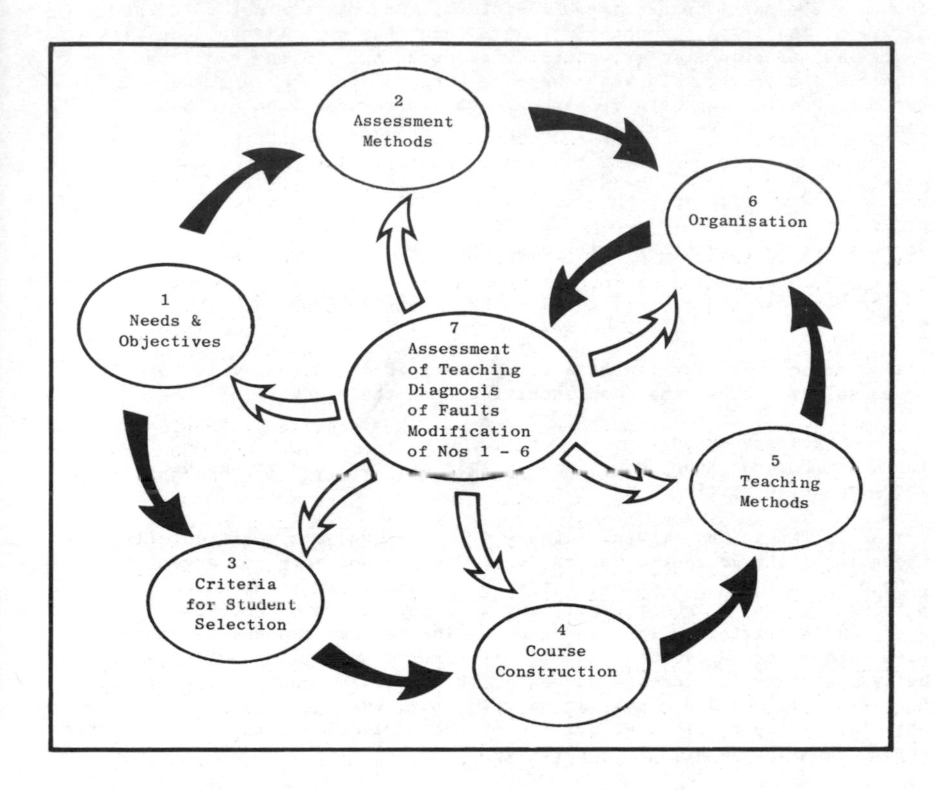

(iii) we cannot decide what to teach so that they achieve it, nor can we decide the best order in which to teach it (Syllabus Construction),

(iv) we cannot choose the best way to achieve it (Teaching Methods) and

(v) we will be limited in testing the effectiveness of our teaching (Assessment of Teaching).

Four further advantages may also be mentioned.

(vi) If we want students to achieve something, or strive towards it, they are most likely to do so if they know what it is; yet it is quite common for courses in Higher Education to be like a steeple-chase in which the participants are blindfolded. Runners are not told the nature of the track, except its length, and they know little about its fences and other obstacles, except their spacing. In the same way students are rarely told what they are supposed to be able to do by the end of academic courses, although they have some idea of the length of the course and the time of examinations.

(vii) The analysis of objectives can reveal assumptions and omissions and thereby provide foci for discussion on which cooperation between staff and with students depends. This is very pertinent in countries where there is student disquiet over courses.

(viii) Students can monitor their own progress thorughout a course; and

(ix) objectives make teachers think about what students will have to do as skills, rather than concentrating upon their own role.

(b) Arguments against

There are however some objections to this approach and it has become fashionable to criticise it.

(i) Intrinsic Objectives. There are some subjects, particularly those involving aesthetic values, where one is not only concerned with an end product of the course, but with certain activities that are intrinsic to it. Thus the military metaphor of the objectives approach is criticised for seeing education only as a means to something else rather than as valuable in itself. For exmaple, it would seem to be a good thing if students can enjoy their post-secondary education. Most teachers would probably agree with this, but few regard it as an objective which requires effort from them, particularly in those countries where education is highly competitive.

It is true that the objectives model seems to fit vocational courses better than those in which people claim to study the subject 'for its own sake', but it is quite possible to have intrinsic objectives like "the manifestation of students' enjoyment". An objective is a product; but not necessarily and end product.

(ii) Unobservable Objectives. Sometimes what we want our students to achieve is not observable. For example, when teaching Industrial Management, Literature or Clinical Medicine, teachers may be concerned with the development of certain attitudes. If these are observable at all, they are not observable in the same way for all students, so it would not be possible to have a standard form of assessment for them.

This is an objection to the narrowest behaviourist approach to objectives and to the rigid specification of methods of assessment. It is not an argument against specifying objectives at all, nor against stating them in behavioural terms so far as this is possible.

(iii) Various Manifestations. Objectives could be too varied to specify. In Business Studies, Teacher Training, Medicine and Management, the teacher is concerned with developing students' inter-personal skills. But there is no one sign of good personal relationships.

This is not an objection against the principle of stating objectives, but it is a very practical limitation on the extent to which detailed planning is possible.

(iv) Modification of Objectives. It may be necessary to modify objectives as the course proceeds. This may appear to be an objection to the model presented in Figure 1.1 because not all objectives can be specifired at the beginning and if they would it would imply that the course is inflexible and never modified to suit students' needs. It is of course true that intermediate and new terminal objectives will become apparent during a course, but this is recognised under (7) diagnosis and modification of Nos. (1) - (6). The belief that you should know what you are doing before you try to do it, does not imply that you can never change your mind.

None of these objections is a 'knock down' argument against the need for teachers to state clearly what they are trying to get their students to do, but they do show that it may be very difficult and there may come a point when the advantages do not repay the effort. Practical difficulties in the use of objectives to evaluate teaching are considered on page

In spite of the objections, when writing this book, it seemed worth finding out how far university teachers do make their intentions explicit. We cannot claim that our survey was large, but we tried to include as many countries, subjects and types of institutions as possible. Although the vast majority of teachers do not appear to have specified what they are trying to do, some have done so in considerable detail to the obvious benefit of their students.

(2) Assessment of students presupposes objectives

We have already seen that professors may be tempted to decide the methods by which students should be assessed before deciding what achievement is to be tested. If teaching is then geared towards success in examinations, the course provided could fail to fulfil its true purpose. This illogical order of decision making may be the result of accepting methods that have always been used in the past and not considering them. It may be because it is easier to imitate examples of examination papers that already exist than to design a course from first principles. For example, African and Asian university courses have frequently been inappropriately copied from an American or European prototype.

Some readers may be surprised that decisions on the methods of assessment should be taken so early. This decision should be distinguished from test construction. It could be that some courses should be modified as they proceed, so that examinations, or other tests, can only be set once the course has begun. Nevertheless decisions on the appropriate *method* of assessment should be taken before students apply for the course.

(3) The selection of students presupposes objectives

In many cases students are not selected for their courses; but if they are, the criteria should normally depend upon the talents and skills required to achieve the course objectives. Hence the specification of objectives should precede decisions on selection criteria.

If doctors and social workers require acceptable personalities, it will be no good selecting students who only have sound academic qualifications, however valuable or prestigious these may be. The specification of objectives is helpful to decide which talents are desirable and which are essential. Perhaps essential skills that are difficult to teach should be rated more highly than others at the time of selection.

(4) To decide curriculum content requires clear objectives and student selection criteria

The differences between the abilities students should have when they complete the course and those they have when they arrive, are the abilities that should be learned. These differences are the students' achievements during the course. Roughly speaking, 'objectives' minus 'selection criteria' equal the course 'content' or 'syllabus'. This is worth remembering when academic subjects are taught in water-tight compartments, because the overall objectives are then frequently forgotten. For example in Medicine, Agriculture, or Engineering, it may be important for the student to relate and apply his knowledge from various sub-disciplines. It may also be important to know how to get on with other people. Teaching these skills is easily omitted beause they are not part of any one academic subject. It will be seen later that there is reason to suppose these objectives are neglected in nearly all countries at every stage of decision-making. The content of courses is too narrowly conceived as a body of knowledge. Thinking and feeling do not receive the attention they deserve.

(5) Deciding teaching methods presupposes teaching content

Because the selection of teaching methods will depend upon what is to be taught, selection can only be made after the syllabus has been constructed. Learning consists of many different psychological processes which are best achieved by different methods. In other words the decision to use a certain teaching method should be strongly influenced by the psychological process required, not by whether the subject is literature or physics or any other, except insofar as these may have different psychological objectives.

(6) Course administration

The administration of post-secondary education will not be dealt with in detail here. The important principle to be emphasised here is that educational administration should serve the teaching process and not the other way round as so often happens. Superficially one might suppose that because administration must exist before courses can be established, administration should appear at the beginning of the sequence depicted in Figure 1.1. Yet the priority of educational consideration over administrative ones is worth making explicit because it draws attention to the need for college and departmental administrations to adjust their organisation once courses have been established. When this requires giving away power, it may be as difficult in educational contexts as in the politics of a nation.

(7) Decisions on evaluation of teachers and teaching

Just as the method for assessing students depends upon what students are to achieve, so the method used to assess teachers' techniques will depend upon the techniques they have used. Decisions on the evaluation of teaching therefore cannot come before general decisions on teaching methods.

It is clear that once an evaluation of any of the decisions categorised under Nos. (1) - (6) has been made, a diagnosis of difficulties may be necessary. This in turn may lead to a modification of some or all of the decisions made. Thus in Figure 1.1 further loop-lines may be drawn ad infinitum from 7 to any of the previous decisions.

II Constraints & limitations of the model

The decisions so far considered are those that are the direct concern of the individual teacher. Like many models, the purpose of Figure 1.1 is to set a simple framework for thinking by breaking down a very complex set of interacting processes. In common with most models it has limitations arising from this simplification.

The teacher is subject to all kinds of constraints and pressures. He must work within his departmental, institutional and national policy (see Chapter 6). He is subject to financial constraints. His objectives are unlikely to be the same as those of his colleagues with whom he must work. Indeed, when colleagues work together to define objectives, they soon find that their conception of their subject is entirely different (Lewis 1971). Academic disciplines are not the established bodies of knowledge we commonly assume. Even supposing colleagues agree, they usually have to work within both the framework of available resources, such as textbooks and timetables, and established practices, including examinations and professional requirements.

For example, many medical courses first require the student to endure two or three years of preclinical study (without any contact with patients) and only to integrate his knowledge and apply it to real living patients later. Yet in some universities (e.g. McMaster) the medical curriculum centres upon a series of pathological problems, so that the theoretical subjects and their application are integrated from the beginning. We may call these the discipline-based and problem-centred approaches. Although the teachers using the two approaches may have precisely the same objectives, an individual teacher working under one system would not be free to change to the other.

In many countries there are social and political pressures for example towards an expansion or contraction of student numbers, which will influence the selection, teaching and assessment methods that are feasible. In the autumn of 1973, the Spanish government suddenly delayed the start of the academic year by one term on grounds of administrative convenience. A new University in Mexico City is built in six campuses each with its own law school. Such factors impinge upon the decisions of all teachers and they are powerless to change them.

In India there are 47 major universities to which several hundred affiliated colleges are attached. The major or central universities fix the examinations and mark them. Teachers in the affiliated colleges may wish to introduce some innovation in the curriculum and be well placed to do so, but be restricted by the examination requirements of the central universities. Examiners in the central universities are loathe to change the system for fear of losing the fees which they obtain for marking several thousand examination scripts submitted by the affiliated colleges. There is conflict here between the maintenance and comparability of standards and the stifling of individual enterprise. This could be overcome if the central universities were willing to accept material submitted and ratified by the affiliated colleges. But not all such conflicts have an easy solution.

Examples of external constraints upon the teacher modifying the applicability of the model in Figure 1.1 could be multiplied indefinitely. There are also some internal limitations. The model appears to describe a predictable dependability of each decision upon a previous one. But this predictability is not absolute. For example, although students can be selected as individuals on the basis of their qualifications, they interact in an unpredictable way at college and become a group. The influence of groups, both on their own members and on others, are quite different from the influence of individuals.

Nevertheless if methods and techniques in post-secondary education are to be rational at all, there must be some rationale. Whatever the shortcomings of the model, it is difficult to deny the argument that before a teacher tries to achieve something with his students he should know what it is. This implies the need to state objectives. Therefore if he accepts the model with all its limitations the next question is how to specify objectives.

III How are objectives specified?

There are two broad approaches. One is to start with general aims, and gradually make them more precise. The other, which is particularly appropriate when training students for a specific vocation, is to carry out a skills analysis of the job, then classify the skills into groups so that the course content can easily be constructed from them.

(1) You can work from general aims to specific objectives

The first approach is more appropriate with courses that are broadly educational rather than concerned with vocational training.

Baume and Jones (1974) recommend four broad stages:

(a) State the general course aim
The first stage is to prepare a brief statement of the overall course aim or objective in about 100 words. This will be rather a general statement but it should say what the students should be able to do at the end of the course. For example, it could include a phrase such as 'The student will be able to use given principles to solve a given problem'.

But this statement is too vague as it stands. Obviously the principles and problems should be specified.

(b) List manifestations of achieving the aim
Therefore the second stage consists of listing a large number of skills which, taken together, will be recognised as involving the attainment of the course aim and overall objectives. The list should be long and the examples specific. But if it is obviously impossible to specify all the conditions in which this achievement could be observable, representative examples can be listed. For example, if it is one of the aims of the course that 'students should be able to think critically', this could include writing three specific criticisms of a theory. If in doubt, a teacher should add to the list because it can always be pruned later. The difficulty is that it can become too long and unwieldy.

(c) Classify these examples
Therefore the third stage involves classifying the examples to produce a slightly more general sample of what students should be able to do. For example, general descriptions of how critical thought is displayed include:
"Distinguishes facts and opinions",
"Draws valid conclusions from given information or facts",
"States assumptions underlying influence and conclusions",
"Recognises the limitations of given data".

(d) Derive further examples from the classification.
Baume and Jones say that component objectives not previously listed can be derived from these major ones. For example, there may be conclusions the student should be able to draw apart from those listed at the second stage.

If the objectives are well specified, the later task of preparing a syllabus diminishes dramatically, not only because the content of the course is determined, but because there is sometimes an evident structure (such as a hierarchy or sequence) which will need to be reflected in the organisation.

Column 2 of Figure 1.2 illustrates this. It is an extract from a course plan in mechanical engineering.

Another example might be the case of a history teacher who had as a general aim (Stage 1) that students should be able to interpret historical events. When he tried to list specific examples (Stage 2) such as explaining why Hitler invaded the Soviet Union in 1941, he found that 'interpretation of this event involved many different skills'. These may be generalised (in terms of Stage 3) as the ability to ask productive questions, to isolate causal factors, to predict 'what would have happened if....?', to relate Hitler's ideas to previous events and his possible strategy, to find information in documents and so on. When these composite skills are distinguished, as in Figure 2, it is a short step to realise that they require different methods of teaching and assessment, and that part of a teacher's job is to know where each student is strong and weak. Many of these objectives from Stage 3 may be applicable (Stage 4) to other events, such as Churchill's decision to bomb German cities. The kind of classification adopted in Stage 3 will depend on the teacher's particular purposes.

Figure 1.2

Preparation of Objectives in Relation to Students' Previous Knowledge, Methods of Assessment and Teaching Methods (from Bligh (ed), 1973(b).)

(1) Objectives	(2) Previous knowledge and abilities reqd.	(3) Methods of assessment	(4) Teaching Methods
Students will be able to: (a) State the Newtonian viscosity law	Higher School Certificate. Applied Maths.	Written exam. (requiring the law to be stated)	Lecture or Private Study
(b) Apply the law to steady fully devel-oped flows	Objective (a)	Continuous assessment using problems requiring application of the law	Private study using problem work sheets; + group tutorials
(c) Calculate the profiles of velocity and shear	Objective (b)	Continuous assessment using problems requiring calculation as part of case	Private study using problem work sheets; + group tutorials

The need to match teaching and assessment methods to objectives was argued on page 2. This tabular technique is one way to do it. Failure to match them produces conflicts (e.g. between students' aim that they are favourably assessed and the objectives of the course. (See student tactics, page 51.)

Column (2) can provide information on how to sequence a course (see page 9.)

Bloom has claimed that all educational objectives can be classified as 'cognitive', (to do with information) 'affective' (to do with attitudes, values and emotions), or 'psychomotor' (to do with bodily movements like setting up apparatus).

He thought that cognitive objectives form a hierarchy in which the student must achieve the lower objectives before he can achieve the higher ones. These range from simple acquisition of information through understanding, applying principles, analysis and synthesis to evaluation. In elementary and secondary education teachers may only be concerned with lower levels; but in higher education, learning, teaching and assessment of skills at all levels are required.

Bloom later suggested a similar hierarchy for affective objectives from receiving, responding to and accepting ideas, to organising them in a philosophy of life and a total change of personality.

(2) Another method is to analyse skills

The second approach to defining objectives is most likely to be used in clinical medicine, agriculture, engineering and other vocational courses.

Mace defined a skill as "an ability to produce an intended effect with accuracy, speed and economy of action". With reference to these characteristics of a skilled worker, it is a good idea to analyse each technique chronologically, asking certain questions:

(a) What does he do? (i.e. analyse his actions as far as possible)
(b) What information does he need to know already?
(c) What information does he acquire at each stage?
(d) How does this information influence what he does?

Answers to (b) and (c) assist the teacher to fill in the second column of Figure 1.2. Using this approach, we may go through four stages similar to those when working from general aims to specific objectives:

Writing a general chronological statement of what the student should be able to do (e.g. examine a patient)
List examples of the skills
Then classify them. (e.g. taking the patient's history etc.)
Lastly, we may see how other skills fit into this classification.

These two approaches raise further questions which will be considered in the next section. If objectives are to be derived from general aims, does post-secondary education have aims that are distinct from those of primary and secondary education? If so, institutions for post-secondary education may be of fundamentally different character to those associated with schooling. There are also questions concerned with the justification of these aims.

IV Attempts to justify aims

If the proponents of the objectives approach argue that objectives should be justified in terms of more general ones, and that general objectives may be justified in so far as they achieve educational aims, how are the aims justified? Ideally this series of justifications of objectives and aims will continue in a regress until they are based upon some ultimate values or some philosophy of life. The aims become based upon policies, principles and philosophies that are progressively more general. Unfortunately most teachers do not have such a coherent set of values. Such coherence has been beyond most philosophers too.

(1) Policies, principles and philosophies

(a) Policies
Although the literature on this subject has been prolific and mostly unclear, it is sometimes possible to discern three stages on the regress.

Firstly course aims could be justified in terms of general statements of policy. These could be made by the individual teacher, his course team, his department, his college, a professional institution, the Ministry of Education or any responsible organisation. Policy statements express values more general than course aims without being fundamental educational principles. For example, the Robbins Report in Britain stated that the purposes of Higher Education are

(i) to promote the powers of the mind,

(ii) to instruct in skills suitable to play a part in the general division of labour,

(iii) to transmit a common culture, and

(iv) to advance learning.

Most teachers in post-secondary education could claim that their courses implement one or more of these statements of policy. Yet the statements each beg further value questions - "What mental powers, Can't the powers of the mind be used for evil as well as good? Should Higher Education not be used for bridging divisions of labour and for continually creating a new culture? And why a 'common' culture? Is not diversity and breadth to be encouraged? Whose learning is to be advanced - an elite of researchers' or the common man's - and what does it mean to advance it?"

(b) Dimensions of disagreements about principles
Behind the policies and the questions they beg, lie educational principles.

Some of these, such as the need to teach what is true and not falsehoods, are often assumed or not explicit. Some, such as the need to make formal education as enjoyable as possible, are sometimes disputed. Others, such as the need to help the students in preference to the teachers or the government, are sometimes unrecognised, ignored or forgotten.

Obviously there are many value questions on which academic staff may disagree, but it is worth picking out three which constantly recur. They are disagreements of emphasis in balancing conflicting principles rather than strict alternatives. Hence they are dimensions of disagreement.

(i) Breadth versus depth

The first disagreement is the extent to which post-secondary education should be general or specialised. Should one aim for 'breadth' or 'depth'? For example, while some academics argue that to pursue general knowledge is to remain superficial and that only the study of a specialist subject in depth can generate the thoroughness and powers of thought of a well disciplined mind, Cardinal Newman (1959) has argued that, as knowledge becomes more specialised and specific, it progressively ceases to be generalisable, until ultimately it is totally useless because, being so specific, it is totally inapplicable to anything else.

(ii) Vocational versus non-vocational

The second dimension is the extent to which post-secondary courses should be vocational or non-vocational. While students in many countries have cried out for some vocational relevance, some educationalists have argued that when learning becomes solely directed towards one type of work it becomes "training", not "education" at all.

(iii) Élitism versus Egalitarianism

A third dimension of disagreement is the extent to which Higher Education should be limited to an elite or be available to all. In USA colleges have an open door and half the young adult population goes to college. In most western countries over 20% of the appropriate age group enter Higher Education, while in Britain's highly selective system it has recently fallen to 12%. In several countries while financial restraint is making full-time post-secondary education more élitist, the development of distance teaching methods, such as radio, television and carefully prepared texts, is extending public involvement.

When considering these dimensions of disagreement, and other value questions on which academics could disagree, the arguments could depend upon contrasting philosophies of education, if not philosophies of life. It is obviously beyond the scope of this book to review all philosophies on which differences in academic opinion might be based.

(c) Philosophies with intrinsic and extrinsic values

However, insofar as it is the function of post-secondary education to seek and transmit knowledge, it may be useful to highlight two contrasting ultimate values with regard to knowledge.

On one philosophy knowledge is valuable in itself. Academics talk about studying a subject for its own sake and of knowledge being its own reward. On the second philosophy, knowledge is valuable insofar as it is useful. On this view the justifications for academic pursuits are not to be found within oneself, but in the world outside the seat of learning.

The philosophies differ over whether knowledge has an intrinsic or an extrinsic value; it may have both. Is education valuable in itself, or is it only to be valued for its contribution to other goals that are valued, such as career advancement for the individual or economic development of the state? Is it an end, or a means?

Apart from the fact that vocational courses are not normally designed as ends in themselves, either of these 'ultimate' values could be used to justify positions taken on the three dimensions of disagreement just mentioned. One could argue that a general education, or a highly specialised one is more 'useful' than the other. Similarly, either could be regarded as an end in itself. For example a highly specialised course in an abstruse aspect of physics could be justified in terms of its useful application in industry, or as an intrinsically valuable mental discipline for its students. A value for knowledge as an end in itself is often associated with an elitist view of Higher Education because most governments cannot afford to let everyone spend time and money acquiring useless knowledge; but there is no logical contradiction in believing that everyone should be allowed to enjoy the pursuits of higher learning.

(2) Two examples

Let us consider two views of a university in the light of these values.

(a) Newman's idea of a university

Cardinal Newman believed that the function of a university is to give a general, non-vocational education as an end in itself to an elite of the population. On his view Higher Education is for the refinement of gentlemen. For Newman intellectual excellence increases with the generalisability, and possibly the abstractness of the principles taught. Not everyone can aspire to abstract thinking, and consequently "intellectual excellence" should be distinguished from "the pursuit of excellence" which is concerned with raising educational standards in general to the limits of each individual's ability.

Much of Newman's writing advocates what he calls a liberal education. That is one that is free from (libre free) the narrowness and constraints of professional education. He valued scholarship highly, but not empricial research. In saying that scholarship and the pursuit of learning should be 'disinterested' from professional and other vested interests, he appealed to the canons of objectivity and other qualities of mind which form the platform for his idea of a university.

It may be objected that as the pursuit of learning becomes dissociated from the practical and professional considerations, it becomes esoteric and retreats into an ivory tower. This objection assumes a principle of utility - usefulness to society - which Newman wanted to reject, but could not entirely escape. In a celebrated passage he relents saying "If then a practical end must be assigned to a university course, I say it is that of training good members of society ..... a university training aims at raising the intellectual tone of society, at cultivating the public mind, at purifying the national taste, at supplying true principles to popular enthusiasm and fixed aims to popular aspirations, at giving enlargement and sobriety to the ideas of the age, at facilitating the exercise of political power, and refining the intercourse of private life. It is the education which gives the man a clear conscious view of his opinions and judgements, a truth in developing them, and eloquence in expressing them and a force in urging them. It teaches him to see things as they are, to go right to the point, to disentangle a skein of thought, to detect what is sophistical, and to discard what is irrelevant."

In modern language we would say that these are cognitive aims. In the same passage he went on to list many that are social. A university education shows a man "How to accommodate himself to others, how to throw himself into their state of mind, how to bring before them his own, how to influence them, how to come to an understanding with them, how to bear with them. He is at home in any society, he has common ground with every class; he knows when to speak and when to be silent; he is able to converse, he is able to listen; he can ask a question pertinently, and can gain a lesson seasonably, when he has nothing to impart himself; he is ever ready yet never in the way; he is a pleasant companion, and a comrade you can depend upon; he knows when to be serious and when to trifle, and he has a sure tact which enables him to trifle with gracefulness and to be serious with effect."

These sentiments would be echoed in many an arts faculty today. They place a strong emphasis upon powers of thought and cultivated conversation. Interestingly many academics today also shift from intrinsic to utilitarian justifications when once seemingly esoteric research suddenly became useful.

(b) Utilitarian discovery and dissemination

A complementary view emphasises specialist research which can be directly useful to all members of society. Hence it advocates extrinsic utilitarian and egalitarian values. It does not necessarily lead to a specialist vocational education, but is likely to do so. According to this view there is a need for some institutions in some society to be finding out new knowledge, to be teaching it and passing it on to others for application. Not all institutions in post-secondary education need be of this kind but research should be one identifying characteristic of universities.

This view is based upon two features of human beings, their mental ability and their conscious desires. In particular they are able to anticipate and reason. By this means they are able to control their environment. "Anticipation" includes prediction, such as scientific generalisations, as well as prescriptions for what ought to be done. These embody science and morals respectively. Even if some powers of anticipation and reason develop naturally in man, it is evident that they are enhanced by teaching and learning.

It is arguable that the cultivation of anticipation and reason ought to be enhanced. Men satisfy their wants, needs and desires, by using anticipation based upon knowledge and ideas. Although the satisfaction of needs, wants and desires may not be the only good things, they are intrinsically good. Some, not now satisfied will require new knowledge for their satisfaction. This can be obtained as a result of discovery or dissemination. Thus one important condition to improve the world is to obtain new knowledge and new ideas. Another is to disseminate the knowledge that is available more widely. Discovery requires thought; dissemination requires understanding. Most education involves dissemination but the cultivation of discovery is often neglected. The definitive nature of universities is that they undertake both dissemination and discovery.

The needs of society undergo continual change. Societies need to adapt to this change and consequently require new knowledge; not any knowledge, but that which is related and hence, coheres. To relate knowledge is to think (which is not to assert the converse, that all thinking consists of relating knowledge.) Since this knowledge is required by persons other than those who discover it, there is a need to pass it on. Dissemination and discovery will need to keep pace with changing needs. With growing aspirations man increasingly needs to control his environment, and to monitor the effects of new technology on the general well-being of the community. The need to adapt has implications for the way educational institutions should be organised.

According to this view the discovery and dissemination of knowledge is an obligation upon all societies because, being influenced by their past history and cultural heritage as well as the levels of industrial, economic and social development, the needs of societies differ. It would be wrong to say that the research needs are the same in all societies. Nor is it easy for one society to do research for another. Similarly we should expect the content of post-secondary education to vary between societies. (For example it may be inappropriate for Asian societies to copy Western curricular.)

Thus, on this view, planned discovery, or "research", is fundamental to a changing society. It remains to be argued that research and dissemination should be combined in at least some institutions, mainly universities. New knowledge, and the ideas that frequently preceed it, are often developed by relating other ideas and knowledge in new ways. This frequently occurs when people with different ideas and knowledge talk to each other. It is most likely to occur if they can be brought together rather than separated either by physical distances or institutional barriers. When separated, the sharing and cross fertilisation of ideas are restricted. The generation of new ideas by bringing people together may best be organised if the institutions exist specifically for this purpose. Universities and research institutes are places of this kind.

The ability to generate new ideas and knowledge need not be left to chance; it can be developed by teaching. Research institutes do not have a formal teaching function; universities do. It therefore seems reasonable to suppose that universities should teach students how to generate knowledge and ideas. This includes research, but is more than research. Research institutes tend to be more restrictive in their methods and outlook by the adoption of specific problems apparently requiring personnel from a limited range of disciplines. While the universities may have this too, both discovery and dissemination are enhanced in an institution where members feel free to meet personnel from other faculties and to speculate along non-traditional lines.

(3) These justifications have implications for teachers

Although these two ideas of a university have striking contrasts, there are also remarkable similarities which have radical implications for teaching, not in principle, but in practice. They both lay a high premium on teaching students to think. Admittedly the reasons are different, but the implication that we use certain principles and techniques when teaching remain the same. These in turn influence the planning of curricula.

(a) The importance of discussion
On the second view the very existence of a university is justified by the opportunities for discussion it offers. On Newman's view a tutor only has his paternalistic influence through the discussion and sharing of ideas. Personal contact is the essence of the university.

The same might be said of other sectors of post-secondary education but notice that neither of the given arguments applies with the same force. The utilitarian argument is half based upon the need for research; and Newman's upon the need for an élite. Nonetheless the importance of discussion to develop powers of thought in all its forms is relevant across the whole of post-secondary education. Thought can be developed if focussed upon a carefully designed progression of problems.

(b) Problem solving is a major function of higher education
A problem-based education is readily applicable to routine vocational and non-vocational situations. It requires active learning and self direction of study skills. It fosters motivation by immediate feedback on the answers given by the student. It allows for individualised instruction, and reinforces memory of information by establishing a set of mental associations so that recall is increasingly facilitated with successive sets.

Students need to have genuine problems to solve. This contrasts with common practice. In physical sciences and engineering the problems students receive are often confined to artificial exercises to which there are right answers and right methods for arriving at them. The students do not experience an adventure of discovery; nor are they obliged to stretch their intellects to consider issues in the wider context of real life. Their role is to learn certain routine procedures by practice, and then to check that their thoughts conform to the established authorities. In lectures the teacher dispenses his authoritative wisdom and too often the students are expected to accept it uncritically.

I am not suggesting that teaching and assessment should not sometimes consist of routine problems, but they should not be these exclusively. We cannot expect our students to produce new ideas, or display responsibility or breadth of vision, if we teach by methods that continually require them to check their thoughts against old established ones.

(c) Research, scholarship and teaching should go together
Participation in a research project is an invaluable part of Higher Education. Similarly, seminars and discussion groups which reopen the questions being asked in research, help to make the latter more meaningful by sharpening its focus. The assumption that research is only a task for postgraduates should be challenged.

(d) New questions should be encouraged
Students should receive encouragement and praise for expressing ideas which are new to them. Numerous examples from the history of science could illustrate the value of encouraging students to dare to consider what appears ridiculous. Confidence is required to develop the kind of questioning that leads to new ideas.

New ideas first require a question. Too often, students are taught to find answers, not to ask questions. It is answers, not questions, that are sought in examinations. Too often tutors see their role as correcting students' ideas by offering criticism rather than encouraging students to think their ideas through for themselves by exploring their consequences. Tutors need an open mind to learn from their students. By this means teaching is a research activity.

(e) Teaching should foster associations of ideas
Although problems are solved through association of ideas, we select and examine students primarily on their factual knowledge. In practice, people from different disciplines do not come together and only rarely do they teach courses together. Newman's plea for a general education is implicitly rejected. Academics feel more strongly for the esteem of their speciality, than for the need to share ideas with others. Teachers need to have a disposition to seek what is good in students' ideas, not a disposition to find fault. Too often teaching is conceived as a process of criticism and correction. Criticism without appreciation stifles speculation, independence, originality and confidence.

Learning is seen as a competitive process rather than a co-operative one in which ideas are shared. We shall see that traditional methods of assessing students are partly to blame for this. Even academics are often not willing to venture ideas before they are 'proved', nor to admit to speculation when they speculate. Yet the common complaint against students is that they are too non-conformist. Their independence of mind disturbs their elders who have fixed ideas.

(f) University teaching necessitates tolerance

This fear of non-conformity highlights a further necessity of university teaching - tolerance. It is because universities are places where new ideas should be generated that they should be the forum for rational discussion. Particularly when there is more than one view opposed to one's own, more time should be spent in listening than in expressing one's own point of view.

The essence of Higher Education, in contrast to primary and secondary education, is that it should be a process in which people search together. Courses are too often conceived as predetermined paths rather than voyages of exploration. Without this, knowledge and ideas will not be evolutionary. The distinguishing feature of an academic mind is not the number of ideas it has absorbed, but its openness to consider more.

In other words, the distinguishing characteristic of universities necessitates an attitude of tolerance towards others. Student frustration is borne of intolerance. In terms of the distinctive function of the universities discussed here, increased participation by students in university affairs is a move in the right direction. Unfortunately this change has often been confined to participation in the political and administrative activities of the universities, rather than in the processes of teaching and learning.

CHAPTER 2: Assessment of Students

CHAPTER 2: Assessment of Students

A question that has to be answered by every course planner is 'How, if at all, should the students be assessed?' One of the purposes of this chapter is to challenge the worldwide complacency on the way students are assessed. This complacency has itself resulted in a lack of research in this subject. Most of the research that has been conducted has investigated newer methods, rather than the traditional methods which still predominate. This is reflected in the fact that much of the research is from North American and British sources; and further inspection shows that much of it is confined to medical subjects.

Yet other methods are widely used even though the proportion of marks allocated to them may be small. A small scale, but worldwide, survey was conducted for the purposes of this book. Replies showed that although almost every department uses written essay examinations, other methods, including objective tests, oral examinations, course work, practical work, and projects, dissertations or theses are frequently used to assess students.

The acceptance of an assessment method should depend first upon its validity - how far it assesses what it is intended to assess - and second, on its reliability - how far it does so consistently. To investigate the validity of a method of assessment therefore assumes some knowledge of its purpose.

I The purposes of assessment

After a review of the literature, Klug (1974) listed 32 purposes of assessment. Many of these may be classified into the following six groups in order of importance for the purpose of this chapter.

(1) To judge the level of achievement

It may be necessary to assess students' level of achievement at the end of their course. These assessments may be divided into 'survey tests' and 'mastery tests'. Survey tests assume there is a distribution of ability, and grades at a number of different levels are awarded to signify these. In mastery tests a simple pass/fail decision has to be made. These are more common in vocational courses where examiners simply have to decide whether or not a student is acceptable to the profession.

Like all other tests, achievement tests may also be divided into 'norm referenced' tests and 'criterion referenced' tests. Norm referenced tests are designed to test an individual's achievement in comparison with other individuals who have taken the same test. These examinations are in effect competitive. Criterion referenced tests are designed to assess an individual's achievement with respect to some criterion or standard of performance. There is a tendency for norm referenced tests and survey tests to go together. Criterion referenced and mastery tests also tend to go together because the question asked by the examiner is not 'how does this student compare with the others?' but, 'can this student do x, y and z?' But these types of test need not always be associated in this way.

These classifications refer to methods of grading; and since a method must be chosen for any test, we shall return to this issue later.

(2) To predict future behaviour

Assessments may be used to predict future performance. Driving tests are of this kind. Satisfactory assessments of this type are extremely difficult to design and take a long time to validate. Consequently most educational institutions do not even attempt to do either properly. After an extensive review of studies investigating the predictive validity of assessment in medicine, engineering, business studies, teaching, scientific research and other vocational and non-vocational courses in North America, Hoyt (1965) concluded that "The present evidence strongly suggests that college grades show little or no relationship to any measures of adult accomplishment". In England, Hudson (1966) has found that a very high proportion of scholars elected Fellows of the Royal Society for their distinguished contributions to research had at some time obtained a university degree with average or below average grades. He claims a similar finding for politicians of ministerial rank and High Court judges; but his evidence here is less convincing. It seems as if university examinations are better predictors for careers requiring high levels of verbal ability than those demanding other skills.

Reporting the career progress made by highly gifted students seven or eight years after they entered college, Watley (1968) found that differences did not appear to be due to scholastic ability. Other factors, such as parents' education, father's occupation, family income and so on, appeared to be more highly correlated.

In another study (Platz, McLintock, and Katz, 1959), although undergraduate grade point averages correlated reasonably well with postgraduate grades, they only had a chance correlation with staff predictions of the students' later contributions to science. Presumably, one or other of these measures must be wrong as a prediction of future performance, but both are commonly used. We shall see in the next chapter that school based examinations are poor predictors of university success. Investigations both in Europe and in North America comparing the grades given to student-teachers and ratings of their teaching ability given some years later, have shown low, and even negative, correlations.

In one sense these research findings are encouraging. In most societies, it would be undesirable if a grade given when young created a complete barrier to preferment in later life. Nevertheless employers and selection boards do, in fact, regard examinations at the age of 23 as predictive of performance even when the individual is more than twice that age. Pym (1969) considers that research in the UK and USA shows no association between achievement at university and subsequent careers. On the results of questionnaires administered to 400 engineers, he concluded that university education has no intrinsic advantage but provides the passport to better opportunities. Those without a degree suffer an increasing social handicap to promotion, achievement and self-realisation. When it is remembered that grades are frequently a cause, rather than a prediction, of later success, there is little room for confidence in their predictive power.

(3) To monitor students' progress

Intermittent assessments may be used to monitor students' progress. Haak (1960) devised a system for measuring students' improvement by using weekly objective tests. At the end of several weeks the most discriminating questions were selected to form a summary test. By comparing the scores for the summary test with the same questions from a weekly test and dividing the actual improvement by the possible improvement to give a percentage, Haak could gauge improvement, not from the beginning of the course, but since each of the weekly tests. He concluded that an 'Improvement Factor' can be identified which is unrelated to intelligence, knowledge at the beginning of the course, or competence in reading.

If standardised tests are developed through a course using the mean scores, their range, and measures of their power of discriminating between good and poor students, they can be used to monitor students' progress. At the Ecole Normale Superieure de St. Cloud, Crouzet and Ferenczi (1973) have developed a course for non-French speaking students which includes forming language classes of participants with the same level of knowledge. Standardised tests have then been designed which will enable the development of an individual profile for each student based on his achievement in comprehension and expression in both writing and speech.

Owing to the speed with which they can give feedback, computers can be programmed to mark objective tests and to provide useful comment on students' progress. They can summarise the results for a whole class, indicating which questions were found most difficult compared with students on previous courses, and which are best able to discriminate between good and poor students. But Groves (1968) has pointed out that the benefits of such technological innovation are wholly dependent upon the quality of the questions devised. Sullivan (1971) has used computer marking of multiple-choice tests as a diagnostic tool to remedy students' weaknesses before the final exam. He found that regular tests reduced examination nerves because teaching and learning were less examination dominated. He claims that more varied objectives may be assessed and less stress placed upon pure memory. He thought that multiple-choice tests were better for monitoring students' progress because, unlike the assessment of essays, the objective marking did not obscure students' weaknesses.

The use of assessments in this way is part of a teaching technique. Consequently, some consideration of these techniques will be made in Chapter 5.

(4) To motivate students

Assessment can also be used to motivate students to work. There is little doubt that it achieves this. Furthermore, it has the unique property that the motivation increases in power as the time of the assessment approaches, while motivation derived from inspiration generally fades with time. For example, there is evidence that students work longer hours in those years in which they have important examinations, than those in which they do not, and the frenzy of activity gets greater as the year proceeds (e.g. Thoday 1957).

Indeed, one criticism of many forms of assessment is that they over motivate students to the point of anxiety and stress. Still (1963) has plotted the incidence of psychiatric referrals month by month throughout the year and has demonstrated that they reach a peak in the month of May when the examinations occur.

It should not be inferred from this that examination performance is necessarily impaired. Indeed, Hallworth (1964) has correlated measures of anxiety and performance in both secondary school children and students, and has found a small but positive relationship in both cases. Hastings (1961) found that students who were more tense performed less well during the examinations; but the relationship was by no means linear.

Many highly tense students performed very well. Malleson (1959) has suggested that examinations are not only a test of academic ability but the ability to keep a cool head under a particular kind of stress. If this is true, it may be over simple. Atkinson and Litwin (1960) have shown that the drive to achieve may be very different from fear of failure, so that the stress experienced by different students may be of very different kinds. Still (1963) has pointed out that the stress bears no relation to students' intelligence or how hard they work.

Ryle and Lunghi (1968) have identified three types of problem student at the University of Sussex : A) Psychiatrically ill, academically adequate students with high neuroticism scores. These often require security and psychiatric treatment because they are disorganised by stress. B) Psychiatrically ill, academically failing students whose performance does not improve under stress. C) Psychiatrically well, academically failing students who, unlike the other groups, do poorly on performance tests but who show a high gain in stress conditions. These tend to be stable extraverts and need to be put under pressure if they are to make the best of their limited capacities.

The question remains, 'If students' stress is something to be avoided, either on humanitarian grounds or because it produces assessments which are invalid, what is to be done about it?' One set of answers would include improving the Student Health Service, making students come to terms with possible disaster by thinking about it (Barzun, 1946), the practice of relaxation and desensitisation (Kondas, 1967), group discussions before examinations (Hall, 1969) and improving staff/student relations.

Another approach is to change the methods of assessment. If course planners are to adopt this procedure, they will require some evidence before they decide which assessment methods cause the least tension. At one time it was assumed that the cause of students' stress was the concentration of crucial assessments at the end of the course. Assessment of work throughout the course was therefore regarded with favour. Subsequent enquiries have shown that far from reducing the amount of anxiety, tension is never reduced to satisfactory levels, and consequently staff/student relationships suffer to the detriment of teaching and learning.

There is some reason to think that the 'open book' form of examination produces less anxiety than traditional methods. In a controlled study, two groups of mature social work students experienced less examination stress when they were allowed to take notes into the examination than when they were not, (Jehu, Pickton, Futcher 1970). There was no direct relationship between examination performance and whether reference to notes was permitted, but there appeared to be a strong interactive effect with the examination subject.

It might be thought that anxiety is caused by uncertainty of what the examination questions are going to be and that the 'prepared essay' type of examination would produce less tension. Available evidence does not support this interpretation. For example, Flood Page (1967) compared students' anxiety during a traditional examination with "prepared essay examinations" in which the question papers were distributed a week in advance. 49% of the students said that they were more worried with the second kind of examination and 31% said they were less worried. Although the purpose of this kind of examination is to give students an opportunity to prepare a reasoned argument, when asked to comment, nearly half the students said that the prepared essay examinations placed too much weight upon memory.

It seems more likely that anxiety is caused by self-doubts rather than uncertainty about the content of the examination papers. For example, in an experiment by Rubin and Tierney (1973) students were able to choose the date of their examination and able students chose earlier dates. Although they tentatively suggest that the residential requirements of universities should depend upon the students' academic abilities, the point to be made here is that examination nerves decrease with well informed, rational confidence of success. If students are not well informed the fault probably lies with their tutor.

At one university it was thought that confidence would be increased, and fear of failure reduced, if each student was offered a grade a few weeks before the final examinations. The students could then either accept the grade they had been offered, in which case they need not take the examinations; or they could take the examinations in an attempt to improve upon the offer. Whatever their examination performance, it was to be guaranteed that they would not receive a grade lower than the one they had been offered. It was thought that anxiety would be reduced because there was not so much at stake in the examinations (Pilliner in Bligh, 1973a).

(5) To test teaching effectiveness

Students may also be assessed to test the effectiveness of teaching. This will be considered in Chapter 7 and need not delay us here, except to note again that assessments are part of the total system of teaching in an institution, not just a method of awarding grades.

(6) To license practice of a profession

Finally, some assessments are used to provide a qualification as a licence to practise a profession. The qualification could be quite irrelevant to the profession. In some countries, for example, the possession of a university degree is sufficient to be regarded as a qualified teacher even though academic skills and those required in teaching may be quite different. Similarly, a medical doctor may have to treat many conditions which were never mentioned in his training and on which he was never examined.

II What makes a good assessment?

(1) Questions of validity

Having decided the purpose of assessing their students, there are a number of questions teachers, course planners and assessment committees will need to answer. (See Figure 2.1)

(a) What mental or other skills should be tested?
Bloom (1956) and others have shown that there is a wide range of cognitive, affective and psychomotor abilities which could reasonably be tested. The problem is that most examination systems only test a very limited range of objectives. For example, Black (1968) surveyed 16 courses in Physics and found that between 80% and 90% of the marks for the final qualification were assigned to the final written paper. Over 40% of the questions tested almost nothing but a good memory for factual information, and another 40% required memory of the information with some ability to apply it in fairly simple routine ways. In other words, the highest grades could be obtained with quite low mental abilities. There were no multiple-choice tests and most of the examinations had the same pattern. Questions were phrased in such a way that external examiners had difficulty in finding out whether the questions really tested memory or the capacity to think, because the teacher and the internal examiner were the same person.

Figure 2.1: A Compulsory Examination for all Examiners

All questions are to be answered. This examination is untimed. Consultation with others (including students) and reference to books and other sources is *recommended*.

1. What objectives do you assess?
2. Justify and criticise your choice of assessment methods. Refer to research in your answer.
3. Describe, justify and criticise your methods of grading.
4. With reference to research findings describe, justify and criticise your marking techniques to overcome the following when using non-objective tests.

   (a) the "halo effect"
   (b) variations in standards on a single occasion
   (c) variations in standards on different occasions
   (d) variations between examiners
   (e) differences in students' handwriting

5. How do you ensure that your standards are similar to standards adopted in comparable examinations?
6. Assess your answers to questions 1 - 5*

* Since this will require you to answer questions 1 - 5 again for *this* assessment, the answer to question 6 is never ending! Nevertheless questions 1 - 5 should be considered seriously by any examiner.

In a study of biochemistry examinations set by ten colleges in the University of London, Beard and Pole (1971), found that the majority required simple recognition and memory of facts. One college had concentrated on 'evaluation of the total medical situation', but only one college had deliberately organised its examinations to cover a wide range of mental abilities.

McGuire (1963) used a taxonomy of educational objectives to analyse the mental abilities required in certain American medical examinations. 78% of the objective test items required 'isolated recall'; 11% needed some ability to generalise, 5% required recognition of facts or concepts, leaving only 6% for all other objectives. One might have expected that medical professions would require people able to apply principles in unfamiliar situations, to analyse complex conditions, and with some ability to make judgements; but virtually no credit was given for these skills. It is, of course, true that factual questions are easier to set and mark because there is usually little doubt whether an answer is correct. McGuire thinks there is an unconscious desire on the part of examiners to seek the security of this certainty.

At the Center for the Study of Medical Education at the University of Illinois she and Levine enunciated two principles: that tests should provide valid and reliable evidence on each component of competence independently, and that the level of performance should be decided before the examination is administered. In other words, that medical examinations should be criterion referenced. It was decided to test four general factors: recall of information, interpretation of data, problem solving, (including clinical judgements) and professional attitudes (Levine and McGuire 1971). For each of these four scores, a computer programme displayed clear passes, clear failures and a marginal group. The Examinations Committee then decided the precise guidelines for future pass/fail sorting procedure within the marginal group.

If a test is to be valid, a very important principle, which McGuire and her colleagues (McGuire and Solomon 1973) do not explicitly state, but which they nevertheless apply, is that examinations should simulate relevant vocational conditions as nearly as possible. Thus, in a series of questions to test problem solving, they describe a 25 year old man who was stabbed and brought to hospital. They give numerous clinical details which the doctor might reasonably be expected to observe and then ask students to select one of five choices of action. Succeeding questions follow the patient's progress. X-rays and other graphic materials that might be available in a clinical situation are provided as data on which the intending physician is required to make his judgements. Examiners are required to classify the multiple-choice answers according to the degree of difficulty they should present to the minimally competent student. From this, the minimum pass level is calculated. There are some possible answers presented which are so wrong that they would be unforgivable in a physician. Similarly there is some knowledge which is indispensable to a physician. These responses are critical in the sense that a student may demonstrate on these alone that he is below the minimum level of competence. Most of the choices are not of this kind and it is on these that the Examinations Committee must decide the pass/fail dividing line.

To be appreciated, the simulation tests devised by McGuire and her colleagues need closer scrutiny than is possible here. Their pass level is clearly criterion referenced. In contrast, Hohne (1955) has shown that, in one country at least, the pass and fail rates have been remarkably constant over a period of time when the entrance standards were known to have been improved. Consequently it was difficult to avoid the conclusion that standards were norm-referenced and that they were variable in consequence.

This procedure can reach ridiculous proportions. In one department a member of staff introduced programmed learning to such good effect that the whole class, with one exception, obtained over 80% on the previous year's objective test. The Head of Department insisted that the usual proportion of students should be made to fail; so that students who reached a standard that would have been a distinction one year, were at the pass/fail borderline another.

In the first chapter I argued the need for society to be continually regenerated by critical and creative minds. Yet in an American study Holland (1961) found no correlation between college grades and public recognition of creative work. Indeed, other researchers, (Hudson 1963, Entwistle and Percy 1973) have shown that there are strong pressures within higher education systems towards conformity rather than creativity.

(b) What is the range of objectives?
The critical nature of some medical knowledge and decisions raises the question, 'What is the range and balance of objectives to be tested?' In medicine a student could have excellent knowledge and be brilliant at solving medical problems but be introverted, tactless and thoroughly incompetent when dealing with patients and other people. The same could be true of students for many other professions. If a medical student of this kind obtained a licence to practise as a doctor because he passed his examinations, he could be a disaster. Yet his knowledge and intelligence could be very valuable in some branches of medicine such as medical research.

The difficulty here occurs when the examiners have an undimensional grading system. Academic abilities are many and varied; professional requirements are more so.

Thus, one of the injustices of the grading system is that it neglects qualitative differences between students. Grades obscure the talents of different individuals and this may be true in any subject. One student may obtain a grade by having a detailed knowledge of all the relevant facts; another may obtain the same grade by exercising his powers of judgement, giving reasoned arguments or propounding original ideas.

Similarly, but in a different way, grades can hide information if the same grade can be obtained by one student who does brilliantly on some of the examinations and poorly on others, and another student who gives a dull, mediocre performance on them all. Deception occurs because unidimensional grades purport to give information when in fact they hide it by aggregation and over-simplification.

One way over this difficulty is to assess students on a checklist of different factors which together provide a profile of his different abilities. This is known as the profile method of assessment. The checklist could consist of the different sub-disciplines that constitute the students' major subject. This has been called a subject-based profile. In practice, it is not very informative because, like school reports, the students' performance could reflect his liking for the teacher or other particular circumstances in which a specific subject is taught. More informative are assignment-based profiles which give different grades according to the kind of work performed. Thus different grades would be given for essay examinations, course work, practical work, projects and so on. Cox (1974) has found that these factors are more influential in the grades obtained than differences between the subjects taken. It is also quite likely that information of this kind will be more useful to the future employer than differences between academic disciplines which are in any case more arbitary than is sometimes supposed. Whiteland (1966) found that less than half the students who obtained a Grade A on their undergraduate thesis in geography obtained marks high enough on the timed written examinations to qualify them to do postgraduate research. Yet we might suppose that the work required for an undergraduate thesis would be more similar to that required for a postgraduate thesis than the writing of timed examination papers. Thus, not only was the predictive validity of the written examinations poor, but an assignment profile method of assessment would have made a better discrimination for the purpose of postgraduate student selection than the unidimensional grades.

The method used by McGuire and her colleagues already described was an objectives-based profile system. Objectives were classified under four headings according to the mental abilities required. The classification adopted would normally depend upon the subject, the social and institutional context, and the similar factors described in Chapter 1. One department of Sociology has adopted three broad dimensions: (i) knowledge of the content of the course with emphasis on recall; (ii) skill in argument, analysis and expression (with no regard to originality) and (iii) ability to produce imaginative or original work. Each piece of work included in the assessment can be assessed on one or more of these three categories according to what the teacher thinks appropriate.

The profile method of assessment appears to be popular with students provided that it is not so detailed that they feel every part of their lives to be under scrutiny. A highly detailed checklist ultimately becomes unwieldy and time consuming. There is little doubt that profiles could be more useful to potential employers than a single number or letter which on its own is meaningless.

Yet it cannot be denied that there are difficulties. In particular there is no obvious way in which performance in various kinds of activities can be translated into judgements about students' mental abilities. For example, the extent to which a student is hard working may be better judged from his project than from a timed examination, but it contributes to both in uncertain proportions. Again, when objectives-based profiles were used in a medical school (Geertsma and Chapman 1967) judgements appeared to be related to one or both of two factors: a cognitive factor, and a non-cognitive factor centring on ethical standards. Yet the objectives ranged more widely than these two categories. Without training, it seemed as if the assessors' judgements suffered from a 'halo effect' within these categories. (A 'halo effect' occurs when an assessor's judgement on one thing influences his judgement on another so that there is a strong, but spurious correlation between them.) Furthermore, clinical teachers tended to give low marks on cognitive dimensions and to be generous on the non-cognitive factors. Geertsma and Chapman believed that may be because ignorance of information may be easy to record, while poorer performance on personal relations may be easier to excuse. This raises a further question that needs to be answered.

(c) What grading system is to be used?
In the United States there has been a considerable debate, not on profile assessment, but on the use of grades. (These, of course, are two separate issues. Grades either may, or may not, be awarded for each of the categories on a profile checklist.) According to Abrams and Byrd (1971) over half the medical schools and associated institutions throughout North America now use a simple pass/fail grading system, and the proportion is increasing. They say that users of this system are more satisfied than those of the traditional grading methods. Nearly all schools use some kind of informal, as well as formal assessment, and about three-quarters use examinations standardised by the National Board of Medical Examiners.

Most students seem to prefer the pass/fail grading system, but not all. At the University of California dental students preferred it, but other students wanted to keep the original five grades (Mumma et al, 1971). At Minnesota, eight times as many students on a management course thought that grading had a worse effect on teaching, private study, work, thought and their own classroom behaviour than the simple pass/fail system (Burke 1968). In response to a questionnaire, students at three American universities agreed that grades encouraged cheating and discouraged independent thought by restricting study to factual material specified by the syllabus. They did not perceive grades as giving feedback on learning (Stallings and Leslie, 1970). At the University of Exeter a campus-wide survey of undergraduates showed a strong dislike of a pass/fail system and a considerable preference for the existing classification of degrees. In a small scale study Philbrick and O'Donnell (1968) tried to see if there were any advantages in having a 12 point rather than a 5 point grading scale, but found none.

Using slightly more objective methods, Johnson and Abrahamson (1968) thought that cramming for examinations diminished when the number of internal examinations was reduced and the specific marking system was replaced by descriptions of performance in course work, together with pass/fail gradings for each course. A self-administered questionnaire, a series of interviews and a medical student attitude test seemed to confirm that students became more interested in the subject rather than simply passing the examinations. These descriptions were rather like a profile method in which grades were abolished and substituted by a statement about the student. The statement had to be supported by evidence derived from a variety of sources and a variety of assessment methods. This last point is important lest descriptions tend to become as stereotyped as school reports. In a college elsewhere a tutor reputedly wrote "Satisfactory without being outstanding" on 29 reports, and "Outstanding without being satisfactory" on the last. Another method used at an ancient university is to allow the student a right to reply to the descriptions given, either in writing or in the presence of the tutor's senior colleagues.

There is some evidence that students are better motivated and study more widely when grades are abolished. Jessee and Simon (1971) compared students' tests and study habits at the University of Illinois, where there is a traditional grading system, and at the University of California, which has introduced the simple pass/fail system with no compulsory in-course examinations. The amounts of time spent in study, leisure and other activities were similar in the two colleges, but the authors concluded that the pass/fail system with no formal examinations produced superior motivation and better distribution of study time. Reiner and Jung (1972) found that a pass/fail system resulted in a lower average mark, but agreed that it encouraged students to study their subject more widely. Hales and Rand (1973) confirm that the average mark of students who opted to take the pass/fail course was less, relative to their earlier grade averages, than those who chose to take a course with a range of grades. Contrary to the findings of other researchers, they interpreted this as implying a reduction in motivation.

(d) What marking techniques should be used?

Usually the arguments about profile and grading systems assume that there is some kind of accuracy in the marking. There is no such accuracy. The very concept of 'accuracy' in marking is a mistake. There is no absolute standard against which students' performance is measured. On the contrary, we talk about the way the standards vary because they are not criterion-referenced. When Natkin and Guild (1967) asked six teachers to grade the performance of 65 dental students, they found that the teachers did not all observe the same thing. In effect, the students had a different examination according to which examiners observed them. Although there was greater agreement between the judgements of the different examiners when they used a common checklist of things to observe, the marks obtained by the students still depended more upon the examiner than on what the students did.

Even if the examiners are agreed, invalidity may occur by giving undue weight to unimportant things and irrelevancies. Chase (1968) found that examiners were more generous in the marking of essays when they had a checklist. He also confirmed the early studies by James (1927) and Sheppard (1929) that the quality of handwriting significantly influences grades. The influence of this factor appears to increase in time as successive essays are marked and it exerts an influence even when examiners are aware of it and try to resist it. Examiners in a study reported by Kandel (1936) were told to allocate a proportion of marks for handwriting and no more. When the essays were typed out and remarked, it was found that the influence of handwriting on marks awarded was greater than the maximum prescribed. This seems to imply a 'halo effect'.

The effect of time has also been demonstrated in other investigations. It is known, for example, that as examiners continue marking a large batch of essay scripts, they tend to be more generous, their powers of discriminating good and bad answers deteriorate and, as if to relieve the monotony, they give more extreme marks. Colton and Peterson (1967) have demonstrated the same thing with oral examinations. Grading became less strict towards the end of each day and also with succeeding days in a series of examinations in medicine.

(e) What validation methods are to be used?
Assessors also need to ask how their assessments can be validated. In many cases this seems to be quite impracticable. Where there are large numbers of students taking basically the same course from year to year, it may be possible either to compare the performance of students in succeeding years, or, where appropriate, to compare their assessment with subsequent professional behaviour. But many courses are constantly changing and have student numbers too small for sound statistical validation.

To most educational institutions this fact provides an excuse for the total neglect of any form of validation. Consequently the validity of their assessments must be doubted by any thinking person.

(2) Are assessment methods reliable?

In an article on university standards Dale (1959) began "One of the biggest obstacles to improvement in the selection of students is the unreliability and uncertainty of university examinations and the biggest obstacle to reform is the ignorance of the staffs at universities about the pitfalls which surround the examiners. The calm assurance with which lecturers and professors alike believe they can carry around in their heads an unfailing correct conception of an absolute standard of 40% as the pass line is incomprehensible to anyone who has studied the research on the reliability of the examinations." He was referring to the British system, but the same is almost certainly true in most other countries.

Unreliability may occur in at least four different ways: (a) examiners may differ either in the range of marks they award, or in their generosity as measured by the average mark awarded by each examiner; (b) the grades awarded by the same assessor may be different on different occasions; (c) different tests purporting to measure the same thing may set inconsistent standards; and (d) the procedure and circumstances in which examinations are taken may be inconsistent.

(a) Consistency between examiners
The first of these causes of unreliability is the most alarming. As mentioned above it has two common elements, the range and generosity of grades awarded.

The French psychologist Pieron (1963), quoted by Cox (1967) has concluded "All experimental data has shown that for a particular performance expressed in terms of an exam script, assessment by different examiners produces marks with considerable variability such that in determination of these marks, the part played by the examiner can be greater than the performance of the examinee". Studies elsewhere have suggested that 10% to 15% of the variations in students' grades can be attributed to differences between the examiners who awarded them, rather than the students (Laugier and Weinberg cited by Cox, 1967). The corresponding percentage for differences in the students' performance on the essay questions is about the same.

In a now famous study by Hartog and Rhodes (1936) the average mark awarded by different examiners for essay questions was similar, but the range of marks awarded for the same piece of work averaged 19.6 when the maximum possible was 100. Mathematics is a subject in which greater objectivity may seem to be possible. But Hartog and Rhodes obtained the same findings at university degree level in this subject, the average variation being 35 marks out of 300. The use of two examiners improved the discrepancy somewhat but the variation remained serious.

We might also expect that in a subject like mechanical engineering the reliability of examiners would be greater. In one study (Hill 1973) students were given problems in fluid mechanics and eight markers experienced in examining this subject used the same marking schedules. The standard deviations of candidates' marks either side of their average marks were within the range of 3-11 (when the maximum possible was 100 marks). This meant that had the examination only been marked by one examiner, over half the students would probably have obtained a grade different from the average of all eight.

When it is remembered that in some countries the prestige associated with the grade obtained in a degree can last virtually a lifetime, the injustice of current examination systems can be appreciated.

What appears to emerge from more detailed consideration of research in this subject is that examiners frequently disagree very little about the majority of candidates, but have a wide divergence of views on either some questions or some students. For example, William (1933) reports marks ranging from 16 - 96 and 26 - 92 given by different examiners to the same examination essays on Mathematics. Bull (1956) found such a low correlation between the marks awarded by different examiners that a random allocation of marks would not have produced a significantly less reliable result. This could have been more excusable had it been in a subject where a proportion of the marks were awarded for reasoning, original thinking, attitudes and powers of judgement; but it was in a factual branch of medicine where variation should have been minimal.

Differences between subjects are most clearly displayed in the range of marks allocated. The range of marks awarded in Mathematics and physical sciences tends to be much greater than the range in literary subjects. This may be of no importance if the results in one subject are never compared with those in another, but they are. It is not uncommon for students who have taken different courses to apply for the same job.

It should not be forgotten that examiners are human. Their subjective judgements in assessment are as vulnerable to social and psychological pressures as any others. For example, because extreme grades are more difficult to justify if they differ from those of co-examiners, there is pressure upon less experienced, or otherwise insecure examiners, to give marks in the middle range. Younger examiners and those wishing to show that their standards are high frequently award relatively low grades.

(b) Reliability of one examiner

Inconsistencies may also occur in the marks awarded by a single examiner. He may mark very strictly on one occasion and be generous on another. This may not matter if the marks on the two occasions are never compared; but they usually are. Students who qualify one year are likely to compete for jobs with those who qualify the next year. When students have to resit examinations it is usually assumed that the standards of the original examination should be maintained. Not only is it very unlikely that examiners can maintain an invariable conception of a given "standard" from one examination to the next, but in some cases, when the examination questions are different, it would be difficult to know what this means unless some system of standardisation has been employed.

There is also some evidence that examiners vary their standards while marking the same set of examination papers. First, there is a tendency for the range of marks awarded to increase as the examiner proceeds. Secondly, there is a tendency to become more generous. The first phenomenon may be explained either by initial cautiousness for fear that scripts very much better or poorer will be subsequently encountered; or by the examiner's need to relieve the monotony of his task the longer he spends at it. It is also possible that examiners gain confidence as they proceed and are more willing to present extreme marks to their co-examiners.

The effect of differences over a period of time can be diminished if examiners mark all the answers to one question before proceeding to the next. Re-marking in the reverse order by the same, or different, examiners may also help to balance these temporal inconsistencies.

(c) Comparability of different tests

It is fairly obvious that the curricula at different colleges may vary even when the name of the subject is the same. Consequently there may be little similarity in their assessments and the qualifications awarded will not be comparable even though they have the same names. Yet on the job market they are compared; employers have no alternative.

In the same way the qualifications of two students graduating from the same department in the same university on two successive years may be regarded as comparable even though the syllabus may have changed and the examination questions were quite different. Again, the qualifications of two students who sat the same examination at the same time in the same department may be regarded as comparable, but if they chose to answer different questions on the examination paper they will not have been judged on identical criteria. In a very real sense they did not take the same test. The fact that students may be able to choose the questions they answer is irrelevant unless the ability to choose wisely is one of the objectives to be tested. There is reason to believe that students are not good judges of their relative abilities to answer different questions on examination papers.

Consequently, though comforting, the existence of a choice increases the chance factor in the marks obtained.

Thus, even where assessments appear to be comparable, a few moments' thought may frequently show that they are not. This may not matter if those who make judgements on the basis of paper qualifications are aware of their limitations. But frequently degree classes and grades are revered as having some mystical objectivity. Professors sometimes speak as if they can identify a first-class mind as a totally different species from one that is second-class. Regulations for research awards and other postgraduate selection criteria are fixed rigidly as if grades were objective measures of potential research or academic performance.

(d) Standardisation of procedure

Examiners may also adopt inconsistent procedures with different students. This is not normally a severe problem with the traditional formal examination, except possibly when the same examination is being administered simultaneously in different places. It is a more severe problem in oral examinations, practical tests and "continuous assessment".

Procedural considerations include those outside the examination room which may influence the student's performance unfairly. For example, when there is a succession of students to be interviewed the conditions of the examination will inevitably vary. Delays may unsettle the anxious student. Examiners may be bored or irritable later in the day. Since such examinations are interactive situations, their procedure cannot be strictly controlled. Many forms of practical examinations involve the same difficulty.

In continuous assessment situations the examination procedure is part of the teaching procedure. The latter may be spontaneous and uncontrollable. Consequently there is no attempt in this kind of assessment to encourage procedural consistency except in mechanical matters such as the processing of marks awarded. This is particularly true where contributions to seminar discussions are assessed.

Thus in many cases it is not a practical proposition to insist upon procedural consistency.

III The choice of assessment methods

We have seen that if course planners are to choose appropriate methods of student assessment, they will need to know the purposes each method can serve, its validity and reliability. This section is intended to give research information to guide the choice of assessment methods.

(1) No method at all

One possible choice is to abolish assessment altogether. We shall see in Chapter 4 that some sociologists have argued that assessments presuppose a way in which human knowledge should be organised. The selection of topics by assessors presupposes a value system and imposes it on students. These values are different in different cultures.

Nevertheless many students enter post-secondary education to obtain a qualification. They enter to be assessed and we have already seen that much of their motivation is derived from this desire. In one survey (Siann and Pilliner, 1974) only 6% of students wanted assessment for the award of degrees abolished and exactly the same figure was obtained from a survey at Exeter. The difficulty is frequently that the assessment methods used are artificial.

Some institutions have attempted to overcome this. In Indonesia there is no post-graduate examination for qualifying paediatric specialists. Doctors training to become specialists have to undergo a formal three year residency programme during which they participate in teaching and research, and take on increasing clinical responsibilities. Towards the end of the training period the Head of Department, in consultation with other senior staff, judges whether a certificate of proficiency should be issued. Thus professional proficiency is judged directly, not by an artificial substitute examination. Such a method avoids artificiality but may be criticised as subjective. In this example we see that the choice of assessment methods almost inevitably requires balancing conflicting principles.

(2) Essays, short notes and other written tests

(a) Increasing reliability by shorter questions
There is some evidence that reliability can be improved if questions are shorter. Mowbray and Davies (1967) believed that short notes demand more concentration from the examiners. If so, this could explain their greater reliability, but it is probable that examiners also have clearer objectives when marking short answers. If questions are shortened to the extent of making them objective tests, the agreement between examiners should be complete. The range of marks awarded for short answer questions is normally less than those for problem or analytic questions (Kelley and Zarembka, 1968). In another investigation, Bull (1956) studied the variation in marks awarded by different examiners. The variation attributable to student performance increased from 19% when students were required to answer four questions in three hours, to 28% for eight questions in three hours and 71% for sixteen questions in three hours. The comparable percentages when the same examiner re-marked the students' answers were 36%, 42% and 65%, with 66% when thirty-two questions had to be answered in three hours.

(b) Increasing reliability by analytical marking
Another way to increase reliability is to use a more analytical marking technique. One complaint about short answer questions and objective tests, such as those of the multiple-choice type, is that they do not give students the opportunity to present a reasoned argument or to propound an original idea. For these objectives, essays are preferred. Heffer et al (1965) have found that the analytical method

of marking essay answers was more reliable than semi-analytical methods. Consultation between examiners also improved reliability but there was considerable disagreement about candidates near the pass/fail borderline. This disagreement was replicated in the complementary oral examination.

There are two broad analytical approaches to marking essays, the points method and the ratings method; but their broad stages are the same. First, at the time that the essay topic is devised, and not later, the major points or characteristics of the expected answers should be set out in writing. This could consist of a model answer, but it need not do so. In the points method a long list of facts may be listed together with the characteristics of the answers required. In the ratings method the characteristics are usually more important than the facts and a series of rating scales of the characteristics should be devised.

The second stage is for all examiners to agree upon the weighting to be given to each of these factors. There will also need to be agreement on the importance attached to peripheral or irrelevant factors. These may include handwriting, linguistic style, spelling, punctuation and so on. It will also include a decision on the treatment of irrelevant information. In a timed examination examiners may choose to ignore it because candidates waste valuable time writing it. But some examiners may think that marks should be subtracted for irrelevant material, particularly if the students write a great deal and expect the examiners to perform the hard task of selecting what is relevant. Again, this stage should be completed before the choice of the examination questions is finally decided, because discussion between examiners often reveals that questions are badly worded, too large or in some other way could be improved. It cannot be stressed too strongly that the time taken to set a good examination paper should be a major timetabled commitment during the academic year. Too often examinations are hurriedly conceived and inadequately discussed. This is particularly true when it is necessary to balance questions because the design of examination papers gives students a choice.

The third stage after the examination is to mark the essays either by the points method in which marks are allocated for points raised, or by the ratings method in which grades may be allocated on a number of different scales. It is usually advisable not to have more than five points on any one rating scale. The rating method is suitable for the profile system of grading. It is also better than the points method when the essays are longer.

Whichever method is used, we have already seen that it is advisable to mark all responses to a given question without looking at the names of their authors before proceeding to the next question. This is more likely to ensure a common standard and the effects of time are more likely to be distributed amongst the candidates. Another technique when marking a large batch of scripts is to select four or five answers as examples representing each major level or grade, and to use them to refresh one's memory of each standard as one proceeds. Any important examination should be marked by two or more examiners. The point at which the cost of examiners outweighs the beneficial effects of increasing their number is a debatable question.

(c) Inter-test reliability

In addition to the reliability of examiners, the reliability of the method of examination should be considered. How far do different forms of written test give the same results? At the University of Copenhagan, Bojsen-Møller (1973) has reported reliabilities as high as .94 when examiners re-marked long and short written answer papers. Correlations between two sets of examiners each marking half the examination papers was .83. Variations depended upon the composition of the question, with higher correlations when the curriculum tested was more representative. These correlations are higher than any obtained elsewhere for marking written answers. Even so the result is confirmed by Starr (1968) who found high correlations averaging .83 between marks obtained in three hour examinations, short class examinations of less than 1 hour, marks for long essays and for course work. The lowest correlation was between course work and final examination marks. This last point is interesting and possibly important.

(d) Prepared essay examinations

The fact that traditional essay examinations only test a small and arbitrary portion of a syllabus may be regarded as unjust because there is a chance element whether students have specialised in the particular topics selected. In addition to increasing the number and spread of questions one method is to announce questions about two weeks in advance of the examination. This is known as the "prepared essay" type of examination. A variation is to announce the topics but not the precise questions. In a study by Siann and Pilliner (1974) 32% of students favoured the first method and 63% the second. In both cases students were more favourable when they themselves had experienced the method. Older students and those who had to resit their examinations were significantly more favourable to these new methods, but there was no difference between students according to their year of study. These findings may be contrasted to those of Flood Page (1967) mentioned on page 27.

Teachers may think that these methods will favour students who only work hard for the fortnight immediately before the examinations but this is only true if the questions set require simple regurgitation of the textbook or are otherwise cognitively simple. Questions that require relating different parts of a syllabus may still be very searching. Thus the solution partly lies in the careful design of questions.

(e) Open book examinations

The "open book" type of examination, in which students may take books into the examination room, is intended to reduce the extent to which examinations are a test of memory, and thereby increase the allocation of marks for higher cognitive skills. There are a number of variations of this form of assessment and the resulting complexity has probably reduced the number of empirical investigations of the method. Sometimes students are only allowed to take a limited number of books and sometimes only certain specified books. The use of dictionaries in language examinations has been widely permitted for some time.

It would be useful to know the range of skills tested by these examinations and how they differ from those of the traditional essay type. What effect does practice have on students' performance? What marking techniques should be employed? Should invigilators be given special instructions? Since reference to books takes time, presumably knowledgeable students will still be at an advantage in timed examinations.

Available evidence (Feldhusen, 1961) suggests that students do as well or better in open-book situations as in traditional examinations. In Denmark Krarup and Olsen (1969) have said the difference is small and confined to recall questions in multiple-choice tests, while in Hawaii, Kalish (1958) has reported that it depends on the student, but he could not say in what way. Students report a reduction in anxiety with this method, particularly when compared with objective tests. In the survey by Siann and Pilliner (1974) eight students in every nine thought open-book examinations reduced reliance upon memory and most thought it was educationally beneficial. Some reported it was better for learning during the examination.

(3) Course work

(a) "Continuous" assessment

Assessment of course work is useful to diagnose which students need help. It can provide a useful check on the validity of examinations, and it may demonstrate at what point in a course accuracy in predicting future performance of students is possible.

If, like timed written examinations, course work also consists of writing essays, as it does in many subjects, many of the same principles will apply to what is frequently, but misleadingly, called 'continuous assessment'. ("Continual" or "Intermittent" assessment would be better names; and in any case the occasional or continual nature of an assessment is only one aspect of this method.) Yet we have seen that there are some important differences. The patterns of anxiety are not the same; and, although many students do equally well on both, the different methods appear to favour different types of personality and study habits (Cox, 1974). Cox found that although grades for course work are strongly related to degree results, they bore little relation to scores on a large number of standardised tests, as if reaction to test-taking situations is itself an important factor affecting scores. Examination scores were positively related to general knowledge and negatively associated with originality and complexity of thought.

Compared with the assessment of course work, timed examinations clearly favour students who can write quickly. Gust and Schumacher (1969) have shown that women can write significantly faster than men. Interestingly the mean speed of writing in their experiment was twice as fast (127 letters per minute) than the normal maximum speed of the general population (60 letters per minute). Whether this is the result of training or an inadvertent result of selecting students on the basis of examination results, it raises serious issues on the validity of timed examinations when writing speed is not a course objective.

While intermittent assessment of course work does not have these difficulties, it has problems of its own. In particular it maintains an authoritarian and strained relationship between students and their teachers which is not conducive to a free flow of ideas between critical and enquiring minds. Bassey (1971) has described a system of assessment without final examinations in which students are formally assessed for work carried out during the course and in which this difficulty appears to have been overcome. Assignments of work were not prescribed by the teachers but agreed between them and the students after discussion in which its purposes were made clear. Although the work could be written, it need not have been, provided there was sufficient tangible evidence of study which could be assessed by tutors and which could be available for moderation by an external examiner. The merits and demerits of students' work were discussed openly with a tutor so that justice could be seen to be done and objectives, including personal and intellectual development, were achieved. In some courses of this kind, grades are only awarded when students and teachers agree what they should be. Although many teachers may find this procedure time consuming, it is part of the teaching process. It could make standards explicit and relieve some of the frustrations felt by students on campuses the world over.

In Dar-Es-Salaam Medical School as much as 70% of the total number of marks of the final assessment are obtained from grades achieved in class work and departmental tests. A somewhat similar approach is used in the Agricultural Universities in India, where at the end of each semester there is an examination which carries 50% of the total marks; a further 30% of the marks are awarded for one-hour tests during the semester; and the remaining 20% may be obtained from surprise tests.

When a student takes one course assessed intermittently and another assessed only by final examinations, work in the latter tends to suffer. A similar difficulty arises when parts of the same course are assessed by these different methods. Elton (1968) has described one method of combining course work with traditional examinations based on a course rating which is obtained by multiplying an index of its difficulty by its length in terms of time. Although the validity of this system can only be judged subjectively, it has resulted in high attendance at voluntary courses.

(b) Projects

Project teaching is increasingly popular for good reason. It cultivates attitudes of critical enquiry, research techniques and thought for which we argued in Chapter 1. Yet precisely because it is a useful teaching technique, the conflict between the teacher's role as an impartial assessor and a committed friendly tutor becomes acute. Since students may do their projects on different topics the problem of incomparability may arise. Group projects are also educationally beneficial because they train students in team work, but such co-operation can impose another set of difficulties for the assessors. Another problem arises when tutors work with students on projects and their aspirations change. Tutors then grade students' performance with reference to their later aspirations rather than their initial expectations. This could be unjust. To overcome this problem one group of British academics (Nuffield, 1974) have suggested that tutors should agree upon 'contract of exploration' with a student at the start of a project and discuss the stages through which the project is expected to pass and the criteria which will be used to assess these stages. This can help to clarify their respective roles. The stages "include the experimental design, the planning of time and resources, the experimental technique, the analysis of data, the presentation of results and what might be called the 'forward look', that is, the ability to see where the project is leading and to make suggestions for further work". The group also suggested that the students' personal qualities, resourcefulness, creative thinking, perseverance, initiative, and, where appropriate, ability to work in a team should be considered.

If the overall assessment system does not require the quantification of grades, a profile assessment is particularly suitable for project work. Because of the tutor's involvement it may be advisable to ask a departmental colleague or an external advisor to assist in the assessments. They are more likely to be detached in their judgements and be able to compare one project with another. In subjects such as engineering an external examiner may be able to represent a professional viewpoint while colleagues will be aware of departmental policy.

In one department of economics (Nuffield, 1974) 25% of the marks are awarded for a student's preliminary draft submitted after the long vacation. After modification following comments and criticisms he presents his final report to a seminar composed of 10 fellow students and two members of the teaching staff. Another student is nominated as a discussant and 10% of their project marks are allocated for the defence of their respective viewpoints. All participants in the seminar can earn up to 5% of their total project marks for their participation in the series of seminars. Thus the final written presentation of the project counts for 50% of the total project marks.

Some colleges have experimented with students choosing their own methods of assessment; in others they do this in consultation with personal tutors. Unfortunately students are not always competent judges of the methods most favourable to them.

(4) Objective tests

A choice which often appears to face course planners is between objective tests and other written forms of assessment. Of course this need not be a choice because many departments use both.

There is some evidence that students prefer a mixture of methods. This was very clearly shown in a survey at Exeter. 82% of students wanted less than half their degree marks to be derived from traditional essay examinations, yet no other method approached the same popularity. Wallace (1974) asked three groups of Irish students whether they preferred the traditional essay examinations or multiple-choice tests or a mixture; and two-thirds preferred the mixture.

Amongst the minorities, science students preferred essays and medical students preferred multiple-choice tests. It is important to note that preferences were unrelated to the different kinds of performance in the examinations. This confirms the view just stated that students are poor judges of the methods in which they are most successful.

When course planners make decisions on the assessment methods to be used it is important that they should have comparative information upon which to make the choice. A number of factors are summarised in Figure 2.2 (page 45). Some of these are fairly obvious but their relative importance is more difficult to judge. For example, one obvious difference between objective and essay tests is that the latter require some writing ability. Yet although this is well recognised, there is good reason to believe that this factor has a disproportionate weight in traditional examination results because there is no satisfactory way of making allowance for it. Objective tests are capable of testing factual knowledge, attitudes and most convergent thinking skills such as those involved when solving problems. They are less suitable for 'synthetic' or creative tasks. Questions appear to be more difficult and time consuming to construct than in some other kinds of tests, but this is only because the standard of construction is higher owing to the existence of standard procedures to test their reliability and validity. In a comparison of essay testing and multiple-choice examinations in the University of Queensland, Lupton and Huxham (1970) concluded that multiple-choice tests are more reliable and valid, although essay examinations could be improved with extra effort and organisation in the way they are marked. Although they believed that essays can test abilities which multiple-choice tests cannot, they concluded that multiple-choice tests are both more convenient and more just.

It is a debatable question how far the abilities tested overlap or how far they happen to occur in the same people. No doubt it depends upon how each type of question is constructed. Nevertheless correlations between scores on objective tests and other methods of assessment are lower than would normally be obtained between examinations of the same or similar type. For example, in one department of dentistry, marks awarded for essays and short notes correlated more highly than with scores for multiple-choice questions (Ferguson, Wright and McNicol, 1971). Multiple-choice test scores in one department of psychiatry correlated highly with general competence in examinations throughout the medical school, yet correlated only .41 with essay tests in the same subject and only .23 with the clinical examination (Walton and Drewery 1967). Students performing badly in the objective tests were more likely to be extraverted, to come from another country, to be moralistic and prone to give advice to patients, to be uninterested in the subject and in psychiatric patients, and to have regarded the subject as irrelevant to their career prospects at the beginning of the course.

Indeed, it seems that the scores obtained by any method of assessment contain a considerable impurity derived from the students' skill and strategy in taking that particular kind of test. In objective tests, these strategies are more explicit and measurable than in many others. This enables researchers and teachers to be aware of them. It does not mean that they do not exist in those methods of assessment where they are less detectable. Lennox (1967) has used 'Games Theory' and 'Mathematical Analysis' to study the possible responses to various forms in which multiple-choice tests can be written. He concluded that while adequate knowledge is the only guarantee of passing, a candidate can improve his score by exploiting the rules. For example, study of earlier question papers will reveal a pattern of questions and the idiosyncrasies of particular examiners.

Advantage can be gained from a careful study of the marking system. For example, if guessing is heavily penalised, no random guesses should be attempted; otherwise an answer should be given to every question. Cooper and Foy (1967) instructed one group of students to guess and another not to do so, and found that although students obeyed instructions, it made little difference to their scores except on difficult questions. The probable explanation for this is that the students had some partial knowledge which eliminated some possible errors, thereby increasing their total score even when the corrections for guessing were made. Rothman (1969) required students to mark their degree of confidence in response to multiple-choice questions. By weighting the scores according to the students' confidence, this technique permitted a more discriminating analysis of students' abilities than the traditional multiple-choice test.

Biggs (1973) has attempted to analyse test-taking strategies in essays as well as objective tests. He has divided these into 'Reproductive Strategies' which were successful for students motivated pragmatically, and 'Transformational Strategies' used by students with more 'Academic' motivation. Success in objective tests was related to a 'Convergent' cognitive style in which the student looks for the one correct answer to problems. Because success on essays depended as much on the examiner as on the students, no one cognitive style or strategy was reliable in essay examinations. Students with high motivation did better than others in both types of examination.

Objective tests have the advantage that comparisons may be made not only between students of succeeding years but between students of different institutions. Australian medical schools are moving towards a system of a National Bank of multiple-choice questions so that all eight medical schools can take the same examinations. Since on initial trials the variations within schools were as great as between them, the system looks promising. Comparable systems exist in some other countries particularly between medical faculties. The existence of question banks can help the teaching process by separating the teacher's authoritarian role as examiner from his more personal role as a tutor.

Most research into objective tests has concentrated on the multiple-choice type. Consequently we should not leave this subject without remembering that there are many different kinds of objective test. Some of these are listed in Figure 2.2. There is little doubt that they will become more popular as ignorance and prejudice against them diminish, and as a greater diversity of types are invented.

Figure 2.2: The Objectives and Merits of Various Types of Assessment (Bligh, 1972b)

TYPE OF ASSESSMENT	SOME POSSIBLE OBJECTIVES	SOME POSSIBLE ADVANTAGES	SOME POSSIBLE DISADVANTAGES
3 hour essay exam	Knowledge of information Verbal fluency	Easy to set	Unreliable marking Emphasis on writing speed Poor coverage of syllabus Poor feedback
Prepared essay exam	Skills in preparation e.g. seeking information Thought	Higher standards set by students Closer to 'real life'	No valid method of marking yet designed
Open book essay exams	Reference techniques Memory Thoughtful preparation Depth of Thought	Less study time spent on memorising Inter-disciplinary answers obtained	Atypical performance
Short answer questions	Knowledge of information	Broader coverage of syllabus More reliable marking	Little opportunity to display argument or originality
Course work	Motivation	Closer to vocational situation	Anxiety through-out course Conflicting roles of tutor as assessor
Projects Disserta-tions Theses	Ability to seek information, to reason Presentation techniques Interest/motivation Originality		No objectivity in marking Grading almost meaningless

(Table continued on page 46)

TYPE OF ASSESSMENT	SOME POSSIBLE OBJECTIVES ASSESSED	SOME POSSIBLE ADVANTAGES	SOME POSSIBLE DISADVANTAGES
Objective tests (of various kinds) including Multiple-choice questions	Information Thought of all kinds Attitudes	A wide range of objectives Broad coverage of syllabus Objective marking Precise feedback Computer marking possible	Difficult to set
Practicals	Practical (motor) skills Experimental design		Written report rather than practical work is assessed
Simulated tasks	Personal interaction Application of knowledge	Closely approximates to professional work	Careful preparation of marker's checklist necessary
Oral situations e.g. viva or group discussion	Personal interaction Reasoning behind personal thought	Flexible Useful to Confirm other assessments	Very subjective 'Halo' effect Examiner's skill needed

(5) Assessment of practical work

Although the marking of practical examinations may appear to be very different from the marking of essays, empirical studies lead to many of the same conclusions. The reliability of marking may be improved with the use of precise checklists where possible and rating scales where not. In some subjects, examinations which are supposed to test practical work are assessed on the basis of experimental reports rather than the practical skills themselves. The skills involved are not the same, and those required to write reports are much the same as may be used in other kinds of written examination. Thus, in spite of appearances, practical examinations do not primarily test practical work. They test it only indirectly.

Indeed, in the training of teachers, there may actually be a conflict between the qualities required for academic success and those for success in practical teaching. Cortis (1968) found that academic success correlated highly with verbal ability, good entrance qualifications and idealistic and tough minded attitudes to education; while good scores in practical teaching were related to previous teaching experience, low verbal fluency and tender-minded attitudes. Crocker (1968) thought that flexibility and ingenuity were very important qualities for practical teaching and devised a test of verbal flexibility. When used in conjunction with an IQ test, entrance qualifications and interview grades, scores correlated very highly with the marks awarded for teaching practice.

Wiseman and Start (1965) have shown that the mark awarded to student teachers bears little relation to their career preferment or their head teachers' ratings five years later. This may be because they were judged on different qualities. Poppleton (1969) has shown that college supervisors give more weight to cognitive qualities, such as the use of visual aids, whereas teaching staff in secondary schools value expressive qualities such as the student-teachers' relationships with pupils. In elementary schools the preferences were the other way round. By producing a checklist of 27 items, Poppleton obtained a correlation between supervisors and schoolteachers' ratings of .64. Because these items gave a profile of students' personal strengths and weaknesses, they provided useful feedback to the student-teachers.

The unreliability of ratings of students teachers can be seen from a study by Doty (1970). Three criteria of academic achievement were unrelated to head teachers' ratings. Ratings of mature female student teachers by class teachers was significantly yet negatively correlated with head teachers' ratings. Furthermore, ratings by college supervisors did not correlate significantly with the students' first head teacher when employed.

Although the use of checklists in practical examinations normally improves objectivity, and thereby the reliability and validity of the evaluations, even this has proved unsuccessful in one college of dentistry (Fuller, 1972). The same has been demonstrated by Houpt and Kress (1973) who made a detailed statistical study of the accuracy and reliability of three groups of examiners of performance in operative dentistry: teachers, dental assistants and the students themselves. Although the teachers could give an accurate and reliable *overall* judgement of clinical performance, their judgements of details were both inaccurate and unreliable and the students were generally as good as the teachers. This seems to imply that 'impression' marking is more satisfactory than the use of checklists, but this is an illegitimate inference because we do not know on what basis the overall judgements were formed. They could have been formed on some irrelevant, and quite invalid, criterion. The solution to this problem may seem to lie in the provision of training for examiners, but in the experiment by Houpt and Kress even this made little difference, except that the dental assistants improved up to the standard of the other two groups.

We can only conclude that much more research needs to be done if the examination systems the world over are to have any measure of validity and justice. The more travel increases and the consequent demand for common standards grows, the greater will be the need for acceptable standards of examining.

(6) Viva-voce and oral examinations

Our survey of a number of universities throughout the world revealed that about one-third used oral examinations at the undergraduate level, and at postgraduate level the proportion was much higher. Yet very little is known about their reliability, validity and the most appropriate techniques.

A report of the British Medical Association (1948) mentions the following precepts for oral examinations.

(i) Treat the candidate with the courtesy which is his due.
(ii) Do not flatly contradict any candidate.
(iii) Try to find out what the candidate knows. If you find a large gap in his knowledge there is no need to find out its total extent. Change the subject.
(iv) Be prepared to receive views with which you may not agree.
(v) Put your question clearly. If the candidate does not answer, it may be because he did not understand what you were trying to ask.
(vi) Be careful how you joke with examinees.

The amount of research into this method of assessment is small and much of it is contradictory, not only in results but in the interpretations given. For example, Colton and Peterson (1967) tried to assess the reliability of oral examinations in Harvard's Medical School. Examiners were in teams of three, and their reliability varied considerably both within and between the teams, but the results were regarded as correlating reasonably well with other measures of performance. Holloway et al (1968) found that the between- and within-examiner reliabilities for scores on oral examinations were similar, reasonably high (between .66 and .74) and of the same order as those reported by Evans et al (1966). They thought these reliabilities compared favourably with those for essay marks; but they disagreed on 20%-25% of the candidates who were given a failure mark. The scores obtained did not correlate significantly with any other assessment method used with the same students and the correlation with multiple-choice tests was particularly low. After reassessing the examinations on the basis of tape recordings, they concluded that some examiners are susceptible to visual impressions and that introverts were relatively handicapped in the live situation. In an earlier study Holloway et al (1967) found that although there was a high degree of agreement between examiners, results of viva-voce tests did not correlate with any factor except with emotional stability. Correlations with multiple-choice tests of factual knowledge were again particularly low.

Kelley et al (1971) have obtained the opposite experimental results. They studied well over a hundred examiners over a two year period and concluded that the disagreement amongst examiners was higher than would be tolerated in other kinds of examination, but correlations with scores for written examinations were satisfactory, although not high. They concluded that oral examinations do not test anything that could not be adequately tested by other means.

Tomlinson et al (1973) suggest that oral examinations should be abandoned, not because they are invalid, but because they correlate highly with multiple-choice tests, and the multiple-choice tests correlate .86 with total examination performance. Correlations with clinical and essay examinations were lower.

Significant positive correlations between multiple-choice tests, essay tests and oral examinations have also been found at the University of Glasgow (Young and Gillespie, 1972). These results were not interpreted as showing that one or other of the methods was redundant. All methods were retained as contributing to a general picture of the student.

Oral examinations are frequently criticised because the examiners' judgements are influenced by the students' personality and visual appearance. Superficially, this appears to be supported by differences between oral examination grades given by doctors and nurse-tutors who examined in pairs. The judgements by nurse-tutors were not significantly different from the results of objective tests. The judgements by physicians were. The explanation for this could lie in the different conceptual backgrounds of physicians and nurses; or, since all the nurses and students were female and the physicians were male, the difference may be sexual (Easton, 1968). Another interpretation is that the nurse-tutors' judgements were influenced by their knowledge of students' usual level of performance on other tests including those of the multiple-choice type.

Other researchers have found low intercorrelations between oral examiners. Hartog and Rhodes (1935) obtained a correlation of .41 between two examining boards assessing the alertness, intelligence and general outlook of candidates. In America, Trimble (1934) obtained correlations between .22 and .40 when students of applied psychology were assessed. Pieron (1963) has quoted correlations as low as .22 between oral and written examinations for the Baccalaureat in Philosophy.

We may conclude that interpretation of empirical evidence on oral examinations is about as subjective as the oral examinations themselves. Oral examinations probably have a place, but they require careful preparation. Miller (1962) has emphasised that each examiner should be explicitly clear as to precisely what knowledge and abilities are to be assessed; questions for oral exams should be prepared in advance; the student should be made as comfortable and relaxed as possible. Arguably the examination should be recorded and be available for both the student concerned and the examiners.

(7) Self ratings and peer ratings

Assessment of students by students seems to be open to obvious criticism, but if students' evaluation of their own work is taken seriously, they too, take it seriously, they learn a great deal and set themselves new standards.

American experience suggests that students' self ratings of their academic performance are usually a little generous at first. This is consistent with findings at the University of Exeter that the majority of students rated their own ability as slightly above average. It is possible that students' judgements are made with reference to their personal standards rather than the standards of students in general, of which they have little knowledge. This interpretation was confirmed by Biggs and Tinsley (1970) in a study in which students' self ratings of performance were adjusted in the light of their scores on academic aptitude tests. When this was done, their self ratings correlated significantly with their performance as judged by the teachers and were also estimated to be highly reliable (.81).

Burke (1969) has produced evidence to suggest that peer ratings in assigning university course grades are more reliable than self-evaluations by students. They had good agreement with teachers' marks, a high degree of internal consistency and a more typical grade distribution than self-evaluations. Self ratings tended to be too generous and to agree poorly with marks allocated by teachers and fellow students. Burke did not, like Biggs and Tinsley, adjust the scores for academic aptitude. Nealey (1969) found that the marks awarded by students for essay examinations correlated .60 to .95 with the marks awarded by teachers. Although there were significant differences on 27% of the marks awarded this should be compared with the normal lack of agreement between the marks awarded by teachers.

If institutions of post-secondary education cannot continue their authoritarian relationships between staff and students, self-evaluation and peer evaluation will need to be greatly developed in the near future.

IV Are assessments fair?

We have seen that current assessment procedures are unreliable and have doubtful validity. It follows that there is a measure of injustice in the way students are assessed. This raises two kinds of questions. Firstly, 'What kinds of students benefit from the present system and who is at a disadvantage?' Secondly, 'What relevant changes take place in students in their college years which are not normally assessed?'

An underlying implication of this section is the need for innovation and experiment in assessment methods. In particular there may be injustice when only a few methods of assessment are used because irrelevant factors may influence success and failure. Variety could increase validity.

(1) Personality influences

There are many studies that show that high-drive introverts perform better in examinations than low-drive extraverts (Furneaux, 1962; Malleson, 1967; Walton and Drewery, 1967; Entwistle and Entwistle, 1970; Entwistle and Wilson, 1970; Entwistle and Percy, 1973). One possible explanation for this is that high-drive introverts work longer; and there is some evidence from the first two studies by Entwistle to suggest that they use 'good study methods' in that they 'work carefully, think ahead, are conscientious and recognise the importance of working conditions'. It should be noticed that intelligence is of less importance, particularly in those countries where a smaller proportion of the population enters post-secondary education. Where post-secondary education is highly selective, the range of ability is narrowed so that the correlation of intelligence with academic success is lower and other factors acquire greater importance.

(2) Student tactics

A second and most important factor is students' attitudes to the examinations themselves. Recently, it has been shown with increasing frequency (e.g. Cox, 1974; Miller and Parlett, 1974) that students feel examinations to be a kind of game which is irrelevant both to real life and to their academic worth. Different students react to this feeling in different ways. Some students study the rules of the game in order to be good at it. Miller and Parlett call these 'Cue-seekers'. For example, they try to find out likely questions in advance by looking for hints in the words of their teachers, observing their teachers' interests, finding out when the examinations were set, studying past papers, doing practice answers and doing all manner of other legitimate activities which are quite distinct from the disinterested pursuit of their subject of study. A second group called 'Cue-conscious' are aware that the game exists, but either ignore it, or deliberately refuse to be corrupted by it. The third group, which was the largest in Miller and Parlett's study, are called 'Cue-deaf'. Unlike 'Cue-seekers' they do not go out of their way to make a good impression upon teaching staff, nor do they deliberately try to pick up hints. They believe in hard work. The interesting, and in one sense alarming, finding is not only that 'cue-seekers' perform better than 'cue-conscious' students, and that 'cue-conscious' students in turn are more successful than those who are 'cue-deaf'; but that some teaching staff deliberately give legitimate hints on topics to be studied. The fact that examination marks are a reflection of how far students deliberately play the 'academic game' to win, dilutes the extent to which they reflect the achievement of educational objectives. Thus, the 'academic game' is a major factor destroying the validity of examinations. The students who do best are those who both work hard and are 'cue-seekers'.

(3) Student failure and related factors

It is to be expected that some students will fail examinations and that the best thing for others is to drop out, but it cannot be stressed too strongly that one of the most iniquitous features of post-secondary education the world over is the high *rate* of student dropout. This needs to be seen not only as part of the responsibility of colleges, but within the context of the invalidity of current assessment procedures. It is not only a question of wasted money and misuse of resources, but the psychological damage and personal adjustment that is required when a student raises his levels of aspiration, isolates himself from his family and network of established friendships at their expense, engages in mental work to the limit of his capacity, only to be frustrated and to have to return to face those who sacrificed for him. This syndrome is less common in western countries than in the 'Third World' where the competition and prestige of higher education, and dependence upon the family unit, are greater. Yet even in Australia and New Zealand wastage rates have been between 30% and 40% of students arriving at university with only 35% - 40% completing their degrees in minimum time. Although it varies greatly from one college to another, up to 50% leave prematurely in the USA and 40% complete their courses in minimum time. Even in England, over 80% of students in one study thought their parents would be extremely disappointed if they did badly in examinations. Only 4% rated their parents as indifferent to their university careers (Musgrove, 1967b).

Some college departments feel that by failing a large proportion of their students they maintain their standards. The reverse is the case. By failing so many they demonstrate their own incompetence in the selection of students, their incapacity to teach, the invalidity of their methods of assessment, or some combination of these three. In England,it seems as if mere awareness of the problem was sufficient to halve the wastage rate to about 13% without apparent lowering of academic standards.

If we consider the factors which relate to students' ultimate academic success at college, many are associated with the students' rate of adjustment to college life in the first few weeks. Hoare and Yeaman (1971) have shown that a survey of students' work habits motivation and academic performance, less than eight weeks after arriving at university, predicted later academic performance better than examinations and a similar survey later in the year. Halpin (1967) has shown that if borderline students are interviewed and counselled at the end of their first term, the rate of their academic failure can be halved. In one small study, Cohen and Child (1969) found that 68% of dropouts were bored by their work, 56% were unsure of their abilities, and 53% were overwhelmed by academic work. Rossman and Kirk (1970) reported that students who voluntarily dropped out at Berkeley had higher verbal ability and were more intellectually oriented than students who continued. Not surprisingly, those who withdrew voluntarily scored higher on tests of ability than those who withdrew because of failure.

The reasons commonly given for student failure by academic teaching staff are either that students lack ability, or that they do not work hard enough. We have seen that there is some evidence for both these views, but it is by no means so simple. Some students fail because they overwork, and others demonstrate that they are not incompetent when they successfully complete comparable courses elsewhere.

Many of the most important factors affecting student performance in examinations are social. When Malleson (1967) asked students to state the difficulties they experienced at college, the three most frequently mentioned were 'social isolation', 'inadequacy or remoteness of teaching staff', 'budgeting between work and social interests'. These are each concerned with students' relationships with other people, not with how they relate to an academic discipline.

The relation of social factors to student wastage is also shown in a recent study by Lohle-Tart-Esser at the University of Louvain (1973). She used a succession of tests throughout the year and the factor which corresponded most significantly with student dropout was the failure to attend the test sessions. Thus involvement or participation seemed to be related to University success.

There is evidence that with the expansion of higher education the proportion of students giving educational stress as a major problem has increased, but this is not to say that the social stresses themselves have increased (Lipset and Altbach, 1966). Again, Astin (1968) has found that high per capita expenditure by students, large research programmes, highly selective student intake, large libraries, high staff/student ratios, highly qualified staff and keen competition among students for good marks, were not institutional characteristics that favoured better undergraduate performance. Students' peer environment, flexible curricula, relatively permissive policies concerning cheating and heterosexual activities were more important. Pervin and Rubin also distinguish between academic and non-academic reasons for dropout. They argued that non-academic dropout is related to mis-matches between self-perceptions and perceptions of other students, self-perceptions and perception of college, and differences between the college and an ideal college. Dropout was also significantly related to its perceived probability (1967).

These studies suggest not only that student dropout is sometimes the result of indifferent teaching, but that it can often be prevented if academic staff consider it as their responsibility and are sufficiently vigilant. After considering students who failed mechanical engineering courses at three London colleges, Malleson (1967) concluded that because they had subsequently done well as measured by income, failure could probably have been prevented by adequate supervision and advice. He concludes that a system of early warning could be beneficial, and that many students would have welcomed a system in which it was easier to change courses. Hecker and Lezotte (1969) have shown that when students who have previously failed transfer to courses with a lower educational goal, their general success rate is extremely high. This suggests that there may be a mis-match between students' aspirations and the courses on which they are enrolled. In one study (Musgrove, 1967b) the main determinants of students' levels of aspiration were present circumstances such as the subjects they were studying and the type of institution they attended, rather than their social or academic histories, their social class or previous academic attainment. If this is generally true it is important because it shows that students' aspirations are not beyond the control of the college authorities and that the responsibility of colleges is therefore all the greater.

(4) Sex differences in performance

A much debated question is whether men or women do better in examinations. There seems to be some evidence that women perform better in medical examinations than men (Tomlinson et al, 1973), but this is not true in other subjects. Walton (1968) found that amongst senior medical students, women were more competent, with significantly higher ability in overall medical school performance. They were more anxious and more introverted. They had more independent attitudes to study and were less moralistic than men. They were more practical and more patient-centred in professional orientation. Men were less critical and inclined to take a more detached view of instruction provided.

Weinberg and Rooney (1973) have observed that although the academic standards of women were inferior in the first two or three years of a medical course, there was no significant difference by the end. They hypothesised that women take longer to adjust to college life than men, and since medical courses are longer than those in other subjects, it is possible that most college courses are too short for women to display their full potential. This is consistent with evidence from a Scottish survey that girls at college need more support from their families than men. At Edinburgh, their failure at University was significantly related to their father's approval of their attendance; girls from lower social backgrounds also performed worse. These differences did not apply to men (Kapur, 1972). Thus, it is possible that women take longer to adjust to the independence and autonomy required in post-secondary education, particularly when they are away from home.

Studies showing the characteristics of successful women students suggest that they have made, or do not need to make, this adjustment. For example, Davis and Satterly (1969) found that successful women student teachers were significantly more tough minded, confident, relaxed and conscientious than student teachers of low ability. In a study investigating birth order and expressed interest in becoming a professor (Fischer, Wells and Cohen 1968), firstborn women had the same aspirations as men, for whom birth order was not a significant variable. These researchers hypothesised that firstborn women learn to adopt role patterns consistent with aspiring to leadership. Again, Gottsdanker (1968) found that gifted women show a distinctively different pattern of intellectual interests from gifted men, and that they diverge more sharply from typical women students than the gifted men. Faunce (1968) has shown at Minnesota University Liberal Arts College that high academic ability in women needed to be associated with appropriate interests to achieve academic success commensurate with their ability. Non-graduates were more interested in business and practical arts occupations and were more troubled by personal problems in the process of growing up.

Thus, successful women demonstrate a certain maturity. As remarked earlier, this is not the same as greater age. Doty (1967) has shown that older women have distinctive problems and characteristics. He compared 40 young and 40 older women students with median ages of 20 and 35 respectively. Older women were inferior in intelligence, they reported more problems in concentrating, reading rapidly and taking notes in class, but less difficulty in remembering academic material and in techniques of study. Doty concluded that mature women can adjust successfully to the demands of an undergraduate course.

In effect, all of these investigators show that current methods of assessment measure irrelevant factors in student performance. While it is also probably true that they reflect the achievement of some relevant objectives, the question must be asked, how many relevant abilities in no way influence assessment results. A study by Newcomb et al (1967) of students 25 years after they had left college, suggests that although students' attitudes and patterns of thought were not formally part of their college assessment, the college had been fairly successful. Newcomb and his colleagues found that students' attitudes had remained fairly stable on the dimension of conservatism, detectable changes being attributable to the influence of husbands and friends. A series of tests suggested that the established norms of the college were individualism, unconventionality, intellectuality and tolerance. Students' adaptations to these norms depended on their questioning attitude, their interaction with fellow students and the extent to which their initial attitudes conformed to those expected by the college community. By a variety of techniques, Newcomb and his colleagues classified students into four categories on the basis of their individualism and intellectuality: 'Creative individualists' (high on both), 'The wild ones' (high individualism/low intellectuality), 'The scholars' (low in individualism and high on intellectuality) and 'The social group' (low on both). 'The social group' constituted a deviant subculture that did not change its attitudes towards college-wide norms. Newcomb concludes that community norms at this college were powerful and their influence persisted.

It should be pointed out, in contrast to the studies of Evans (1967) and Morrison and McIntyre (1967), that these students were not necessarily immediately subject to counter norms immediately upon leaving college. Morrison and McIntyre re-tested student teachers on three scales of opinion about education (naturalism, radicalism and tender-mindedness) after one year of professional teaching. On all three scales the scores for graduate women decreased while those for graduate men remained the same. Non-graduate women increased in naturalism and radicalism. During training there were increases in naturalism, radicalism and tender-mindedness, and these decreased again after a single year of teaching. This reversal was least for teachers in progressive primary schools. Evans (1967) looked at changes in values and attitudes of 78 students during their post-graduate certificate-in-education year. Both men and women increased their scores on a test of teachers' attitudes, but there were few differences on Allport's Study of Values, except that men had increasing social and economic values compared with women.

V Conclusion

A large number of studies have been cited in this chapter to show that things other than the achievement of course objectives affect students' assessments. The resulting invalidity of these methods is not sufficiently appreciated either by educational institutions themselves or employers or others who attempt to interpret them. A drastic change in the attitudes of authorities in post-secondary education is long overdue.

In many respects examining students should be regarded like a piece of research. Many of the same precautions should be taken, and many of the same questions should be asked. "What, precisely, is to be tested?" "What test design is to be used?" "What controls are to be observed?" "Has the test been piloted?" "What research has been conducted that would justify the approach being adopted?" "What measuring instruments are to be employed, what scales do they give, and what is their margin of error?"

Many contemporary methods of student assessment predate the Renaissance, and academic inertia has continued to be stronger than the scientific revolution. On the other hand, new methods do exist and are being introduced by scattered enterprising individuals. There is a need for experiment and variety in methods of assessment combined with explicit accounts of what assessments consist of. If a certificate does not say clearly what it certifies, how far does it certify it?

This chapter has been mostly concerned with "summative" assessment; that is assessment that summarises a lot of judgements such as judgements about a student's knowledge, abilities or character. It has not been primarily concerned with "formative" assessment; that is assessment which forms the basis of future policies decisions or actions. It has been more concerned with retrospective judgements than with guidance for future change. Chapter 7 reverses this balance.

CHAPTER 3: Selection methods and students' circumstances

CHAPTER 3: Selection methods and students' circumstances

As we have seen, the next task for the teacher is to decide the criteria by which he will select his students. Student selection has several functions. One is to guarantee the quality of students. Others are to limit numbers, to obtain information, to compile records, to assist administration and, most of all, to foster personal approaches in teaching.

Those teachers who do not select their own students will have to use other means to find out what they are like, for those who try to teach students without knowing their characteristics, will probably be less effective than they should be.

It should also be remembered that selection procedures are two-way processes. Not only do colleges select their students, but applicants select their colleges. The latter is much the more powerful determinant of who goes to college.

Therefore in this chapter we ask "Who enters post-secondary education?" This involves consideration of the methods by which students are selected and research evidence on students' general circumstances.

I Selection methods

(1) Academic examinations

(a) Varied requirements of a similar nature
Although in many countries individual colleges may lay down their own entrance requirements and this leads to great diversity, when we look at the overall pattern there is a remarkable uniformity. The most common criterion for selection of students is previous academic attainment as measured by academic examinations. In most cases these consist of a Baccalaureat or a Higher School Certificate or some other examination taken at school. Where this is not the case applicants usually sit an entrance examination set by the educational institution or a professional organisation.

The school examinations vary not only from country to country but from one state to another within a country. In India there have been recent attempts to make a uniform system of college requirements, but elsewhere the independence of colleges to make their own regulations has been closely guarded. For example, at Brock University in Canada, outstanding students in the Ontario Junior Matriculation may be accepted into a special summer course and, if successful, will be admitted to the University's first year course.

Most college requirements result in an age restriction and many universities explicitly will not accept students until the age of 18. Again, there are many exceptions. In Australian Universities, for example, there is no age restriction, although students usually do not enter before the age of 17.

Most colleges have different regulations for different subjects, and these are usually less stringent in arts than in science subjects. In Bangladesh Universities, for example, there are no special requirements to take an arts degree, but for other courses, the Higher Secondary Certificate is classified into groups of subjects and applicants need to have passed in an appropriate group. Nigerian universities permit entry at two levels: 'Direct entry' for those who have passed the Higher School Certificate in at least two subjects, and a 'Lower level' through a 'Concessional entrance examination' for those who hold the Lower School Certificate qualification in at least five subjects, including English.

Universities are increasingly requiring a demonstration of competence in the language of instruction for foreign students. Applicants sometimes perceive such requirements as obstacles imposed by college administrations to obstruct the achievement of their personal ambitions. Consequently, even before the student arrives at college, he has some antipathy towards college authorities as those who frustrate and obstruct his achievement. Yet these language regulations are in the applicant's own interests. For example, language tests can be a diagnostic tool to help the applicant make his choice of college, not a method by which colleges can reject a proportion of applicants.

Because foreign students are selected at a distance it is easy to make mistakes and difficult to give advice. Consequently foreign students in many countries are less happy and less successful than native students. For example it has been shown in Belgium by Delfosse (1972) and De Vittorelli (1972) that about one-third of the foreign male students had financial anxieties. It is not the regulations, but the methods by which they are administered, which is sometimes unsatisfactory.

One way over these difficulties would be to establish common standards. Although there is a considerable world-wide variation in requirements, there is sufficient in common to form the basis of comparable standards, and students' interchanges in the future. This is illustrated by an international university entrance qualification called the 'International Baccalaureat' which is being developed to meet the needs of multinational communities who work for agencies such as UNO (Peterson 1971). The idea originated in Geneva. The examination is set in French and English and has been recognised by universities and Ministries of Education in many countries for an initial six year period from 1970-76. The qualification is based on a course structure leading to a six subject examination at the age of 18, which consists of multiple-choice and other 'objective' questions, short answer questions, essays, auditive tests and oral examinations. Three subjects must be taken at a higher level and three at a lower level. These should include two languages, mathematics, at least one science, at least one arts or social science subject, and one other optional subject. There is a choice in the direction of specialisation, because any combination of subjects may be taken at the higher levels.

When using previous academic examination results as a criterion for selection, there are many questions on which selectors should be informed. One of these is the social implications of this criterion. Another is to know whether it is any good, and if so, what it is good for. It is to these questions of consequence and validity that we will now turn.

(b) Some social implications

Which is the more important, to select students on the basis of previous academic attainment, or on the basis of national, or other needs? Is it possible to over-select? Should selection be used for social engineering?

For example, most medical schools in developing countries admit students on the merits of grades obtained on a state or national examination. Such a system is biased towards the urban middle-class because better schools and colleges are usually confined to urban areas. Despite the effort to build new schools and to improve the existing ones in the rural areas, fewer than half the children in most rural areas, and as low as 10% in many, complete four or more years of primary school. Dropout rates are high and the great majority never reach secondary school. In the present circumstances, schools in rural areas function as filters transferring a small number of able and motivated young people from the rural world to urban universities.

Yet when considering post-secondary education it should never be forgotten that the majority of the world's population lives in rural areas of developing countries. A bias for selection of students with an urban background produces an elite of qualified personnel unlikely to accept work in rural communities. This has led to an over concentration of health professionals in cities with the result that in some instances there has been a heavy expenditure on curative and hospital based medicine at the expense of preventative services and rural health centres. A further result is that deep seated professional attitudes are established by university selection procedures.

To avoid far reaching implications of this kind many countries are attempting to create a balance in the student intake by reserving places for students from socially deprived groups (e.g. preserved places of up to 30% for scheduled caste students in India) or for those from rural areas (e.g. reserved places for students of Malay descent in the University of Malaya). Students from such groups feel the need to be convinced that what they are being taught has a direct connection with the needs and aspirations of their families and communities.

(c) Predictive validity

If success in college examinations is regarded as the standard of success, school examinaitons predict college performance as well as any other criterion. Nevertheless, the correlations with final examinations are low. How low they are depends upon the proportion of the population entering post-secondary education and the subjects taken in the school and college examinations being correlated.

In the United States, where up to half the population proceeds to some kind of college education, correlations between high school achievement and first year college grades average about .5. This correlation decreases as the time between school achievement and college achievement increases. Thus the typical correlation between high school achievement and the final college grades is about .4 (Humphries 1968). A similar result has been obtained at the University of Kuppio, Finland, in the Department of Community Health. Previous grades predicted subsequent grades very accurately, and correlations of marks between examinations were higher, the closer in time the examinations were held. In England, where only 8% of the population enter university, the correlation between university entrance qualifications and university degree performance averages about .3.

Broadly speaking, the greater the mathematical content of the two sets of examinations, the higher the correlation. Correlations of .6 between school achievement and university achievement have been obtained in Physics and Mathematics, while typical correlations in arts subjects are around .2. On average, less than 10% of the variance between students on final examinations at college is related to differences in performance at school leaving examinations. Thus, over 90% of the variation needs to be accounted for by other factors.

One reason for these low correlations is that school leaving examinations frequently measure an inappropriate mixture of abilities. For example, after an analysis of Advanced Level General Certificate in Education papers in Physics in England, Spurgin (1967) concluded that they place a considerable emphasis on factual knowledge such as memory work, book work, description and simple problems, while the Scholarship Level papers require higher levels of understanding. Scholarship Level papers should therefore be better predictors for university work, but these are usually ignored by university selectors, and fewer candidates are taking them. While there may be some truth in this argument, we have already seen that university examinations also place a heavy emphasis upon factual knowledge.

Therefore if final examinations measure anything at all, the variation in marks needs to be accounted for by other means. In a survey at the University of Edinburgh, Kapur (1972) has shown that academic success was related to achievement at school and participation in sporting activities, while students who failed were more likely to be Scots than English, over the age of 20 and to have experienced some emotional disturbance at university. Wilson (1968) claims that students with two or more of the following factors could be reliably predicted as at risk of failing the first year examinations: low vocabulary score, high neuroticism, high extraversion, poor entrance qualifications, and inadequate or partly inadequate lecture notes. Research in Scandinavian universities is producing basically similar results.

Entrance qualifications are one important predictor of university success, but by no means the only important factor. Sherwin and Child (1970) have also found that grades upon leaving school bear some relation to performance at university, but the best predictors of final degree qualifications were other examinations taken at the same university. This may be partly explained by the greater consistency between the examiners at the same institution than between those at school and university levels.

There is also increasing evidence that environmental factors play an important role in academic performance; and, of course, these factors are held relatively constant when the examinations taken at the same university are compared. Teachers from many universities in different parts of the world have remarked that students with apparently excellent entrance qualifications completely fail when they reach university.

A further factor is the degree of similarity between the criterion taken as an entrance qualification and the criterion of success at college. For the selection of post-graduate doctoral students, Stricker and Huber (1967) found that grades on undergraduate *courses* were the best predictors of grades of post-graduate *courses* and the time taken for completion. Graduate examinations were poor predictors. We have already seen in Chapter 2 that motivation and skills required for course work are fundamentally different from those required for success in set examinations.

There is also a question of how far entrance examinations should be taken in the same subjects as those to be studied at college. It is frequently assumed, for example, that students who have studied history at school, will be better students of history at college than those who have not. Consequently, previous experience of the subject is made obligatory. Colleges who have such regulations are forced to be inconsistent when many subjects, such as psychology and the applied sciences, are not taught at school level. Some experiments have been conducted in the United States, England, and elsewhere, in which subject requirements were waived for a proportion of applicants. Broadly speaking, the greater the importance of Mathematics in the subject, the more difficult it was for students to catch up or compensate for their lack of experience at school level. When students with arts backgrounds have been admitted to medical courses, they have performed just as well as those with science backgrounds except that they sometimes take one year longer. There appears to be little difficulty for applicants with science backgrounds transferring to courses in the arts and humanities. This is consistent with the different power of prediction of college entrance qualifications in these different subjects. It also helps to explain the observation by Phillips (1968) that in France and Germany, where there is no faculty entrance requirement and students are permitted to change courses between school and university, there is an overall drift from science subjects to the humanities. In the Netherlands and Britain, where faculty requirements demand experience in related subjects, the proportion of first year entrants in university science is higher than in France and Germany and is not so disproportionately less than at school level as in those two countries.

We may conclude that although previous academic attainment is one of the most widely used criteria for student selection, it does not have great predictive power and selectors would be wise to use other criteria as well.

(2) Standardised tests

We have seen that the mathematical component in applicants' previous academic experience is the most influential predictor of later performance in scientific subjects; that students who are not competent in the language of instruction experience academic difficulties; and that the selection of students is not simply a question of picking the best, but of selecting those most likely to do well in a particular college environment. It might be thought that each of these factors could be measured better by tests specially designed for the purpose. Such tests could be standardised and easy to administer.

This method has been used more in the United States than in any other country. After looking at hundreds of research studies, Fishman and Pasanella (1960) concluded that both high school achievement and aptitude tests correlated about .5 with first year college grades, but their correlations are much lower when enquiries are restricted to students of very high ability. Lunneborg et al (1970) have investigated how well these tests predict performance at various stages of a four year college course. As with academic examinations, they found reasonably good predictions for the first few years, but by the students' final year the correlations were nearly zero.

A much debated question is whether the standardised Scholastic Aptitude Test (SAT) discriminates unfairly between negroes and whites. After a six-year investigation, Stanley and Porter (1967) claim that it predicts future performance equally well for both races, and have obtained correlations between .55 and .70. While aware of Stanley and Porter's results, Cleary (1968) wondered whether the SAT consistently overpredicted the performance of one racial group. In two tests he thought it did not, but in a third he thought that it flattered the future achievement of negroes.

One of the reasons for the disappointing predictive validity of school based academic examinations is that they may place very variable weight upon different mental abilities. For example, when comparing Caucasian and Negro high school students, Green and Farqahar (1965) reported that Verbal Reasoning correlated .62 with future academic achievement for the Caucasian students, but bore virtually no relation to the future achievement of negro men. Impressed by the American results, Australian universities combined to produce a test battery involving a very wide range of materials and skills, but so far its predictive power has been little better than the traditional school based examinations (Rechter, 1970). A ten-year investigation in Scotland including a survey of all university entrants in selected years produced substantially the same results: the specially designed Tests of Academic Aptitude predicted college performance slightly less well than the traditional school examinations. A possible reason for the relatively disappointing Australian and Scottish results is that their universities accept a smaller proportion of the population than their counterparts in America, and we have seen that this tends to lower the predictive correlations obtained. The reason for this could be that it is more difficult to discriminate between students with a narrow range of ability, or it could be that the questions in the test require modification to discriminate well between people of high ability.

Chauncey and Hilton (1965) looked at the college careers of people with very high scores on standardised tests of academic ability, including the SAT, and concluded that they could validly predict subsequent levels of achievement such as obtaining a doctoral degree. By a long series of modifications to standardised tests, French (1964) tried to improve their predictive validity in colleges with very able students. Although his tests were not as reliable as the SAT, he thought the inclusion of questions requiring a knowledge of General Information and Insight for Reasoning made the test more useful with these students. It is possible that the colleges in which French worked valued critical thinking more highly than other American colleges and that information and reasoning are necessary for students to achieve this objective.

It was argued in Chapter 1 that critical and creative thinking should be a major objective in any institution of higher education. This raises the question of whether standardised tests of critical thinking could be developed. Shatin and Opdyke (1967) found that Watson-Glaser's Critical Thinking Appraisal Test showed no significant correlations with students' overall performance in first-year medical courses in New Jersey, nor with their study habits. They therefore recommend that subject specific tests of critical thinking should be developed; but their implied criticism of the Watson-Glaser Test assumes that their first-year medical examinations were an adequate test of medical thinking. This seems highly doubtful. Lysaught (1970) reports that a combination of I.Q. scores and the Watson-Glaser Critical Thinking Test successfully predicted people to train as computer programmers. But this is not necessarily an argument against Shatin and Opdyke, because the type of thinking that can be tested in the standardised set of questions is more likely to be of the deductive kind as is required in mathematics and computing than the inductive reasoning required in medicine. Therefore how far it is possible to produce standardised tests of critical thinking in specific subjects is still an open question.

To some extent students select courses in which they find the mode of thinking most congenial. McComisky and Freeman (1967) found that students of architecture, especially those concerned with architectural design, were significantly superior to economists in tests involving concepts of size and shape. In England, Hudson (1966) found that boys in selective secondary schools who specialise in science subjects were superior to boys studying arts subjects in questions requiring deduction and one correct answer ("convergent" thinking), while boys who specialised in arts subjects were superior to their science colleagues in questions requiring many possible answers ("divergent" thinking). It is of course possible that the specialisation had trained the mode of thinking, but some self-selection is also likely.

Standardised tests of knowledge of specific subjects do exist and are used by some North American colleges. The predictive validity of the

American 'College Qualification Tests' seems to be vindicated in a study by L. Smith, (1971). On the basis of questionnaires five years after entering college, compared with low achievers, high achievers were significantly more likely to obtain a college degree, were less likely to have changed their major academic discipline, and were more satisfied with their income, their intellectual growth, the standard of teaching they received at school and the number of friendships they experienced with college tutors. Both groups felt their values had changed significantly. This study is interesting because, unlike the others so far considered, it was a follow-up study two years after the students had left college, and because it considers other factors than academic success as objectives of a college of education.

We have now seen not only that academic success may be partly predicted by non-cognitive variables, but the question has been raised of how far academic success is the only objective of higher education. It is fairly clear in many professional courses that academic attainment is not the only important objective. For example, after using the California Psychological Inventory, Gough et al (1968) report that successful male teachers are conscientious, practical, rational, moderate, methodical and plan their actions in advance. Successful female teachers are dominant, persevering, serious, opinionated and ambitious. Unsuccessful men were reckless, daring, pleasure seeking, spendthrift, irresponsible and flirtatious, while unsuccessful women teachers were curious, affectionate, careless, easy going, unconventional and dreamy. Similarly, using the 16PF test McClain (1968) claimed that successful male teachers exhibit control, sobriety, steadiness, responsibility, non-competitiveness, and freedom from tension; while successful women teachers are competent, energetic, enthusiastic and spontaneous.

If these tests genuinely do predict success at teaching, rather than someone's subjective opinion of their success, they could provide suitable methods for selecting students in Teachers' Colleges. Again, Leeds (1969) claims that a modification of the scoring system of the Minnesota Teacher Attitude Inventory could improve its predictive validity of student success after one or more years of teaching to .55.

Outside the United States, professors responsible for training teachers have been cautious in the use of such tests, perhaps with good reason, for it is a very debatable question of policy how far the teachers of the future should be selected from a limited range of personality groups. There is also some reason to think that the academic and the personality requirements of students entering the teaching profession are actually in conflict. If this is so, it is possible that selectors should consciously choose students with diverse talents and use a profile of assessments in which these are explicit.

In spite of the relation between personality factors and academic achievement, there is reason to think that academic and non-academic accomplishments may be independent. Using the American College Testing Programme and Non-Academic Achievement Score records, Richards and Lutz (1968) claim it is possible to assess and predict non-academic accomplishment with some success, but their predictions bears no relation to academic achievement. Similarly, R.D. Brown (1968) has questioned the assumption that the best students academically are also the most active in cultural and intellectual activities. He used four scales of intellectual activity based upon the Omnibus Personality Inventory and a self report. None of these indices was significantly correlated with academic performance.

In conclusion, it may be said that standardised tests predict academic achievement as well as other methods but little better. Their use begs many questions of educational values; and while other methods of student selection are inordinately time consuming, selectors who commission the construction and validation of standardised tests will be wise to consider their cost-benefits.

(3) Recommendations

Rather less than half the respondents to our questionnaire reported that they paid attention to recommendations by head teachers or other persons when considering the selection of students. In vocational courses there is frequently a professional institution which either recommends certain candidates or has reserved places. For example, the Ghanaian Ministry of Agriculture reserves the right to fill a proportion of places in some university agricultural courses. Applicants for postgraduate medical courses normally require the support of a medical practitioner to give evidence of their medical competence.

The interesting feature is that, although this method is widely used, there seems to be virtually no research on its effectiveness. The obvious weakness in the method is that recommendations for different candidates usually come from different people who may have different standards. Recommendations provide useful information, but judgements of different individuals about different applicants are essentially incomparable.

It is equally true that colleges vary, so that a headteacher's recommendation for an applicant to one college may be more or less valid than the same recommendation to another. Bloom and Peters (1961) have suggested a way over this difficulty. Scholastic Aptitude Test scores can be used to define the scale of standards. The range of ability of students at particular schools and colleges can be placed upon these scales. The predictions for particular students may then be adjusted up or down according to the school from which they come and the college to which they apply. By having this information about their own standards, schools and colleges will be assisted in finding *appropriate* places for students and thereby reduce dropout and wastage. Whether the increased competitiveness between schools and between colleges to raise their mean position on the scales would be wholly desirable is open to question.

(4) Students' motives and expectations

(a) The education conveyor belt - motivation lacking
It might be thought that one reason why students enter post-secondary education is that they want to and that they then decide to apply to a

number of colleges. But it is a consistent finding of researchers in this field that a considerable proportion of students in Western countries have no strong desire to enter post-secondary education and they arrive because they are on an educational conveyor belt and they do not decide to get off. Morris (1969) has shown that the most important factors influencing choice between full-time work or full-time education are parental expectations and the perceived usefulness of college education to their general career. Potential students do not think about these issues until just before the decisions have to be made. They have a little knowledge about the colleges to which they apply and know little of their selection procedures. They expect interviews to be a confirmation and not a test of their suitability. Morris calculates that one-third of the people capable of benefitting from higher education in England never apply; but if data from intelligence tests is relevant, the figure could more reasonably be half or two-thirds because higher education in England attracts about 8% of the population from the top 25% of the intelligence range.

After an extensive survey of university entrants, McPherson (1973) reported that about one-third had no wish to attend. "They experienced from very early on in their secondary school career strong expectations from teachers and from parents that they should go to university and if they had no alternative in mind, it required considerable strength of character to disappoint those who had authority in the only social environments they knew: home and school. Such students were frequently relatively able, had parents with professional occupations who went to University themselves, and wished their children to experience the things that they valued." This finding applied equally in vocational and non-vocational courses. Indeed, in one prestigious school of medicine, just over half the students had entered with no strong desire for a medical career. Last and Stanley (1968) have reported that the majority of medical students do not decide their eventual career until the end of their training, and even five years after qualifying only 50% had definitely decided. Furthermore, their intentions are remarkably changeable, two-thirds having changed their mind within the period of five years. Similarly, a large proportion of girls entering teachers' colleges did not want to be teachers. Closer enquiry showed that, when children, they were allocated to classes from the age of 13 onwards according to their teachers' judgements of their potential academic ability. These judgements are unconsciously, if not deliberately, conveyed to the children, who then feel under pressure to succeed on a predetermined path.

(b) The 'decompression syndrome' - motivation lost

Upon arrival at college, these students frequently experience the 'decompression syndrome'. At school their life was planned and regulated for them. They did their work conscientiously and being able, received a consistent stream of encouragement and praise. At college they are *suddenly* required to regulate their own working habits. Work does not have to be submitted the next day, but only after a few weeks, and the tutors do not give the same encouragement. Consequently, the motivation that dominates the pupil at school, is neither fostered nor satisfied at college.

In Germany, Spindler (1968) concluded that the German university structure motivates students negatively. He said the students study too little when they come to college first; they receive too little counselling; they do not plan their work; they work little on their own and rely chiefly on lectures; they do not take an active part in seminars; and do not know how to prepare for examinations. The importance of motivation is shown by a study at the University of Tampere by Laitos (1973) in which it is shown that achievement at the end of the first year depends to a large extent on whether the student has been accepted by the University to study fields he originally wanted to study and which are of primary interest to him. This factor was a better predictor than the previous grades and achievement. Students did not know how to plan their study and their stated intentions were frequently unrealistic even when the time spent with tutors appeared to be adequate.

It was argued in Chapter 1 that independence of mind is an important objective of higher education, and to say that this can impose a stress upon new students may seem like a contradiction; but the need is to make the transition to college more easy, not to change the objectives of higher education.

Thus, students not only need to be selected on the basis of their motivation, but to be counselled at the time of selection on the kind of motivation that is appropriate at the particular colleges to which they have applied. To supply the second, colleges require a measure of introspection to understand the service they can offer both to students and their community.

(c) Motivation for a career

Students who do have definite career intentions upon arrival at college frequently change them. Werts (1967, 1968), analysed, in relation to their fathers' occupations, the career intentions of over 70,000 male students from 248 heterogenous colleges on entering college and one year later. Three broad types of occupation appeared to be passed from father to son: Physical sciences, Social sciences and Medical occupations. Of those who changed their intended careers during their first year at college, those who switched out of high socio-economic status careers (such as medicine and law) were less able and of lower socio-economic status themselves. Those who wished to move away from lower socio-economic status careers (such as teaching, business and accounting) were more able and of higher socio-economic status in origin. Hind and Wirth (1969) have shown that many students are discouraged from pursuing careers which require extensive academic training. Although the proportion of students in their sample who intended to be engineers was 20% upon arrival at college, it was only 7% upon graduation. On the other hand, the 7% intending business careers had increased to 21% upon graduation.

(d) Interest and prestige in the subjects to be studied

These findings are symptomatic of a phenomenon reaching serious proportions in Western Europe and North America in the early 1970's: the drift of students' interests from science to arts and social science courses. Butcher (1969) says that clear patterns of preference for science or arts subjects are evident at the age of 13 and that potential pure scientists and applied scientists are also clearly distinguishable. Although more British boys in his study wanted to be engineers than anything else, they perceived the relatively low prestige of this career. For children of both sexes the career of science teacher was not highly regarded. Upon arriving at college, science students found their courses more difficult than arts and social science students and became less interested as the course progressed, while the reverse was true of social science students.

(e) The satisfaction of achievement

Butcher's study is interesting because, when other investigations have shown student achievement to be related to occupational motivation (e.g. Smithers and Batcock, 1970), it has been assumed that students' motivation was the cause of their success, not the other way round. If motivation is the cause of success, selectors should have some means to assess motivation. If success is the cause of motivation, there are implications for teaching methods.

This causation works in both directions so that motives tend to be reinforced. Students who perform badly are discouraged and steadily enter a vicious circle of depression and poor performance. Conversely, Coombs and Davis (1967) have found a significant relationship between ratings on motivation and conformity and grade point averages. In one course in Business Studies (Morea, 1969), students who were interested in people as individuals were more likely to withdraw than students interested in codifying, classifying and arranging data.

This could be a comment on the content of the course, but it could equally be a factor that should be borne in mind when students are selected. Reed (1968) has found that over-achievement of students in academic work corresponds to the extent to which they can relate it to their own life.

(f) The desire to understand oneself

Increasingly, research is showing that students' motivations are not directed towards some external goals such as career preferment, power, financial rewards or even self satisfaction, but towards an understanding of themselves and their own psychological development. Brown (1967) thinks that student stress and unrest in American universities follows from the increased incongruity between students' desires and expectations of college and its reality. This is heightened by their own psychological development while at college and by the increasing size, complexity, impersonality and anonymity of the American university. He thinks administrators are aware of this and try to devise environments to help rather than to hinder emotional and intellectual development for students. Some efforts are being made in this direction at Michigan. In England, Cox (1974), after extensive surveys and interviewing of students, thinks that many students are asking the question "Who am I?" There is revulsion at the feeling that they are playing a meaningless academic game.

To satisfy this motivation, at Lancaster University many students take a course in the study of higher education so that students can see their own role in relation to the rest of society.

The drift from science to arts and social science subjects can also be interpreted in terms of the desire for self-discovery. Thus, students may select their subjects of study, not because of their academic interests, but in the light of their personal, private and unconscious motives. In one investigation, engineers and scientists had significantly higher levels of aspirations than arts and social science students, but they were less academically qualified and came from families with lower occupational standing. Engineers and physical scientists saw themselves as being more successful, tough, important, logical and adventurous than male social scientists (Musgrove, 1967a).

(g) Conclusion
We may conclude by saying that although motivations and expectations are important predictors of students' future academic performances, and to this extent college selectors cannot afford to ignore these factors, it is necessary to evaluate how far the college courses and environment will influence students' motivation. Thus, student selection not only involves judging the applicant, but judging oneself.

(5) Selection by interview methods

(a) What role can interviewing fulfil?
The interview method permits applicants to see a college for themselves. It provides an opportunity for counselling and gives selectors an opportunity to judge applicants' personal qualities.

It is often forgotten that the interview is a two-way process, students selecting colleges as well as colleges selecting students. Students are prospective clients, not slaves, and as such they are entitled to form their own judgements of the persons and places with which they will be associated for some of the most important years of their lives.

The college authorities should be professionals who keep themselves well informed both on changes in the pool of potential students and on research into techniques of selection. The applicants are amateurs and need counselling. This humanitarian role is neglected by post-secondary institutions in virtually every country of the world. Student selection is conducted like choosing fruit in a market place, rather than a consultative process.

Since we have seen that motivation, expectation and personality are the most influential factors upon students' success at college, and these are least easily assessed by other means, an evaluation of applicants' motivation should normally be an important objective of the interview method. The use of interviewing as a technique for selecting students, varies widely, not only from one country to another, or from one college to another, but within colleges.

Many do not interview at all. In some cases, candidates come from too great a distance for this to be practicable. The process is extremely time consuming and therefore very expensive, and is consequently impracticable when there is a large number of candidates. Furthermore, there has been an increasing distrust of the methods during the past fifty years. For example, seven interviewers in a University School of Architecture showed consistency when considered together but their individual reactions to interviewees with particular personalities was not consistent (Stringer and Tyson, 1968).

(b) Methods and styles of interviewing
There are four broad methods of student interview for selection. The most widely used is a "single interview" where the would-be student meets one interviewer. This method is used by 59% of medical schools in the United States (Kelly, 1957), and although I have no appropriate data, it is probably the most extensively used elsewhere. In a "board interview", one candidate meets several interviewers. In a "group interview" several applicants meet one or more interviewers. This is not widely used except in social work and management courses. Fourthly, a candidate sometimes receives a series of "single interviews". The last method allows interviewers to make independent judgements and to be less influenced by colleagues.

It is interesting that mere knowledge of interviewing technique will not make someone a good interviewer. Ware and his colleagues (1971) showed a film which significantly increased the knowledge of students on interviewing technique, but then found that the actual interviewing ability of students varied inversely and significantly with the amount of knowledge obtained. This finding is not unusual, but there could be many explanations for it. It could be a temporary phenomenon immediately following cognitive learning, or it may be that people who are good at learning factual information are weak in those affective skills essential to good interviewing technique. Another possibility is that it is not easy to learn both these things at the same time, and that some learned one, and some the other. Such hypotheses require further testing.

We have seen the importance of motivation on student performance. The difficulty with students' motivation is that it is commonly covert and unconscious. Interview methods such as provocation, disagreement and cross examination are sometimes used to detect it, but it is doubtful whether these are appropriate for the kind of motivation that is connected with academic study. A more appropriate technique known as 'Amplified Agreement' requires the interviewer to extend and agree with a candidate's value statement in order to test the degree to which the value is held because the candidate must either agree, disagree, or ignore the generalisation. Some interviewers try to adopt a variety of attitudes or introduce an element of surprise in order to gauge the candidate's own attitudes and reactions.

Most authorities (e.g. Anstey and Mercer) think that a good selection interviewer should be slightly introverted yet display sincerity and warmth. Vernon and Parry (1949) think that a good knowledge of the applicant's intended academic discipline is essential, and stress that the interviewer should be emotionally mature.

Members of academic staff meet students in one to one situations, both in tutorials and in oral examinations in addition to selection interviews. The techniques required in these three situations are quite different; yet not having any training in the use of appropriate techniques, there is a tendency for academics to use inappropriate behaviour transferred from one of the other two situations.

II Students' circumstances

(1) Student environments

(a) College Characteristics
It seems reasonable to argue that teachers should understand the characteristic environment of the college in which they work before they select students to spend some of their most formative years in it. This should lead student selectors and counsellors to ask "What are the characteristics of my college environment and which students are most likely to thrive there?" The study of college environments has received a great impetus since the early 1960's, largely owing to three American researchers: Pace, Stern and Astin.

After using factor analysis, Pace (1962) described four groups of college environmental factors which he called the College Characteristics Index. The first of these was the intellectual, humanistic and aesthetic climate of the college, the second coupled personal status and vocational orientation, the third was the extent of group, community and social responsibility and the fourth factor was the college's independence, rate of change and scientific emphasis.

On the basis of intercorrelation of these factors, Stern (1963) formed six scales: A) intellectual orientation, B) social effectiveness, C) amount of play, D) friendliness, E) the degree of constraints and F) dominance-submission. For example, students in colleges with a high intellectual climate displayed better understanding of social and political issues, were less dependent on others, displayed more spontaneous emotional expression and were less self-indulgent than students in low intellectual college climates.

Stern (1963) has also developed an Activities Index to measure psychological needs in college environments. On the basis of this work, Boyer and Michael (1965) identify three kinds of college in the United States: denominational colleges, which emphasise conformity, constraint and dependence; small private prestigious liberal arts colleges, encouraging high intellectual independence; and colleges where social pleasure was valued at the expense of intellectual rigour.

More recently, (1969) Pace has developed seven scales with which to characterise colleges: Practicality, Community, Awareness, Propriety, Scholarship, Campus Morale and Teacher/Student Relationships.
Although this book has emphasised the methodological decisions to be taken by teachers, it is also true that these College Characteristics should be borne in mind by students when applying to enter college.

There is a tendency for colleges to attract students of the kind they already have and thereby perpetuate their character. This may be because the need for adaptation to a new environment, and the feelings of insecurity when leaving home to go away to college, are less if students are amongst people like themselves. Astin has classified college environments in a number of different ways, and in two of his studies, (1964a and 1964b) he found that the characteristics of freshmen were distinctively similar to other members of their college when compared with students elsewhere on scales of Intellectualism, Aestheticism, Status, Leadership, Pragmatism and Masculinity. Astin thought this suggested that students select colleges to suit their own characteristics. If this is generally true, the reader may wish to consider the characteristics of his own college and students when deciding selection policies or when counselling applicants.

In another study (Astin, 1963) the aspiration to take a Ph.D was negatively associated with the number of students and the proportion of men among them. The reason for this is not obvious, but it suggests the influence of the social climate of a college on the academic aspirations of its members.

In a later series of observations, Astin (1965) attempted to classify classroom environments and the behaviour of teachers in various subjects. Factor analysis produced three bi-polar scales: foreign languages versus social sciences, natural sciences versus English and the fine arts, and business studies versus history. This implies that college environments will be strongly influenced by the proportion of students studying the various disciplines.

In yet another study (Astin, 1967), the potency of the 'Protestant ethic' was the most important factor in the college environment. Colleges which were religious, conservative, moralistic and with a strong administrative policy, were contrasted with those in which high intellectual standards and behavioural freedom permitted drinking, sexual and aggressive behaviour. Although the nature of college environments may be expected to vary widely from one country to another, and most research so far conducted has been in the USA, McLeish has also found that religious values are a major determinant in the environment of teachers' colleges in England (1970).

Chickering (1967) has said there are four types of college. The 'rocket' trains students quickly for a vocation or profession. The 'Cadillac' liberal arts college provides luxury, leisure and self-gratification, and prestigiously offers broad, verbal and intellectual skills to a limited elite of students. 'Horse and Buggy colleges' offer a wide range and depth of courses with no special sophistication and which students can help to modify. In 'junkyard colleges' students make their own decisions and have great freedom to assemble courses of their own choice. 'Rocket' and 'Cadillac' colleges overuse the lecture method and do not promote reflection and critical thinking although the high ability of students at Cadillac colleges provides some stimulus for reflection. 'Horse and Buggy colleges' develop intellectual competence, while 'junkyard colleges' are non-competitive and emphasise personal development.

To some readers it may seem strange to discuss college environments in a book on methods; but, not only may the environment impose limitations on the methods that may be used, in a wider sense it is a complex of methods in itself. What makes a college is not a collection of buildings, but an association of activities and the way it performs them. This point may be made clearer with examples. Hammond (1957) has reported that participation in small informal discussions and attendance at small group activities is associated with examination success at the University of Melbourne. Abercrombie (1966) has quoted studies which suggest that accessibility of teachers is an important environmental factor in the learning situation because it provides opportunity for feedback on learning, both to and from teachers and students. Thistlethwaite (1962) has shown that students' levels of aspiration are strongly associated with factors of the college environment such as enthusiasm, humanism, friendliness, achievement, independence and vocational orientation.

(b) Students' residential environment
An important aspect of the students' environment which may affect their methods of study, is their place of residence. Prior to the expansion of higher education in the 1960's, considerable attention was paid to this factor in England and Australia.

Although it is commonly assumed to be an advantage to live in a hall of residence, there is little evidence to support this view. For example, the pattern of performance in final examinations has been found to be almost exactly the same for students in halls of residence, students in lodgings, those living at home, and small groups of students sharing local accommodation (Howell, 1955; Holbraad, 1962). There is some evidence that students in halls of residence make more contact with members of the academic staff, attend more student activities, and have more college based friendships. But it is quite possible for students to live in social isolation, surrounded by other students in a hall of residence, if the potential community interaction is not realised.

First year students value the opportunity to live in residence before they have established college friendships, but living in flats is later perceived as an opportunity for independence. Living at home is not popular and restricts the number of college based friendships. Brothers and Hatch (1971) point out that the educational value of living in halls of residence is difficult to test, that halls of residence are expensive unless they are carefully designed to restrict labour costs, but that lodgings are not a satisfactory alternative.

It is true that Holbraad (1962) found that the proportion of students who complained their accommodation was unsatisfactory was twice as high amongst college failures as those who succeeded; but it seems reasonable to suspect that these students would be more likely to have complaints anyway.

Holbraad has cautioned that generalisations cannot be validly made about residence except with reference to specific colleges. Howell (1962) reported greater dropout for students living at home than for those in halls of residence, but Studdarth (1957) found the precise opposite. The most successful students, and those with the fewest dropouts were those who lived in sororities and fraternities. Students in lodgings, those living at home with parents and those in halls of residence showed decreasing success in that order. By contrast, Albrow (1965) claimed that students in halls studied slightly longer hours per week and performed a little better than those in lodgings.

In Australia, Anderson and Priestley (1960) also thought that students in halls performed slightly better but, in strong contrast to some British studies, (e.g. Brothers and Hatch, 1971) they believed the physical facilities and comfort to be no better than those in lodgings. Yet in another Australian study (Schonell, 1963) performance by students in halls, especially women, was markedly inferior to those in lodgings.

Acland and Hatch (1968) found little evidence to suggest that academic performance is related to residence factors. They have also observed that students in halls are not entirely representative, Jews and Catholics being under-represented and middle class and fee paying school origins being over-represented. This needs to be taken into account if counselling, student selection or policy decisions are to be made on the basis of research on the effects of residence. Halls seem to encourage participation in organised student activities, especially Christian activities.

Punch (1967) subjectively identified four sub-groups in a hall of residence - the lads, the Christians, the sensitives and the non-entities. The 'gentlemen' ideal was the dominant norm. It is obvious that these sub-cultures will vary with the wider culture of which they are a part. Hence the need for every college to study itself.

(c) Conclusion

The study of students' environments is in its infancy. Consideration of specific factors in isolation produces apparent contradictions. The broad image of a post-secondary educational institution appears to influence students' applications to it. If teachers are to select and advise applicants wisely, they will need to know whether the image is accurate. On this their own judgements are usually subjective while the judgements of applicants are usually based upon very little information.

(2) Social factors affecting student applications

In most countries of the world, applicants for courses in post-secondary education are an atypical sample of the community in their social class, age and sex.

This is, in part, a reflection of the influence of parents on applicants which has already been noted. A survey of students entering the University of Bradford (Musgrove, 1967) showed that for half of them, one or other parent was the most important person in their lives. ('Mother' and 'Father' were each mentioned by 25%). Child (1970) also found that parents were the most important persons in the lives of students throughout their time at university. Towards the end of their course, engaged partners and friends of the opposite sex assumed greater importance, while university teachers became significantly less important.

In the USA, Stout (1967) has shown that the support by blue-collar parents for their child's attendance at college varied with their social background, the social status of close friends and neighbours, participation in out-of-work activities and the father's type of employment. A newly introduced selection procedure in Czechoslovakia awards 20 bonus points out of a possible 100 to an applicant with at least one parent of worker or peasant origin. Since the student would thereby become a member of the intelligensia, his own children would not have the same benefit. Thus, if continued, a strange social oscillation could theoretically result. Whether there will be resentment at such a system is difficult to predict. Much depends on whether it is seen as a system of privilege and how it operates in practice. It could be a useful corrective to parental discouragement. In a recent study by King, Moore and Mundy (1974), students in England, France and the Federal Republic of Germany came chiefly from the higher social groups, but in Sweden and to some extent in Italy, students represented a more even spread of social groups. King and his colleagues found some evidence that a higher proportion of parents in France and Italy had received an education at upper-secondary or higher education level than in England, Germany or Sweden. Parents in France and England appeared to encourage their children to go on to higher education more than their counterparts in Italy, Sweden and Germany. Mothers in all social groups, and families where the father's occupation was professional or higher managerial in level, appeared to give more encouragement. It was clear that in most European countries parents do not give much information or advice about higher education and the children do not find it helpful. On counselling, King et al conclude that there was almost unanimous dissatisfaction with counselling services. There were frequent complaints that insufficient information and advice was available and that what was provided tended to be unrealistic, subjective and out of date. Both French and British students had suggestions on the training and recruitment of counsellors.

Sewell and Shah (1967) found both socio-economic status and intelligence related to the decision to go to college. For girls, socio-economic status was more important; and for boys, intelligence was more important. At college, intelligence was more strongly related to the degree of success than social class, although social class continued to have some positive relationship. In the same way, Armstrong has confirmed that about 70% of children in the USA with IQs above 135 at the age of 11 proceed to full time higher education. Of these, about three quarters are from professional homes (1967). Campbell and Siegel (1967) claim that the number of eligible candidates enrolled for higher education in the United States has remained a relatively constant proportion of the total population from 1919 to 1964. But when Spady (1964) examined the educational attainments of American men in relation to the educational backgrounds of their fathers, he concluded that although the attainment levels for men in all status groups have improved over time, the relative chances of men from low status origins reaching and completing college courses has actually deteriorated when compared with men from high status origins. Attainments for whites exceeded those for non-whites for students of all socio-economic levels and ages.

There is some evidence (e.g. Altman 1968) that mature students training to be teachers tend to come from working class backgrounds, whereas young students come from middle class backgrounds. Altman has suggested that 'mature' students tend to be 'people-oriented' and anxious to find scope for self-expression in their work. 'Mature' students in his study had already 'moved up' socially before applying to college.

Most college teachers agree that even a small number of older students can have a disproportionate beneficial effect upon college climates. Australian universities have supported this opinion by giving more favourable entry conditions to students who have spent at least 23 months between leaving school and applying for university. Of course, although the word 'mature' is sometimes used to describe older students, 'maturity' is not the same as 'age'. The latter can only be an imperfect guide to the former. Kipnis (1968) has claimed that socially immature students, as measured by a socialisation scale on the California Inventory, have a higher absentee rate. In his study they under-achieved in introductory mathematics, but not in an introductory psychology course. He says that when they first enter college, they tend to be more disruptive, but in later years they contribute more to discussion.

The characteristics of students applying to a college depend upon its prestige. For example, when one college of technology became a university, the proportion of middle class students increased, a higher proportion entered with traditional qualifications, more had long-term intentions of undergoing post-secondary education, fewer lacked parental support to go to college and the image of the college as having direct links with industry faded (Couper and Harris, 1970). The same conclusion may be drawn from the work of Hatch and Reich (1970) who chose eight institutions as a cross-section of British higher education and found that students at Cambridge came from the highest status backgrounds while at a polytechnic and a technological university about one-third came from the working class and a high proportion from overseas. But even these most accessible institutions of higher education were far from representative of the population as a whole. Even where the qualifications of working class students were the same, they took less prestigious courses. Hatch and Reich wondered if this was associated with the dissatisfaction and low morale of students from working class backgrounds, but it could also be associated with the low parental support received by these students.

It is difficult to appreciate the difference in impact of a crowded university campus on students from rural backgrounds compared with those used to urban life. Crotty (1967) has shown that freshmen who were members of small groups and who came from small town or rural areas were more likely to change their attitudes during their course than other students. This may partly be a reflection of the fact that rural areas are frequently conservative and the dissonance and incongruity between attitudes in these areas and lively university attitudes may require greater adaptation and change by rural students if they are to conform to university group norms.

Yet the differences are not confined to attitudes. In a Canadian study, Janzen and Hallworth (1973) showed that students who attended city as opposed to rural schools, and students with an English-speaking background as opposed to any other language background, had significantly higher mean scores in mechanical accuracy, fluency and the complexity of sentences they were able to write. Presumably this could affect their performance in examinations and possibly in group discussions as well.

(3) Student dissent

Since post-secondary education has been dramatically disturbed by student unrest during the past ten years, and inevitably some people have blamed selection policies and the expansion of this sector of education, it may be asked how far potential 'trouble makers' should be deliberately eliminated at the selection stage. Apart from the obvious difficulty of detecting who is likely to be a 'trouble maker', Bay (1967) points out that students active in protest movements tend to do better academically. They also tend to be more intelligent and more intellectually disposed compared with apolitical students. Bay says this statement may be justified, first with reference to the social psychology of attitudes, especially the works of Newcomb and Stouffer, secondly by examining work on authoritarian personality, dogmatism and political attitudes, and thirdly by looking at more recent work on political activists.

There is also some evidence that leaders of student dissent are not natural leaders, and derive their leadership from qualities which have not developed at the time of entry to college. These qualities grow with their intellectual development at college. Jansen et al (1968) at Indiana University found that the socio-political action group leaders were different from 'religious', 'resident', 'activity' and 'fraternal' leaders in that they appeared to have less formal leadership and experience than the other campus leaders and they emphasised personal interests or knowledge of group goals as their reason for election, rather than personality or leadership ability.

M.B. Freedman (1969) argues that the majority of American college students are unsophisticated and stable, and rather more in need of stirring up than calming down. Generations of students emerge having greater commitment to liberal views than they had when they enrolled. Student unrest on the campus is in some ways the result of the very success of administrators and teachers in liberalising students, he says. Universities and colleges need to provide society with leaders who have been critical and questioning during their college years.

Freedman also shows that, contrary to popular opinion, sexual behaviour of college students is characterised more by restraint than licence. Sexual attitudes and behaviour of college women in the past several decades show a considerable decline in strictness and prudery, and this in itself exemplifies the revival of love and affection, or respect for human dignity amongst young people. The use of drugs he sees as part of a rejection of American society. Freedman sees unrest on the American campus as an attempt to restore a viable sense of community in colleges and universities, to re-assert the unity of intellect and personality and to establish the ethics of social service and the free 'impulsive life'. Freedman thinks intra-college strife will soon diminish, but relations between college and society are not likely to be so smooth. This could be because the attitudes of college and university staffs could become more in harmony with the students than with the rest of society.

Trent and Craise (1967) say that although different forms of discontent may be observed among present day college students across the American continent, the committed and informed intellectual dissent that takes the form of students' activism, is typical of only a small minority in a few academically elite colleges and universities. They suggest that educational as well as political activism may enrich educational experience and foster personal development. Political and social apathy and conformity to an established norm appear to be a characteristic of most college students of this generation as with students in the past. However, despite this general apathy and conformity, college students do seem to possess a more intellectual disposition and greater autonomy than their peers who do not attend college. Since these are precisely the traits which to a more intense degree distinguish student activists from other college students, and we have argued for encouragement of independent, critical, enquiring and tolerant minds in post-secondary education, potential student activists should certainly not be excluded, and possibly should even be encouraged to go to college.

III Conclusion

We have seen that no method of student selection is very satisfactory. Like most educational decisions, those of student selection require making the best of a difficult job in the light of an informed humanity. Throughout this chapter we have stressed the importance of the counselling role by college selectors. It is frequently neglected. Obviously the interview method is important for this function, but so too is the active dissemination of accurate information about college life.

CHAPTER 4: Organising the content of the curriculum

CHAPTER 4: Organising the content of the curriculum

When a teacher has some idea of the abilities and other characteristics of his students he will be able to estimate in what ways and to what extent their knowledge, skills and attitudes should develop to achieve the course objectives. The teacher will then need to design the order in which the objectives should be reached, possibly in cooperation with the students themselves. This chapter is therefore concerned with two decisions: the selection of the students' tasks and the sequencing of them.

The first decision will involve (1) philosophical assumptions about what is to be learned and (2) will probably be influenced by certain social pressures. We will look at these two factors separately before (3) considering this decision. They will lead us to consider three dimensions of curriculum style: (a) the continuum between courses which emphasise the curriculum as a 'given' body of knowledge and those emphasising the students' learning processes; (b) the extent of 'depth' or 'breadth' and (c) how far students can influence decisions about their own curricula.

The second decision, sequencing the course, (1) will probably make both logical and psychological assumptions. Some people have said there is a logical order in which objectives can be achieved. Others have attempted to describe stages in students' intellectual development which seem to imply that some mental skills can *only* be achieved in a certain order. These are briefly described before (2) some generalisations about the sequencing of courses are attempted.

I Choosing the content of the curriculum

(1) Philosophical assumptions

(a) Content = subject matter + processes
In this chapter we will assume that the "content" of a course includes both the subject matter and the mental processes it requires. This is perhaps unusual. It is commonly assumed when one is choosing the content of a curriculum that one is only selecting subject matter. "Content" is taken to mean the information, concepts, principles, techniques, topics and literature on which attention will be focussed. But it was argued in Chapter 1, and indeed it is commonly believed by teachers in higher education, that the factual content of the curriculum is less important than the development of students' skills in thinking. In other words, processes, particuarly mental processes, are more important than the subject matter itself. What is more, these processes are shaped to a great extent by the teaching methods and assessment system.

In contrast to our use of the term "content", some course designers would draw a distinction between the "content" of a course and its "process". The processes may include the learning of particular skills (e.g. in laboratory work, interviewing, essay writing and so on) as well as the give and take of an academic discussion. But in this chapter both the "subject matter" and desired mental, or other "processes" associated with it, will be regarded as curriculum "content".

The distinction between "subject matter" on the one hand and these "processes" or attitudes on the other, is not a clear one. Science, philosophy and some other subjects are essentially activities, or processes, and not primarily bodies of knowledge. In any case, in order to learn some "subject matter" a student must engage in some kind of "process" when communicating, learning or practising. Nevertheless, even though the distinction may be a fuzzy one, we will use it later as a dimension to contrast the emphases of different kinds of curriculum.

Both these emphases assume the importance of the academic discipline. In this sense they are subject-centred. Later in the chapter we will consider reasons for supposing that some curricula should be student-centred. A major assumption of these courses is that their content and sequence reflect the needs of the students taking them rather than the nature of their academic disciplines.

(b) Does knowledge have natural boundaries?
A further assumption when selecting the content of the curriculum is that some knowledge or activities can be classified as relevant to a particular subject while others cannot. It is as if academics walked around with a map of academic knowledge on which certain boundaries are drawn. Is there any justification for this? If so, this map of knowledge may tell us what to include in a course and what to leave out. In other words, are there natural boundaries dividing knowledge into areas, so that a teacher can know what the content of his course should

be and which parts should be grouped together?

Philosophers have long been engaged in an exploration of the nature of different forms of knowledge and have attempted in various ways to distinguish them according to their 'implicit forms'. For example Phenix (1964) describes six "fundamental patterns of meaning" each of which has its own basic ideas, structure and method. They are:

symbolics - ordinary language, mathematics
empirics - physical and life sciences, experimental psychology and social sciences
aesthetics - arts, literature
synnoectics - personal knowledge of self or others as in existential forms of philosophy, psychology and religion
ethics - areas of moral and ethical concern
synoptics - meanings which integrate man's experience such as forms of history, philosophy and religion.

Phenix thinks that these realms of meaning form a logical order and a pattern of human development and maturation. He believes they are not separate and isolated, but inter-related and complementary.

Hirst (1974) has classified knowledge into "forms" and "fields". Forms of knowledge include mathematics, physical sciences, human sciences, history, religion, literature and the fine arts, and philosophy. He has claimed that each of these, unlike fields of knowledge, have distinctive concepts. While this may be true, it is also arguable that they may be distinguished by the characteristic methods of explanation they adopt. Fields of knowledge may be theoretical, practical, and may or may not include elements of moral knowledge. They include geography, engineering and business studies. Fields of knowledge are "held together simply by their subject matter, drawing on all forms of knowledge which can contribute to them."

But it is hard to justify the customary boundaries between the academic knowledge taught in different departments on the basis of these classifications. In fact these philosophers explicitly deny that their classification should be used in this way. Most academic disciplines use several patterns of meaning and forms of knowledge. Indeed it is arguable that teachers should consciously include a variety of forms of knowledge and thought when designing the content of their curriculum.

Consequently the work of philosophers does not *directly* help us in this decision. There are no clear boundaries between academic disciplines, and even if there were, it is doubtful whether a teacher should ask himself "what is the area of knowledge covered by my discipline?" and then try to cover every part of it when deciding the content of the curriculum.

The value of philosophers' work is indirect. It can provide frameworks for curriculum designers to think about the balance of mental processes (as distinct from subject matter) required in their courses. For example a psychologist or sociologist may need to decide on the balance between an experimental emphasis and techniques based more on subjective experience. Teachers of languages or music may need to decide the balance between analytical skills and aesthetic appreciation. What level of mathematical, statistical, or computing competence should be assumed or taught in physics, geography or economics courses? These are only some of many such judgements. The design of interdisciplinary courses will clearly require many more.

(c) The hidden curriculum
Snyder (1972) has pointed out that decisions of this kind frequently imply a "hidden curriculum" of which teachers are wholly unaware. Consequently the requirements of a course perceived by students frequently conflict with aims explicitly stated by teachers. Teachers say they like students to write thoughtful answers in examinations, but they choose the content of their courses in a way that emphasises the memory and regurgitation of "facts". Universities wish to encourage enquiring minds and research, but their laboratory teaching frequently prescribes fixed recipes rather than the discovery or creation of new ideas. Institutions which claim to be meeting the "needs of industry" and its desire for team work develop a deeply based sense of competition between students with their assessment systems. Teachers say they want students to have critical minds, but feel threatened if they criticise the course. In addition the very selection of facts, the way they are organised, and the methods they imply, assume a set of values, procedures and tasks which the students are not supposed to question. "These covert inferred tasks, and the means of their mastery, are linked together in a hidden curriculum. They are rooted in the professor's assumptions and values, the students' expectations, and the social context in which both teacher and taught find themselves". (Snyder 1972).

Since a hidden curriculum of this kind restricts the nature of enquiry and therefore frustrates one of the major purposes of higher education as argued in Chapter 1, it is necessary to make the hidden curriculum explicit. Therefore each teacher should teach his students to be aware of the nature of his bias and to encourage them to develop their own values, organisation and methods. It is part of the teacher's job to reveal what is hidden. The hidden curriculum is a form of indoctrination, not least in the limitations imposed by the language of the subject and the assumption implicit in the metaphors it uses. Academic enquiry requires freedom; the teacher must give it.

(2) Social influences on choice of content

If the boundaries between disciplines are 'fuzzy' and not sharply defined by their logical characteristics or some other generally recognisable and acceptable features, the teacher's task in choosing the content of students' learning is not only an academic one, but will be affected by the social and political context of his work within the college. We will consider five factors which influence the divisions and boundaries of academic knowledge in courses and of which the teachers must therefore take notice.

(a) Five factors
Institutional factors. Institutional factors include the formation of

subject-based academic departments and the consequent bureaucratisation of the subject area, administrative convenience, the career structure of teachers where it is defined in terms of specialist expertise, the need for small social groupings with which to identify, and the formation of blocks of knowledge when timetables sub-divide courses.

Relevant associations. Studying frequently involves focusing on one aspect of knowledge to the exclusion of others. When studying a topic in depth attention is necessarly withdrawn from knowledge irrelevant to it. Conversely common associations of knowledge are established and boundaries become drawn by common usage. In this way distinctive fields of knowledge evolve.

Professional classifications. Professional bodies also influence the organisation of knowledge by sub-dividing it for assessment purposes and by classifying students' perception and ambitions when they specify professional roles.

Unifying concepts. Some bodies of knowledge can be distinguished as having central unifying concepts. Very often these may be perceived as the forms or realms previously described on page 83. These will be considered further on page 90.

Common interests. Teachers and researchers may share interests across faculty divisions. These could include research (and even teaching!) methods or interests in certain information or its application.

These five factors are probably most influential on those adopting traditional approaches to the choice of course content; but they may not be aware of it. In some senses they are most evident, because they are most problematical, in courses demanding cooperation across the usual boundaries. Such cooperation cuts across the social forces which establish the boundaries and leads us to consider the social control of knowledge.

(b) The social control of knowledge.
Sociologists have considered the way knowledge is associated to satisfy the needs of those who use it, the manner in which boundaries between areas of knowledge are socially established and maintained, and the causes and effects of hierarchical systems of knowledge.

Bernstein (1971) describes the sort of course where there are sharply defined boundaries between parts of the subject typically supported by a hierarchical departmental organisation with little horizontal communication across the subject by junior teachers, but stronger horizontal working relationships between heads of departments. Junior staff tend to prefer vertical loyalties and working relationships within their subject area. Knowledge becomes compartmentalised.

Naturally, this insulating effect spreads to students who become similarly bound to subject allegiances and are reluctant to become involved with students of other disciplines except for sporting and social activities. They perceive their identities and their future careers as shaped by their specialist subjects, especially in professional courses.

On some courses it almost seems as if academic knowledge becomes the "property" of those who teach it. Access to the most highly valued knowledge, and the possibility of creating new knowledge, is often restricted to postgraduate and research students. Knowledge then becomes stratified so that a hierarchy is established. Because there is a tendency to restrict access to knowledge to those who progressed upwards through the hierarchy, access to knowledge reflects status. The excuse commonly given for this stratification is that restricted knowledge is dependent upon first learning other things. But in most subjects observation will show that research discoveries and new concepts can quickly pass downwards through the hierarchy to undergraduate and school level courses. The dependence is frequently a myth. Ideas can be understood in many different ways. The fundamentals of atomic theory and set theory may serve as examples. We may shortly expect elements of computer science, contemporary psychology and systems thinking to make the same downward journey.

The compartmentalised curriculum is typical of many designed on traditional lines. The students often experience disjointed courses, competing priorities, and considerable mystery about the rationale of the curriculum and its assessment procedures. However, these experiences are likely to occur in any style of course if special effort is not made to integrate with other students and teachers across the boundaries of knowledge and status, not just socially, but in terms of their learning, teaching and research. Integration also implies the encouragement of an open dialogue between teachers and students in continaully developing the curriculum. These dialogues are as important in a single discipline course as in a multi or interdisciplinary one. The implication of this for curriculum innovations is of course considerable significance. Pity the innovator, however, who does not allow for the hostile reactions to such changes.

Young (1971) has argued that any attempt to gain access in a horizontal plain acros the hierarchy could be construed as a threat to the ordering of knowledge. The availability of expert knowledge across disciplines is also a threat to the authority of the subject specialist in controlling access. Thus interdisciplinary courses could be viewed as threatening, especially when bridges between established disciplines are sought. Where students are given access to the control of knowledge, and where they build up their knowledge as in experimental learning or project work, there is an implicit threat to the established hierarchy of knowledge and to its custodians, the academics.

Like the contributions of philosophers, the work of sociologists does not offer prescriptions or formulae to guide the choice of course content, but it does provide considerations that will inform this decision by making the course designer more aware of what he is doing.

(3) Three dimensions of curriculum style

These philosophical assumptions and sociological considerations draw attention to three dimensions within the content of a curriculum. The first dimension runs from a concentration upon subject matter to an emphasis upon students' mental processes. The second runs from specialisation in a single form of thought to the variety of inter-disciplinary studies. The third varies according to who chooses and controls the content of the curriculum. Strictly speaking this third consideration is multi-dimensional because many agencies may be involved, but we shall be particularly concerned with the extent to which students decide their own curriculum content.

In an ideal world these would not be dimensions at all, but in practice they are. For example, a curriculum containing a large amount of factual subject matter to be remembered does not necessarily prevent students from thinking about it, but in practice there is a limit to what students can achieve in the duration of a course.

(a) The subject matter - mental processes dimension
The traditional curriculum. In many colleges teachers and students are under pressure to conform to the "traditional" emphasis upon subject matter. In the "traditional" academic approach to the curriculum, information, principles and techniques have been accumulated over the centuries, their indissoluable and distinctive unity remains unchallenged and their benefits to students and humanity are not questioned. Within each subject there is supposed to be something unique in the way it orders or explains experience. Its unique quality is believed to "train" students' minds irrespective of the way they learn it.

Particularly when a teacher himself was taught in this way, there is a tendency for him to imitate the "traditional" curriculum simply because he has never learned to think about any alternative. In the same way, students readily accept this style at college when they have experienced a similar curriculum at school.

In the "traditional" approach the selection of course content arouses great controversy and rivalry at all levels. The selection of specific content implies certain values, educational aims and the pursuit of specific ideologies. These are rarely made explicit enough to be tackled.

In higher education the range of information taught in a subject defines its academic territory. It affects the number of students who take courses in the appropriate department and conseqeuntly reflects college politics and departmental power. If courses are designed with the students' mental processes in mind, then it becomes clear that these can be equally well developed in a variety of subject areas.

Thus there are strong pressures for a syllabus to be designed in terms of factual knowledge, not for the benefit of the students, but for those who teach and administer the courses. These pressures tend to make the classification of academic knowledge clear, rigid and exclusive. Consequently even within a single course some students receive knowledge as if it was a "collection" of isolated facts. Such classifications, Bernstein remarked, result in a compartmentalised curriculum and emphasise the division of labour between teachers. They restrict teachers designing their own courses. Consequently, without the permission of teachers in other departments or the sanction of high-level superiors, curriculum innovations within an individual teacher's courses are sometimes limited. In this way creative thinking arising from the novel association of knowledge and ideas is inhibited. The ability to think across subject boundaries is not encouraged and significant innovations involving the whole course are enormously difficult to achieve.

Thus the "traditional" conception of the curriculum is a conservative force for cultural inertia. For example, science is frequently conceived as a body of knowledge rather than a method of enquiry. Far from enjoying an exciting adventure with academic curiosity and discovery, students are expected to absorb the dogmas of "established scientific practice" from authoritative sources, to find solutions to problems with known "right" answers, and to conduct "cookery book experiments" to obtain "correct" results. The student has little freedom to develop his own knowledge outside the prescribed framework.. What is to be learned is equated with what is to be taught.

Figure 4.1 is an extract from a syllabus of the "traditional" type. Its vagueness allows teachers and examiners great freedom in their choice of methods and general approach. It is also less public by being less specific than other approaches so that teachers' effectiveness is less open to inspection. Teachers may believe they achieve a wide range of objectives under these headings, but their achievements may be limited because the pressure to include a wide academic territory may make coverage superficial through concentrating on teaching information. The knowledge explosion also results in a crammed syllabus and superficial coverage. Furthermore, the syllabus does not tell the student what he should be able to do with the knowledge or what he should achieve by the end of the course; yet he must strive to achieve it. From his point of view it is a boring list of headings which mean very little.

Figure 4.1: Part of a 'Traditional Curriculum'

General Subject: The Sociology of Industrial Society

1. The concept of industrial society. The nature of the major institutions - the family, economy, polity, military, religious education etc. Changes in their structure and functions.

2. The process of industrialisation, modernisation and development. Historical and contemporary approaches to social change. The future of industrial society.

3. Social stratification and mobility. Historical and contemporary theories of stratification e.g. Marx, Weber, Warner, Davis and Moore etc.

4. Bureaucratisation and organisational development. Organisational theory, professionalisation and changes in the occupational structure.

5. Social problems of industrial society and societal responses to them. Social disorganisation and social deviance.

Process-centred curricula. In the process-centred approach the emphasis is not so much on the subject matter or learning methods as on the development of psychological processes. In such courses the aim might be to develop not only high level cognitive skills such as creativity, originality, problem solving, communicating, and decision making; but also affective qualities such as valuing, caring, cooperation, commitment and the development of personal relationships. Students are encouraged through participatory learning (e.g. in discussions, games, simulations, T-Groups, etc. see Chapter 5), to examine their own part in these activities and thereby their feelings about academic knowledge, and not just to accept it as given. It is thought that in curricula of this kind, students will develop the skills and attitudes that are prerequisites for learning and intelligent behaviour. This should encourage them to be more innovative, as well as developing more harmonious motives and values (cf. Berman, 1968; and Heron, 1973).

If it is thought that this emphasis upon attitudes and other affective objectives is only appropriate in a few courses, such as postgraduate Management Studies, it should be remembered that all education from the cradle to the grave includes education of the emotions. If nothing else, this argument should stand as a corrective to the common neglect of this aspect of human nature in many courses in higher education.

Other styles of process-centred curricula include those based on the techniques to acquire, interpret, communicate and apply knowledge proposed by Parker and Ruben (see page 93 and the problem based courses described on page 98.)

Whatever position on this dimension a curriculum designer may take, in most subjects he will still be faced with a series of conflicts in selecting the subject matter. The selection of what should be learned on a course will always be artitrary in some respects. The specification of objectives does not eliminate these decisions. However, clear objectives can help decide, and even reduce, the content, because some objectives can be achieved equally well regardless of the subject matter. Wheeler (1968) suggests the following diagram as an aid to clarifying this procedure:

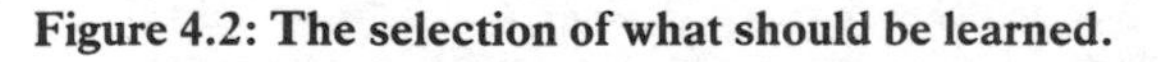

Figure 4.2: The selection of what should be learned.

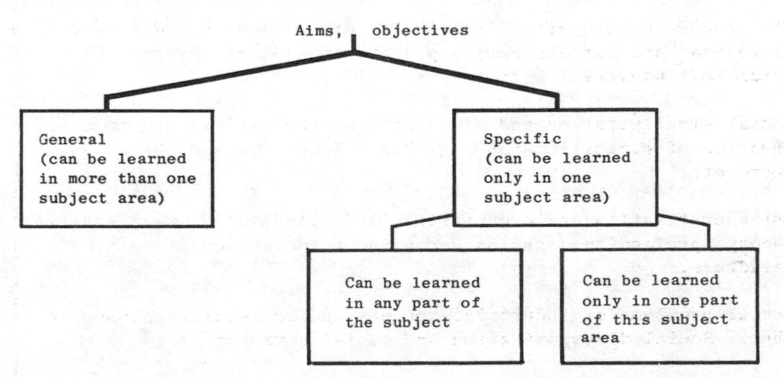

Presumably the selection of content should reflect what is relevant and of value not only to the teacher, but also to the student. Bruner (1977) argues that the most important criterion for the inclusion of a piece of knowledge is the extent to which it will encourage the transfer of learning. That is to say it should exemplify a principle which can be generalised across a range of knowledge. Phenix (1964) places less emphasis upon subject matter and suggests that the content of a course should exemplify a method of enquiry and should arouse the imagination of the student.

There is reason to believe that the "traditional" approach is still the most commonly used, but it is clear that the preference expressed in this book is towards developing students' powers of thought. With the increasing expansion of knowledge subject matter becomes out-of-date more quickly than the mental processes associated with it. Nevertheless the choice of a position on this dimension is a value judgement that each course designer must take for himself and assumes that he, at least, has the mental skills to do so.

(b) The "conceptual unity - interdisciplinarity" dimension

(i) Specialisation.
The arbitrariness and fragmentation of the "traditional approach can be reduced if the body of knowledge to be taught is selected on the basis of some fundamental rational principles. These principles will then give this "subject" a unity and the boundaries of the subject are defined by using them. This is not to say that the boundaries of subjects may not overlap. The principles often entail fundamental concepts. For example "time" in history, "atom" in chemistry, and "form" in art are fundamental concepts without which these subjects would have no unity and no boundaries.

Since most subjects have more than one fundamental concept, their relationships are thought to give a basic structure to which later knowledge is related as the subject grows. Thus the body of knowledge which forms the subject is seen as organised around a unifying structure of concepts, knowledge and principles. For example, in addition to "atom" simple numerical concepts "pattern" and "valency" are basic in chemistry. They are related in fairly precise ways, and the whole subject has been organised around them. If knowledge is to be taught in an interesting way "there must be some relational idea, a supra-content concept which focuses on general principles at a high level of abstraction" (Bernstein, 1971). For example if the relationships between sociology and biology are to be opened up, problems of order and change could be examined through the concepts of genetic and cultural codes. The important point is that whatever these relational concepts are, they will act selectively upon the knowledge to be included in a subject.

Teachers who take this view commonly assume that the organisation of the curriculum should reflect the fundamental organisation of the subject. As in the "traditional" approach they emphasise the acquisition of knowledge, but they pay particular attention to how far students understand the relationships between items of knowledge. Examination questions are set which cut across a variety of lecture topics.

The proponents of "the curriculum as organised knowledge", such as Bruner (1977), say that if knowledge is organised or "structured", not only is it remembered more easily, but is is more readily applied to wider issues so that problems may be solved and advanced topics may be attempted sooner. In short an organised curriculum leads to efficient learning.

However, as Northedge (1976) suggests, one possible danger of careful structuring is that courses are often taught in a manner similar to building a house where bricks are laid on top of one another in a carefully planned way, so that the laying of the first brick seems to bear little relation to the finished product and the house is unfit for use until completed. A more dynamic and flexible analogy, he suggests, is cultivating a garden. The gardener is a catalyst and must provide continual encouragement to bring the plants to their prime. Moreover although the garden may not be mature, it does have recognisable and meaningful forms and people can enjoy it from the first day.

To assist the reorganisation of knowledge, Lewis (1972) lists one set of questions for purely theoretical subjects and another for applied subjects. These are shown in Figure 4.3 and 4.4. Answers to these questions will produce a syllabus that is 'static' in that it does not change knowledge according to students' needs; but it does at least offer knowledge in an organised form. The presentation of the knowledge to the students requires the course designer to decide how to lace the separate strands of knowledge together to benefit both students and teachers. Since the people who design courses are not always the same as those who teach them, there is a possible source of conflict here.

Figure 4.3: Questions to be put to courses in areas of fundemental knowledge such as physics, chemistry, geology, biology, psychology, sociology, economics, political science and linguistics (Lewis, 1972)

(i)	What are the names of the laws and theories, or their equivalents, that give structure to the knowledge covered in the course?
(ii)	What are the postulates, theorems, and other propositions that are central to each of the theories?
(iii)	What are the headings of the classes of facts inter-related by each of the laws and theories?
(iv)	What are the references to the key works in which these laws and theories were first stated in the form taught in the course?
(v)	What are the major limitations of each of the laws and theories?
(vi)	What are the key references that discuss and explain these limitations?
(vii)	What knowledge is presented in the course that does not fall within the limits of applicability of the laws or theories enumerated?
(viii)	What methods have been used to organise this knowledge?

Figure 4.4: Questions to be put to applied courses such as agriculture, medicine, business, education, geography, horticulture, marketing, microbiology, public health, resource development and social work (Lewis, 1972)

(i) Upon what body or bodies of fundamental knowledge does this course draw?

(ii) What are the names of the laws and theories, or their equivalents, in the fundamental knowledge that give organisation to the knowledge being applied?

(iii) What are the postulates, theorems, and other propositions that are central to each of the theories?

(iv) Cite examples of how the laws and theories in the fundamental knowledge have been fruitfully applied.

(v) What practical forms of organisation in the course take precedence over the organisation that stems from the structure of the fundamental body of knowledge?

(vi) In what ways does the practical form of presentation increase the pedagogical efficiency as compared to a presentation based upon the structure of the fundamental body of knowledge?

(vii) What classes of facts in the course fall outside the limits of applicability of the laws and theories in the fundamental body or bodies of knowledge upon which the course is dependent?

Answers to these questions will produce a syllabus that is static in that it does not change according to students' needs but it does at least offer a structure for the organisation of knowledge in a subject. (see pages 91-93)

Parker and Rubin (1966) point out three difficulties in regarding the syllabus as "organised knowledge". The unifying "structure" of a subject is not always agreed or easy to find. Secondly the relationship between knowledge in different parts of the main subject may be of quite different kinds so that the subject as a whole has no overall coherence or "structure". In any case the description of the "structure" of a subject varies with the viewpoint of the specialist teacher. Furthermore it is doubtful whether anyone has ever fully described the "structure" of a subject and it is certainly more than can be expected from the ordinary teacher who has to prepare the syllabus for a course. Consequently, while it is clear that many disciplines do have some central concepts, the extreme view that a syllabus should consist of explicitly organised knowledge seems to be limited in value and practicality.

(ii) Interdisciplinarity

A further difficulty is that if courses are to possess a unifying concept, the possibility of interdisciplinary courses is frequently excluded. Yet interdisciplinary courses may be educationally valuable. The complexities of the modern world increasingly require our educational assistance to produce persons with a broad outlook, not narrow specialists, and people who are flexible, adaptive and seeking new links between areas of human understanding, rather than enclosing themselves within the confines of narrow and often trivial erudition.

It is possible to distinguish six kinds of interdisciplinary courses. In *multidiscipline* courses subjects may be studied without any apparent connection between them as in the modular, unit or credit system. They may be described as "open" if the choice of subject is unrestrained (except for certain necessary sequences) as it may be in project-based studies. They are said to be "schematic" if the choice is limited to certain combinations of subjects as in the traditional pre-clinical medical curriculum.

In *auxilliary*-interdiscipline courses certain subjects provide the theoretical support for others. For example philosophy, psychology and sociology frequently support the study of education in this way.

Overlapping interdisciplinarity occurs where two or more subjects are applied to the same information as in psycholinguistics; or when subjects begin to use the same theoretical and methodological approaches as in biophysics.

Method interdisciplinarity includes a study of similarities and differences in the philosophy and methods of different subjects. *Historical* interdisciplinarity exists when there are common historical, metaphysical and ideological foundations of different subjects within the same course. Courses are said to exhibit *focussed* interdisciplinarity when a problem or topic is studied from a variety of standpoints. For example "urban living" or a period of history such as the "enlightenment" may be studied from a sociological, psychological, systems theory, ecological or some other viewpoint. (Berger, 1972). Another example of focussed interdisciplinarity occurs at Maastricht, Netherlands, where for six week blocks, medical students study a symptom, such as a pain in the chest, and various subject specialists contribute knowledge from different perspectives.

The sixfold classification is not exhuastive and the types may overlap. Only the last three provide an integrated study programme for the student. The first two place the total responsibility for forming any inter-disciplinary links with the student. This is not sufficient to achieve interdisciplinary thinking. It may be doubted whether students are the best people to integrate subjects unless they are given appropriate tools to do so.

One of the principal tools is time. Doyal (1974) estimates that students need roughly one third of their formal study time allocated to inter-disciplinary thinking. Such courses also need a team of teachers committed to interdisciplinarity. Whatever the organisation it should always be remembered that integration should ultimately occur in the minds of the students. The integration of ideas is the result of student activity, consequently teaching methods such as projects, syndicates simulations and group discussion become the most important aspects of such courses.

Interdisciplinary courses cannot be successfully conducted if their teachers do not have interdisciplinary attitudes. One of the greatest obstacles to interdisciplinary teaching is that the previous education and training of post-secondary teachers has not equipped them for this role and we have already seen that many are subject to pressure to define the boundaries of their subjects more precisely, rather than break such barriers down.

The foundation of new universities has given opportunities to rethink the organisation of knowledge to be taught before traditional departmental barriers become established. The Open University of Great Britain has been particularly original both in the way it has structured and presented its courses and in the careful way it has attracted the interest of mature students. It also decided to offer degrees within a "credit", "unit" or "modular" based system.

The "modular" system, which has been used in North America for some time, is being increasingly adopted in other countries. Students are required to take a certain number of "units" to obtain their final qualification. Courses are assigned a value in terms of number of "modules" or "credits" their students receive on completion. Although some courses may not be taken without the successful completion of others, the "unit" system is very flexible and allows students considerable freedom of choice. They are not necessarily or irrevocably committed to courses in a particular department (at least in theory!). The disadvantage of "unit" systems is that they divide knowledge into discreet parcels and it is difficult to see how students can gain a sense of integration in their learning without stringent efforts by both themselves and their teachers. Project work and "synoptic studies" surveying a range of disciplines are two possible solutions, but there is little evidence yet of their benefits.

In Western Europe the growth of knowledge, and the decrease in student numbers in some disciplines has made rethinking a necessity for courses in science and technology; and many other innovations have resulted.

The difficulty with interdisciplinary and modular courses is that they can be superficial. Thus the choice of a position on this dimension is part of an old educational problem; the conflict between the demands of a specialist and a general education. Whether he knows it or not, every course designer makes a value judgement on this dimension.

(c) Who controls the curriculum content?
This dimension is not entirely independent of the previous two. If it is decided that the curriculum content should concentrate upon subject matter or should focus on some central unifying concept, teachers and others who are authorities on the subject matter and concepts will presumably be authorities in choosing what subject matter and which concepts should be included. But as soon as courses are conceived more widely in terms of students' thought processes and the variety of desirable vocational skills, it is more natural to focus upon the students who will have the thoughts and pursue the vocations.

Indeed according to one argument courses should be designed bearing the needs of individual students in mind because however much one tries to give students the same course content, they will interpret it differently. In other words, far from suggesting the dangers of conformity, indoctrination and stagnation of ideas resulting from a traditional curriculum, it is claimed that students are inevitably different in their understanding of ideas and teachers may as well accept the fact and provide curricula which allow for the individual differences. We all learn by perception and each person's perceptions are different from another's. This is partly because of the uniqueness of the individual, but partly because we all have varying experiences through occupying different positions in time and space. What we learn is therefore different, and unique to each one of us. The learned content of any education will therefore vary from one individual to another, and while it may be important that students should share a common understanding of what they are learning, it is equally important that the course, and its form of assessment, should allow for the necessary variation in the personal nature of the students' learning.

Furthermore, what we learn is related and selected according to what we have already learned, and our personal feelings and emotions, so that each of us has a different frame of reference for the organisation of knowledge. If a student's personality is integrated, his learning cannot be divorced from his emotions. His emotions should therefore be the concern of his teacher.

Similarly, the framework of a syllabus necessarily reflects the perceptions of the individuals who design it. It will also be interpreted differently by the teacher. The so-called "facts" of an academic syllabus are therefore not impartial. This not only has implications for the courses, but for the way this book and any other is written and for the differences in interpretations readers put upon them.

Again, it should be clear that even where curricula are apparently the same, what is learned will vary according to language and culture. Consequently when Western courses are 'transplanted' to developing countries, they are not only often inappropriate, but are perceived quite differently by both teachers and students from those in its country of origin. There is a strong danger that a course which is based upon content and standards drawn from another culture with vastly different needs and priorities, will only serve to divorce the thinking of the educated elite from the rest of the country's inhabitants.

When those in authority in colleges have differing perceptions of what should be included in the curriculum they commonly discuss their differences to work out an agreed programme. If it is accepted that students' perceptions are also relevant, it is a short step to include them in the discussions. Yet staff-student cooperation in the construction of curricula is remarkably rare notwithstanding that some decisions may need to be taken before students arrive at college. For students the sharing of ideas about a subject when designing their course is itself part of the learning process. The design meetings help students to understand their subject, to understand their teachers' views of it and to take responsibility for their own course. The methods and assumptions in the curriculum construction become more explicit and teachers and students work with a common purpose. In traditional curricula it is quite common for students to see themselves in opposition to their teachers and for teachers to think of students as lazy and uncooperative.

More recently several attempts have been made to devise curricula which are more student-centred than teacher-centred. In some cases the student, with careful tutorial advice, is expected to organise his own programme of study to suit his interests and needs. Perhaps the best known example is at Hampshire College, Amherst, Massachusetts where "students are expected to devise their own program of classes, make up their own tests, and pace their own degree progress" (Heis, 1973). The universities of Iowa, Minnesota, New York and Lancaster, UK, are amongst others where some students, in consultation with a tutor, select the ingredients of their courses on non-traditional lines. In so far as Oxford and Cambridge have traditionally allowed students to select their own course activities in consultation with a tutor, there is little innovatory in expecting students to take some responsibility for designing courses to satisfy their individual needs. Nevertheless, in many institutions, it is commonly assumed that only teachers know what is good for their students. Having chosen their subject of study students are only allowed "options", almost as a privilege, in their final year.

II Sequencing the course

(1) Logical and psychological assumptions

If, in order to learn one thing, students must first learn another, there will be a necessary order in which these two things should be learned. Thus in Figure 1.2 in Chapter I we saw that achievement of objective (a) was necessary to achieve objective (b), and achievement of objective (b) was necessary to attain (c). Hence, at least in some contexts, there is a desirable sequence in which objectives should be attained. Notice that this reasoning makes logical and psychological assumptions about learning. In some contexts these may conflict. The belief that "you cannot run until you can walk" may seem fairly obvious in the context of physical skills and it has been commonly assumed in the context of subject matter. It has been less obvious in the context of mental skills.

(a) Bloom's cognitive taxonomy

Where the recent emphasis upon mental processes associated with a subject has been different from its forerunners is the classification of a hierarchy of thinking skills with the tacit assumption that lower level skills have to be learned before those at a higher level. For example, in Bloom's Taxonomy (1956) it is assumed that a student will need (i) to *know* a principle before (ii) he can *understand* it. (iii) He must understand it before he can *apply* it. (iv) Skills of *analysis* are said to presuppose the ability to apply principles and to be a pre-requisite for relating them. (v) He should be able to relate *(synthesize)* it to other principles before (vi) he can *evaluate* it and so on. (Bloom's Taxonomy of Cognitive Educational Objectives has been set out in many textbooks and will not be repeated here).

(b) The affective domain

Krathwohl et al (1964) proposed a similar classification of 'affective' objectives from attitudes in which a student is aware of, or willing to receive, a value judgement, right up to a full characterisation of his personality. For example, suppose that a teacher has a general aim that his students should be open-minded. (i) At the lowest level *(receiving)* they should at least be able to listen to other people. (ii) Only if they have listened can they *'respond'* showing that they have considered what has been said. (iii) It is a further step to *value* what has been said sufficiently to *'accept'* it; (iv) and a further step again to incorporate the idea into their framework of ideas (*'organisation* of ideas'). (v) The final level would only be reached if students normally behaved in an open-minded way, for example if they are willing to change their opinions, or face contrary evidence.

(c) Gagne's types of learning

In the same way Gagne (1965) has classified different types of learning from (i) the simple association of two stimuli (signal learning), (ii) through stimulus response learning, (iii) chains of stimulus-responses, (iv) verbal association, (v) multiple discriminations, the learning of (vi) concepts and (vii) principles, leading to (viii) skills in problem solving.

Gagne's work was an attempt to synthesize theories of learning varying from Pavlov's physiological studies to the intuitive concepts of Gestalt psychology in problem solving. Since these theories make different philosophical presuppositions, educationists who use Gagne's hierarchy for purposes for which it was not intended, run the risk of conceptual confusion.

Again it is assumed that students must acquire the lower level skills before they will have success at the higher levels. Consequently teachers are supposed to design their curricula so that the skills acquired are sequenced in this heirarchical order starting at the lower levels. While there is undoubtedly some validity in this assumption, and it has probably been neglected in the past, it is by no means always true. Nor does it take into account the problem of motivating students to learn at the lower levels where there is typically less challenge to their intellects. It may sometimes be a good idea to present students with a problem first and let them work back to the facts required to solve it, rather than present facts and only later expect them to be used, related or communicated in some way. Furthermore, it is not always clear whether this assumption only applies to the application of specific facts and principles, or whether the ability to apply principles is infinitely generalisable. It is probably true that to apply specific or non-specific principles involves abilities that need to be taught. If this is true, teachers in post-secondary education need to give much more thought not only to the thinking skills they intend to teach but to the order in which they intend to teach them. This may include teaching students how to learn from the teaching methods they expect to use.

(d) Parker and Rubin's stages in the curriculum
Parker and Rubin (1966) argue for an organisation of the curriculum based on the way knowledge is manipulated. One of the models they suggest contains four stages. (i) The first stage is concerned with the way knowledge is acquired. In this students observe phenomena, read expository material, collect evidence and listen to presentations. (ii) The second stage is concerned with interpretation. Students derive meaning from what they have learned; they relate new knowledge to old. The skills include analysing, reorganising and experimenting with information, and relating it together. (iii) In the third stage, which Parker and Rubin call "attaching significance", students infer the information in new ways. These types of activity are required for communication. (iv) The fourth and final stage is concerned with the application of knowledge. Students use information to recognise, clarify and solve problems.

Thus, like Gagne, they see problem solving as the apex of cognitive activity. However, each stage of the Parker and Rubin model demands a variety of skills from the student and thus avoids the danger of boredom which any sequence of increasing complexity is likely to induce in its earlier stages.

(e) Perry: Intellectual and ethical development
When the ideas of Bloom, Gagne, and Parker and Rubin are used as guides for sequencing subject matter in a course, it is assumed that the necessary pre-conditions for learning are cognitive. But this is not always so. Sometimes it is students' attitudes and emotional development that prevents them from developing certain lines of thought. Perry (1970) suggests that (i) students start with a simplistic state of thinking in which "us-right-good" is polarised with "others-wrong-bad". Right answers for everything exist and it is the job of teachers and other authorities to dispense these truths. (ii) Later, uncertainty and diversity of opinion are first perceived and then (iii) accepted because "authorities haven't found the answer yet". (iv) After recognising some subjects in which "anyone has a right to his own opinion" (v) students are said to perceive "all knowledge and values (including authority's) as contextual and relative". (vi) The need to orientate themselves in a relativistic world leads to (vii) an initial commitment in some area such as a political or academic viewpoint. (viii) Finally

students identify themselves in terms of many on-going commitments which all characterise their life style.

(f) Growth of critical thinking

In a hitherto unpublished paper, Bligh has emphasised the importance of students' confidence and emotional security through ten stages in the development of independent reasoning in arts and social sciences. He argues that when at school these students progressively learn how to learn (i) facts, (ii) explanations, (iii) issues and (iv) standard arguments or criticisms. Independence of mind is not encouraged because it challenges the authority of teachers, it is difficult to assess fairly in mass examinations, and children are not deemed ready for it.

(v) When at college their independent thought is at first negative, critical and destructive. (vi) Only later does the typical arts and social science student develop a commitment to a constructive viewpoint of his own and learn to argue for it. (vii) The appreciation of the value of opposing views, and (viii) the merits of arguments against his own opinions, require greater maturity. (ix) The practice of these skills slowly develops intellectual objectivity culminating in (x) relativism.

In many teaching situations it is part of the teacher's role to wean students from one stage to the next. With this thought in mind it is instructive to look at tutors' critical comments at the end of students' essays. The fact that anxiety tends to make people regress to relatively simplistic levels of thinking, shows the importance of developing students' confidence and emotional security, particularly at the beginning of their course and during examinations.

Unlike Perry, Bligh sees at least some forms of useful commitment as preceeding a more objective detachment and relativism. But if detachment leads to non-involvement and an inability to act, Perry may be right to include some measure of commitment in his final stage. Bligh's account is more concerned with thought than action. It works fairly well in the social sciences, but his later stages are beyond the reach of most students in the physical sciences. He conceives of his stages as cumulative rather than transitory, but not all subjects require this sequence.

For example students of law require considerable factual knowledge and objective detachment without developing extensive personal opinions. Emotional commitment to the subject matter or a client's particular case is discouraged. Unlike the authors mentioned in (a) to (e), Bligh does not attempt a general account of intellectual development. He sees student developmental types varying with home background and subject of study as major variables.

(g) Conclusion

If it were possible to produce a hierarchy of psychological objectives on the basis of logic, a general taxonomy would be produced. If it is further assumed that easy or simple tasks should be learned before difficult or complex ones, the taxonomy could provide guidelines for sequencing the content of the curriculum. It has been claimed that the work of Bloom, Gagne and others can be used for this purpose; but it should be pointed out that they themselves have not made this claim.

The trouble with all these hierarchies is that they are not easy to apply in curriculum construction on a large scale. They seem more realistic when applied to restricted subject matter or specific topics. This is because they emphasise the sequencing of mental processes rather than subject matter. But no matter what position one may take on the "subject matter - mental processes" dimension, the subject matter of a course must be sequenced too.

(2) Some common patterns for sequencing subject matter

Subject matter does not lend itself to general logical taxonomies, in the same way as "mental processes". Subject matter will vary with every course. Consequently it is difficult to make sound generalisations about the way subject matter can be sequenced. They usually assume that one bit of subject matter is somehow connected with another, perhaps by having certain concepts in common. Sequences are then chosen for their "connectedness" making sure that not too many concepts have to be taught all at once. Two psychological assumptions here are that familiarity with the concepts of a subject assists the understanding of it, and that understanding is essential to academic learning.

(a) Chains
Sometimes the structure of a subject may suggest a chronological sequence or a chain of cause and effect. The difficulty with this kind of organisation is that a chain is only as strong as its weakest link. Every member of a class must attain objective (A) before proceeding to (B) etc. This is particularly evidence in mathematical subjects. Their consequent high student dropout and failure rates are well known. Inbuilt methods of assessment and feedback are therefore particularly important in subject matter with a chaining structure or that which builds upon itself. Of course some subjects which appear to have a chaining structure do not suffer from this difficulty when later objectives are not wholly dependent upon the achievement of earlier ones. For example it is possible to have some understanding of baroque music without a profound understanding of that which preceeded it. This is because there is more than one way of understanding baroque music (but it might be said that a 'full' understanding can only be had with some knowledge of its antecedants.)

(b) Students' motivation and the structure of a subject
The example of music shows that logic and understanding are not the only criteria for sequencing the subject matter of a course. If a three year degree course in music was treated only chronologically, students' motivation would suffer. The same would be true if a course was built up from first studying the minutia of detailed musical analyses. Such a breakdown and build up would assume, or create, a hierarchic logical structure of knowledge. It is relatively obvious in the study of music that the sequence of a students' course must take account of their initial interests. The same is true in other subjects, yet courses are commonly

sequenced without even knowing what the students' interests are. Thus motivational factors have to be balanced against factors affecting the ease and accuracy of understanding a subject as its logical structure.

(c) Spiral curricula
The spiral sequence is a form of chain and is particularly useful in some traditional courses emphasising the learning of subject matter. In a spiral sequence the student touches on a set of topics in a preliminary form before returning to the same or similar topics at a deeper level, possibly coming back to them again in yet another context. For example the problems of soil erosion could be considered from various aspects: the rocks, soils, microclimates, vegetation, economics, hydrological cycle, government planning and history.

(d) Network analysis
Many subjects do not seem to have an obvious sequential, hierarchic or logical structure. They have a multitude of concepts all interconnecting in a network. Network analysis is the technique that makes these interconnections explicit. By mapping these relationships Wyant (1971) and others have attempted to show the range of possible sequences in specific subject matters.

(e) Problem nodes
Another way to sequence the subject matter of a course is to build it around a series of problems. Each problem may be centred upon a node of the network. That is to say each problem may bring together a wide variety of subject matter. The treatment of an academic may not be systematic or complete by this approach; but no teacher can teach every aspect of his subject. This approach should make the students think by selecting and using knowledge relevantly, it may be interdisciplinary and could stimulate interest. The medical curriculum at McMcaster University, Canada, is becoming well known for its problem based approach on this pattern.

(f) General principles to particular applications
A common assumption when designing a course is that fundamental concepts have to be taught first. This is an analytical approach. The concepts tend to be abstract and it is assumed that students will later be able to relate them together with great ease in a multitude of ways. It is an approach that moves from general principles to particular applications. There is an element of deductive reasoning from abstract general elements of a subject to particular concrete complex situations in which it is applied.

(g) Teaching generalisations from particular examples
Some students prefer to work the other way round. They prefer to consider practical problems before studying the abstract principles that govern them. They work better from the particular to the general, than from general principles to particular examples.

It is suggested by Chanan and Gilchrist (1974) that there is some virtue in alternating these two approaches. This, they observe, has the advantage of exercising both the 'convergent' and 'divergent' faculties of the students' minds. In other words these two approaches do not teach the same thing. One requires application of principles, the other teaches powers of generalisation. Both approaches are used with traditional curricula.

Goodlad (1975) recommends alternating "practical action" with periods of "structured reflection". He argues that such a balance between the 'real' world and academic work not only helps the student to relate thought to action and to appreciate the strengths and weaknesses of theoretical ideas, but also keeps an academic subject relevant to practical, non-academic contexts.

(h) Backward chaining

Instead of teaching a chain of reasoning by beginning with its intial assumptions and premises and proceeding forwards with each step in turn, Gilbert (1962) has recommended what he calls "backward chaining". The student is taught the last link in the chain first, then the second from last, and so on. For example students might be given the results of an experiment and be required to make the final inferences of interpretation. Then the student might be given the scientific problem, a hypothetical solution, and an experimental design to test it; but be expected to carry out the experiment and make the inferences of interpretation. At the third stage the student might be expected to design an experiment; at the fourth to consider the formation of hypothesis; and to consider underlying assumptions and the basic problems only when other steps in the chain of reasoning have been learned. This "backward chaining" sequence has been represented by Rowntree (1974) in Figure 4.5.

Figure 4.5

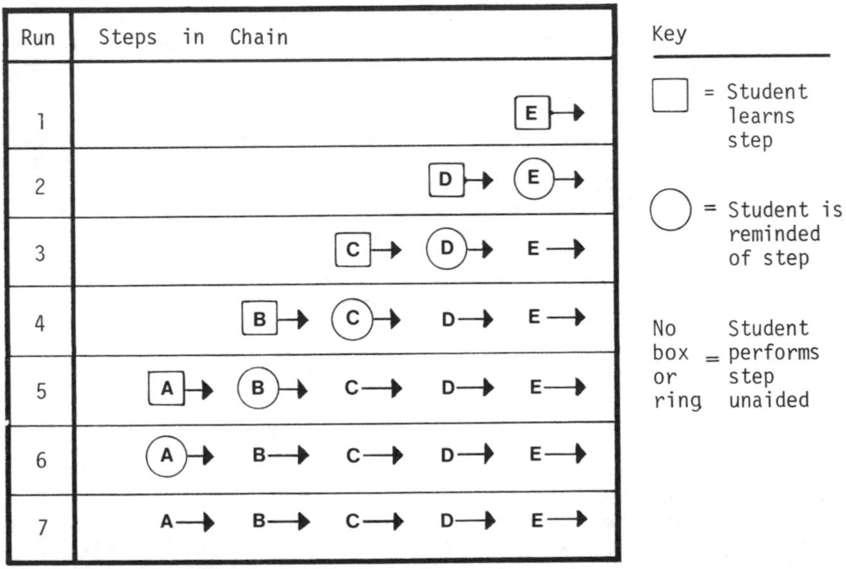

Run	Steps in Chain				
1					[E] →
2				[D] →	(E) →
3			[C] →	(D) →	E →
4		[B] →	(C) →	D →	E →
5	[A] →	(B) →	C →	D →	E →
6	(A) →	B →	C →	D →	E →
7	A →	B →	C →	D →	E →

Key

[ ] = Student learns step

( ) = Student is reminded of step

No box or ring = Student performs step unaided

Gilbert claims that all kinds of sequences can be taught by "backward chaining" and that there are motivational benefits from the procedure because the students have the satisfaction of achieving the final goal at each stage. Motivation is difficult to maintain when courses require students to work very hard on basic material before being shown that the fruits of success can be obtained. Although research has shown that "backward chaining" is not always more effective than "forward chaining", Gilbert's work is a strong statement in favour of a psychological, rather than a logical, approach to sequencing a course.

III Conclusion

To attempt to discuss how subjects could be organised is to enter a meta-subject. It assumes we can step outside, and take an aerial view of, our disciplines with some detachment. But in practice this is not usually possible. We are biassed through habitual patterns of thinking. Perhaps it is for this reason that the philosophical, sociological, logical and psychological assumptions discussed in this chapter can be disentangled. If there is a meta-subject concerned with curriculum content it is neither well integrated nor well developed.

Hence, this chapter, like the others in this book, presents considerations but no right answers. With these considerations in mind, the reader is left to take his own decisions when organising the content of the curriculum.

CHAPTER 5: Teaching methods

I. Methodological problems in the study of teaching methods

II. Presentation methods

CHAPTER 5: Teaching methods

The results of our limited, but worldwide, survey of teaching methods show that the lecture is by far the most commonly used. Although there are wide variations, the typical university teacher gives about 5 hours of lectures per week to an audience of between 30 and 100 students. He usually spends rather less time, 3 to 4 hours a week, using discussion methods. As may be expected, the amount of time devoted to practical teaching varies considerably with the subject taught, from none at all in some arts subjects to 30 hours per week in fine art and engineering. But these are extremes. The average teacher spends between 5 and 10 hours per week teaching practical classes. Geologists spend irregular amounts of time in fieldwork and the amount of time spent by teachers of clinical medicine actually teaching, rather than treating patients, is hard to determine.

It is, however, more relevant to consider the time spent by students. Again it is difficult to generalise, but the typical student receives 10-15 hours of lectures per week and spends 2-5 hours per week in discussions. Many universities and institutions of higher education suffer from large student-teacher ratios, with the result that there are few opportunities of personal contact and only those teaching methods that permit one teacher to communicate with a large number of students are possible. Thus, lectures, seminars and panel discussions are preferred to small group discussions and individual projects. In a questionnaire survey of 884 medical students in Middle Eastern countries (WHO 1972), it was found that only 26% met their teachers outside the class; of these, 82% met for academic reasons, 3% for personal reasons and 5% for social reasons.

The entire teaching and learning process is often aimed at passing examinations which provide a passport to an elitist world. The students develop a tendency to depend upon lecture notes rather than texts and reference books. In the above mentioned analysis, many students asked for lecture notes to be dictated and as many as 27% felt that they could do well in the examination if they depended solely on lecture notes. Clearly in such a climate of teaching and learning there is no place for critical thinking and for testing the applicability of what is learned.

It has not been widely appreciated that when teaching and learning occur in a foreign language there is little scope for the student to read widely in his subject and explore it along different avenues through research literature. His reading gets narrowly confined to the prescribed texts and to lecture notes. For the same reason libraries are not used enough and education becomes too didactic. Such factors restrict the practicality of some teaching methods.

The central question for teachers is "What method shall I use?". This should be decided on evidence of what can be achieved by different methods and on what methods are practical. Thus, the two crucial questions we shall attempt to answer in this chapter are "What do the various teaching methods achieve?" and "What are the practical advantages of the different methods that achieve the same thing?".

I Methodological problems in the study of teaching methods

There is a methodological problem in answering the first question. What is acceptable as evidence? Subjective judgements of the effectiveness of teaching methods have been shown to be reliable in the sense of giving consistent results, but only have a chance level of validity (Bligh, 1974). Students are poor judges of how much they learn from one method compared with another, and teachers are poor judges of what, and how much, they teach by different methods.

Many of the studies which purport to show a significant positive correlation between students' judgements of how much they have learned and what they have actually learned as measured by objective tests, depend upon a logical fallacy. They neglect the level of difficulty of the subject taught. When students are taught a difficult subject, less able students will learn little or nothing and will know they have; similarly able students will learn something and will also know that they have. Consequently, there will be a *positive* correlation between how much students think they have learned and how much they actually have learned. But when the topic is easy, able students still learn more than the less able ones but are bored, thinking they have learned nothing. They consequently rate the amount they have learned less favourably than the less able students, who realise they have learned more than usual. Thus, when a teacher does his job well by making his subject easy to understand, there is a *negative* correlation between students' judgements of how much they have learned and the amount they have learned as measured by objective tests. The direction of correlation depends on the difficulty of the topic. When this logical error is corrected by correlating students' *relative* judgements of how much they have learned with how much they have learned as measured by objective tests, the correlations are found to be virtually zero. A large number of research papers which appear to give comfort to teachers who trust their own subjective judgements of their teaching effectiveness can be dismissed for failing to consider this logical error.

A more logical approach appears to be to carry out an experimental comparison. This, too, has its difficulties. Teaching situations are social situations. They are intrinsically uncontrollable because they involve the interaction of one person with another. Their results are difficult to generalise because they depend upon individual differences of personality, intelligence, age and sex, as well as differences between institutions and between subjects taught. Nevertheless, if a large number of experimental comparisons point in the same direction, some generalisations may be tentatively legitimate. This is a "picture building" approach.

This was the procedure adopted by Dubin and Taveggia (1968). They conducted a literature search and found 91 studies comparing lectures, discussion, lectures with discussion, supervised independent study and unsupervised independent study. Although individual comparisons may have favoured one method or another, when calculations were made to allow for the extent of differences observed in all the experimental comparisons, they concluded that no one method was superior to any other.

However, their study pays little attention to the varied criteria employed by the experimenters they reviewed. The majority of these experimenters used performance in end of course examinations as their criteria, but even this knowledge does not tell us what psychological objectives were examined. For the purposes of this volume we have searched the literature and found over 100 comparisons of the various teaching methods in post-secondary education. Although statistically it is a less satisfactory procedure than that adopted by Dubin and Taveggia, we have tabulated the results of experiments comparing lectures with reading and private study, lectures with discussion, and lectures with irrelevant activity or none at all, when the acquisition of information gained was the criterion of effectiveness. It will be seen that the first two comparisons confirm Dubin and Taveggia's conclusion that there is no difference in the effectiveness of these methods. The third comparison suggests that lectures are effective in teaching some information. Of course, three comparisons are not very many on which to base a general conclusion, but many of the comparisons in the previous two tables include gain scores, derived from the differences between pre-tests and post-tests, which are positive. It therefore seems reasonable to conclude that lectures, discussion, reading and private study are effective methods of acquiring information. We cannot conclude that one method is superior to any other.

Figure 5.1: Comparisons of lectures and other methods using knowledge of information as the criterion

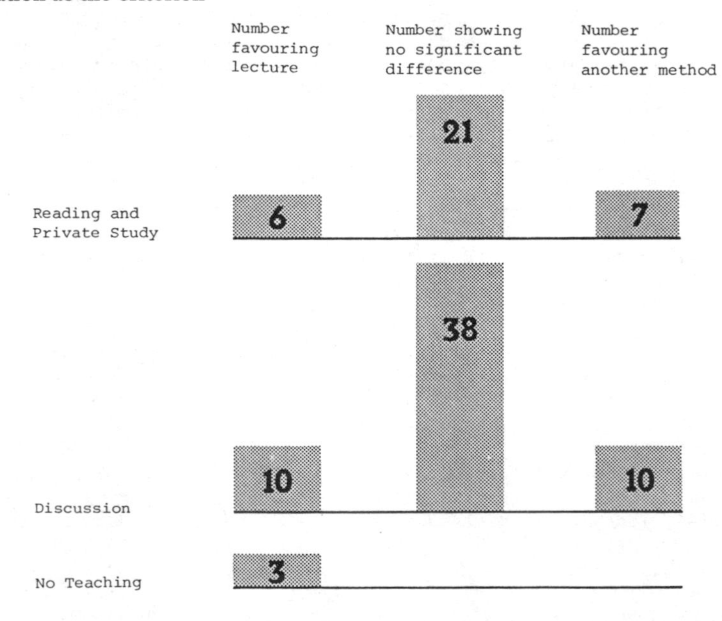

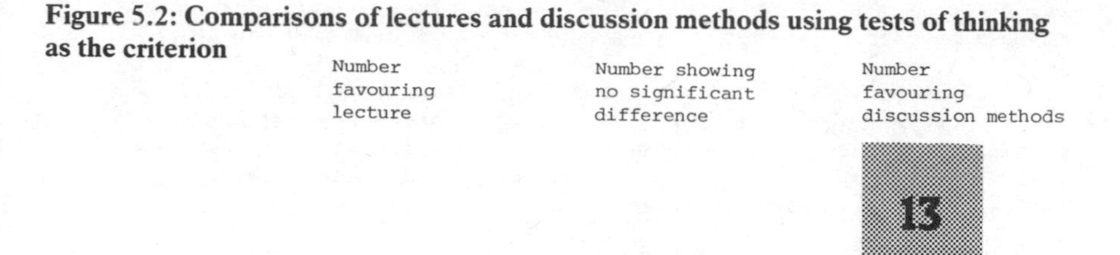

Figure 5.2: Comparisons of lectures and discussion methods using tests of thinking as the criterion

Figure 5.3: Comparisons of lectures and discussion methods using attitudes as the criterion

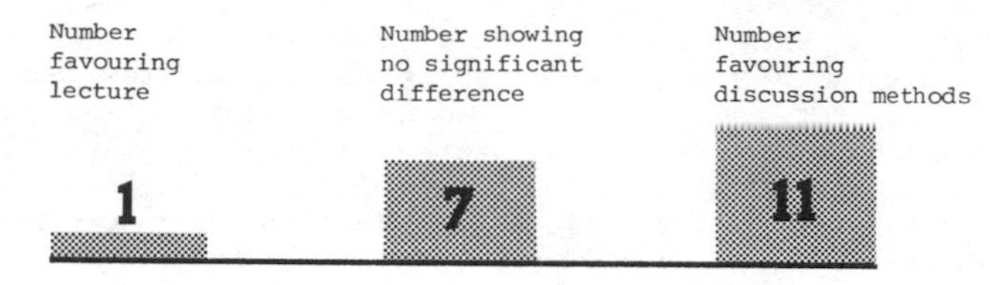

However, when different kinds of objective are considered as a criterion of effectiveness, the picture is very different. A similar literature search revealed 15 studies in which comparisons of lectures and discussion used some kind of thinking as the criterion of effectiveness. In most cases, the thinking involved problem-solving, but in some it required analytical thinking and in others, decision making. On balance, it is clear that discussion methods are more effective than lectures for teaching students to think. (Fig. 5.2)

A similar, but less certain, conclusion may be drawn from experimental comparisons of lectures and discussion when the criterion of effectiveness involves some kind of attitude change. The criteria for attitude change include standardised tests such as the Minnesota Teacher Attitude Inventory, measures of enthusiasm for the subject including students' electing to take further courses, and some specially prepared questionnaires. (Fig. 5.3)

It will be appreciated that these are very gross comparisons. The terminology describing teaching methods is not precise, and it is almost certain that different experimenters mean different things by the terms, 'Lecture', 'Discussion', 'Private Study' and so on. The comparisons involve a wide and unbalanced range of academic disciplines. No attempt has been made to differentiate between different kinds of students. Most of the experiments were conducted in North America, and while we have no evidence that there may be cultural differences affecting the effectiveness of different teaching methods, this possibility cannot be discounted.

Nevertheless, on available evidence it seems difficult to escape the conclusion that, if teachers in post-secondary education wish to teach their students to think about their subject, they will need to use discussion methods rather than lectures.

Yet a closer scrutiny of the literature suggests that the crucial difference is not between lectures and discussion, but between presentation methods in general, of which lectures are but one, and active methods which require problem solving, of which discussion methods are a very important group.

Thus, the prime function of books, films, television, audio tapes, radio and lectures is to give a presentation. All that can be presented is information. The products of attitudes and thought can be displayed; but they can only be displayed as information. Consequently it is not surprising that what students obtain from these methods is information.

To put it rather crudely, the acquisition of information is a process of input, but the processes of thought and attitude change are internal. They do not consist of an injection from outside the person's mind, but a manipulation of what the mind already 'contains'. Therefore it is not surprising that to achieve thought or attitude change teachers need to use methods that require the students to carry out these mental 'processes' or 'manipulations' for themselves.

Arguments were presented in Chapter 1 that teaching students to think is a major objective of post-secondary education. Yet inspection of the methods of teaching and learning currently used in post-secondary education shows that a student spends most of his working time receiving presentations, not thinking about what he has learned.

We saw in Chapter 3 that if students are to be psychologically healthy (and this is essential to the success of their education) they need the security and social interaction of friendships. Yet the dominant methods of teaching and learning used in the world today prevent social interaction and expression of ideas. A member of a lecture audience may be in the presence of 100 fellow students, but the method does not permit his interaction with them; and private study is essentially private. Particularly in the 'Third World', where places in higher education are keenly sought, the learning process is competitive rather than co-operative; and solitary, rather than interactive. Humans are naturally gregarious and sociable. There is a desperate need for the teaching methods of post-secondary education to become more social and thereby more humane.

Thus there is a basic contrast between presentation methods and group discussion methods. With this broad generalisation in mind, we may now review the evidence available on various teaching methods which may be pertinent to teachers' decisions either to use one method rather than another, or to adopt specific techniques within particular methods.

II Presentation methods

(1) The recent development of presentation methods

Educational innovation tends to go in phases of enthusiasm followed by a period of disillusion in which the previously vaunted methods resume a more appropriate place in the esteem of teachers and administrators. As the merits and disadvantages of each craze become more clear, a residue of knowledge and principles remains in the consciousness of the teachers. This results in a very slow process of change in teaching methods.

The craze for visual aids took place in the 1950's before the rapid expansion of higher education. Consequently, most of the experimental work in this sphere is with secondary or pre-secondary school pupils. Post-secondary education has been relatively neglected. There remains a tacit recognition that it is 'a good thing' to use visual aids, but there is little understanding of their proper use. Sturwold (1973) has suggested that even in the USA, lack of knowledge of available visual materials and local technical provision are reasons for the sparse use of audio-visual materials. In his survey, he found that most teachers use audio-visual aids occasionally, but the majority use them less than five times a year, even in apparently visual subjects like dentistry.

Although the basic principles were enunciated much earlier (Pressey, 1926; Skinner, 1958) the craze for programmed learning occurred in the early 1960's. I shall present evidence to show that, while many of its principles have some value, they are not absolute and consequently, programmed learning has not proved to be the saviour that was once expected.

Two of the principles of programmed learning, the needs for self-pacing and feedback on learning, led to a growth of interest in self-instructional techniques in the late 1960's and early 1970's. These include the Keller Plan, correspondence techniques, tape-slide presentations and the use of mass media. They have been greatly assisted by a revolution in reprographic techniques (for example, the widespread use of photocopying machines) and the increasing availability of tape recorders and television equipment.

Indeed, we are still experiencing the craze for television and great claims are being made for its use. Exaggerated hopes for the use of computer assisted instruction (CAI) are beginning to be expressed. Unfortunately, each successive craze requires greater expenditure than the previous one with little obvious sign of direct benefit. The indirect benefits, which include the residue of the knowledge of principles previously mentioned, are probably greater but less measurable. The benefits lie more in the techniques of presentation, such as ways of reducing students' memory loads, rather than in the development of macroscopic methods. What is required is many small scale projects to slowly build up a picture of effective teaching, rather than a few large scale projects which are expensive and which tend to produce results that cannot easily be generalised.

Most of the rest of this chapter will consider these and other methods roughly in the order mentioned, with the precise intention of building up such a picture by the assembly of available evidence. It will be appreciated that many areas have been only patchily investigated by educational researchers and many of the experiments reported reflect the enthusiasm of the experimenters for a particular method rather than strict objectivity.

(2) Lectures

(a) Their role
It is sometimes remarked that lectures were invented before the printing press, when appropriate reading materials were not widely available and many students could not read. It is forgotten that in many parts of the world the same is still true today. It has been estimated that approximately one-third of the world's adult population is illiterate and many countries are short of educational reading matter, particularly in rural areas. Even in countries where the reprographic revolution is well advanced, the expansion of student numbers ensures that written resources are never totally adequate. It therefore seems likely that the lecture method will continue to be important for the dissemination of information in the forseeable future.

Lectures continue to be one of the most economic methods of teaching information when the presentations need to be adapted to the requirements of large and specific audiences. These conditions are particularly fulfilled in some of the countries of Asia. These have large rural populations and basically agricultural economies with little, if any, economic surplus with which to expand an education system. Yet they wish to broaden, if not industrialise, their economic base within a generation. For this, they need to expand their trained manpower upon a very small educational base. The agricultural, industrial, economic, medical, legal and social problems of each region, let alone each country, are sufficiently specific to guarantee that imported educational programmes are inappropriate.

In these conditions the lecture method has an important role. It is cheap, adaptable and relevant. Where courses are introductory, non-local and remain the same from year to year, a better case can be made for imported programmes.

(b) Their limitations

(i) Students' misunderstanding
Given that the lecture method is sometimes appropriate, the task is to overcome its well known limitations. Students' perceptions of what is said are normally inaccurate, as judged by the notes they take, because their previous understanding of the subject is necessarily limited. Students' inaccuracies in perception may be reduced if the lecturer re-states his material in different ways, if students can supplement

the lecture from other sources, if arrangements are made to consult with fellow students and if they can check their understanding by answering questions or solving problems.

(ii) Students' fading memories

Memory of information presented fades very rapidly at first, and more slowly later. In one study, Jones (1923) found that students' memory of information faded from 60% immediately after a lecture to 23% eight weeks later. Bassey (1968), like Jones, has shown that this loss can be drastically reduced if students are made to go over the information learned as soon as possible after its presentation. Obviously, there is no more immediate time than during the lecture itself. Yet even lecturers who are aware of this are frequently loathe to use interrupted lecture techniques.

(iii) Linear form

Thirdly, lectures are linear in form while the understanding they are intended to promote increases with the extent to which ideas are cross-linked in 'multi-dimensional forms'. (See for example, Johnson, 1967). It is sometimes claimed that lectures can be used for 'opening up' and 'providing a framework for a subject' (e.g. The Hale Report, 1964), and certainly lecturers try to use them for this. But if the students do not already possess a framework of relevant ideas, the linear form of the lecture is quite inappropriate to teach it. This is less true of books because a reader can proceed at his own pace and turn backwards or forwards to relate ideas at will. Where students already have a framework of ideas, the lecture method becomes more viable. This consideration is of central importance in adult instruction outside traditional educational institutions. In one post-graduate medical centre (Stansfeld, 1971) 45-minute non-participatory lectures were given to general practitioners and other hospital staff at lunch time. The lectures were not part of any formal course. They were not examined and there was an element of relaxation about the situation. When multiple-choice questions were sent to all the doctors in the local district, one-third replied, including two-thirds of those who had actually attended the lectures. Results showed that the lectures had been effective in teaching information to those who attended. The doctors learned because they already had a framework about the subject. Students frequently do not have this. Lecturers who talk under a very clear hierarchy of headings can teach a classification of information, and this is a framework of an elementary kind; but this clarity is usually achieved by a visual display which overcomes the natural linearity of a lecture. It is also true that some topics naturally lend themselves to a linear or sequential form (Bligh, 1972).

(iv) Declining student attention

There is also the problem of declining attention. From the results of multiple-choice tests, Thomas (1972) has concluded that the proportion of information retained during a lecture declines steadily after an initial settling-in period. This decline continues until near the end of an hour lecture when a sharp rise in attention occurs. Lloyd (1968) obtained the same pattern when he inspected the lecture notes taken by students. Bligh (1972) obtained the identical pattern when students' heart rates were recorded during lectures. But measures of students' learning and thinking, when the same information was systematically presented at different times in lectures to matched groups of students, did not show the same decline (Bligh, 1974).

The basic solution to the problem of declining attention is the introduction of variety into the lecture. This includes varied voice, varied methods of presentation, the use of different kinds of visual aids, the introduction of other teaching methods such as small group discussions, general discussion, question and answer sessions, individual problem-solving, rest pauses for students to look through the notes they have taken, requiring students to write down and anonymously submit statements of what they have not understood, completion of teacher evaluation questionnaires and so on (Bligh,1972).

(v) Poor feedback

The lecturer obtains little immediate verbal feedback on his effectiveness. By its nature, verbal feedback from students to the lecturer is not easily possible in lectures. If it occurs, ipso facto the teaching method has changed. Nevertheless, non-verbal feedback is possible. In an interesting French study, Guyot (1970) has shown that there is a relationship between the positions occupied by students in a lecture theatre and their feelings towards their lecturer and their fellow students. These positions were the result of several psychological forces in which motivational and emotional factors were stronger than cognitive ones. In particular, there was an ambivalent attitude towards the lecturer, who was seen as both an obstacle and as an aid to learning. It is well known that some students sit where they believe they cannot be seen. Others sit at the side or at the back where they can observe others. The observant lecturer should notice which students are isolated and which commonly cluster in the same group. Such groups often have unofficial leaders and lecturers who can identify and observe them can more easily gauge the reaction of the whole group to their lectures and thereby obtain non-verbal feedback more easily. Students who regularly sit in the front are also likely to have different motives. Many lecturers fail to realise that their own position and their distance from their audience is a powerful factor affecting their mutual relationships.

Observations of variations in students' gaze and posture can also produce useful feedback on the lecturer's performance. Unfortunately, too few lecturers regard students' reactions to their lectures as their responsibility, and still fewer study it systematically. Yet a lecturer who fails to study his students' reactions can hardly be regarded as doing his job properly.

There are mechanical methods of obtaining feedback on learning. For example, the microbiology department at the University of Ghent has equipped a classroom with an electrical answer system for students, not only to establish communication with a large number of students, but to make students active in the classroom. This is known as a "feedback classroom". They have used multiple-choice tests with up to 250 students and have also assessed the attitudes of students in the light of the believed inadequacy of the current oral examinations.

Taplin (1969) obtained basically the same facility using a cube with different coloured sides. Students could indicate their responses to questions by displaying an appropriate colour to the teacher.

(vi) Ineffective for important objectives
We have seen that lectures are relatively ineffective to teach students to think about a topic and have doubtful effectiveness in developing attitudes and values. Although students have little opportunity to think during lectures, lectures built around problems which are clearly expressed at the beginning appear to be more successful in achieving this objective. However, problem centred lectures are the most difficult to give and require extremely careful preparation of the inter-relation of the subject matter.

(vii) Improved effectiveness often temporary
There are innumerable experiments which show that improvements in presentation can lead to an increase in immediate learning, but that this advantage is lost in the ensuing week if no techniques are used to consolidate it. This is frustrating for teachers who strive to improve their teaching.

The use of buzz-groups provides a partial solution to all these problems and will be briefly described later. Because some detail is given in the book "What's the use of Lectures?" (Bligh, 1972) a full account is not given here.

(c) Dialogue lectures
Betts and Walton (1970) provided varied stimulation when one delivered the formal theoretical aspects of a subject while the other interjected critical and humorous comments. Thus, the lecture was a dialogue which gave well organised theoretical information in one voice, but alerted students to debatable issues, and may even have stimulated later thought, with another.

(d) Step-by-step lectures
One method known as the 'step-by-step' lecture involves structuring the lecture in a series of stages with short periods of discussion after each stage. The discussion may be by the class as a whole with the teacher or within smaller groups with the teacher observing or moving swiftly round from group to group. Another method is to set a problem or question for students to answer individually after each stage. Again, the lecturer may observe or go to those who require help. In this way he can obtain some information on his success and the students' difficulties. McCarthy (1970) has attempted to structure lectures around a series of multiple-choice questions at the University of Sydney. This method proved to be significantly more effective than conventional teaching involving lectures and small group discussion some time later. Students were also well satisfied with the method, which is well suited to factual subjects with a crammed syllabus.

These methods appear to be effective because they require some activity from the student. This activity seems to require or result in the transference of information from students' short-term memories to their long-term ones. Note taking probably has the same effect.

(e) The use of notes and handouts.

Why do students take notes? A 2 x 4 matrix gives eight possible reasons. The process of taking notes could help students at the time, or the notes could provide a useful record later. Notes can also aid students' attention, memory, understanding and organisation of a lecture. Consider first the advantages of note-taking at the time notes are taken. (i) Note-taking may aid concentration during a lecture by focussing attention on the material noted, but there is some evidence from experiments by Aiken et al (1975) and Thomas et al (1975) who asked students to take notes between rather than during sections of a lecture, that note-taking divides students' attention at the time of writing. (ii) Hartley and Davies (1978) provide very clear evidence that on balance note-taking aids recall, so probably the losses from divided attention are outweighed by the gains resulting from improved recall. Hartley and Davies reviewed 35 studies. In 17 note-takers did better than non-note-takers on tests of recall, in 2 they did worse and in 16 there was no significant difference. In an interesting experiment, Howe (1970) found that the mean probability that a student could recall an item of factual information he had recorded in his notes was .34, while the mean probability of recalling an item he had previously failed to record was less than .05. (iii) No empirical investigations have been found to test whether the act of selecting information to be noted aids thought or retention, or (iv) whether note-taking helps students see the development and structure of a topic.

Turning now to the use of notes after a lecture, (v) some colleges have used submitted notes as evidence of students' attendance at a course. (vi) In the review by Hartley and Davies of 16 studies used to answer the question "Is recall increased by reviewing one's notes?"; 13 indicated 'yes', 3 found no significant difference and, none suggested notes are a hinderance. Presumably the use of inaccurate notes for revision could hinder test performance, but apart from a tendency reported by Howe and Godfrey (1977) for students to make lecturers' negative statements positive, reasonable accuracy is reported in most studies that have considered this question. (vii) Particularly in mathematical subjects students report that, when they cannot understand the content of a lecture at the time it is delivered, they take notes to obtain a record of the syllabus covered by the lecturer. If one totals the man hours involved one must think that there could be more efficient ways of conveying the content of a syllabus. (viii) However the use of lecture notes as a record of ground covered by a lecturer can give students an opportunity in private study to consider the relationships of one part of a course to another and thereby gradually obtain an overall view of the syllabus structure. However there is no evidence that students use notes for this purpose and it is difficult to estimate the benefits of doing so.

Clearly there are many other factors that could be investigated in students' note-taking. Buzan (1974) has recommended the use of a branching structure of lines linking associated notes. A number of studies confirm that women and third year students take more notes than men and freshers, but women do not, in general, learn more from lectures. Possibly women take notes with more redundancy. Very little work has been conducted on note-taking styles, notes from different forms of presentation such as lectures and books, notes on different kinds of subject matter, differences between note-takers such as motivational factors and the personal relevance of the subject matter, the use of structural and other cues by presenters, and the intellectual level or other characteristics of the notes taken.

Are handouts better than students' notes? Freyberg (1956) gave four groups of students the same lecture. One group was instructed to take no notes at all; a second was told to take only brief notes; a third was required to take full notes; while the fourth group was given a duplicated summary. On an immediate test, students who took notes did best, and those with the duplicated summary did worst. After two weeks they were given another test without warning. The students who took no notes performed significantly better than all the other groups. On the sixth week, a short revision of ten minutes was allowed; but of course, the group with no notes had nothing from which to revise. The results of a test on the eighth week showed that their memory continued to decline slightly, while all the other groups made very marked improvements. The group with copies of the teacher's duplicated summary performed best probably because it contained all the important points and no errors.

Gallagher (1971) has substituted handouts for a full course of lectures and found few detrimental effects upon students' learning. Of course, such a finding raises all the usual problems of how far students compensated for lack of formal teaching, how far the tests were strictly based on the handouts, and so on.

I am sometimes asked by university teachers whether it is better to give handouts before a lecture, at the beginning of a lecture, or afterwards. There is little experimental evidence on this subject. McDougall et al (1972) has found that students given handouts before lectures performed significantly better on immediate post-tests than students given handouts immediately afterwards. There was no difference seven weeks later. There may be many reasons for this latter result: for example, students may have engaged in compensatory study; they may have forgotten the content of handouts; or they may have had some other intervening levelling activity. Much depends on the nature of the handouts, how the lectures are organised, their clarity, and how these factors interact.

(f) Some other factors in lecturing.

Obviously there are many other factors influencing the effectiveness of lectures. Few can be mentioned here and the reader should be warned against his own prejudices. Empirical evidence is usually more trustworthy.

In the USA, the credibility and prestige of a lecturer or broadcaster has been shown to influence students' esteem for what was said (Aronson, Turner and Carlsmith, 1963). But Oleron (1959) has obtained contrary results in France. A prestigious person and a high school student were judged according to what was expected from each. In contrast to the American experiment, the literary style of the high school student was regarded as superior and there was no difference in the ratings of their literary knowledge. Oleron concludes that an audience adopts different frames of reference and different standards according to the prestige of the person being judged.

In an earlier study, Oleron (1953) showed that parts of a talk are forgotten once it exceeds four minutes. Concrete ideas are remembered better, especially if they are isolated either vocally by a change in the voice, or by brief pauses. Facts are difficult to remember when placed at the beginning of a sentence. Short sentences with subordinate clauses at the beginning are easier to understand. Oleron thinks facts should either be introduced within a body of information with which they are related, or they should be repeated. The direct style which calls upon the listener to take sides in an issue is most helpful and variations in intonation and intensity of the voice are necessary to break up monotony and to aid memory.

A world wide problem is the large size of lecture classes. These are more difficult for lecturers to observe, but contrary to common opinion, available evidence (Bligh, 1972) does not suggest that they are less effective. Indeed most investigations have found them slightly superior.

A more severe problem is the tendency of lecturers to go too fast. Up to a point this makes no difference, but after that the amount of learning declines very rapidly (Bligh, 1972; 1974).

(g) Static pictures and diagrams

During the Second World War it became necessary to train large numbers of people quickly who were not highly proficient in verbal skills. Since many of the subjects from artillery to engineering involved spatial concepts, it was immediately evident that a much greater emphasis upon visual teaching would need to be made than was traditional in universities. After the War many of the war-time military personnel became undergraduates and lecturers in post-secondary education and gave a great emphasis to visual teaching.

It seemed obvious that visual presentation could maintain attention, partially overcome the linear temporal form of the lecture and simplify complex subject matter. Indeed, this emphasis produced a naive association between visual aids and good teaching. Educational technology and visual aids were regarded as almost synonymous.

Yet research studies at the time were already casting doubt on these facile assumptions. For example, it is often assumed that statistical data is easier to understand when presented graphically than when presented in a verbal description. But M.D. Vernon (1946) had already shown that the ability of adults to understand and remember the data depends upon their ability to interpret graphic material, to understand and use language, to generalise from particular instances, and to think relevantly without being swayed by preconceived ideas. A similar experiment conducted with secondary school pupils came to the same conclusion and emphasised the importance of a coherent argument connecting isolated data.

Thus a verbal accompaniment to visual presentation appears to be more important than a visual accompaniment to verbal presentations. In another experiment in the same series M.D. Vernon (1951) found that a purely verbal description presented to intelligent 16-18 year-old girls was remembered better than one supplemented with visual material. She concluded (1952) that 'comparatively intelligent and well educated people can derive some factual information from graphs and charts presented without written text; but with less educated, unintelligent and immature individuals, or with complex data, understanding and remembering may be rather poor. A short descriptive heading may be of some assistance but will not clear up difficulties inherent in the data. No all round advantage is obtained by using charts instead of graphs'.

Even when specific factual information is understood from graphic presentation, many people find it difficult to accommodate this information to knowledge they already possess. A verbal argument assists this process. It should also be noticed that a written argument will not be made easier to understand and remember by presenting visual factual data except in certain circumstances. Hall (1950) has taken this a stage further by showing that language not only assists but influences visual perception. Graduates were required to reproduce drawings or written passages each with various verbal titles or no title at all. The verbal titles influenced what was remembered and how much. Like Vernon, he found that the intelligence and attitudes of the students were important in what was remembered. Vernon (1950) concluded that the accuracy of perception of graphic material depended upon the students' intelligence and educational experience. Insofar as the latter is important, this is something that can be taught. In the Vernon experiment (1953) pictures were little help to readers in understanding what they read and they were less effective than graphs to demonstrate relations and explanations, although they were sometimes helpful in remembering a particular part. Pictures sometimes aroused emotions but these did not necessarily lead to appropriate action. If the reader had not learnt to interpret graphic representations, they could actually confuse him (Vernon 1954 a and b). Laner (1956) has come to a similar conclusion when teaching a manual task to young adults by film or still pictures. He concluded that visual presentations are not necessarily more effective than conventional media. The most important variable affecting their effectiveness was the adequacy of the accompanying verbal exposition.

However, not all the evidence is in one direction. Oztilman (1963) has shown that the use of pictures is important in teaching Turkish vocabulary to American students. Although there was some immediate advantage in asking students to write the words, speaking them did not seem to be very effective, contrary to some of the latest theories. This is a surprising result because one might have expected that verbal methods would be at an advantage compared with visual methods when teaching verbal material. It provides a warning against simple theorisation about teaching methods.

It is clear that very often the distinction between visual and verbal presentations is too simple. For example, Dwyer has shown in an extensive series of experiments that different objectives are achieved if the same subject is visually presented in different ways. For instance, in one experiment (1971) he showed that if students were required to draw a diagram, simple line visuals in colour were most effective for learning; but if only recognition of anatomical parts was required, shaded drawings in colour, were the most effective. Like M.D. Vernon he found there was little significant advantage in adding visual aids to verbal presentation. Also, increased realism in diagrams did not always result in an increase in learning.

A lot of experiments in this field use methods of recall or student preference; but Laner and Sell (1960) have shown that these are not very reliable guides to the effectiveness of visual presentations upon actual performance. They presented a series of posters on industrial safety and found they were effective as measured by the safety workers' industrial behaviour. They thought the posters worked by being perpetual reminders and by reinforcing correct working habits to the point where they become self-maintaining.

There are many publications listing the merits of various methods of visual presentation. These considerations will therefore not be repeated here. Many of them are fairly common sense, so that only reminders are necessary.

The traditional chalk blackboard has few advantages compared with the overhead projector. Seymour, as long ago as 1937, showed that students can perceive dark letters on a white background more easily than white letters on a black background. This finding has been repeated since (e.g. Foster, 1969). Yet, even when overhead projectors are readily available, blackboards are still widely used. With both methods, presentations may be built up in the presence of the class. Spontaneous explanation, repetition and erasure are easy, and little technical assistance is required. Overhead projectors may provide a larger image, greater visual contrast and a wider range of colour. Large areas of board are not required. Use of the overlay facility permits easy analysis and re-assembly of complex diagrams at will; it is less dirty; and teachers who are poor artists may trace or prepare their diagrams in advance. Overhead projector transparencies are particularly valuable for the visiting lecturer.

The use of blackboards and overhead projectors is personal to the particular teacher. This may be why Peters and Scheffer (1961) have found in the Netherlands that the teaching of technical subjects was slightly less effective with film strips than with traditional teaching. When a film or film strip was used as a starting point for teaching, the results were better than when it was shown at the end. The teaching *techniques* used by teachers in conjunction with the films and film strips (e.g. making notes and stimulating class participation) were notably worse than when they talked without them, even though they had been instructed in the use of visual aids. This may be related to the way the visual and verbal presentations were combined.

The simplicity of the blackboard and overhead projector is also an advantage. Peters and Scheffer reported all kinds of administrative difficulties connected with the use of audio-visual aids. Films sometimes arrived too late; distributors often gave insufficient or inaccurate information; not all buildings were suitably equipped, (e.g. with blackout); room changes caused confusion and many teachers were not competent in handling the projection equipment.

In some subjects the use of coloured slides is increasingly popular. They can present intensive colours and pictures of high quality. Remote control facilities enable the teacher to act as projectionist, but this requires careful planning and is only suitable in subjects where the slides will be presented in a fixed order. This is a handicap if the teacher welcomes interruption and questions from the class. Thus, slides are not very flexible; they need maintenance and facilities such as blackouts. We may see from Dwyer's work that insofar as they are used to present realistic pictures they may teach recognition of symptoms, minerals, land forms, mechanical parts and other recognition skills; but compared with an overhead projector, they are not as convenient and are no more effective when teaching new concepts. The size and clarity of the image obtained is an advantage. In one department of dentistry, (Gordon and Morgan, 1971) students preferred projected slides substituted for work using a microscope.

As with other methods, care should be taken when combining verbal presentations with slides. When students of microanatomy were offered lectures, unstructured laboratory sessions, laboratory exercises and sets of slides with written guides, they all used a variety of methods, but the slide-guides were the most used and exam results correlated highly with the extent to which they were used, not with any other method. Attendance at lectures and laboratory sessions decreased during the course (Elwood and Haley, 1974). It seems likely that the words of the guides were more carefully prepared than for the other methods.

The visual demands upon the students are probably too great. Some brief points about students' vision should be made. Parnell (1951) found that one undergraduate in three at Oxford wore glasses. Compared with conscripts in the armed services of the same age, four times as many had unsatisfactory sight.

Ollerenshaw (1962) has suggested that the width of a screen in a lecture theatre should be between one sixth of its distance from the back row and half the distance to the front row. If the screen contains 45 letters in a line of writing, the angle they subtend to the eye of the student in the back row would be too small if he was any farther away, and too large for the student in the front row if he was any nearer.

A great deal of research has also been conducted into light intensities, styles of lettering, the use of colour, eye movement, quantities of information, viewing angles and methods of layout. Some experimental evidence on these factors is summarised by Ollerenshaw (1962). They are mentioned here as factors to be considered, but the everyday teacher could spend more time attempting to gain perfection than the gains in learning merit. In the heyday of the craze for visual aids, many enthusiasts ignored this cost-benefit factor and brought their work into disrepute.

We may conclude that the benefits of visual aids depend upon the kind of learning that is required and will not be evident unless appropriately tested. To be effective they need careful integration with other methods of presentation.

(3) The declining importance of Programmed Learning issues

Even as recently as ten years ago many people had great hopes that programmed learning would bring about a revolution in education, especially in developing countries (e.g. Komoski, 1962). Schramm (1964) believed it was particularly appropriate in countries where teachers are short, and envisaged the wholesale translation of American programmes. Indeed, Stewart even thought there were dangers of a 'neo-colonialism' from the use of American programmes. Watson (1964), Bunyard (1968) and Martin (1965) were particularly optimistic for the use of programmed learning in Africa. Morgan (1965) and Leith (1966) thought the method was particularly appropriate where there are learning problems, and remedial adult education in remote parts of Africa seemed to be an example.

In many cases, programmes were introduced, but never greatly developed. The well known programme by Holland and Skinner (1961) was introduced into an education degree at the University of Botswana, Lesotho and Swaziland. Mathematics courses at the University of Zambia had a programmed element. Programmes were used in genetics and statistics courses at the University College of Rhodesia. Practical work in physics at Ahmadu Bello University, Nigeria, consisted of conducting experiments by working through a programme. Programmes in chemistry and genetics were also used at the University of Malawi. Elsewhere in the world the use of programmes was spasmodic and depended on the interest of the few enthusiasts. Nevertheless, there was widespread interest. In many parts of Europe the interest was more theoretical, especially in Germany, and did not lead to widespread production of programmes. The development of programmed learning was greatest in the North American continent and least in South America.

Yet the revolution never happened. Programmed learning has too often been associated with expensive hardware and was deemed too sophisticated for immediate use in countries suffering more basic educational problems through lack of resources. A programme validated in one country cannot necessarily be transplanted to another. Okunrotifa (1968), obtained significantly better results in Nigeria when a programme on map reading was modified from the original imported version. Lawless (1969) has argued therefore that "if programmes are to be used in African countries, they need to be re-validated". Another difficulty which is frequently forgotten is that students in developing countries, such as Africa, normally work in a second language. Consequently, not only is the content of the frame frequently not understood, but responses requiring fine distinctions of meaning are difficult, particularly when the students' vocabulary is limited.

In the early 1960's the United Nations Special Fund supported the initiation of an extensive plan for the development of programmed learning in Central Africa based at University College of Rhodesia. Courses to train programmers in the Armed Services, the Civil Service, Railways and Mining Companies, as well as schools and other educational institutions, foundered in the mid 1960's in a sea of political troubles following the Unilateral Declaration of Independence by Rhodesia (now Zimbabwe).

Programmed learning has been justified upon theoretical principles emanating from psychology rather than empirical data based on teaching conditions. Most of these principles are important in themselves and have had an influence upon other methods of teaching and learning. Yet there is contrary evidence on almost all of them suggesting that they are not in any sense absolute principles of the type that might be expected in the physical sciences.

(a) Success breeds motivation
One of these principles is the principle of success. In most countries of the world, with the notable exception of the USA, this principle is grossly neglected. 'Nothing breeds success like success' is a better dictum than 'we learn by trial and error'. Students gain encouragement from success so that their motivation is enhanced and we have seen that motivation is, in many educational climates, the most important correlate of examination success. Educational systems which are competitive and elitist successively eliminate potential students at each examination hurdle so that all but the most able people in society finish their education with failure.

In programmed learning students are supposed to gain motivation by successfully responding to 90%-95% of the frames. This is perfectly consistent with research findings at school level. For example, Kennedy and Willcutt (1964) reviewed a large number of studies and conducted eleven experiments of their own, and concluded that praise improved performance while blame led to a deterioration. Leith and Davis (1969) have shown the same in a programmed learning situation, whether the pupils are introverts or extraverts, and regardless of their level of anxiety.

Yet there is counter evidence that students in higher education, especially able students, become bored with programmed learning. It appears to deaden originality and creativity by requiring fixed answers from the students before they can proceed to learn from the next frame. To this extent, programmed texts are instruments of conformity and run counter to the ideals expounded in Chapter 1. Macdonald-Ross (1967) has suggested that the questions in programmed texts should be open-ended to allow for student creativity and critical thought. In this case there would be no "correct" answers and the principle of success would be less obvious if not inoperative.

Furthermore, although Elley (1966) has shown that when doing a rote task, such as learning a vocabulary list in a foreign language, students who make fewer errors learn more, the same has not been found with other tasks. For example, Elley, in the same experiment and Leith (1968) have found no relationship between concept learning and the number of errors made. Thus the relationship between success and learning, though important, is not a simple one and may depend upon the level of the cognitive skill required.

(b) Small Steps

A second major principle is that the text should proceed in small steps. Small units of information should be presented one at a time and then tested before proceeding to the next. In this way students are not allowed to proceed very far without discovering their misconceptions.

Again, at school level there is evidence that programmes teaching concepts in a large number of small steps are more effective than those using fewer but bigger steps (Middleton, 1964; Coulson and Silberman, 1960; Evans et al, 1962; Goldbeck and Campbell, 1962). It seems a fairly common sense principle that if something is difficult, or the students are not very able, a subject will be easier to understand if it is taken in small stages. But these techniques do not seem to work so well with students who have high ability either through background knowledge or intelligence. Wright (1967) has shown that part of the boredom with programmed texts experienced by able students is caused by the small steps and the frequent and repetitive testing. Their intelligence consists of the ability to relate the various aspects of a subject together without being led by the hand. Indeed, there is some evidence that students in higher education work faster and longer if the material is presented in larger chunks without testing every item of information.

Similarly, programmed learning has placed an emphasis upon students' active performance and the provision of feedback from it. But there is reason to believe that students, especially older students, object to frequent testing, and find it actually interferes with their learning (cf Gessner, 1974).

(c) Linear versus branching programmes

One possible solution to the problem that students of different ability require different step sizes may be to use a branching programme which offers a choice of answers to each question so that students proceed to different frames according to the answers they select. Students who choose wrong answers may then be led along the correct path in a number of small stages. There are a number of ways of doing this. The number of frames per concept taught can be increased; an element of redundancy can be introduced by increasing the number of words used to explain a concept, thereby making the programme less concentrated; the number of responses per frame may be increased; and hints (usually called cues) for the correct response may be introduced.

Because students are told whether their answers are correct, they receive immediate feedback on their learning, but Stones (1967) has argued that there is no fundamental difference between linear and branching programmes, because 'all the branches and remedial sequences are related to a hypothesised linear path'. In one programme Senter et al (1966) found that only 6% of the possible 'wrong' branches were used with Crowder's original programme, 'Arithmetic of Computers'. Kaufman (1964) could find no significant difference in the amount of remedial material between the two different kinds of programme. Biran (1966) and Biran and Pickering (1968) have shown that if the branching text is 'unscrambled' so that all branches from a given frame are placed on a single page, it is more effective in teaching knowledge and the students are more favourable to it. They followed this up by removing the branches that would be followed by students who gave incorrect answers and substituted an explanation of the correct answer. This decreased the length of the text, took much less time to complete and was equally effective.

It may be that the time spent looking for an appropriate branch could be saved by the use of teaching machines, but after reviewing the research available, Tobin (1968) could find little advantage in mechanical presentation of branching programmes. He concluded that the most important factor affecting success of the programmes was how well the subject was analysed in the first place. This could equally well apply to lectures, films, television or any other kind of presentation.

There are clearly many factors which influence a programme's effectiveness. Foote (1973) has used what he calls an audio-visual response teaching machine to teach engineering and has concluded that the use of colour and rest pauses assist learning, that students' viewing angles should be about 30 - 60 degrees from the horizontal, that background noise can affect attention but humour, animation and irrelevant subject matter do not help to regain it.

There is reason to believe that programmed learning can be quicker than conventional teaching but the experience is too intensive for students to maintain it for very long. Cavanagh (1963) et al, compared the use of a teaching machine with the conventional lecture and found no difference in effectiveness except that the machine took about half the time. Intelligent students did better than others by either method but the machines were not popular. In the same series of experiments, Knight (1963) observed that students missed not having access to the teacher. He therefore argued that the role of teachers would have to be reconsidered. In spite of the effort required to construct a branching programme in electro-cardiography, Owen et al (1965) found it was no better than lectures. Stretton et al (1967) used the same programme and found that the use of textbooks was slightly quicker than the use of a machine with no loss in learning.

Thus the research here suggests that there is little advantage in using branching programmes or machines.

(d) Problems of Thinking

Programmed learning is based upon Skinner's Theory of Instrumental Conditioning and it appears to be effective when learning is by association; but when, as in higher education, 'the teachers' are concerned with students' gains in thinking, the theory does not apply. This is shown in an experiment by Leith and Wildbore (1968) concerned with children's spelling. 'The experiment showed not only that the amount of over-responding was related to improvement scores but that this was a linear function of the number of responses made. "Time spent in learning was also directly related to gain, and an extrapolation of this line to the vertical axis gave the agreeable conclusion that, if no time was spent on learning, then no gain in performance would result." But what is important within the context of this book is that this relationship was not evident with conceptual topics. These require thinking; spelling only requires simple associations.

This is consistent with the finding by Leith and Buckle (1965) that overt activity is less important for students with background knowledge of the subject than for those who have little or none. Leith (1969) has related this to an experiment in a Swedish university by Szekely (1950) in which one group read a text explaining certain principles and then observed a demonstration of them, while a second group received these two treatments in the reverse order with the demonstration being presented as a problem requiring explanation. When students were given a similar problem, the second group were markedly more successful. The problem required thought. When they were required to regurgitate the principles in writing, the first group was more successful. Thus the objectives achieved depended on how the topic was introduced. Programmed instruction tends to be expository rather than problem-based. Consequently it teaches facts and principles, not the ability to use them in problem solving.

(e) Self pacing

One of the basic principles of programmed learning is that students should be able to proceed at their own pace. Yet when experimenters have presented a programme to a whole class so that all must proceed at the same speed, there has been no significant loss of effectiveness. For example, Moore (1967) found no difference between those who had to work in a group and those who had to work individually. Hartley (1968) reviewed a number of studies comparing individual use of a booklet with projection using film strips or television. Most showed no difference between the two methods. Experiments by Stones (1966) and Gallegos (1968) lead to the commonsense conclusion that students can go a little faster than their inclination without any loss of effectiveness.

(f) Working in groups

The principle of self-pacing appears to require that students work on their own. Yet, although there appears to be conflicting evidence whether self-pacing is more effective than working in groups, these conflicts can be reconciled by noticing that work in pairs is reported as more effective than either working with larger numbers or singly. For example, using a programme on advanced algebra with university students, Dick (1963) found that students who worked in pairs scored higher than those who worked alone on tests after one year; but there was no difference at first. If we suppose that a member of a pair can talk more than members of groups of any other size, this is consistent with findings on discussion methods to be considered later. James (1970) compared managers and apprentices working on programmes in groups of three or four with those who work singly, and concluded that the individuals had an advantage on immediate tests which had diminished four weeks later. Thus the time of testing and the amount of discussion appeared to be important factors in the size of groups working with programmed learning.

(g) Teachers' attitudes
In Europe, programmed learning aroused some hostility in teachers. This was probably because they associated it with a behaviourist philosophy which they found threatening. Yet, even in America, Tobias (1968 and 1969) found that teachers perceived programmed instruction and audio-visual aids of various kinds as competitors rather than aids. In these circumstances hostility to innovations is hardly surprising. This is consistent with the research of Hopper, Evans and Littlejohn (1972) who have shown that the attitudes of teaching staff to programmed instruction varied significantly from one department to another and that 'Elitist Teachers', 'Elitist Researchers', 'Expansionist Researchers', and 'Expansionist Teachers' have attitudes increasingly favourable to programmed instruction in that order.

(h) Conclusion
Although I have painted a picture of programmed learning as a thing of the past, many new programmes are still being developed. For example, six programmed texts in pathology have recently been successfully introduced at the University of Iowa (Kent et al, 1972). Programmed texts are still used in Germany and extensive plans for their use have been made in the Soviet Union (Severtsev, 1974).

Castle and Davidson (1969) concluded that programmed learning was 'effective to bring groups of people varying widely in social, ethnic and academic backgrounds in a new medical faculty to the same high level of attainment' at the beginning of a course. In other words, it is a good 'leveller'; but Stavert (1966 and 1969) and many other researchers have shown that courses based exclusively on programmed learning are not popular and consequently may rapidly become ineffective. There are signs that programmed learning techniques can make a complex subject easy to understand (e.g. Croxton and Martin, 1968).

Most studies comparing programmed learning and conventional teaching have found little significant difference, but this is possibly because of the way experiments and courses are conducted. For example, the discipline of writing a programmed text is likely to improve the teaching of the same subject by traditional methods by clarifying and organising the subject in the teacher's mind in a clearer and more suitable way for the student.

Many studies that have shown an advantage to programmed learning have done so because the tests used have been the criterion tests of the programmed text. The more the tests require thinking, the greater is the advantage of traditional methods. It is possible that programmed learning is superior on immediate tests. For example, when comparing a lecture and programmed text in clinical pharmacology R.N. Smith (1971) found the programmed text group significantly better after four days but not significantly different after 20 weeks. If this is generally true, it is incumbent upon teachers to follow up this advantage and to consolidate it by discussion methods which will be more suitable for teaching students to think about the subject.

(4) Individualised instruction

In countries where programmed learning is a thing of the past, its importance lies in the methods it has generated. Many of these have maintained the principles of individual self-pacing, the careful specification of objectives, frequent testing and immediate knowledge of results; but they have used much larger blocks of information and have introduced personal contact with tutors or fellow students.

(a) The Keller Plan

One of the most popular of these is a method variously called 'The Keller Plan' and a 'Personalised System of Instruction' (PSI). In this method, a year's work is divided into about 30 equal units approximating to one week's work. The students are assigned reading, which may include programmed texts, material only available from the library, and handouts. It always includes questions and exercises. As with other courses, students may go to particular rooms at specific times; but if they do, they will find other students working at the reading materials, not a formal period of teaching. In scientific subjects the rooms may be laboratories and the tasks and exercises may include the conduct of experiments, or other kinds of observations. 'Proctors', who are undergraduates who have been chosen for their mastery of the course, their maturity of judgement, their understanding of learning problems, and their willingness to help, are students from more senior years, and are available to help with any difficulties that may arise. Laboratory work is normally under the direct supervision of a laboratory assistant.

When a student thinks he has completed one of the thirty units of work he may report for a test at one of two times per week. These tests may typically consist of about ten short questions and one which requires a more discursive answer. Upon completion, the student takes his test to a proctor who marks it in his presence and asks questions to find out why certain answers were wrong, to correct the misconception and to test the depth of reasoning in some questions for which correct answers were given. If he does not reach a satisfactory standard, the student will be required to go away and re-study the assigned materials. If his score on the test was a borderline failure, he may be allowed to take the test again the same day after at least half an hour. If his score was satisfactory, he will be given the next assignment.

Lectures and demonstrations are provided as an added bonus to the course for those students who have completed a requisite number of units successfully. Thus attendance at lectures and demonstrations is not compulsory, but a privilege earned by successful study.

In Keller's original course, 25% of the course grade marks were obtained from the final examination which partly consisted of questions the students had already received either as part of the assignments or in the follow-up tests. (Keller calls a follow-up test a 'readiness test' because it indicates a readiness to receive the next assignment). Because the course is criterion referenced, the number of readiness tests passed counts to their credit, but the number they fail is not held against them. Nevertheless, each student's progress can be monitored throughout the course to permit counselling where necessary. This counselling is initially given by the proctor, but the teacher may help as required.

This system results in the students feeling that they receive a great deal of personal attention although, by the stop watch, they receive less than in a typical course with lectures and discussions.

The teacher's role is to select reading materials, to organise their presentation, to design the tests and to make the final evaluation of students' progress. He will also provide the lectures and demonstrations and act as a clearing house for complaints and disagreements.

This method has become extremely popular in the USA and is attracting considerable interest in Europe. The Keller Plan is now one of the most thoroughly investigated methods and there seems little doubt that it is superior to traditional teaching. Over 100 comparative studies have been published. A common feature of these reports is that very few students obtain the middle grades. It seems as if students who would have obtained these grades by other methods reach the highest levels of mastery, and there is also some evidence that fewer students fail. The method appears to be universally popular with students, largely because there is a continuing sense of achievement, they receive individual help, teaching and assessment methods are not divorced, and because it provides training in regular study habits.

It will be seen that in addition to using some well established principles from programmed learning, the Keller Plan embodies four distinctive, though not unique, principles: (i) Advance depends upon attainment. Students must achieve certain objectives before they can proceed to others. (ii) Lectures and demonstrations are used to control motivation. (These first two are aspects of what has been called 'Contingency Management' or 'Contingency Contracting').
(iii) The use of proctors permits "Repeated testing, immediate scoring, almost unavoidable tutoring and a marked enhancement of the personal-social aspect of the educational process" (Keller, 1968).
(iv) Teaching and assessment methods are made to be part of a single process, thus avoiding students feeling that examinations are irrelevant (see Chapter 2).

For teachers intending to use this method, Lewis and Wolf (1973) have given the following advice: texts and references should be at the student's level; make the first units easy to establish confidence and then gradually increase the level of difficulty; do not include too much material in one unit because units must appear manageable to the students; include summaries and questions where possible; make the questions comprehensive, consistent with unit objectives, brief and suitable for rapid grading; keep a separate folder including tests and a progress chart for each student and permit students to review their folder at any time; start in a small way and expect to spend a long time writing assignments and tests.

Although the Keller method has been used with a very wide range of subjects, it appears to work particularly well with subjects requiring practical work. This is an unusual feature because practical work is not always easy to integrate thoroughly with self-instructional methods.

(b) Contingency Management and Contingency Contracting
In the sense that teachers have always said that "if you do 'x', I will give you 'y'", contingency management has always been part of education. Students go to lectures and do assignments because they want good grades or to enter a certain profession. L.K. Miller (1970) used this principle in a course on Community Relations. For example, students were given a reading list consisting of 32 books and 85 articles, tests were designed on each, and a specified number of credits awarded. Attendance at 9 of the 30 class meetings was required to earn an 'A' grade; but attendance was only permitted by paying a certain number of credits earned as a result of test performance following the reading. Students were also required to complete a pre-test and post-test attitude questionnaire, pass a short test on the contingency management system of the course and take, but not necessarily pass, further tests on at least one further book and two further articles. Grade points were subtracted if requirements were not fulfilled. The course was run and organised by 7 students who received extra credits for doing so. Not all students reacted well to this system but over half attended more than the nine classes required and performance on experimental tests of achievement were extremely high.

Lloyd (1971) has described the principles involved in contingency methods but they are perhaps best summarised by Homme (1970) who says that the rewards should be immediate, frequent, small and given for achievement of objectives, not for anything else. Contracts with students should be fair, clear, honest, positive and systematic. At New College, Alabama, students are selected on the basis of their intellectual independence, their curriculum vitae and an admissions conference. Each student selects his own Contract Advising Committee which usually comprises the Core Tutor, the student himself and two other people who are not necessarily members of the university. After assessing the student's wishes and abilities, the Committee designs a programme which may include interdisciplinary centred seminars, in-depth projects, attendance at lectures and off campus work. This constitutes a contract with the student. He is responsible for his own self-evaluation, which may be supplemented by traditional examination results and specific comments from the course tutor which are subject to periodic review by the Contract Advising Committee.

The independence required for these courses does not suit all students and the colleges select their students with this in mind. Yet because the purpose of post-secondary education is often to stimulate students to explore their own ideas for themselves, what is sometimes required is the opportunity for an exploratory digression for inquisitive students within traditional courses in such a way that students may obtain their qualification in the same length of time. This is possible at Tufts University. The assessment system and grades, if any, are negotiated between students and their contractual tutors. A similar system operates at Hofstra University, USA. Students design their own course of study in collaboration with a tutor and there is special provision for an "Encounter" year in which the student may study a special topic off-campus. A similar scheme at the University of Hawaii requires the student to work off-campus or to travel, and to produce a major thesis of his own during the last two years of a four year course.

Of course, in terms of some traditional theories of education it is highly debatable whether students should study a subject for immediate reward. It is certainly hard to imagine that good researchers could be trained this way. But in this book we are concerned to report innovations that have been found to work, rather than expound the polemics of educational theory.

(c) Audio-tutorial

A method, which has received a great deal of publicity, developed at Purdue University by Postlethwait and his colleagues (1964), is the audio-tutorial system. This is intended to have the advantages of programmed learning without some of its limitations. For example, programmed learning methods do not seem to encourage the scientific spirit of enquiry because there is immediate feedback of "correct" answers. In the audio-tutorial system, audiotape presentations are available in carrels at a learning centre. The presentations are supplemented with textbooks, a laboratory manual, specimens, experimental apparatus, and so on. The students are therefore encouraged to carry out experimental work alongside their actual learning rather than separated by the timetable as is commonplace in traditional teaching. In short, it is an attempt to integrate scientific activities. The centre is open from 7.30 a.m. until 10.30 p.m. so that students may come and go as they please. The approach is a multi-media one in that films, lectures and demonstrations are available, and there are weekly discussions and question and answer sessions.

Although the combination of media and experimental equipment varies, this method has been widely used and probably did not originate at Purdue University. For example, at Exeter University, England, courses in engineering have used a similar method for many years, with the added sophistication of computer assisted instruction. The computer performs complex routine calculations, giving the students encouragement from immediate results to realistic problems which can be used for tutoring.

As with the Keller Method, Postlethwait reports a general improvement in students' performance when using the audio-tutorial method. It is clear that the 'normal distribution' of grades is inappropriate because virtually all students can master the subject if they spend sufficient time studying it. Postlethwait et al (1969) found that students with high analytic ability could obtain more knowledge in nine hours than less able students could in twenty.

Yet, if it is true, as Novak (1970) claims, that all students can master the material, and if this is true of other methods of Individualised Instruction, this is a serious comment upon traditional methods of teaching. It in no way justifies the complacency which is more excusable when comparisons between teaching methods reveal 'no significant difference'.

Owing to the modern complexity of educational planning, an increasing aspect is, and will continue to be, co-operation between institutions in the planning and development of courses. This is particularly true where a combination of expensive media is used. For example, the University of Lund in Sweden and the University of Oslo in Norway, have adopted an anatomical text originally devised at Erasmus University, Rotterdam, which is supplemented by an Audio-Visual programme, group discussions and clinical material supplied by each institute. The student is asked to keep a diary recording his views and his impressions of his personal and intellectual growth. He is also asked to submit criticism and comments on the course to the editors of the basic text.

These methods show that the boundary between classroom instruction and private study is no longer a sharp one.

(5) Reading and independent study

(a) The size of the problem

Investigations published in Britain in the past fifteen years have been remarkably consistent in finding that, on the average, students work a 36-39 hour week, partly in class, and partly in private study. Of course, there are wide individual differences. In one study, (Thoday, 1957) there were significant differences between students who had no examination that year and those who had. Another study (Clossick 1968) showed that students resident in a tall tower block worked fewer hours than students elsewhere. There are marked differences between students in different subjects in the amount of timetabled instruction they are given but not in the overall time spent. In other words, it seems that if students are given less formal instruction, they make up for it in independent study. At one extreme, students in art and architecture may spend over 30 hours a week in studio work. Engineers and physical scientists with a large amount of laboratory work average 20 timetabled hours per week.

Generally, the timetabled hours of students in arts and social sciences may decrease from about 15 hours in their first year to about 6 in their third, but Entwistle (1972) found that, on the average, the number of hours spent in class was 14 in universities, 19 in teachers' colleges and 22 in polytechnics. These figures may reflect the subjects taught in these places rather than different attitudes of course planners, but a similar study ten years earlier suggests that students in polytechnics and teachers' colleges now receive about 5 hours less formal instruction than they would have done then. Consequently, the amount of private study time has increased. Thus, a typical student in Britain spends 20 or more hours a week in independent study.

Research in other parts of Western Europe gives similar figures, but findings in North America and Australia suggest that students work longer. For example, in the Netherlands, Muggen (1972) developed an instrument for measuring the time students spend in study and applied it to good effect on the schedules required for specific courses. The majority of courses investigated required less time than had previously been estimated. This is contrary to findings obtained in other countries where teachers, underestimating their own erudition, usually do not appreciate students' difficulties. The average weekly time a student spent in private study was 24 hours in Chemistry and 23 hours in Economics. Correlations between study time variables and student achievement were between .35 and .66. In the Australian study by Clift and Thomas (1973) students in arts subjects spent from 46 to 51 hours per week on academic work in their first three years, but this dropped to 36 hours for students in their fourth year. They report that a typical student spent 7½ hours per day on study, 4 hours on some other activity, 8 hours asleep, 3 hours on routine activity such as eating and dressing and one hour a day on travel. The 7½ hours on academic work comprised approximately two hours in class, one hour in preparation and follow-up work, one hour in general study, and three on assigned work. These figures are averages. Apart from the contrasting requirements mentioned between different subjects, there are wide differences between individual students. Using a self-paced study in mechanics, Verreck (1971) found students needed very varied times to complete a course. Although the average study time was objectively less, students subjectively felt that they were spending more time than with traditional methods, possibly because they had to be more active. It should be remembered that, compared with most workers, students spend a high proportion of their time near to the limits of their abilities. This suggests the need to distinguish between ability, learning style, time and effort.

Nevertheless, from these figures it will be possible for governments to estimate the number of hours spent by their student population in private study. Even assuming that students never do any work during the vacations and completely fail to transfer any of their study skills to their later working life, a mere increase of 1% in their efficiency would justify a considerable investment in research and training. Students' independent study is a major industry in any moderately developed economy. Thus, if it is objected that institutions in post-secondary education cannot afford to train students in study methods, it must be replied that they cannot afford not to do so.

(b) Research into study methods

Research into independent study is fraught with problems. Firstly, it is a private activity, so how can a researcher know what goes on in students' heads? Secondly, there are no fundamental parameters. There are no fixed criteria because we want many different things from our students. We want them to remember information, but we also require many different kinds of thought and the relationships between them are many and unclear. Thirdly, in practice the questions asked by researchers have become entwined.

Sometimes researchers have asked 'Who is successful at studying?' hoping that methods can then be discovered and recommended to all. To get at this question some researchers looked at the study methods of successful students, but even if it were true that people who use good study methods are successful, the converse, that successful students use good study methods, is not necessarily true. The natural abilities and personalities of students are other variables affecting their success or failure. If it were possible to hold these factors constant, it might be possible to look at the study methods of students who do better or worse than their natural abilities and personalities would lead one to expect. In other words one could look at the contribution of study methods to over or under-achievement. However, how can we decide what the expected level of achievement of a student should be with a given personality, intelligence and other abilities? One could answer, "By finding the mean scores on examinations or some other measures of achievement for students with the given personality and abilities", but is it really possible to separate the individual characteristics of a student from his manner of studying? Isn't studying a personal activity of which one's personal characteristics form a part? For example, motivation and powers of concentration are as much part of a student's personality as his study technique. In any case, if studying is a very personal activity, supposing it was possible to separate study methods from personal characteristics, will the conclusions drawn from one group of students be applicable to others? This will be particularly doubtful in those courses which aim to cultivate students' independence of mind and approach.

A developmental approach holds individual variables constant. If growing independence during college years is assumed, one could observe students periodically and generalise the ways they have matured. Section (e) on page 98 summarises Perry's (1970) interpretations of four annual interviews with 67 students at Harvard. He recognises that students may delay, regress or even diverge from this path of development. He assumes that the search for self-identity, intellectual and ethical development are all integrated. That may depend on a student's subject.

Until the mid-1970s much of the research into study methods consisted of trying to identify the differences between successful and unsuccessful students in terms of their personalities, abilities, and study habits. First in the field were Brown and Holtzman (1955 and 1966). By successive piloting and modification they evolved the Survey of Study Habits and Attitudes (SSHA) containing four scales: Work Methods which are effective, Delay Avoidance in submitting work, Teacher Approval by the student, and Educational Acceptance of the aims of the course. The first two factors combine to form a Scale of Study Habits while the latter two form a scale of "Study Orientation". Although there have been some recent criticisms of its reliability (e.g., Bray et al 1980) the SSHA has been well used and usually correlates significantly with academic success, but not, of course, more highly than other measures of academic performances. Although Brown and Holtzman included some items on the mechanics of study technique in their pilot questionnaire, it should be noticed that techniques have emerged as less important than motivation and attitudes to study. This could be because they did not know what study techniques were likely to be most important, or it could be that study techniques are too specific to have a general influence; but in either case we are taken little further forward in discovering what techniques are most important.

In his early work Entwistle (1970) used the SSHA to establish relationships between personality, study methods, and academic performance and concluded that the average successful student plans his work carefully, thinks ahead, is conscientious and seeks suitable conditions for work. Developing his own Student Attitude Inventory (Entwistle et al 1971) he found that four scales: motivation, study methods, lack of distractions, and exam technique appeared to predict academic performance. The reader may feel that these factors do not tell us anything we do not know already, but they do give an emphasis by excluding factors we might have expected to be present.

Essentially what these researchers were trying to do was to find simple bipolar scales which would distinguish students who were good at studying from those who were not. In the late 1960s and early 1970s a host of such scales were proposed. For example Hudson (1966) has described convergers as those who are better at problems with one right answer and a correct path to obtain it; and 'divergers' who perform well on questions with many possible answers. In another bipolar scale 'levellers' tend to blurr distinctions and to omit details of information, particularly when they seem contradictory or ambiguous, while 'sharpeners' exaggerate differences (Gardner et al 1959).

Some students are naturally cautious while others take risks. Kagan (1966) has contrasted impulsive children who blurt out the first answer that come into their heads, with 'reflectives' who are more willing to suspend their judgements and tolerate ambiguities, but who would rather not answer at all than be wrong.

People who are field-dependent orient their judgements to their perception of their environment; while field-independents are better able to restructure their thoughts and impose their own organisation on ideas, they are better able to develop their own hypotheses, have superior powers of analytical thinking and seem to experience flashes of insight rather than accumulate ideas gradually by steady methodical work and practice (Levine 1976).

Parlett (1969) contrasted two different styles of studying. Students who were described as 'syllabus bound' tended to agree that "Without the stimulus of exams I doubt whether I would do much effective studying", "I prefer not to be left to work in my own way as I get nothing done", "If I think about the amount that has to be covered and learned in my coursework, I sometimes get harassed and anxious", "If I were to go to graduate school, it would not primarily be because I was really excited about finding things out". Students described as 'syllabus-free' were more likely to agree that "I don't like to be closely supervised in my work", "I spend too long on certain topics because I get very involved in them", "I frequently think of experiments for investigations I would like to tackle", "I like to play around with certain ideas of my own, even if they do not come to much" and "Often, I try to think of a better way of doing something than is described in a lecture or in a book". Parlett thought that 'syllabus-bound' and 'syllabus-free' students are contrasting types on the same scale; but Entwistle (1974) and others have concluded that these are two different dimensions and students may score high or low on both.

The limitations of attempts to find any predictive relationships between simple scales and study methods or academic performance were soon evident. It was not long before Entwistle (1974) was looking at classes of characteristics in relation to academic performance. Entwistle identified four groups of students according to their attitude to work. 'The Disorganised and Dilatory' agreed that they were slow in starting work in the evening, tended to put off work and hand it in late, were not good at organising their study time and did poorly in their examinations. 'The Cynical and Disenchanted' sometimes wished they had gone straight into work after leaving school, could not see the relevance of their work and did not think text-books worth buying. A third group displayed 'syllabus freedom', conscientiousness, but fear of failure. They worried about examinations and work which they should have submitted, they regarded their friends as more competent, they preferred to listen in tutorial discussion groups. The last group displayed a 'Masculine Competitiveness and a rather ruthless efficiency'. They were syllabus bound, determined to do well and played the 'academic game' to win. Students in the last two groups tended to perform better in examinations than students in the first two groups.

Meanwhile, using ever more complex factor analytic techniques, and questionnaires with over a hundred items, Biggs (1976, 1978) was trying to identify study processes. He identifies ten of these (1978): (i) "Pragmatism" - in which the student is grade oriented and sees university qualifications as a means to some other end; (ii) "Intrinsic academic motivation" in which the student sees university study as an end in itself; (iii) "Academic neuroticism" in which the student is overwhelmed and confused by the demands of course work; (iv) "Internality" - where the student uses internal, self-determined standards of truth, not external authority; (v) "Study skills" including consistent work, regular reviews and scheduling of work; (vi) "Rote learning" - in which the student centres on facts and details; (vii) "Meaningful learning" - where the student reads widely and relates material to what is already known so that he is oriented to understand what he reads; (viii) "Anxiety" - when the student is dominated by fear of failure; (ix) "Openness" - in which the student sees the university as a place where values are questioned; and finally (x) "Dependence" - where the student needs a class structure, and rarely questions lecturers or textbooks.

Biggs sees these values, motives and strategies as interacting upon the student's personal and institutional background. The former includes his cognitive style, his personality, his intelligence and home background; while his institutional background includes his subject area, teaching methods, methods of evaluation, and course structures.

It is interesting that when Biggs used factor analysis to try to predict students' performance in different faculties, the resulting scales could predict a student's performance equally well whatever his faculty. Thinking that having ten scales is rather cumbersome, Biggs carried out a higher order factor analysis. This resulted in three study processes: Reproducing, Internalising and Organising. It seems that the items contributing strongly to these three factors could themselves be divided into three groups concerned with the students' values, motives and strategies.

Biggs' work is stimulating for those concerned with students' study methods, but is a little daunting for the ordinary teacher in higher education. Like the work of Entwistle and numerous other researchers too many to mention, he uses questionnaire methods to probe the essential privacy of independent study.

Another method is to interview students immediately after giving them a passage to study. This is the approach adopted by Marton and his colleagues in a series of investigations at the University of Gothenberg. While the number of students interviewed is usually less than a hundred, this method has the advantage that the interviewer can question them more thoroughly, the questions can be related to a specific study activity rather than general introspection, and the students' experiences are fresh in their minds. This last point is important because, when concentrating on the subject matter, a student cannot be clearly aware of the process of concentration and other mental processes. His memory of these will quickly fade if it is not soon recalled. Some objectivity was introduced by the use of independent judges to interpret the interviews which were tape-recorded.

Marton classified students as either depth or surface processors. Depth processors are more thoughtful, try to see the meaning of the passage as a whole, make links between its parts their personal experiences and other disciplines, and generally adopt a more active, searching strategy. Surface processors are relatively passive and concentrate upon rote memory and covering the ground in preparation for reproducing the knowledge. Depth processors concentrate upon relevance, and construction of meaning, while surface processors concentrate upon recording.

Although Marton emphasised that these labels constitute poles of a dimension, in practice they are commonly regarded as categories and, perhaps unwittingly following psychometric assumptions, there is an inclination to categorise the students as either one or the other. Marton's work also made implicit assumptions which are probably valid, that depth processors are in some sense better students than surface processors, that they will score better in examinations and that surface processing precedes, either logically or chronologically, the ability to process at depth.

Not surprisingly it has been found that the same student may be superficial on one occasion and think more deeply on another. Laurillard (1978) has shown that students might use either approach according to their interpretation of what is required of them. In this way she rightly emphasises the context of academic study, a point which should not be ignored by teachers.

Another dichotomy in students' approaches to learning is Pask's (1975) distinction between "serialists" and "holists". Serialists work sequentially and consequently do well when learning 'string-like cognitive structures' such as rules, procedures, chains of reasoning, taxonomies, chronological sequences and following a programme. As the name suggests, "holists" interrelate ideas in complex and individual ways, and recall them in groups, possibly together with irrelevant detail.

The serialist/holist distinction is really part of a wider contrast between "operation" and "comprehension" learning. Operational learners quickly grasp methods, rules and details, but fail to place them in their widest context. Comprehension learning is marked by the use of analogies. This involves the perception of similarities between ideas within different contexts and each student builds up his own personal network of associations and meanings. When a student's mind wanders off either by using "vacuous" analogies or misapplying valid ones, he is said to be "globetrotting".

The distinction may seem the same as that between Marton's depth and surface processers, but it is not. Holists are not better students than serialists; they score equally well on tests. Nor does one strategy logically or chronologically precede the other. Pask argues that serialisation and seeing things as a whole are both necessary strategies for the most versatile students. More important, he has shown experimentally that the way subject matter is structured in teaching needs to be compatible with the serialist or holist predisposition of the students. A mismatch between a teacher's and a student's cognitive styles results in markedly inferior learning. Similarly a mismatch in the strategy demanded by an examination question and the student's personal meaning (cognitive structure) will result in impaired performance. Since most groups of students will contain both serialists and holists, there is an obligation on the teacher to present his material in both ways. Yet such an obligation becomes increasingly impossible if teachers have to take all such dichotomies into account.

Indeed it is increasingly doubtful how long personal tutors specialising in other fields will be able to offer students up to date professionally informed assistance. Knowledge of study skills and study habits is becoming a highly specialised field. The importance and intrinsic interest of reading and independent study have led to sudden rapid developments in research. Because these are complex processes, the research is becoming fairly technical. The findings cited here are only a very small fraction of recently published work.

Consequently we should anticipate the appearance of a new specialist profession in institutions of post-secondary education - the study methods assistant. Before considering how they might work, we should know the need for the service they can offer.

(c) The need for training in study methods

Any systematic attempt to provide a training in reading and independent study is neglected by the vast majority of post-secondary educational institutions. There is reason to think that students should be taught how to study as an integral part of their course. There are very few teachers who would not agree that one function of post-secondary education is to develop students' capacities to continue to learn in later life. If this is so, it is hard to deny that post-secondary education should be a training in independent learning. Therefore, if study techniques can be learned, teachers should teach them, or at least create conditions in which students can learn them.

At undergraduate level it is clear that students' study problems are not well recognised even by the very people at present responsible for dealing with them. For example, in one university, (Reid 1970) 60% of the teachers thought that undergraduates should be mature enough to work with only general guidance. Since students cannot be expected to change their study habits immediately upon entering college, the patterns of work established at school are inevitably transferred to post-secondary education. These are often inappropriate. Even at post-graduate level, Rudd (1968) discovered in interviews with 696 research students, that 38% of Arts, and 63% of Social Studies students said that they had received no instruction in research techniques. Arts students in particular had difficulty in finding suitable places to work and in obtaining books. More than other groups, they complained of the lonely life of the researcher. Nearly all groups remarked that supervision was inadequate. Bradley and Hindmarsh (1968) classified the activities of post-graduate students into 'leisure', 'living' and 'research'. There were few differences between subjects and universities. They typically spent less than one hour a week with supervisors or participating in informal academic work.

Another investigation showed that most students have periods when they cannot concentrate and 70% reported that personal problems interfered with their studies. Nearly all students set unrealistically high standards of concentration and believed that they concentrated poorly (Appleton, 1969). In addition to motivation and interest in their subject, concentration was found to be strongly influenced by the study environment. Training could make students more realistic and could give guidance when and where to study. Hammond (1957) has reported that the distribution of study time, the use of the library and attendance at classes were important; and he also mentioned the importance of small informal discussion groups.

Doctors concerned with student mental health have observed what is sometimes called the "Decompression Syndrome" (see chapter 3). When students are at school they are subject to pressure of examinations for college entrance, teachers closely monitor their progress and they are told what to do and when to do it. On arriving at college, this pressure, and the pressure of parents who are ambitious for them, is removed. Yet there are pressures of a less tangible and familiar kind. Firstly the abruptness of the change can create uncertainty and anxiety for some students. Secondly there is the pressure of the pace of work which is sometimes easy when students have been well prepared at school, but at other times there is a sudden increase in the gradient of difficulty. Yet, because no one wants them to hand in work the next day, they have a feeling that no one cares if they fall behind. Elton (in Bligh 1973) has remarked that this is an unnecessary uncertainty in students' lives, and is exactly the point at which we should not 'throw them into the deep end', but should be more authoritarian than universities have been in the past. "And this is particularly difficult at a time when we all agree that basically we must be less authoritarian with our students'. His judgement is reinforced by 75% of the students in Child's study (1970b) who said that their relationship with their tutor was an important factor affecting their attitudes to their subject and their methods of study.

The attitude of a student's tutor has a special importance in courses which combine academic and industrial training. In Eastern Europe great emphasis is placed upon this integration; and Milton (1974) has reported that such courses are increasing in number and success in the USA. Outside the universities, courses of this kind have been extensively used in Western Europe too; but Cohen (1970) has pointed out that if an agreed objective of such courses is a closer relationship between academic studies and their practical application, it is necessary that some person is responsible for its achievement. The majority of students in Cohen's study reported that their supervisors made no effort to integrate students' academic and industrial work. The majority of industrial supervisors were primarily 'job-oriented', rather than 'student-oriented', and they thought the students should be the same, rather than spend time in private study.

The important point here is that study methods require adjustment to the social and academic climates in which students have to work. Working habits are influenced by cultural conditions and these include the sub-cultures of the college environment itself. Child (1970a) has shown in one British university that, although when at school, students study in the evenings and at the weekend, they prefer to confine their work to weekday evenings when they reach university. Students prefer not to study in the library. Study sessions are usually between one and two hours and methods are developed by trial and error. At Exeter we have repeatedly found that first years work more at weekends, second years work shorter hours, and third years work little at weekends but average about 40 hours per week on the remaining five days.

Course design is a major determinant of academic climate. In Australia, another study by Clift and Thomas (1973) highlighted the need for teachers to consider the capacity of students when designing courses and assessing students. Like other studies, it shows the need to give tuition in study methods. Students in the faculty of science complained that too much material was covered in lectures, that it was frequently too difficult and that too little time was assigned for tutorials. They had plenty of time to follow up formal class teaching and to prepare assignments, but did not seem to know how to use it. Students had competing demands from teachers in different subjects and this created a stress when they were formally assessed. There was generally too little time to write up results of practical work.

Some of the most disturbing findings are on postgraduates' use of libraries. For example, Wood (1969) has shown the importance of training in the structure and use of scientific and technical literature for modern scientists. He reports surveys of scientists and engineers working in industry and universities, which show that libraries are often used only casually, and that abstracts indexes and other sources of information are often completely ignored. In one official government survey, 28% of physicists and chemists experienced delays in their research owing to their ignorance of earlier work.

The difficulties encountered by undergraduates in using library resources is reflected in a study by Durey (1967) in which students completed a questionnaire one day when leaving the library. 44% did not have to look for books either because they used their own, or because they had located their requirement on a previous visit. The survey showed that students who had to look for books frequently had inadequate or inaccurate information. 17% did not know the author or title of the books they required. 43% were unable to find what they wanted, and a quarter of these could not find it in a catalogue. Only half those who failed to locate books on the shelves, asked whether they were on loan, and only a third of these asked for the books to be recalled. Wood (1969) advocates courses on the use of libraries on three levels: when students first arrive at college, when given project work in their third year and at the beginning of postgraduate research; but I don't think this proposal will answer the problem. The difficulty is not that students do not know how to use the library; but that they don't do it.

Training in study methods needs to be an integral part of a student's course, firstly because study habits require some practice and secondly because learning to study a subject is an integral part of its discipline. However it does not follow from this there is no place for specialists in teaching study methods. It implies the need for co-operation.

Indeed since writing the first edition of this book I have entirely changed my opinion from believing that tutors should be taught to give advice on study methods, to the belief that giving study advice requires such detailed knowledge and special skills, that colleges should appoint specialists for this work. It should not be thought that because someone is a specialist in a certain subject, that he will necessarily be an expert in the study methods of that subject. Many gifted professors may be unaware of the techniques they use, and be even less aware that they require to be learned. Nevertheless, experience in learning a subject is one, but only one, of the qualifications for teaching others to learn it.

(d) Study methods can be taught

It may be objected that study methods cannot be taught; they can only be caught like a disease. It may be said that students can only be told what to do; they can't be taught to do it.

This is simply not true. There are numerous studies showing the effectiveness of all kinds of provision including the use of courses, counselling, peer groups, contracts, manuals on how to study, self monitoring of study behaviour and the use of behaviour modification techniques.

There have been over two hundred studies investigating the effectiveness of these various methods in the past ten years. The overall impression is that these methods can and do improve students' study habits and techniques; but nearly all the investigations are open to some criticism. Firstly it seems likely that simply being made to pay attention to study methods results in some imporvement and it is not always possible to disentangle these effects from the direct consequences of the programmes, remedies or treatments reported by researchers. Secondly reports showing no significant difference are not likely to be published; and since study methods programmes are unlikely to be harmful, it is not surprising that the majority of published reports show some benefit from such programmes. Thirdly, while not suggesting that research is deliberately biased, it is known that the enthusiasm of experimenters for their particular hypotheses to be confirmed, can sometimes unconsciously influence results if the necessary controls are not observed. Finally criteria of the effectiveness of study programmes do not always include tests of 'depth processing' and other higher mental skills which Marton, Pask, Biggs and others have shown to be important.

(i) Manuals. Interestingly the most popular method for improving study habits, namely the use of 'how to study' books, appears to be the method with least empirical support. Indeed the study by Gadzella and Goldston (1977) showed that the use of study guides combined with classroom discussions did not benefit less able students who, presumably, are those whom the study guides are most intended to help. This is consistent with the remark that students who don't know how to study are precisely those who will not know how to study a document giving advice.

In view of the differences between subjects, some reservations should be held about the general recommendations made in books on how to study. Most of these are written from the point of view of students in the humanitites, social sciences and biological subjects. The aesthetic needs of students of literature and the particular requirements of students of the physical sciences are less well catered for. Thus most of them are concerned with digesting a large body of information.

Although there are nearly as many recommended study methods as there are authors, their recommendations have certain features in common. They nearly all recommend that students should first obtain an overall view (a 'Gestalt') of the material. They then suggest a number of stages so that the student progressively considers more detail, culminating in note taking and revision. After each stage the student may decide that the book or article is not worth further study. Some authors suggest that students should ask questions about the subject they are studying either before they begin or after the first brief overview. This is particularly important in arts subjects where the questions asked are, in a sense, more important than the answers obtained. Nearly all authors recommend some method by which students are tested or are required to recall the content of what they have read. Some suggest that students should graphically represent the relationships between various aspects of a topic.

Perhaps the best researched scheme is the SQ3R System of Study (Robinson, 1961). This stands for Survey, Question, Read, Recite and Revise. At the "Survey" stage, the student is advised to study the table of contents, read the author's preface, read chapter summaries and skim rapidly through the book. The student should keep his purpose clearly in mind and if the book does not fulfill it, he should look for a better one. If the student then writes down questions that occurred to him, his study will remain relevant and it will be easier to relate the isolated facts. These questions also enhance motivation and encourage a more critical attitude. Only at the third stage is the student encouraged to read the book and even then, he should keep the headings and sub headings clearly in mind. Particular attention should be paid to graphs, tables or other methods of visual presentation. The fourth stage in which the student is required to recite or recall the content of what he has read is important for the consolidation of memory, but it does not encourage creative or critical thinking. It should be noticed that revision, the final stage, is not something done just before the final examinations, but is another important way of seeing the subject as a whole.

There is some evidence that a subject is easier to remember as a whole if students work quickly. It is possible that slower working makes association between the first and last sections of work more difficult. In an interesting experiment, Carmichael and Dearborn (1948) showed that if a reader was required to answer questions every 25 minutes on what he had been reading, an acceptable level of attention could be maintained for up to 6 hours compared with 1½ hours without such tests. Since tests are not always available for students, they should be trained to test themselves with this degree of frequency.

(ii) Courses. The research into study methods repeatedly shows the importance of individual differences and personal approaches to studying. The provision of the same course to a large class of students is unlikely to be effective with more than a small number of them. There is also the danger that precepts offered at the beginning of the academic year will soon be forgotten if too much advice is given at this time. Having a once-only course at the beginning of the academic year also neglects a very important principle. Any respectable industry, not only inspects its final product, but monitors the production process and constantly strives to make it more efficient. In education, we examine the product, but we scarcely ever monitor the learning process. We examine what students have learned, but we do not worry how they have learned it.

Furthermore when the material for study methods courses is drawn from disciplines outside the students' interests, motivation falls. The study techniques required by students in different subjects will be very different. 81% of students in a London psychology department wanted advice on how to read reports of experimental research given in journal articles. Students of literature require different techniques according to whether they are reading a literary work or literary criticism. In the latter, they need to extract major arguments or points; but to use these selective techniques when they wish to savour the language of the whole work, would be as inappropriate as listening to only some of the notes in a piece of music. Mathematical calculations appear to have a sequential form; but mathematical expressions are often understood more easily if students observe their relation to both the previous, and the following, lines of a calculation. This attempt to see a mathematical expression in its context requires jumping ahead in the sequence and looking at it in both directions. In the social sciences, the student needs to learn to discriminate between facts differing in importance and generality. He also needs to know techniques to deal with a large body of information by organising it, yet at the same time, to be able to re-organise it in different ways.

If students are to be taught practical skills of this kind, it is no good merely telling them what to do. They must *do* it - particularly when it requires unlearning the bad habits they have practised for some years. Many experiments have shown that merely giving people information whether in lectures or in a book, is quite an inappropriate way to teach practical skills. Continuous practice is required because the habits of years cannot be changed in a few hours. This is a further argument for the integration of study training with the students' academic course.

Despite these reservations there is some evidence that courses in study methods are effective. For example Larkin and Reif (1976) were able to train students of physics to abstract quantitative relations, such as definitions or laws, from textual descriptions and they also learned to apply them. Although Robyak and Downey (1978) found that the effectiveness of a Study Skills course varied with students' personality type and previous levels of academic achievement, there were overall gains in the use of study skills. There are several studies showing that courses in Study Methods improve study attitudes as measured by the SSHA, but these are unconvincing unless there are also measured changes in study behaviour.

Poulton (1961) has suggested that the main problem for many students is that the rate of reading never catches up with the maximum rate of comprehension. There are two well known rapid reading courses. The Carborundum Course uses film of a passage of which one small section is in better focus and moves continuously along the line while the Harvard films use a jumping technique in which the student is required to fixate on one phrase for a prescribed time before shifting his attention to the next section. Each section consists of a phrase that may be understood from a single fixation. Multiple-choice tests of comprehension are an unsatisfactory feature of the Harvard course because they test recognition rather than comprehension.

To justify the benefits of training courses for students in rapid reading, we need to consider the time spent on the course with changes in comprehension and the time saved by rapid reading. It is probably true that commercial companies make extravagent claims for the efficiency of their methods. Reading speeds of over a thousand words per minute have frequently been reported, but after surveying available evidence, Poulton (1961) concluded that the average reading speed was between 160 and 280 words per minute before training and between 340 and 500 words per minute afterwards. These improvements ranged from 40% to 130%. If we assume a mean of 85% interacting with a mean improvement of 10% in comprehension scores (MacMillan, 1965) the gain in efficiency is just over 100%. Poulton's calculations are based on the Harvard courses while Berry (1965) has only found 40% improvement with Carborundum films. Fry (1963) only expected a 25% improvement from students who read his book. It is a general finding that after considerable initial improvements, students' reading speeds tend to regress but some improvement remains. It is probable that Poulton was not able to allow for this factor so much as Berry and Fry.

Even so, if we suppose that the average improvement is 20%, less than any of these researchers have reported, a student can gain two terms' work in a four-year course. This calculation discounts any benefit to vacation study or reading in later life. Put another way, a student who spends 20 hours per week reading in private study, would save four of them by taking a course in rapid reading. Therefore, only if the course in rapid reading takes more than 4 hours per week for the whole of his time at college, is it not a worthwhile investment. If this increase in efficiency is maintained in a student's working life, it is an investment no college and no government can afford to ignore.

(iii) Study Counselling. There are numerous reports of the effectiveness of counselling upon study behaviour but the methods of counselling vary so much that it is difficult to draw any general conclusions. Counselling varies with the needs of the students and the theories of the counsellors. It may be given to individuals or groups. What most counselling has in common is a recognition of the importance of emotional, motivational and personal factors upon cognitive study processes. For this reason much of the work is concentrated upon developing independence, self-discipline and efficient planning in use of time. One common procedure is for the counsellor to negotiate a 'contract' with the student that he will undertake a certain amount of work. Gradually the counsellor can withdraw by lengthening the term of the 'contract'. In this way the student exerts increasing self control.

A related procedure uses behaviour modification techniques in which, by a process of conditioning, students take increasing responsibility for the organisation of their study time. Reports suggest that these techniques are very effective (e.g. Groveman et al 1977), but the research is difficult to interpret. When the reward or 'reinforcement' of the conditioning process is offered by an external agent such as a counsellor or experimenter, it does not seem like a process of self-control.

When a student gives himself his own 'reinforcement' he already has some self-control which is not a random activity needing to be reinforced. The languages of self-control and behaviourism may not be incompatible but they have long been thought to be so and it is difficult to understand the relationships between their concepts. Furthermore there is considerable and growing evidence that the mere act of monitoring one's own study behaviour results in considerable improvement. It is easier to explain this in terms of rational behaviour following self-awareness than to assume the effectiveness of some conditional external reward. More probably the reward is internal - the personal satisfaction of having done the necessary work.

What conclusions can be drawn from this review? Manuals are most easily provided but have the greatest limitiations. Systematic advice, both in separate courses and as an integral part of academic programmes, results in improvements, but do not take account of individual needs. The benefits of personal counselling are the most difficult to prove and the most expensive to provide, but seem likely to be the most effective.

An assignment for teachers

Teachers often complain that students do not do precisely what is asked. Are they always in a position to do so? Before setting an assignment complete the following checklist.

(1) How will you make clear to the students what is most important: for example is it factual knowledge, coherent argument or well supported opinion? Are you prepared to accept the students' interpretation of what is important?

(2) Is the assignment intended to test or to teach?

(3) Do students know how long the assignment should be?

(4) Is it important what sources are used and if so have you checked whether the material is available to students?

(5) Schedule the assignment:

- (a) Make a realistic estimate of the time it will take the *students* to complete.
- (b) Check their commitments including the time required and deadlines for assignments from other teachers.
- (c) Set deadlines for students to submit the work and deadlines for you to assess it.
- (d) Plan how and when you will give feedback to the students.

(6) Tell the students what support is provided for those experiencing difficulties in completing the assignment.

(7) Will you grade it absolutely in terms of the standard required at the end of the course or relatively in terms of the students' present level of attainment?

(e) Correspondence study

Moore (1973) has classified methods of independent learning and teaching according to the distance of the student from the teacher or teaching media. He hypothesises that more autonomous students will be attracted to more distant methods of learning and teaching and, therefore, that measurable differences will be found in the autonomy of learners in courses varying in teaching distance. This does not seem to have hampered recruitment for correspondence courses.

In recent years there has been a great increase in the number of courses of private study to be taken at home. At first, these were correspondence courses but later, radio and television services were also brought into use.

Governments have seen these methods as cheap and quick ways of achieving 'higher education for all', 'education permanente' and other social and economic ideals. In most countries of Eastern Europe, particularly East Germany, it was thought that correspondence methods could achieve ideological and economic objectives. The University of Sierra Leone hopes to make a significant contribution to the cultural life of the country and also to satisfy the requirements of the professional and semi-professional groups such as social workers, business executives and trade unionists, by providing lectures, courses, seminars and general information for the public on academic, professional and cultural matters at various levels of presentation. In order to provide middle level training, the University is considering admitting non-degree students to the relevant parts of degree courses.

Most countries of Western Europe use correspondence courses to provide training and further qualifications for teachers. This is even more important in Brazil, where about 50% of teachers in schools are unqualified. Since there is a young and rapidly expanding population there is an urgent need for quick and efficient training of a large number of teachers. The Brazilian government hopes to achieve this by a modified version of the British Open University. The Institute of Space Research in Brazil has instituted an ambitious programme to develop a completely integrated system using the latest cost-benefit technology. The system includes the use of radio, television, a new system of programmed instruction and computer management of student programmes, a satellite system and special TV receivers capable of receiving signals directly from the satellite. All these components work together in a system, so that the amount of information presented over the duration of a course is rather like a parabolic curve. At first a small amount of information is presented on television, this increases rapidly and is maintained by intensive programmed instruction, and towards the end radio is used to diminish the information rate and to raise issues.

Correspondence education in Sweden dates back to the Hermods School of 1885. Today, the state schools, folk high schools and industrial and commercial training establishments provide an opportunity for supervising teachers to explain difficult points, suggest additional reading and organise group work. Degree level courses are provided by university teaching staff under the auspices of the University of Lund. Throughout Scandinavia there is a wide range of folk high schools, adult education centres, Workers' Educational Associations and other institutions providing an excellent and varied educational service of which these countries should be proud.

In Sweden nearly one person in eight is engaged in some form of correspondence study. Established institutions providing further education have received subsidies and state grants to expand existing courses, especially in Business Studies, and to make laboratory facilities available for students studying science by correspondence. Professor Husen at the University of Stockholm has designed aptitude tests for students intending to study by correspondence. Research has been conducted into the use of programmed learning techniques for correspondence students. Sweden was also responsible for some of the early experiments in university level correspondence education, considering success and dropout rates, characteristics of students and the effectiveness of various methods of presentation including radio and television.

Then, following a suggestion of the Education Commission in 1968, Sweden attempted a decentralised system of regular university programmes. Students who took these courses were more likely to have a family and a professional appointment than students in an ordinary university; and 50% said that they would not have gone to the Regional University if the decentralised courses had not been initiated. The attitudes of the students were favourable and their performance in examinations was slightly better than that of students in an ordinary university, although their academic aptitude and intelligence were no different. The use of the tape recorder for personal communication between the tutor and student has been found more satisfactory than writing. This may be because mature students prefer the personal touch and find writing difficult. Andre (in SRHE, 1973) recommends that the heterogeneity of students should be reduced before entry and that adequate information on the minimum requirements should be given during the course. No doubt this would improve the general level of academic performance, but it would also change the social function of the system.

The Soviet Union has several million students studying by correspondence and more than any other country. Courses in economics, industry and building, and 'Public Education' are particularly popular.

An underlying theme of this book is that methods cannot be appropriately chosen before a fairly precise specification of course aims and objectives. The aims of governments are not precise enough. Yet a feature of correspondence courses is that the organisers are committed to a particular method regardless of its suitability for the objectives appropriate to a particular subject.

This leads to enormous difficulties. It is difficult to stimulate students to think or to be creative with methods which basically consist of presentations. The range of student activities is small. The time spent in marking students' work is greater and possibly less effective, than in situations where face-to-face contact is possible. Students need face-to-face tuition at the beginning of their courses when they first meet the challenge of studying on their own; but in most correspondence colleges this is the time at which it is most difficult to provide. The high demands upon students' motivation and attention leads to a very high rate of student dropout. Consequently the need for training in private study is particularly acute; but because this requires practical work, it is extremely difficult to carry out. Laboratory and other practical work is difficult to arrange. Finally, correspondence courses do not easily fit in to a national system of academic awards.

Correspondence courses also require a reliable postal service and a literate population. Expansion has been less rapid in many developing countries where these requirements cannot be satisfied and where a large proportion obtaining secondary education are able to gain access to higher education. Consequently the examples which follow of attempts to overcome these difficulties are drawn chiefly from Europe.

In the Soviet Union, East Germany and other parts of Eastern Europe, the students typically attend a regular one day 'consultation session' every two to four weeks, consisting of lectures, seminars, exercises, laboratory practice and individual tutorials. Residential courses are also held once or twice a year for which the state guarantees full pay and a 75% reduction in travel expenses.

Desirable as these supplementary measures are, they remove the à la carte feature of correspondence courses in which students may enrol at any time of the year and proceed at their own pace. However, there is some evidence that the imposition of a time schedule makes students work harder and complete their courses sooner. The East German system, which includes oral tuition, consultation sessions, residential courses and blocks of full time teaching, compels students to work at a similar pace but probably permits the achievement of objectives that would otherwise be impossible.

In East Germany, as in many other countries, the need for students' personal contact with tutors and fellow students is recognised. Individual tutorials are available on request and radio, television and programmed learning techniques are extensively used, both individually and in combination as supplementary methods. Seminars and laboratory work are also arranged where practicable. In any case, complete isolation is avoided because industrial training and shop floor practice are compulsory for those not receiving such instruction as part of their occupation. In East Germany a larger element of face-to-face teaching has been included than elsewhere.

In West Germany, H.F.L. of Hamburg recognises the difficulty of organising groups of students or providing face-to-face tuition, and refuses to mount courses in subjects such as engineering, which they consider unsuitable to the correspondence method. S.G.D. of Darmstadt has reacted by incorporating periods of residential face-to-face tuition and instituting local student associations which are thought to reduce the rate of dropout considerably. Elsewhere in West Germany it has been shown that dropout is very high (up to 80%) in semesters in which only correspondence methods are used. This reinforces a point repeatedly made in an earlier chapter that education is essentially a social, as well as a learning activity. Course organisers and governments who choose correspondence and mass media methods will increasingly need to recognise that group methods are a necessary complement to presentation methods.

This raises the question of student dropout. In spite of their large numbers, dropout and wastage rates in the Soviet Union are low compared with other countries. They vary with the subject of study and are usually between 2% and 15%. In France, the Centre National de Télé-Enseignement (CNTE) is a vast state controlled organisation with limited support from the radio and television networks. Intending students have to show that their needs cannot be satisfied at an ordinary institution and a strict check is maintained to see that they work regularly. The organisers estimate that the annual dropout rate of 25% per year compares favourably with similar institutions in other countries.

The incorporation of correspondence courses into national educational systems appears to take time. In Europe, Sweden, France, The Netherlands, as well as Australia, where there was a rapid expansion of correspondence courses after the Second World War, these courses are fairly well integrated into their national systems. This is not so in West Germany where growth was less rapid. In The Netherlands there is a system of inspection and accreditation of correspondence courses. An inspector visits a correspondence college at least twice a year to see that course designers and tutors are fully qualified, to ensure that the colleges' promises and the students' obligations are reasonable, and to see that the college is sufficiently financially solvent to fulfil its obligations to its students. Examinations are also inspected to ensure that academic standards are adequately maintained.

There are many and varied innovations using the principle of correspondence. The University of California, for example, has recently experimented with courses by newspaper in which 20 lectures, constituting a course, are published in over 100 newspapers across North America. There are three kinds of participant: the casual reader, the curious reader and the serious student who wants a college credit. The last group have to register with the university, meet on campus four times a year, receive a reading kit and take examinations administered by a local college. A study guide, bibliography, self-tests and other materials are also provided.

There seems little doubt that teaching and learning at a distance will continue to grow, that techniques will be increasingly sophisticated, and that the world wide sale of learning materials has scarcely begun.

(6) Mechanical presentations by radio, tape, film, television and computer

(a) Radio

Radio has been widely used in the United States, Australia, Britain, Japan, Thailand, Mexico and to some extent in Spain, at the school level. At university level, radio has been used extensively in

England to supplement written materials provided by the Open University. In Australia, the Radio University of New South Wales, beginning in 1965, used the short-wave bands of The Flying Doctor Service to teach students isolated in the 'Outback Regions'. Each outback community purchased a transmitter and, for a short time each day, the students were able to speak to the teacher about their correspondence material.

The 'Radio College' (Funk Kolleg) at Frankfurt in West Germany provides short courses in social science and modern languages consisting of 20 radio lectures and 20 radio seminars, each lasting 45 minutes. The number of registered students is small (under 2000). A survey in 1966 showed that 46% were interested members of the public, not aiming for any specific qualification, 31% wanted to take university entrance examinations, 31% were people who had done well in their occupations and wished to go to university but were unable to do so through lack of entrance qualifications, while the remainder were either trained or practising teachers or university teachers wishing to broaden the range of their studies. 48% were in the age group 20 - 29 and 29% were from 30 - 39. Although the supplementary written material includes some practical exercises, it is mostly reference material, and since even the radio seminars are really presentations for the majority of students, constructive and critical thinking about the subjects must rely heavily on the students' initial ability.

An important difference between sound presentations on tape and on radio is that in the latter, students cannot replay the sound at will. Consequently, problems of attention and clarity of presentation are even more important on radio than on tape. Most of the important research in this area was conducted over 20 years ago. Philip Vernon (1949) investigated the factors affecting comprehension of broadcast talks by army recruits in Britain. The interest aroused by the topic was by far the most important factor. Comprehension was better when the topics were not abstract, when they were treated in a concrete way, were familiar to the listener, and involved the audience personally. Comprehension decreased when more than half a dozen points were made, and when the sentences were complex and unduly literary. A conversational style was not necessarily more effective, because a good speaker could be understood even when he used quite a different language. The number of abstract nouns and the proportion of passive verbs in a sample of 100 words provided a rough indication of difficulty. Belson (1952) tested the understanding of a five minute news topic broadcast to a typical sample of the British population. He claims that people leaving school could only understand 21% of it, the average for the population as a whole was 28% and university graduates only understood 48%. While these figures give a spurious objectivity, it seems clear that the comprehension of the broadcast material is much less than is commonly assumed.

Schneider (1954) compared the attention span of pupils and students of various ages when listening to broadcasts. Children from 8 to 10 years could attend for about 15 minutes; between 10 and 12 years their attention lasted for 20 minutes; from 12 to 15 years, 25 minutes; and from 15 to 18 years students could attend for over 30 minutes. A similar gradation has been found in the proportion of material that was remembered by children of various ages after listening to radio broadcasts. When active work was carried out immediately after the presentations, significantly more information was remembered in tests up to one year later. There is no reason to believe that these results would not be replicated if adult students had been used. They show how important it is that active methods of learning should be used in conjunction with presentation methods.

(b) Tape-recordings

There is relatively little work comparing the effectiveness of radio broadcasts with live lectures. Evidence from Australian study suggests a tendency for students receiving traditional instruction to do better on an immediate post-test while radio students do better than others after a delay. There have been a number of comparisons of tape recordings with traditional teaching when repetition of the taped material has been disallowed. In one study (Bligh, 1970) tape recordings of live lectures were more effective on tests of high level thinking; but this finding has not been repeated (Bligh, 1974). Frank and Lesher (1971) found tape recordings and live lectures equally effective. Snyder et al (1968) obtained a similar result but students did not like the disembodied voice. In a similar experiment Popham (1961) divided a graduate course in two groups and taught one by the lecture-discussion format and the other by a tape-recorded version of the lecture followed by a brief teacher-led discussion. He later taught the two groups by audiotape. With one group the audiotape was followed by a lecturer-led discussion; with the other the discussion leader was an untrained student. There was no significant difference in the effectiveness of any of these methods on measures of students' learning, but students preferred the audiotapes because they thought they were better organised and they felt free from distractions. However, they disliked their inability to question or disagree with the lecturer.

An experiment by Menne et al (1969) suggests that tape recordings may be better with less able students. 290 students who chose to receive a course on audiotape were given a tape recorder and a complete set of taped lectures together with blackboard notes in a prepared booklet. 408 other students chose to go to live lectures. In terms of post-test scores and final grades, the two groups were no different; but when the comparisons were controlled for differences in students' performance at school, audiotapes were clearly beneficial to the least able students. For others there was no difference. Furthermore, only 5 of the students who received the audiotape dropped out of the course, while 58 attending lectures did so.

The problem of declining student attention is as pertinent when listening to tape recordings as broadcasts. The work of Lavach (1973) suggests that the careful use of stimulating language can ameliorate this difficulty. Lavach played 20-minute tape-recorded lectures with arousing words preceding selected passages. Recall scores on short term and long term memory tests confirmed the hypothesis that high arousal during the acquisition of learning results in good long term memory and poor short term memory. Wakeford (1972) has shown that it does not matter whether an audiotape is read by a professional broadcaster or a college teacher, but students prefer the voice of someone they know.

In Sweden, Agar (1962) has studied the effectiveness of training newly recruited industrial workers by tape recorder. He thought it an advantage that the same teaching can be given to successive groups of workers. Since the presence of a teacher is not required, recruitment may be staggered or at any time. Agar's students can consult the tape at any time without feeling embarassed, and this is particularly important with older workers. Management can ensure that the quality of instruction is good. The time taken for training has generally been halved, permitting more direct contact with the trainer. After use, the tape can serve the same function as a reference book. It leads to the desired quality of work and is suitable for the instruction of foreign workers because they can repeat sections they do not understand.

(c) Language laboratories

A particularly important use of tape recorders is in language laboratories. Influenced by programmed learning and Skinnerian psychology, early users of language laboratories believed that languages could be learned most efficiently if students received the stimulus of hearing the language spoken properly, actively responded, possibly by imitating what was said, and then received feedback by hearing their own performance for themselves. Unfortunately, this alone is not enough. The students must then be capable of detecting the weaknesses in their performance, or have a teacher available who can do so. The first they are sometimes unable to do; the second, requiring the presence of the teacher, removes part of the attraction of the method.

The cause of this difficulty is the need for variable immediate feedback. This may be partially obtained by linking the audio system of two or more students so that they may converse; but the danger that students may practise their bad habits as well as their good ones, remains. Solutions of this kind depend upon the electronics of the system established. It is not the purpose of this book to describe these in detail, but to point out that before the decision to install a language laboratory is taken, a clear understanding of its use should be envisaged. How far will it be necessary for courses to include remedial loops and specialised branches? If multiple access to many sources is required, multi-channel wiring and centralised tape-replay facilities will probably be necessary. How much storage space can and should be available? Thus, many crucial decisions are taken before the language laboratory is built.

Another important question is whether the language laboratory will be any more effective than traditional teaching. Apart from a careful, but limited, experiment by E.S. Freedman (1969), and an expensive programme of experiments by Banathy and Jordan (1969), there has been very little empirical work to study the effectiveness of language laboratories. Freedman's students learned some aspects of French grammar better in the language laboratory than by the traditional lecture, but she concluded that students' superior motivation, interest and attitudes to the subject was the major advantage of the new method. The superiority of students' motivation has been confirmed by Stock (1966) who reported that students wanted to go on using a language laboratory at the University of Adelaide regardless of its limitations.

Language laboratories require students to speak the language, while in traditional methods they have a more passive role. Consequently, it may not seem surprising that the military personnel in Banathy and Jordan's experiment were judged to be seven times more expressive in their foreign language than a control group. This shows that students learn what they are taught and not another thing; and teachers therefore need to match their teaching methods with their precise objectives very carefully. Nevertheless, the difference reported is remarkable.

Chomei and Houlihan (1968-1969) have shown that the immediacy of feedback is an important factor in the effectiveness of language laboratory teaching. Therefore the system devised must take account of this and may require more intensive activity by the teacher than is commonly supposed. On the other hand, Brown (1968) has described a method in which a conversation with a teacher is simulated. Students reply in the foreign language during silences left on the tape recording. Another method is for the student to switch over to a second channel while he responds. The second method enables the student to take his time and to reply at length. By either method the teacher's next pre-recorded contribution may seem unnatural. Nevertheless, students practise articulation of the language even though feedback, if any, is not immediate. Brown does not report a thorough evaluation of his method, which is unfortunate. Had he done so, some judgement of the relative importance of feedback and expression might have been possible.

It is worth pointing out that the studies of the effectiveness of language laboratory teaching at school level in the United States by Keating (1963) and P.D. Smith (1970) have either found no difference or found traditional teaching to be marginally superior. Insofar as results in post-secondary education are different, it may be supposed that language laboratories are particularly appropriate with older students.

(d) Telephoned lectures
Beckman (1970) has reported a series of lectures given by telephone at the University of Pennsylvania. Facilities, talent, time and money prevented the use of videotaped recordings. 300 students were divided into 10 classes, each with two loudspeakers, and a student talk-back unit which had to be placed carefully for smooth running. It was necessary to pay attention to acoustic and temperature conditions to ensure that students maintained attention. Printed material such as textbooks, tests, maps, a list of course objectives and evaluation sheets were provided. A 'classroom attendant', who may have been a graduate or a member of the academic staff, was always present to attend to the needs of students and to be prepared to stop a lecture to clarify points if necessary. He also had to make sure

that two-way telephone communication was maintained and that the lecture was effective and interesting. The lecturer himself visited the college every six weeks, gave a lecture and answered questions. It is clear from Beckman's Report that this method is not in general to be recommended, and it needs very careful organisation and planning; but it did overcome the enforced absence of the lecturer and the experience shows that the method is not impossible. After initial problems were overcome, students became more favourable to the method.

McKeachie (1969) has reported a number of instances in which the telephone was used "to guide students into contact with well-known public figures". The results of the only well-controlled comparison of telephone lectures and face-to-face teaching show no significant difference in students' learning and attitudes (Cutler et al, 1958). This is consistent with recent experiments comparing tape recorded and live lectures, but it is not consistent with early experiments (e.g. Paul and Ogilvie, 1955; Wilke, 1934) which suggest the importance of visual, and preferably face-to-face tuition. Ristenbatt (1968) has shown that pictures can be transmitted along ordinary telephone wires, but, of course, the students will require a 'blackboard-by-wire' receiver and the pictures received have to be more static than those obtainable by television.

So far as I am aware, no country has yet introduced a method by which anyone can dial a specific lecture on the telephone; but there is no technical reason why this should not be possible. If nationally instituted, such a method would be cheaper than most other forms of education, but it would have obvious disadvantages compared with other methods. There would be no 'classroom attendant', no obvious means of feedback, telephone acoustics are not conducive to prolonged attention, visual teaching would not be easy, and the method would need to be used in conjunction with others if students were to submit or to discuss their work. Nevertheless, this method could be a public service and could be available in each person's home at any time of day or night. For this reason it could be valuable for people in remote areas, the blind, and those who are housebound either because of physical handicaps or domestic duties.

A limited system of this kind has in fact been used by the Department of Postgraduate Medical Education at the University of Wisconsin; but its use has been restricted to practising doctors. 230 tapes are available to any doctor in Wisconsin State, 24 hours a day. They have been well used and have influenced medical practice. Meyer et al (1970) have argued that this system could play a valuable role in assessing the needs of continuing medical education.

One section of Britain's Open University has experimented with a multiple telephone link-up for group discussion with about five students in each group. By saving travel costs and rent for a meeting room, the method proved cheaper than traditional group teaching in spite of telephone charges. Group interaction normally depends upon visual cues, but their absence was not a handicap after the first two or three 'meetings'.

(e) Tape-slide presentations
The use of tape-slide presentations as a substitute for lectures could be a major development in post-secondary education in the next ten years. It has all the advantages of self-instructional techniques so far considered. Students may work at their own pace by stopping the playback and repeating it if necessary. They may work at any time of day or night. Questions and other self-testing devices may be introduced to provide consolidation of learning and feedback. The supporting visual illustrations can be very attractive, display concepts not possible in language, relieve the load upon students' short term memory, show the organisation and relationships of different aspects of the topic and all the other advantages usually quoted for visual aids. Tapes are more easily modified and brought up to date than printed books. Above all, tape-slide programmes are cheap to produce.

The usual method is to construct small cubicles, each with a small screen, a table, two chairs, the play-back part of a tape recorder and a projector. Tapes are designed so that an inaudible signal provides an electrical impulse in the projector so that the next slide is shown. In this way a synchronised tape slide presentation is produced.

There has been remarkably little research on the effectiveness of tape-slide programmes. Goodhue (1969) and others have shown that the provision of tape-slide programmes in laboratories can reduce the time taken by students to conduct experiments to one half or one third that required by traditional methods. Furthermore, practical work is found to have fewer errors. Pullon and Miller (1972) have reported that the use of audio visual aids in individual carrels has proved slightly more effective in the laboratory teaching of biological subjects than conventional methods. Engel et al (1972) have successfully developed a range of teaching materials (including tape recordings, 8mm films, scripts and illustrated booklets) for use in England. They found the materials just as useful in New Zealand. There was no difference in the effectiveness of the various methods except that students who used tapes appeared to learn a little quicker.

An interesting feature of tape-slide programmes is their portability. More than one company in England produces medical programmes which have been sent all over the world and have been particularly useful in remote parts of Africa and South America. This is possible because compatibility between one make of tape and another is better than in the case of tele-recordings.

Tape-slide programmes appear to be popular with students too. At Harvard, for example, multiple-choice questions have been introduced into the middle of tape-slide presentations in haematology, together with discussion of the right and wrong answers. Students warmly approved of this innovation and even some members of staff found it helpful (Reich, 1972). As with programmed learning, there appears to be some evidence that learning is more successful when students use tape-slide presentation in pairs. The reason for this appears to be the same. Discussion between pairs allows greater participation than any other number; misconceptions are likely to be questioned by partners and programmes are completed more quickly. Obviously the same discussion is not possible with "individualised instruction". In many subjects tape-slide presentations combine well with the work required in laboratory practicals, especially on difficult topics when students need a series of short instructions which can be repeated as often as they like.

As with other self-instructional devices, teachers have more time to give individual attention to students, with obvious beneficial effects.

We may say, in conclusion, that tape-slide presentations may not be spectacular, but they probably have more value than any other generally applicable teaching innovation at the present time.

(f) Films

In terms of their educational effectiveness, films and television may be considered together. Broadly speaking, things that can be learnt from one can be learnt from the other. The major differences lie in the technical problems of their production. The minimum initial capital outlay for film production in educational institutions is probably less. The pictures usually have better definition, and at the present time colour productions are both better and cheaper on film. On the other hand television technology is developing more rapidly. In particular, editing and modification of videotapes is relatively easy and this is an important consideration in post-secondary education. Because videotape can be erased and re-used, once the necessary capital equipment has been obtained, television can be used for many purposes which would involve unthinkable expense if film was used. In Higher Education films are soon out of date and inappropriate.

For these reasons, television is rapidly surpassing and replacing film in Higher Education. Consequently virtually all the research on film reported here was conducted before 1960. The exceptions are concerned either with film loops or combinations of media, including film. Nevertheless, many of the early findings on film are equally applicable to television.

There are numerous studies using children showing that films are a suitable method for teaching factual knowledge, but there are fewer in post-secondary education. For example, one French study has shown that films can play a part in the acquisition of knowledge, but that children have to be taught not to be passive when they are shown. Bacquet et al (1954) compared three methods of giving 13 and 14 year old children vocational guidance: a pamphlet, class teaching, and films combined with discussion. The pamphlet was read chiefly by parents and did not promote discussion between parents and children. Class teaching resulted in small gains in the children's knowledge, while the third group, who had films combined with discussion, acquired more knowledge, showed greater development in their attitudes towards their careers and more decisiveness in their own choice.

Of course, Bacquet et al's experiment does not show whether it was the film, the discussion, or the combination of the two, which was effective in teaching knowledge or changing attitudes. In an extremely well designed experiment, Lewis and Steinberg (1951) showed that film gave significant increases in knowledge to students and could prove a popular teaching method.

As in all experiments on teaching methods, the timing of the test is an important variable. In an interesting experiment with children, Paulsen (1957) showed that, when tested immediately after the presentation of a film, many details were remembered but the story as a whole was not clear. Two years later, many details were omitted but the story as a whole was remembered much better. This suggests not only that information absorbed is organised subsequently but that if the teaching by film presentation is immediately followed up so that the details are related to the story as a whole, the optimum teaching effectiveness could be achieved. Thus, once again, we see the importance of combining film with other teaching methods. Using an immediate test of factual recall, Van Der Voorde and Fraleigh (1971) demonstrated that a group receiving film was significantly superior to those receiving the same information by lecture or by reading the film script. It is doubtful whether this result can be generalised; the films were a novel method. Nevertheless, that films can be effective over a long period of time has been shown by Foy and McCurrie (1973) when teaching Pharmacology, by using multiple-choice pre-tests, post-tests and delayed post-tests.

Fraisse and Montmollin (1952) point out that memory of presentations is mostly a process of reconstruction rather than recollection. This is why the meaning of a presentation is all important. Fraisse and Montmollin have conducted experiments on students' memory and attention during the presentation of films. More than one-third of the visual content of the films in their experiments was forgotten immediately, and what was retained lacked precision. Only one-third of the shots were specifically recalled. Several factors influenced immediate memory, among them the meaning of the film and the importance of these shots. For example, shots essential to dramatic action were well remembered. In a newsfilm, the shots which illustrated the commentary clearly were retained. Memory was influenced by the time and length of the shot used, long shots being better remembered in newsreels. There was a much greater loss of memory of sound. Only about one-third of the commentary was remembered and this was mostly associated with the action.

The fact that films are either as good or possibly better than other methods to teach information, does not imply that they are better at teaching students to think about it. Indeed, the concentration of information often prevents thought. An interesting example of the inability of students to manipulate ideas from presentations such as television and films has been shown by Gibb (1970) when student teachers, who observed one classroom situation, were quite unable to transfer the same principles to a second situation presented 20 minutes later. Yet the thought required for this transfer was relatively simple, and the concentration of information was probably not great.

An interesting French experiment by Tardy (1960) shows, contrary to popular opinion, that although films were effective in teaching information, they did not bring about significant changes in attitudes. This implies that it was the discussion in Bacquet's experiment that resulted in attitudinal change.

Systematic observations of the attitudinal effects of films give inconsistent results. These may be partly explained by the temporary nature of attitudinal changes. For example, many experiments finding aggression after seeing films, may not have detected deep seated changes in attitudes, but an immediate need for expression following inactivity while viewing. Stückrath and Schottmayer (1955) have shown that the effect of a film depends on the extent to which the action in the film corresponds with the student's personal situation and the degree to which he can identify his own ego with it. Wölker (1955) has suggested that young people and students may identify with films on two different levels. There is identification with individuals, and identification with the film as a whole. In the latter, the student considers the way the film forces him to think. He has no opinion of his own; his thoughts and emotions are absorbed by the wider action of the film and it is from this that identification with individuals in it develops. There are not 'thoughts' in the academic sense, but a high degree of involvement with the total situation depicted. Thus, Wölker's view does not conflict with my earlier claims that films are ineffective to teach students to think.

It may be thought that films can provide an excellent substitute for demonstrations of manual, and other practical skills. Demonstrations can be made virtually perfect. They may be seen by many students at the same time, however small the objects shown. The span of time depicted can be lengthened by slow motion, compressed, or edited. Repetition is easily possible and does not waste materials in the same way as repetition of a demonstration in chemistry or cookery. In one experiment (Weiss et al, 1971), dental students taught a manual technique by film loops performed significantly better than a similar group taught by conventional lectures and demonstrations. Furthermore, the group experiencing the film loop took 42% less time. This is a similar result to that obtained by Goodhue (1969) with audiotapes.

However, although there is not much evidence to suggest that films are less effective than live demonstrations, some studies show no difference. In Turkey, film has been used to give demonstrations of practical teaching, and as a means to overcome the shortage of science teachers, their lack of up-to-date knowledge, a curriculum thought to be out of date and a serious shortage of laboratory and demonstration equipment (Nelson and Ozgentas, 1961). Film was found to be useful as an in-service teacher training device but, although it was popular with students, it did not improve upon the performance of experienced teachers or do more than might be expected from satisfactory textbooks. Hughes et al (1953) compared a silent coloured film on 'How to inoculate a plate' with live demonstrations of the procedure. They found no significant difference in the way two groups of students performed the task. They concluded that the choice of method should be based on class size and other factors of convenience. Obviously one such factor is expense; and another is the fact that films cannot easily be modified later.

This raises a general difficulty when deciding whether to use films, multi-media programmes, teaching machines or other modern methods. Their effectiveness appears to be related to very specific situations. One example of this occurred at the Minnesota Medical School where a System Analysis Index for Diagnosis was designed using multi-media methods, including films, to teach clinical psychopathology. Students in experimental groups were significantly better at performing a diagnosis of a filmed patient, but they were no better than a control group in diagnosis with actual patients (Cline and Garrard, 1973).

The success of educational films is dependent upon the finer points of teaching technique as much, if not more than the choice of methods itself. Although there may be some overlap, the criteria used to judge films on the cinema screen and educational films, are not the same. When the latter are judged according to their teaching technique, much of the research on film technique seems to make sense. These points may be illustrated by examples: One of the much vaunted advantages of film and television is their ability to show the real moving world rather than still pictures or cartoon animations, but Laner (1954) has shown that to provide instruction for a manipulative task, a series of line drawings was more effective with military and university graduates than a film of the task being performed. Again, it has been shown by Kanner (1968) and others that the use of colour has no beneficial effect unless it is directly relevant to the content. In a later experiment, Laner (1960) concluded that although some techniques of film production are more important in making it an effective teaching method than others, realistic pictorial portrayal contributed little to its teaching effectiveness.

As with static visual aids, Rey (1954) has shown that films with too great a cinematic complexity should be avoided in educational contexts and that the importance of repetition should not be underestimated. Lajeunesse and Rossi (1960) have compared films with a predominance of close-up shots with others containing a predominance of long shots or a mixture of the two. Close-up shots giving an analytical structure brought about the greatest gain in knowledge; but the authors concluded that in certain cases, each of the three types of film was suitable for presenting information at different levels.

One of the difficulties of hiring films is that they are made by people who do not know the precise circumstances in which they will be used. The teacher, or more often the student, must adapt them to his own needs. This is consistent with evidence (e.g. Mackintosh, 1947) that a teacher's commentary to a silent presentation is superior to a sound film, provided the teacher is familiar with the film and has prepared his commentary well. For background teaching, the sound film is superior to the silent one; but where film is to be the major form of presentation, it should be short and deal with specific points.

The importance of precise needs and circumstances makes it difficult for the ordinary teacher in post-secondary education to use hired films effectively. Yet the importance of the finer techniques of production make it unwise for him to produce his own. The use of short films can overcome the problem of course relevance. Repetition and the problem of keeping students' attention makes short films or film loops desirable. Francis et al (1963) concluded that universities and colleges of advanced technology should be encouraged to develop a central photographic unit to form libraries of single concept films for inter-institutional distribution when suitable. This would appear to be a reasonable solution to all these difficulties if film is to be used. To a large degree the same arguments apply to television.

(g) Television

In addition to the advantages compared with film mentioned earlier, television has the advantage that it can be received in many places simultaneously. Many universities with large classes relay lectures from one hall to another. In London all the major colleges in further and higher education are linked by television cables. Programmes are produced centrally more cheaply and with greater expertise than would be possible in the individual colleges. When the programmes are relayed, the colleges may either show them directly to students or record them for future use at their convenience. Programmes may also be borrowed from the central audio-visual service. Video-taped lectures on closed circuit television have been widely used in Canadian universities. Alberta and Ontario have conducted some small scale projects. Newfoundland has offered credits for courses on videotape which have never required the presence of teachers (B.L. Moore in Packham et al, 1971).

The ability to relay a picture by cable is also an advantage when the television camera can observe in places where students cannot. It may observe under water, in confined spaces, from the air, in inclement conditions, and where the students' presence would affect the observation. For example, observations of marine life, the movement of a stomach wall, field and vegetation patterns, the flow of molten steel, and patient behaviour, can all be observed more conveniently by television. The use of cameras sensitive to infra-red light may permit the observation of life in an underground cave without disturbing light-sensitive animals.

Of course, television can also be transmitted to many receivers without the use of cables. Being a large country with a widely dispersed population, Australia was one of the first countries to experiment with broadcasting adult educational programmes. Beginning in Sydney and Melbourne in 1956, a daily educational TV service to all capital and provincial city areas had been developed by 1963. The University of the Air was inaugurated in 1961 as an extension course rather than popular education, to bring university education to a wide audience. Research revealed that the viewers ranged from graduates, professional groups and students in adult education, to the intelligent lay public. School-university bridging courses were also broadcast and the extension of television coverage to remote areas has begun.

It is also true that cameras can be taken to remote areas more easily than students or other viewers. This is of great advantage in the presentation of topical items and has led to a great increase in the geographical knowledge of adult populations.

The cost of television teaching is likely to increase less in the near future than the cost of teachers' salaries. Clearly the cost-benefit of television teaching becomes greater with larger numbers of students. With smaller numbers traditional teaching is cheaper. In 1968 Harrington and Knobblett concluded that the cut-off point was 350 students for their courses in business studies. With the relative decrease in television costs, this figure is now probably high. Indeed, work by Vaizey in Portugal and Layard with reference to USA and Britain seems to confirm this (Layard, 1973).

These calculations assume that television and traditional teaching are equally effective. On balance, the weight of evidence suggests that like other presentation methods, television is useful to teach information, but is not very effective for promoting thought or changing students' attitudes. For example, an investigation by the BBC in 1958 enquired how far viewers' knowledge, attitudes towards medical questions and worries about their health were changed by a series on medical practice. The series had no effect upon people's worries and did not affect their attitudes towards doctors or hospitals in any way; but did increase viewers' knowledge of the National Health Services.

Chu and Schramm (1967) surveyed 421 comparisons of television with traditional instruction reported in 207 separate studies. The table following shows that overall there was no significant difference between television and traditional instruction. Of those studies which did show a difference, there were more favouring television with elementary and secondary school children, but more favouring traditional instruction at the college level.

Television versus traditional instruction

Institution	Television Superior	No Significant Difference	Traditional Instruction Superior	Total
Elementary School	10	50	4	64
Secondary School	24	82	16	122
College	22	152	28	202
Adult Education	7	24	2	33
	63	308	50	421

Dubin and Hedley (1969) have reported as many as 191 comparisons at the college level. Although most of the differences found were insignificant at the standard 5% level, when all investigations were considered together there was a slight but significant difference in favour of traditional instruction.

Chu and Schramm have also surveyed attitudes towards instructional television. They conclude that administrators are more likely to favour television than teachers; and that college level students prefer small discussion groups to television classes and television classes to large lecture classes. There is evidence of a "Hawthorne" effect amongst students in which they feel stimulated by the novelty of televised instruction at first, but it later wears off. However, there is no firm evidence that attitudes towards television improve or worsen with time. As with lectures, liking television is not always correlated with learning from it. Dubin and Hedley also reviewed students' attitudes towards television and found wide differences between colleges. While most students became more favourable towards television after they had experienced it, two-thirds preferred live lectures. After only a five week course using television, Greenhill et al (1956) found students evenly divided in their preference.

It should be emphasised that these results have been obtained from college students. Evidence on the educational effectiveness of television with ordinary people receiving programmes in their homes is slightly different and this is pertinent when we consider the claims for mass education by television.

There is some evidence that although a considerable amount of factual knowledge is acquired, it is superficial, and adults are often imperceptive of the deeper significance of the programme presented. A reasonable explanation of this is that they simply do not think about what they see. This is consistent with evidence already presented on the effectiveness of live lectures for promoting student thought. Daines and Neilson (1963) have ascribed this to a kind of 'tele-hypnosis' which occurs even in viewers of high intelligence.

Yet although young people may not think about the contents of programmes, there is some evidence that they can be critical of them. In a German survey (Divo, 1961), young men preferred sports programmes and crime stories while girls preferred light programmes; but they all objected to the bad quality of presentation although they thought the medium was excellent for topical information. In an interesting British study, Belson (1959) has shown that viewers' breadth of interests was reduced in the years immediately after acquiring a television set both in terms of their own feelings and their actual behaviour. Although there was a gradual recovery after five or six years, it was remarkable that even personal interests did not revive greatly when featured on television. Acts of initiative were also reduced during the first five years after owning a television set. In another study, Belson (1956) showed that programmes on France and the French language increased viewers' knowledge of words and phrases and they gained information about France; but their anxieties about language difficulties and visits to France increased too. Once again we see that presentation methods can only present information and consequently this is all the viewers acquire.

Thinking and attitude change are mental processes that require activity. This activity can be generated if television viewing is combined with discussion or some other active method. In two UNESCO studies, Dumazedier has studied the potential of television to stimulate modern ideas in rural areas. Programmes were viewed in community groups and followed by organised discussions in which questions were asked on general problems and the answers recorded. He concluded that although there was no evidence that audiences participate more actively with tele-recordings than with films, tele-recordings promote a reflective attitude, stimulate co-operation between television authorities and adult education groups and television can be an educational instrument in rural areas. Because presentations were followed by discussions, there were considerable changes in attitude on some problems. Viewing in groups resulted in more self-expression than private viewing and we shall see later that self-expression of attitudes is frequently a prerequisite for changing them.

There have not been many studies comparing film and television as teaching methods. Since they are similar kinds of presentation one might expect little difference in their effectiveness and this expectation has been confirmed by Mundy (1962). Tardy (1963) has also found no significant difference in the effectiveness of live television and films. However, knowledge that a programme was live made a favourable influence on students' attitudes to the message and their attention to ideas expressed.

As television equipment becomes cheaper, the provision of individual self-pacing programmes on videotape will become increasingly popular. A system of this kind has already been tried at the University of Mississippi (Suess, 1973) and was just as effective as a parallel lecture course.

(h) Computer Assisted Instruction (CAI)

Like other pieces of hardware, computers may assist teachers but not replace them. They are convenient tools for some jobs; but they cannot do everything. This may not seem a very surprising assertion. Yet it should be appreciated that there are some teachers in post-secondary education who fear such innovations and assert, without careful consideration, that they can have no place in the teaching of their subject. Equally there are those who see CAI as the instrument of a revolution in education in the near future. Compared with their programmed learning counterparts one or two decades ago, the sceptics are more open to conviction by practical demonstration and the optimists have made fewer exaggerated claims.

The jobs computers can perform include the presentation of information and questions, the provision of immediate knowledge of students' performance, routine calculations and bibliographic searches, demonstrations, the production of complex data for students, participation in games and simulations and the monitoring of student performance for teachers.

When using computer assisted instruction, Sokolow and Solberg (1971) found that cognitive objectives were achieved but affective ones were not. Students learned to make a diagnosis of certain medical and dental disorders but they were dissatisfied with the standard of the computer programmes. When presenting information, there is little doubt that computers can be programmed to perform all the functions of a teaching machine and can be better than the most sophisticated of them. With programmed learning in declining favour, this seems a small advantage for the obvious difference in cost, particularly as there are few teachers sufficiently competent to write branching programmes of such complexity that they require computer control. Computers have some advantage over most teaching machines in that they may be linked with television presentations and other electrical equipment. By performing routine analyses of students' responses they can provide immediate information for the improvement of programmes.

Combined with its "immediate feedback" facility, a computer may be programmed to give students instructions for repeated practice at such skills as routine calculations. By contrast, students' enjoyment of some subjects, such as engineering, can be frustrated by small errors in repetitive routine calculations. Computers can remove this drudgery and leave students free to concentrate upon principles. This facilitates a more rapid coverage of principles and enables students to conduct small research projects near to the frontiers of their discipline. This is both rewarding and instructive.

The computerisation of library catalogues is a relatively simple task and, if a series of key concepts is appended to each reference, appropriate references may be presented to any student who requests them for a particular combination of concepts. The Teaching Services Centre at the University of Exeter, England, is developing a system of this kind with reference to the literature on Higher Education. On payment of a small fee the service is available to anyone in any country.

Goldberg and Suppes (1972) have shown that computer assisted instruction is suitable to teach mathematics. Computers can give mathematical demonstrations to show the working of conceptual models. For example, mathematical models showing economic, psychological or mechanical interactive systems may be demonstrated. If students arbitarily change one variable, consequential changes in other variables may be quickly shown. Similarly interpretative analyses of graphs may be demonstrated.

We often claim in Higher Education that we want students to think for themselves. We want them to be original and to propound their own ideas. Computers cannot be creative for them, but they can store vast quantities of data which can be presented in a form that enables students to test their own ideas. For example, if a student wanted to propound some new ideas in the field of demography, data stored in a computer could be processed so as to check the student's opinions.

Games and simulations in management and economics can reach new levels of sophistication with the aid of computers. Computers can be programmed with the rules of games and by the use of random numbers they may simulate chance elements affecting managerial decisions, such as the weather in agriculture. At Beliot (Wisconsin, USA) attempts have been made to simulate chemical behaviour. Several colleges have simulated international power politics. In one project, computer assisted instruction was used to train medical students to interview patients. The computer was programmed to simulate patient reactions. When students who had received this form of instruction first met patients, they performed better than students who had not; but later on there was no difference (Brody et al, 1973). Anaesthesiology has also been taught by computer simulated patient behaviour.

Signs of incipient student dropout, failure or distress which could be remedied by counselling are often slight unless the information available to teachers on a given student is put together to form a general picture. With the expansion of student numbers in post-secondary education it has become increasingly difficult to monitor student performance. The storage, relation and retrieval of such information by computers provides a possible way over this difficulty. Thus, although they may be feared as tyrannical instruments if used to process human data, computers can perform a humane role to diagnose where counselling may be worthwhile.

A major doubt of any college contemplating the use of CAI is its cost benefit. The calculations of educational economists give very varied answers, and current costs could change dramatically in either direction in a short time. Layard (in Lumsden, 1974) has reported that the PLATO IV system at the University of Illinois cost $0.34 to $0.68 per student hour if each of 4,000 terminals were used for 44 hours per week for 45 weeks per year. This intensity of usage seems optimistic. In New York City, California and Wichita State Universities estimates ten times this have been made. If computer instruction can be linked with telephone networks, many savings are immediately apparent. For example, the demand for college buildings and their maintenance is reduced. All that can be said now is that the doubts on cost benefit cannot be confidently confirmed or denied.

The second major doubt about CAI concerns its effectiveness. Here again it must be said that too little is known. Studies in the USA at Stanford, Illinois and Florida State Universities indicate that CAI was quicker for the same results. Attempts to compare learning from computers and other methods show the usual crop of insignificant differences; but when it is remembered that computers may be used for a wide range of educational objectives, close inspection is quite encouraging (Levien et al, 1972). Nevertheless, it would be misleading at this stage to suggest that a sudden revolution is imminent through the widespread use of CAI.

III Discussion Methods

Throughout the earlier part of this book there has been an undercurrent leading towards emphasising the importance of discussion methods in post-secondary education. It has been argued that the major objectives of post-secondary education are concerned with students' ability to think in certain ways, to foster certain attitudes and to develop satisfying personal relationships, rather than the acquisition of information.

Earlier in this chapter we saw that when the results of a large number of experiments are considered together, there is evidence that these things are best achieved by discussion. It has been shown that students spend most of their working time either in private study or listening to presentations such as lectures. These are rather solitary activities even though a hundred people in the room may be doing the same thing. Yet part of the purpose of having colleges at all is to permit students to meet and talk to other people, to share ideas and to work out their own ideals by testing them against those of others. Learning is more effective when it is a co-operative, not a competitive, activity. These things imply discussion.

Again, part of the function of post-secondary education is to facilitate students' personal development. Many students at the age of 18-21, before entering a wider world, are trying to understand their own relationship to it and within it. They are trying to understand themselves.

We have seen that there has recently been a considerable growth of interest in individualised learning and self-instruction. There is obvious merit in these developments; but in my own view self-instruction in small groups is even more important. In Belgium, Dupont and Servais (1973) compared students of Economics working in autonomous groups with students working independently within the framework of a course. Both methods reduced students' dependence on authority, but group work facilitated personal development, the growth of cognitive complexity and greater educational and intellectual development. Students need a social, as well as an academic, experience. Because language is the vehicle for both of these, I think discussion techniques are essential for the teacher in post-secondary education in a way that lecture techniques are not. Discussion is the essence of the process of post-secondary education. The process of presenting information is necessary, but not in this sense essential. It is often said that discussion techniques are inappropriate in the physical sciences, but in a course for 1st and 2nd year engineers in Belgium information was taught by the use of library techniques together with audio-visual presentations. Modern computing techniques were taught with the aid of computing machines and basic principles were introduced in a more or less programmed form in seminars. The students then discussed selected problems in small groups in the presence of the entire teaching staff. They were also told how to write a report about their own findings. The use of computing machines was integrated into the whole course. Although the course has been running for about 18 months, it is clear that most students appreciate the special atmosphere and the active methods. There is little doubt that it is highly effective.

Because teachers tend to use the methods which they were taught, they are often unaware of the diversity of group methods available. Figure 5.5 indicates some of the methods available. It ranges from buzz-groups to T-groups, but it may be better to think of the methods as a continuum along which the skilled tutor glides imperceptibly from one method to another and back again according to the needs of his students.

Figure 5.5: A Hypothetical Continuum of Group Methods

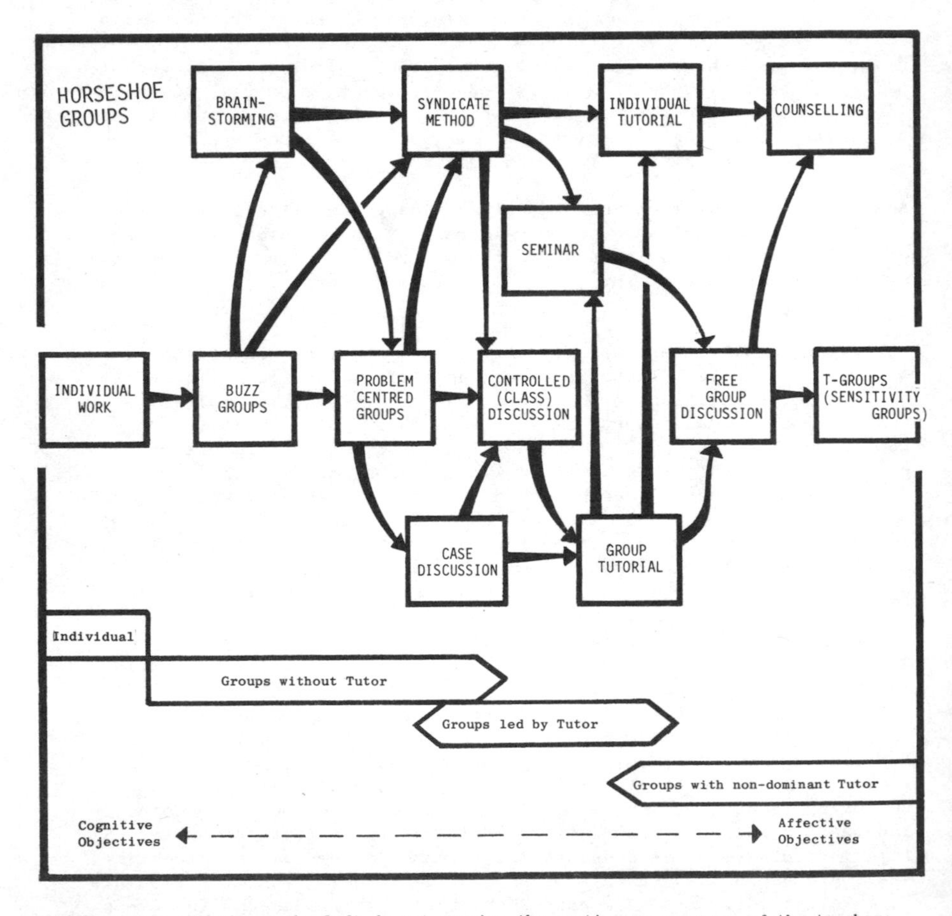

The first six methods on the left do not require the continuous presence of the teacher; the remaining seven do. In the last four on the right the teacher's skill in observation and listening are particularly important; while his leadership in controlled discussion, seminars and group tutorials is more evident.

(1) Groups without teachers

(a) Buzz Groups

Buzz groups are tutorless groups of 2-6 students meeting from 2-15 minutes. Provided the co-operation of students is enlisted first by explaining their purpose, buzz groups may be formed by asking students in alternate rows in a lecture to turn around and face those behind. This is shown in Figure 5.6. If the lecture theatre is too steeply terraced a group of two or three students may be formed on a single row as shown in Figure 5.7. If groups are formed of four or more students in the same row, insufficient eye-contact is generated.

This is one of the easiest and most versatile of all teaching methods. It has been used with up to 400 students, and there is no reason why it should not be used with more; but obviously when there are large numbers the teacher cannot visit every group to give help or obtain feedback. As we shall see, it can also be used with tutorial groups.

It is the method in which students can most easily express their thought. Consequently, in my opinion, it should be the basic method from which students learn how to learn in other teaching situations. It is frequently not appreciated by teachers in post-secondary education that their authority, derived from their status, their superior knowledge and their role as examiner, inhibits students. Thus, even teachers with the best of intentions are frequently obstacles to learning.

Students can practise all kinds of thinking according to the problem they are asked to discuss. For example, a problem requiring knowledge of another subject could encourage interdisciplinary thinking. Some problems can train students in analytical thinking by requiring them to write down similarities and differences between concepts. A subject can be made relevant to a student's career if he is asked to apply principles that have been taught in a lecture. If the teacher wishes to train his student's powers of judgement, he must give problems that require it. If the task simply requires the student to go over what has been said in a lecture, it may remind students of certain facts or practise the use of new concepts and terms. Essentially, the nature of the objectives achieved will depend upon the task the students are asked to carry out.

Buzz groups are essentially a method to be used in combination with other methods. It is remarkably rare in post-secondary education for teachers to use combinations of methods within a single teaching period at all. Timetables are arranged by heads of departments or administrators and teaching periods are labelled many months in advance by a single teaching method such as 'lecture', 'seminar', 'practical' or 'tutorial'. Consequently there is an expectation that this method, and only the prescribed method, shall be used. It is equally remarkable that these long term prescriptions remained unchallenged by the supposedly intelligent sections of the populations that have to endure them.

Figure 5.6: Buzz Groups

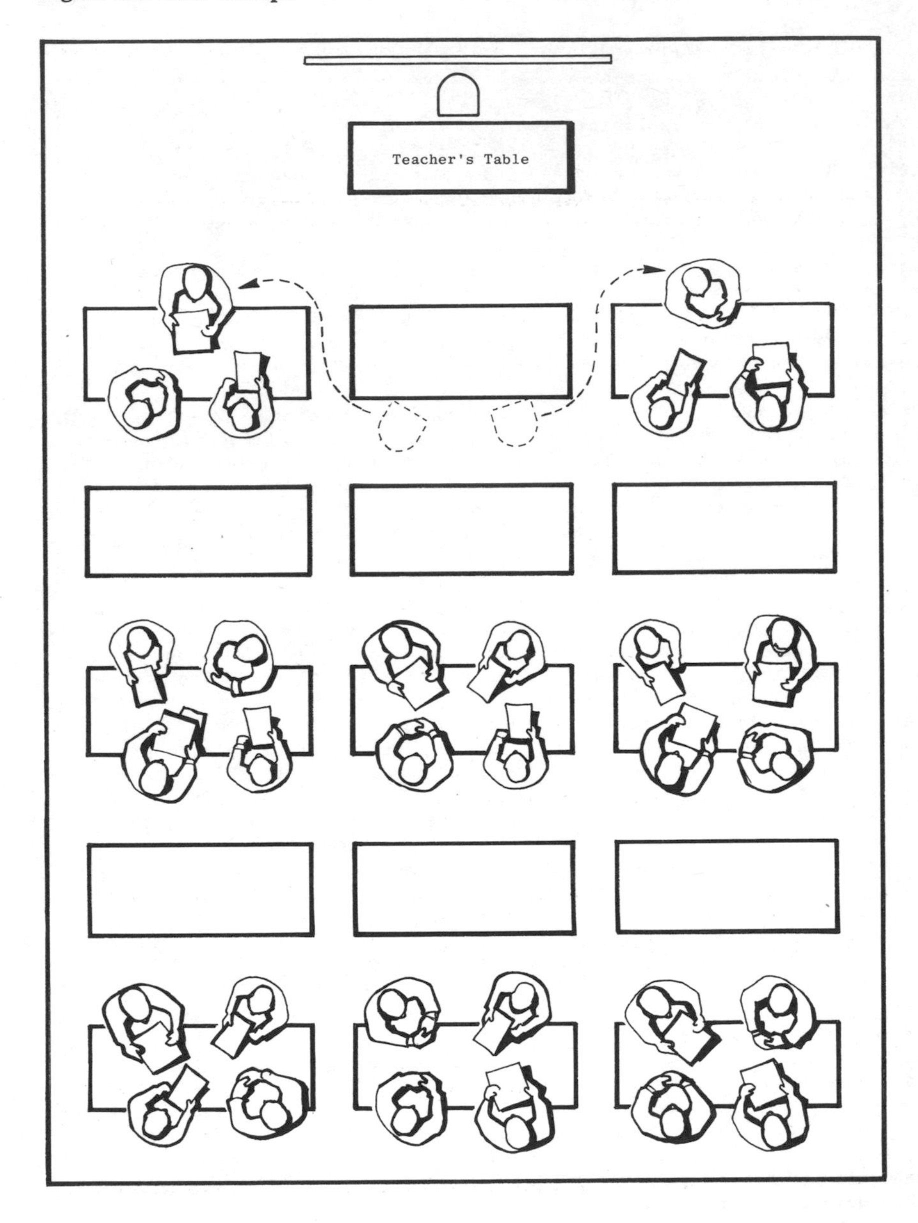

Figure 5.7: Buzz Groups in a formal lecture theatre

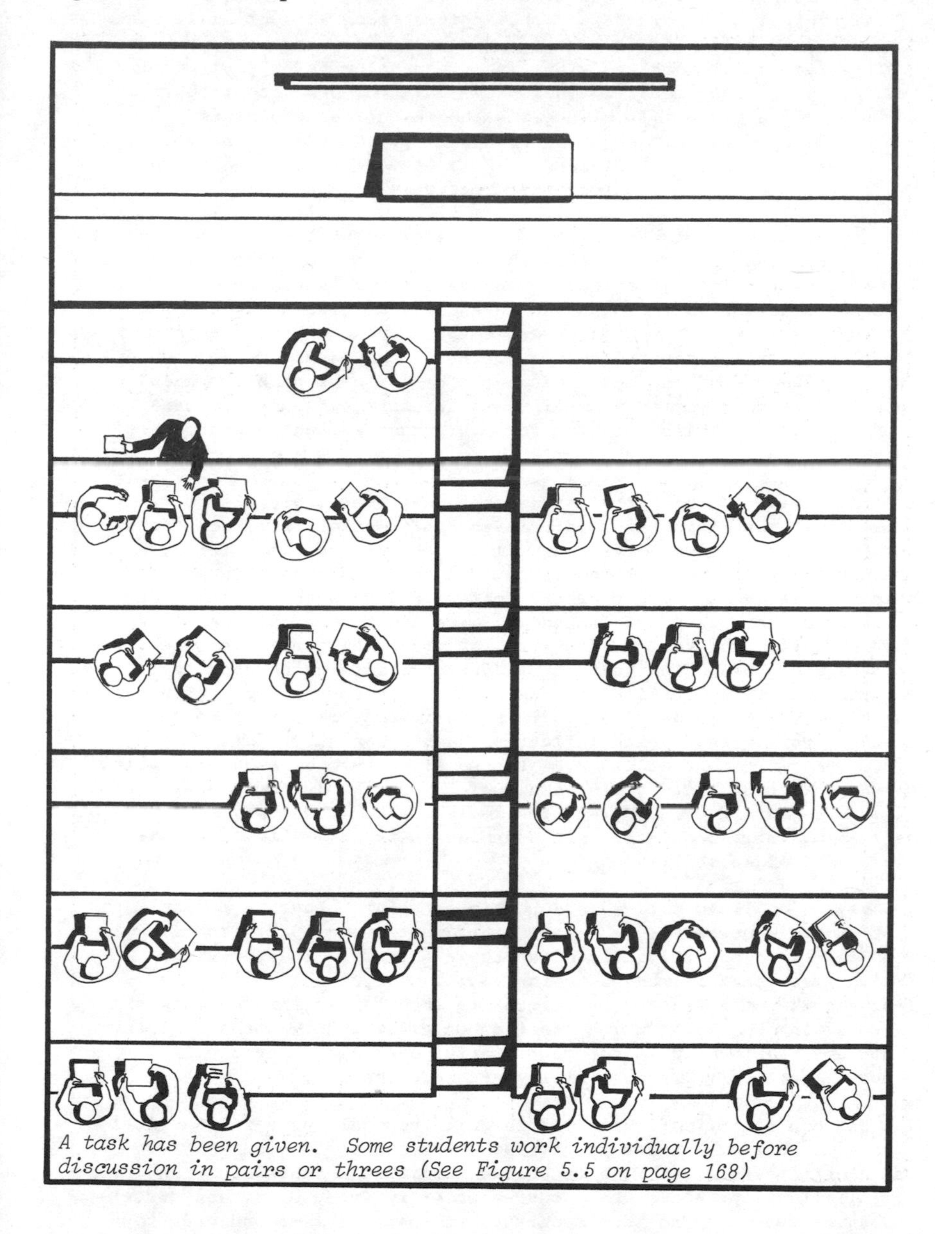

A task has been given. Some students work individually before discussion in pairs or threes (See Figure 5.5 on page 168)

When a combination of methods is used, the pattern shown in Figure 5.8 is typical. The brevity of the lecture takes account of students' declining attention and is used for a purpose it is known to achieve. Asking students to work individually on a problem before introducing buzz groups ensures that each does some work and has a contribution to make to the group. It also gives the teacher an opportunity to deal with the difficulties of individuals without disturbing a group. A similar pattern shown in Figure 5.9 is useful at conferences when it is important for participants to become quickly acquainted.

The technique shown in Figure 5.10 is useful to deal with questions of common interest amongst students which are not answered by a lecture. The easy and foolish questions of individuals are answered or eliminated in the buzz-groups and no individual student is stigmatised as stupid when a question is presented by a group. Indeed anonymity can be preserved if questions are written on paper and passed to the front at the end of the buzz session. The use of a panel to answer questions permits varied viewpoints to be expressed and is a gentle introduction to public speaking for postgraduates and potential new teachers.

It is sometimes thought that students cannot profitably discuss a topic until they have received relevant information from the teacher. But the pattern shown in Figure 5.11 can be very useful. Teachers are not the source of all knowledge. In most subjects, students do have some relevant background information and need to be placed in situations where they are forced to think and to use this knowledge. When students have varied industrial or other relevant experience the pattern shown can help the teacher develop his teaching upon this experience. It is particularly useful in literary subjects where the teacher's aim is to develop students' individual reactions to an author's work before being influenced by his own judgements. Uren (1968) reported that students of French literature were able to think of the most important points on a topic before he lectured on it, so that this technique saved lecture time and made students more involved. By sharing their knowledge this technique acts as a "leveller" with classes of mixed ability.

The saving of lecture time is a pertinent point because a common criticism of buzz sessions is that they waste it. Apart from its doubtful truth the criticism often springs from an inappropriate attitude of teachers, based on the belief that students are only learning when the teacher is talking to them, that learning consists of acquiring the information the teacher gives and that the teaching-learning relationship is an authoritarian one. It undervalues students' activity, responsibility and independence.

The pattern shown in Figure 5.12 is quite commonly used in practical classes. Buzz-groups are used first for students to plan their work and then to assess it. The technique eases the teacher's organisational problems that occur when every group of students wants the same piece of practical apparatus at the same time and when they are ready for the teacher's concluding remarks at different times.

Figure 5.8: Typical combination of methods using group work in large classes

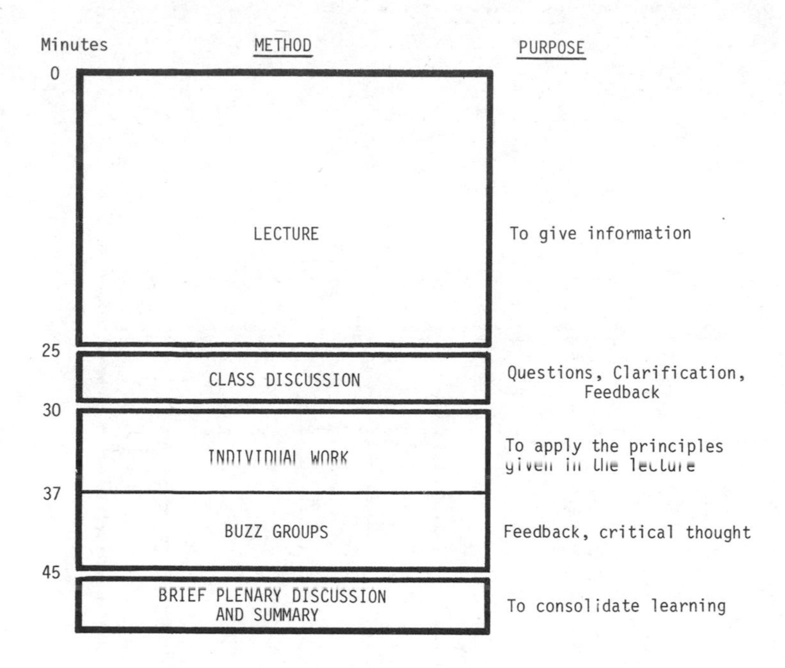

(b) Square Root Groups
A variation of the buzz-group method, which I shall call the 'Square Root Technique', is useful for developing a cohesive class spirit. The teacher forms groups consisting of roughly the square root of the total number of students. For example, if there were 27 students in the class, he would form 5 groups with roughly 5 students in each group. Each student is given a card with a number in the series, A1...E5 (Fig. 5.13). After a short period of discussion, each student may report what has been said to another group consisting of one student from each of the initial groups. In this way, each student meets two less than two times the square root of the total number of students; he is trained to concentrate and keep a record of what is said in the first discussion; each student is required to 'break the ice' and say something; not a great deal of time is consumed, and it is in any case spent discussing the content of the course. This technique is particularly valuable with older students, with part time, day release, sandwich or evening courses, and in teaching which has an important social function. It has also been found to be very useful when teaching foreign languages without the teacher concentrating on only one student at a time.

(c) Brainstorming
Fear of ridicule is one factor that is thought to prevent students from expressing imaginative or original ideas. The brainstorming method is thought to overcome this difficulty. Students are asked to express ideas or germs of ideas as freely as possible in response to

Figure 5.9: The Use of Buzz Groups to Create a Cohesive Class

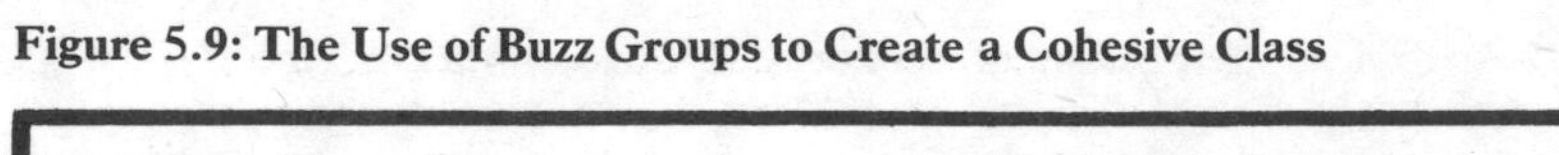

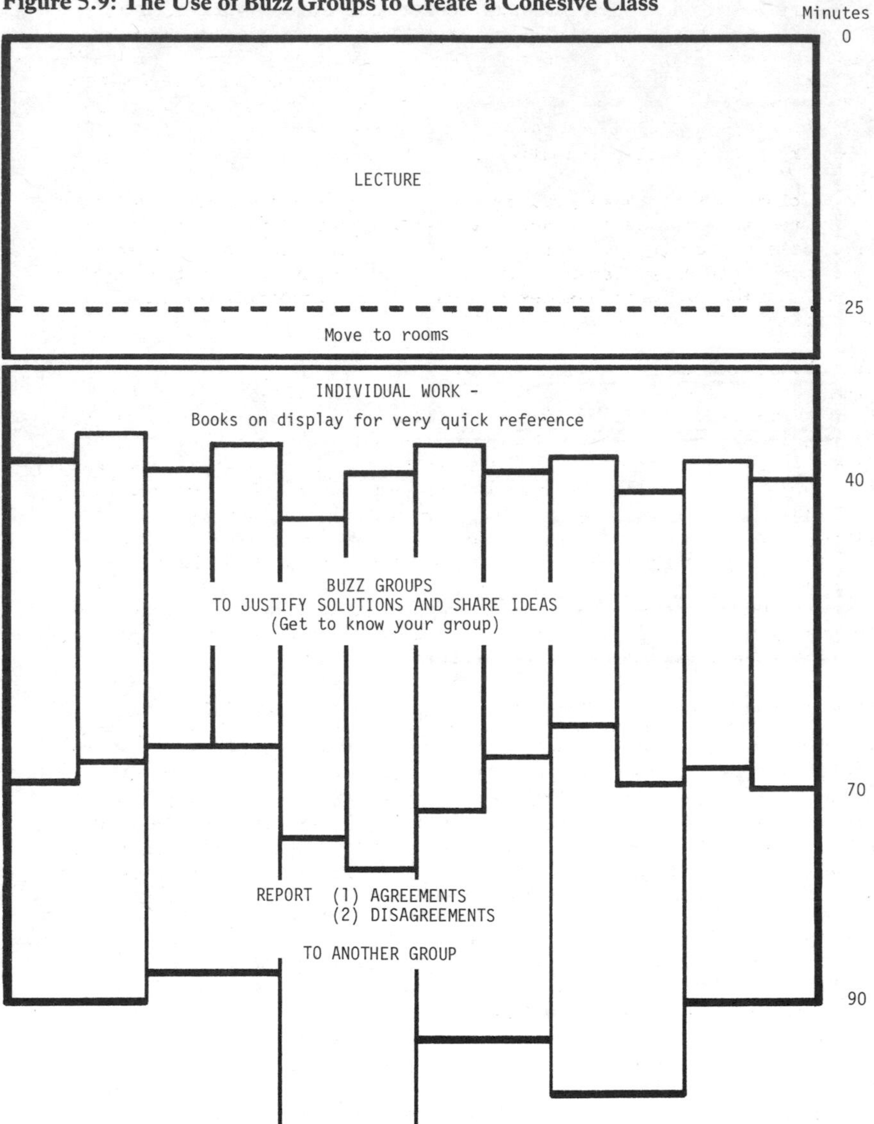

Method particularly suitable for part-time students to get to know each other. The last group discussion can be open-ended.

a creative problem. They are instructed *not* to be critical of the ideas of the others. In this way it is intended that free association of ideas is encouraged. Ideas expressed are written down in any order no matter how ridiculous they may seem. They are only considered more critically later when the idea can be dissociated from the person who had it. The groups may be larger than buzz-groups because diversity of backgrounds facilitates diversity of ideas.

It is claimed that these groups produce more creative ideas, but it is controversial whether they actually teach creativity. It may be that they only encourage the expression of creative ideas rather than increase creativity itself. Alternatively it may be that the cross-fertilization of ideas enables groups to be more original than individual, but even this is questionable.

(d) Horseshoe groups

Another method is to arrange several chairs in each of a series of horseshoes with the open end towards the blackboard or screen as in Figure 5.14. In this way a lecturer can talk formally, but switch to group tasks, such as observing specimens or answering questions on a handout, and he can then resume the lecture again. This method can be used with classes of up to 90. The teacher can easily move from group to group because a gap has been left for him, and his presence can even bring a sense of unity to the group by closing the circle. If groups write their solutions to problems on an overhead projector transparency, the teacher can draw their conclusions together without tedious group reports and use them to develop his lecture or a controlled discussion which involves the whole class.

By having more students than in a buzz-group, greater diversity of opinion is available to horseshoe groups. This is an advantage when the group is asked to prepare answers to examination questions. Students find that their peers either interpret a question differently or answer it in quite a different way. In this way they are taught to see the breadth of questions and to relate ideas they have previously not associated. Teachers in higher education frequently claim these objectives to be important, but they never use appropriate methods to teach them. In this way, horseshoe groups have a useful role.

(e) Case discussion

Case discussion can be developed, with or without the presence of the teacher, from horseshoe groups by presenting problems based upon real-life situations. Normally, these are more complex than theoretical examples with which students are usually confronted. Case study method is therefore useful to teach students how to apply principles they have learned, to understand how they may interact in practice, to recognise their practical limitations, and thereby be forced to develop powers of judgement.

Case discussion methods are useful in courses which study the complexities of human interactions. These include Law, Medicine, Education, Economics, Management Studies, Social Work, Literature, Geography and History. They may also be used in Engineering, but the relatively well established methods of verification in subjects of this kind restrict the areas for expression of personal opinion.

Figure 5.10: Buzz Groups to ask questions

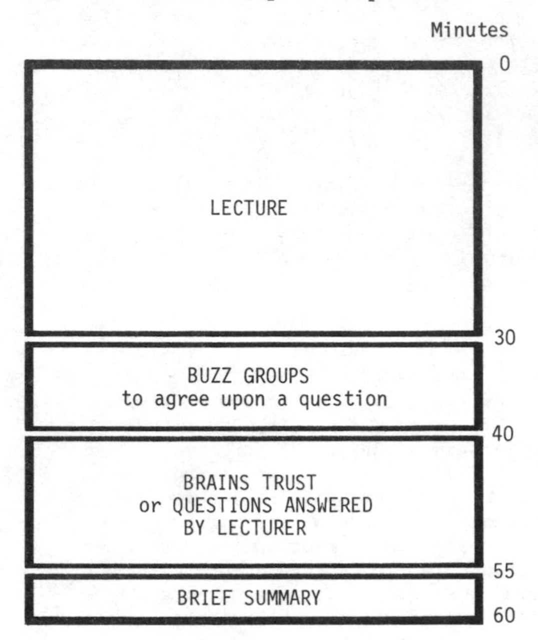

Figure 5.11: A technique to promote thought before lecturing

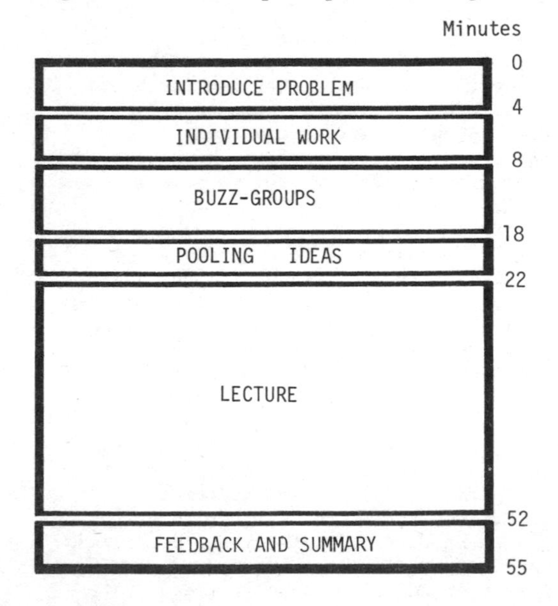

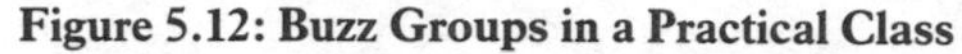
Figure 5.12: Buzz Groups in a Practical Class

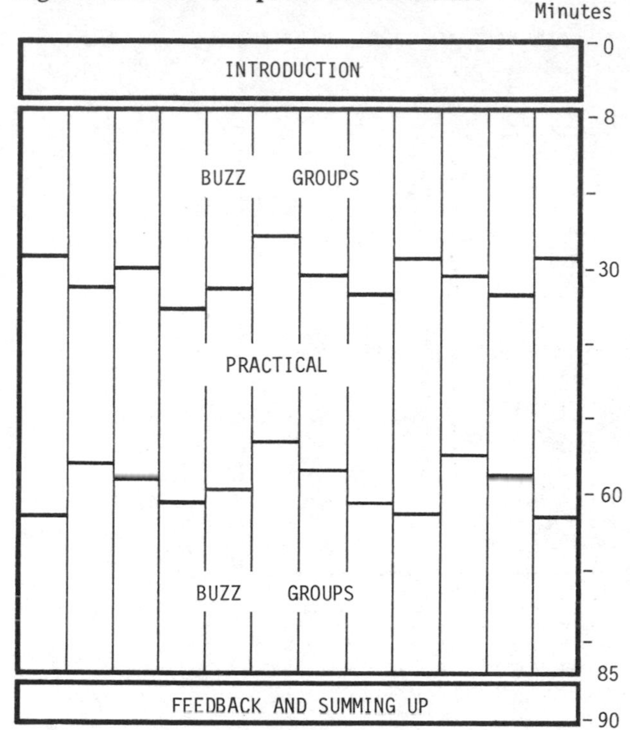

Consequently, the form of the discussion and the preparation of case material may include sections of mathematical calculation.

The problem posed by the teacher normally requires an element of commitment from the students. They may be required to give an answer to a problem, to prescribe a course of action, to demonstrate a proof, or to state a preference. Although most case study problems involve some decision making, the kinds of thought learned during the discussions leading up to the decisions will inevitably vary. By relating principles from different academic subjects, case discussion is useful for inter-disciplinary thinking, and students with different experiences and patterns of thought may broaden the outlook of their peers.

It is obvious that the success of case discussion depends greatly upon the resource material presented to the group. If the case is not a genuine one it is very easy either to overlook important details or to include some that are inconsistent. While it is not possible to generalise for all subjects, case material may often consist of a history, a description of conditions in which a decision must be taken, and certain practical constraints. A teacher preparing case material may bear these three categories in mind together with a fourth, which is not apparent to the students, namely, information which is unavailable. This last category may be important if it is necessary for students to learn to ask pertinent questions, to act intelligently

Figure 5.13: Square Root Groups

When, as in this case, the total number of students is not 9, 16, 25, 36 or some other number with a convenient square root, extra students (F1 and F2 in the diagram) will have to accompany a colleague. This means that they will therefore not be forced to concentrate so hard in their first.

when there is insufficient information, or to recognise that pertinent information sometimes cannot be known. In such subjects as Medicine, Education or Law, the principle of simulation may be employed if information in the other three categories is provided in the form of patients' notes, children's records or clients' files.

Case discussion can be organised in various ways. Horseshoe groups may be given the same, or different cases. There may be a single discussion group with the teacher acting as leader. In a class of up to 30 students, they may be required to peruse the case material and take a decision first; and the teacher, by receiving suggestions and questioning, may then control a class discussion to elicit the major points. Another technique requires each student to write up the case notes for submission to the teacher according tc the decisions and actions he would have taken.

The case conference method requires participants to bring their own case material for discussion by the rest of the group. This method has several advantages but also some drawbacks. It can make the students feel personally involved. It requires them to use their own experience directly. By using the students as a resource, each case can be studied in considerable depth. Quiet members of a class may be required to take a more prominent role. On the other hand, much depends upon their powers of presentation of the case. The cases selected by one student may not be suitable for others, particularly if they are selected on the basis of their difficulty rather than

Figure 5.14: Horseshoe - Groups

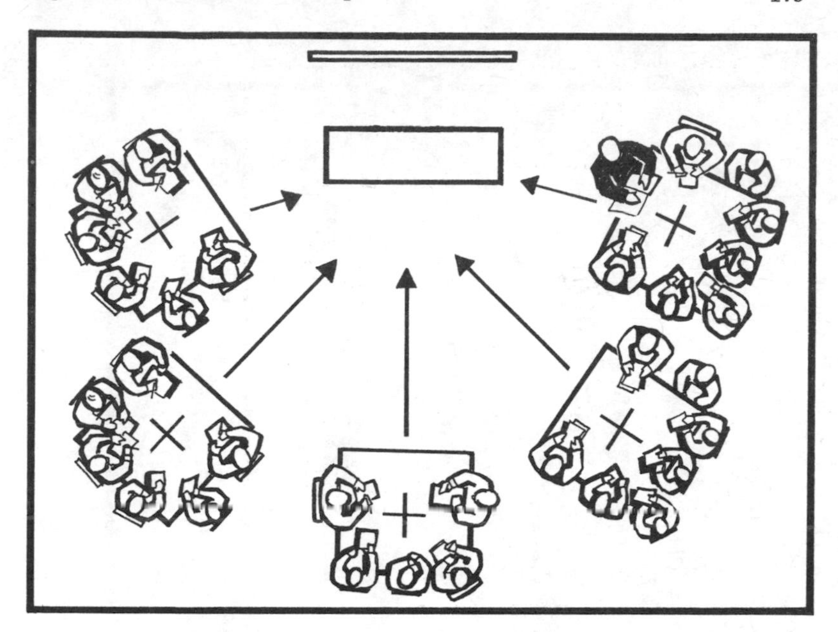

This method requires preparation, a level floor and suitable furniture. It is useful as an introduction to case discussion, when specimens are limited, and for discussion of examination questions.

their power to instruct. In some vocational courses, such as those concerned with training teachers and social workers, it is frequently necessary to build up the students' confidence and the case conference method can undermine this if not discreetly managed.

(f) Syndicate method

In the syndicate method a class of about 30 students is divided into groups of about 5 or 6 and required to write a joint report upon either the same, or different, topics. Each group, called a "syndicate", is like a government committee commissioned to conduct an enquiry and to report back to the minister. Each student syndicate is given a reading list in which the items are wide ranging in subject matter but short and precisely specified. For example, a group required to give recommendations for the route to be taken by a new town by-pass may be expected to read short extracts on concrete engineering, the psychological effects of traffic noise, the economics of road transport, meteorological reports, local geological maps, legal documents, even, maybe, a poem on village life. The syndicates usually distribute the reading amongst their individual members and will assign other tasks amongst themselves. For example, the prescribed reading is usually insufficient to write an adequate report. Students will need to search the college library for further information (Fig. 5.15) and possibly carry out experiments or make other observations on their own.

Figure 5.15
Representation of the Syndicate Method

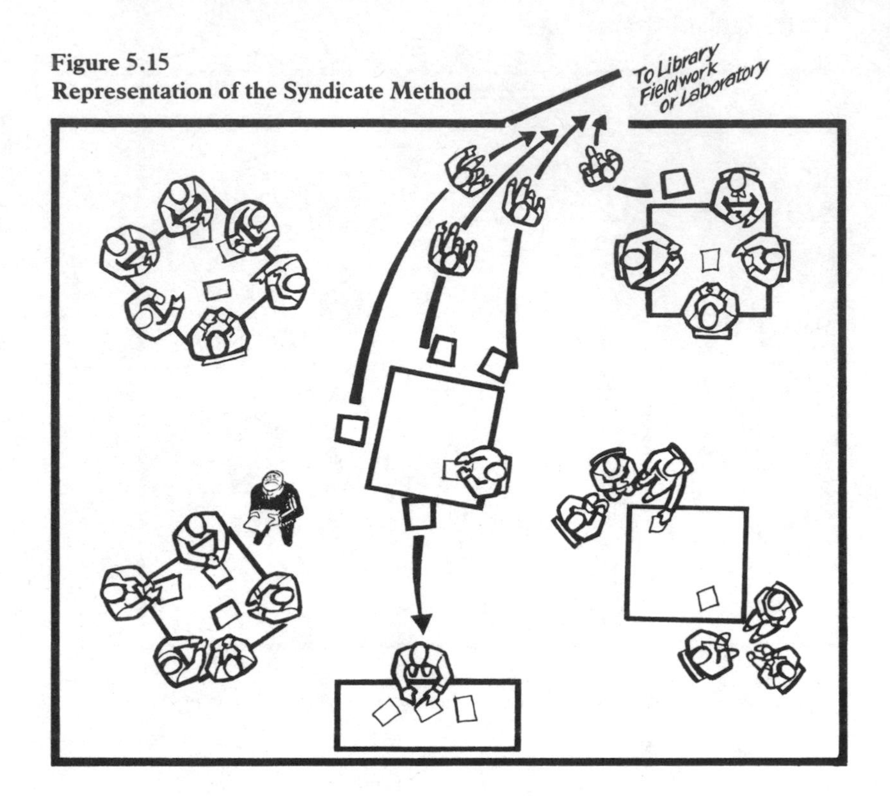

In this way the syndicate method can be used to teach students team work, committee procedure, library skills, complex problem solving, and interdisciplinary thinking. It can provide a useful, and much neglected introduction to research techniques. It is a popular method with older students, particularly when they have industrial, or other experience which may contribute to the enquiry.

The major difficulty of the syndicate method is that students may not write a *joint* report, but five or six separate reports which are then placed one after the other. The solution, as illustrated in Figure 5.15, is for the teacher, when circulating amongst the syndicates, to challenge any individual to justify any single statement written by any other member of the group. If the student cannot justify the statement he should have written a minority report. It is essential that students understand this early or much time can be wasted.

Although there have been some enthusiastic reports of this method, so far there has been little empirical evidence to support or deny the enthusiasms.

The methods so far considered involve the use of small groups in medium or large size classes. The teacher only enters the groups

Figure 5.16: Technique to Introduce Syndicate Work to Students Gradually

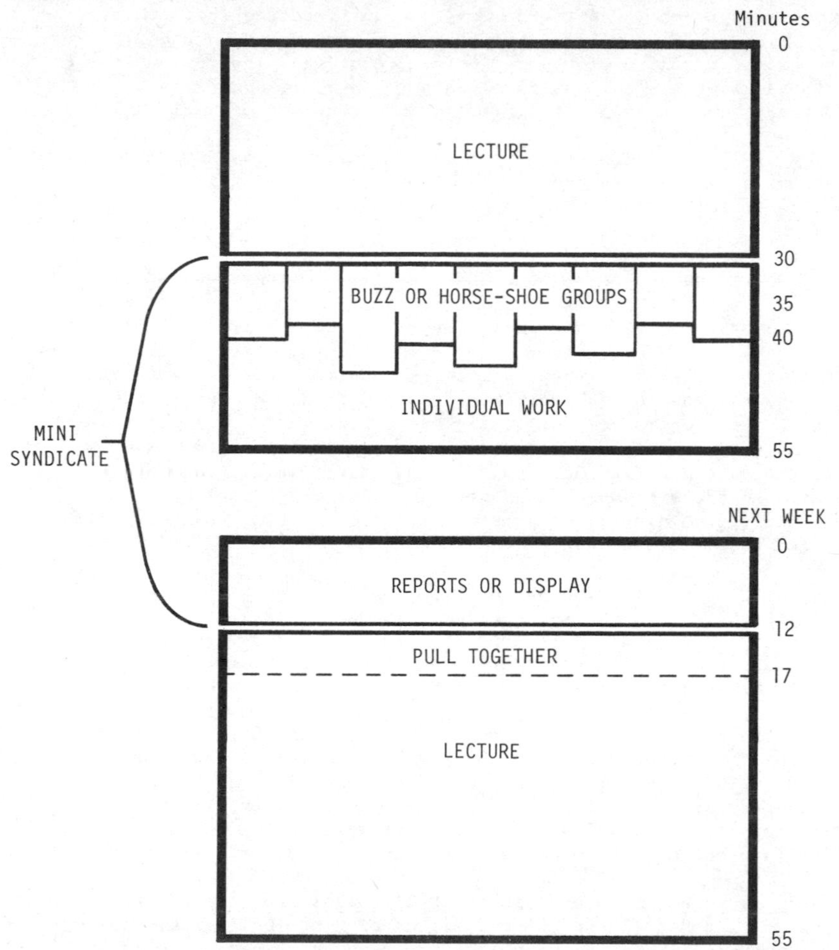

temporarily and his control of them is consequently indirect. There are three common methods by which a teacher may control discussion in classes of more than 15 students: step-by-step discussion, controlled discussion, and the lecture-discussion method.

(2) Groups with teachers

(a) Step-by-step discussion

As its name suggests, the step-by-step method is particularly useful to take students in easy stages through difficult subject matter. The teacher may lecture for a while, say, 5 minutes, and then allow 1 or 2 minutes for students to answer a question either individually or in small groups. The question could be one of the multiple-choice type.

SDTS-M

By immediately asking students to report their answers, and asking questions about them, the teacher may obtain immediate feedback on his teaching, clarify points that have been misunderstood and prepare the way for the next 5 minute period of lecturing. The method is easy to use when the subject involves a chain of reasoning, a historical sequence or naturally falls into a number of small units.

McCarthy (1970) has used the method in medical subjects and found that attention is well maintained because students have committed themselves to certain answers (see page 115).

(b) Controlled discussion

Controlled discussion is often used at public meetings when after a lecture members of the audience ask questions which may be immediately answered by the lecturer or taken up by other people from the floor.

Because in the classroom the teacher takes on the role of chairman as well as the role of subject expert, there is no separate person to prevent the lecturer from dominating his class. Unfortunately this often happens, with the result that the discussion is formal and rigid, and does not flow freely. Indeed, it frequently gets no further than the students asking questions for clarification. Consequently, the discussion does not promote thinking and does little more than teach information.

This domination should be apparent to an observer when alternate contributions are made by the teacher. It should be evident to the teacher if he occasionally records his own teaching. Unfortunately, too few teachers in post-secondary education ever attempt to assess their teaching in this way.

However, the causes often lie deeper. Teachers frequently learn their techniques by copying their own teachers and teaching in the past has been bad in this respect. It has been authoritative and students have been expected to be absorbent and passive. Even today, lecture theatres are built with rows of fixed seats all facing one direction so that interaction between members of the audience is restricted.

Whatever its value in scientific and public meetings, controlled discussion is generally not a good method of teaching. Stones (1970) has shown that although third year student teachers should be used to hearing the sound of their own voice in a classroom, 70% said they would be unwilling to ask a question in the presence of more than 30 people. Thus, it seems likely that this method only satisfies the needs of a minority at a low cognitive level. It is easily abused and maintains an unhealthy distance between teachers and students.

(c) The Lecture-Discussion method

In school this may simply be called 'teaching'. Instead of an uninterrupted formal lecture, questions and answers are asked and given by both the teacher and students. The teacher's skill lies in his ability to develop his subject in a logical fashion while maintaining a free interaction with his students. It is not enough for the teacher to know his subject well. He must be able to re-structure it in different ways according to the responses obtained from his students. His relationships with his students should be easy, friendly and encouraging.

(d) Group Tutorials
I use the term 'group tutorials' as a general term to describe the situation in which a small group of students meets a tutor for discussion. The number of students is normally less than 15 and if it is only one, I class it an 'individual tutorial'. The word 'seminar' will be restricted to group meetings of a similar size in which there is an initial presentation which is then discussed. The topic is therefore decided before the meeting, and while this may be so in some other group tutorials, it is specifically not the case in 'free group discussions' in which students should be free to raise any issue they please at the time.

The most common difficulty in group tutorials described by tutors is to get the students to talk at all. There are a number of techniques for this. It is important if students are to interact that they can all see each other; therefore the arrangement of chairs in a circle, or a similar shape, is essential. It is important for the teacher to withdraw himself from a position of authority so that students have sufficient psychological security to risk making mistakes. If a tutor can withdraw, he will find that the students take over some aspects of his role. One may concern herself with maintaining the harmony of the group and another with ensuring that the discussion is relevant and that the task is accomplished. By this means, students become more independent and responsible for their own learning. When a teacher sees himself as a dispenser of information, his contributions tend to alternate with those of the students who seek it. If he sees his role as encouraging interaction his contributions are likely to be fewer but more varied. He will be more concerned with reconciling differences and accepting what is said by facial expression. He may redirect discussion by clarifying, elaborating or focussing on a point. He will ask questions such as, "What do you feel about such and such?" rather than questions with a right or wrong answer, so that the students are not threatened.

There is reason to believe that some tutors are too afraid of silence and always wish to fill it. Others think that controversy is necessary. Possibly the model in their minds is a 'debate'; but if students are lacking in confidence in expressing their ideas, they need support and encouragement of all their good points, not destructive criticism of their weak ones. If tutors attempt to present controversial points, either no student will dare to challenge them, in which case the silence may continue; or someone will challenge them, so that he is left talking half the time in order to defend them.

Part of the difficulty is that teachers in post-secondary education are selected on their ability to express themselves in speech and writing, but in discussion techniques they need precisely the opposite virtues. They need to listen and observe. The tutor's skill in facilitating discussion lies, not primarily with knowledge, but with his sensitivity to the emotional climate he produces. This is created by small acts which may pass unnoticed by the inexperienced eye. For example, the experienced tutor may be prepared to give way on a point; he may allow himself to be interrupted; he is always a vigilant for likely contributors and then uses eye contact at the right moment to encourage them to speak. The use of buzz-groups for a short while is a more obvious but very effective technique to withdraw from a position of authority.

It should be noted that many of the techniques for managing small group discussions require considerable subtlety and genuine human understanding. They are essential teaching skills in post-secondary education, for we have seen that personal interactions to develop thinking should be the essence of the post-secondary educational experience.

(e) Seminars

At a research or postgraduate level when new ideas and proposals for research procedures can be briefly presented and usefully discussed by other researchers and postgraduates in the same field, the seminar is a useful method. An idea is presented and discussed amongst equals. Participants will have gained some confidence in their subject, they are more likely to speak when they have something worth saying, and they will have no reason to feel that they are being assessed by a tutor.

When the seminar method is transplanted into the teaching of undergraduates none of these conditions apply and it is simply inappropriate. Yet it is at undergraduate level that it is remarkably common. That there is dissatisfaction with it is hardly surprising. Undergraduates are not able to express themselves easily in the language of their subject. The system in which students take it in turns to write essays and read them to the group leans too heavily upon one student's attendance and satisfactory completion of the essay in time. Such essays are not necessarily good introductions to a topic and reading them to a group may waste time. Because the tutor is present, students may feel reluctant to criticise one another in case their assessments are affected. Furthermore, the seminar method unsettles the natural development of group dynamics. In one sense, the teacher is the leader of the group, but in another, the student who has written and read his essay may temporarily be regarded as an authority compared with the other students because he has probably studied the topic more thoroughly. The following week a different student may have this role. Unless the ignorant students are prepared to risk a contribution, discussion will be dominated by the teacher and the essay writer. This is undesirable in a method where students are supposed to learn from their participation.

We may conclude that, although it is much used, the seminar method either requires skill from the teacher or is usually inappropriate in post-secondary education.

(f) Free-Group Discussion

In free-group discussion the tutor's role is essentially non-directive. He may literally take a back seat outside the circle of students. He may contribute very rarely to the discussion but Barnett (1958) has shown that his contributions may be more varied than those of a tutor in a more traditional type of group discussion. He may ask or answer questions, unblock an obstruction to the flow of discussion and generally foster a harmonious spirit; but his main activity is to listen and observe. By this means his few contributions are more likely to be effective.

Free-group discussion is based upon the assumption that different individuals have different preconceptions and modes of thinking which fundamentally influence their understanding of any proposition. Consequently each student's understanding of his academic discipline is different, and different from that of the teacher. No amount of didactic teaching will overcome this difficulty, indeed, it will only exacerbate it. What is required is for students to become aware of their different presuppositions and understandings. The same is true of their attitudes.

This self-awareness is only possible if students first express their ideas, because only then do the ideas become overt, and only then can they be considered rationally. They will only be expressed if the group climate is sufficiently free to allow them to do so. Thus the method requires considerable humility on the part of the tutor.

Proponents of this method (James et al, 1956; Barnett, 1958) point out that, in time, students learn to appreciate the conceptions of others so that they become more broadminded. Where there are misconceptions they are corrected by other members of the group. Group members acquire more responsibility for their learning and therefore learn how to learn. It will now be seen that the objectives of the free-group discussion method involve the acquisition of self-awareness, the development of perceptual skills, the growth of reasoning, attitude change, learning how to learn, and the development of open minds. Yet there is frequently hostility to this method at first. Students are unfamiliar with it. They expect the tutor to play his traditional role and feel unsettled by his silent presence. They are frequently aggressive towards him and other students and the aggression only decreases as the group learns to control its members by establishing an unwritten code of rules. It may be thought that this could be avoided if teachers explained the purpose of the method at the first meeting. Tutors usually do this but it is part of the very nature of the problem that students do not understand what is being said. They only understand that different people see the same thing in different ways after they have experienced discussions in which these differences were evident. Without this experience, the teacher's words are meaningless. Consequently, tutors often need considerable inner self-assurance. It must be emphasised that the objectives of this method take a long time to achieve and tutors should not become despondent with students' hostility too soon.

Nevertheless, in my opinion, it is a mistake to use this method in the face of student opposition to it. In these circumstances it is better not to use the method in a predetermined way, but to prepare for a seminar or group tutorial and to drift in and out of using the free-group discussion method as occasion may arise. This can be done by letting the discussion drift away from the initial topic when the tutor feels that students' irrelevancies reflect a hidden concern. As with all such methods, this technique requires more skill on the part of the teacher than is felt to be apparent. Nevertheless, Abercrombie (1965) has shown that the free-group discussion method can be effective for the objectives mentioned and it is difficult to see what other methods could achieve them so well.

(g) Sensitivity groups

There is a wide range of group methods variously known as 'Sensitivity groups', 'Encounter groups' and 'T-groups'. These methods can be used to provide recreation, psychotherapy and mystical experiences. They can also usefully serve education.

Ideally, the groups have 8 to 12 members with fewer if time is restricted; but frequently circumstances force the groups to be much larger than this. The participants discuss their feelings and perceptions of each other; but strictly it is not the individual who is analysed and discussed, but his place in the working of a group as a whole.

In T-groups the 'T' stands for 'Training'. Smith (in Bligh, 1973) has said that the purpose of T-groups is to increase students' sensitivity, diagnostic ability and action skills. The first means that they become more aware of the reactions of other people to their behaviour. The second is the ability to make valid inferences about the kinds of behaviour that take place in a group; action skills consist of the ability to use this knowledge.

These methods are most appropriate in subjects such as Medicine, Education, Management and others where it is important that students learn how other people react to them. It would be appropriate in the study of Law, but to the best of my knowledge it has not been used in the teaching of this subject. Unlike any other teaching, the content and the process of the teaching are the same. Consequently the immediacy of feedback on the students' behaviour is important. The taboos of ordinary society should be discarded so that frankness replaces tact, and self-expression is encouraged.

Variations of these groups have been used in California, Boston, The National Training Laboratory at Bethel and the Tavistock Institute in London. With an almost missionary spirit the ideas have spread to France, the Low Countries, Scandinavia and to a lesser extent elsewhere.

The question remains whether these methods are effective in achieving their purposes. Back (1973) cites no less than 141 research reports evaluating sensitivity training published between 1945 and 1970. Yet the picture is by no means clear. As with other teaching methods, assessments have been made by proponents of the method; but it is also sometimes claimed that a person who is not part of the 'Encounter Movement' cannot understand the experiences of insiders sufficiently to evaluate them. Experimental comparisons of the usual type appear to be excluded; yet proponents are anxious to extol the scientific underpinnings of the method. On the other hand, the submission of a group to any assessment method infringes its liberty, and freedom is part of the essence of the method.

In the educational context, the prototype of the sensitivity group method was in a course on 'Social Relations' at Harvard, in which Cabot assigned readings and began the discussion on interpersonal relations and only considered the relationships of class members at the end of a session. The T-group method has been developed by using only the last technique. The teacher is responsible for the conduct of the whole class, including any harm that may result. Yet he will not wish to take a prominent role and his comments are normally of a general character.

Yet, even without the assigned readings it is pertinent to ask when the T-groups are successful, whether the groups conform to expectations because they knew T-group theory. Back (1973) has described courses in Italy, Israel and the USA which have not been successful in reconciling national and ethnic differences. Furthermore, it is interesting that in one study involving the discussion of their national border disputes by intellectuals from Somalia, Kenya and Ethiopia, the participants judged the T-group to be a miserable failure in their reports, while the American organisers perceived all the encouraging aspects and were moderately satisfied with the encounter.

At the University of Boston, Massachussetts, Benne has used what he calls 'Confrontation Groups' in which the leader forces participants to contemplate their own ethnic, sexual, age or other differences by remarks such as "You are reacting to him in this way because you are white and he is black." or, "He is a man, and you are a woman." and so on. The intention is that participants will come to terms with their fundamental differences by being made hyper-conscious of them. This may be successful if the course is sufficiently long, but in shorter courses it is highly doubtful whether strong identification with one's own group will lead to more sympathetic perceptions of other groups.

We may conclude that although there is great interest and enthusiasm for these methods on the part of some people who have experienced them, the evidence of their effectiveness is ambiguous and the skills required by the trainer are so great that the method should not be attempted by any teacher who has not himself considerable experience as a participant.

(3) One-to-one teaching

There are three major types of method in which one student meets another person: individual tutorials, student counselling and student-to-student counselling.

(a) Individual tutorials
The tutorial system as it evolved from the medieval university required each student to meet a tutor individually for perhaps one hour per week. Traditionally, a student would read an essay to his tutor who would make comments upon it. The method was not rigidly used. Discussion could wander widely and deeply and could include non-academic counselling.

Although there have been few objective investigations of the method, there seems little doubt that it can be effective for a wide range of objectives. It forces the student to work and to express himself in writing. It allows him to develop his ideas in an individual way, yet be disciplined by the need to justify them to someone thoroughly conversant with the subject. By judicious questioning, a wide range of cognitive skills, from the clarification of concepts to complex evaluations, can be developed. Furthermore, attitudes, personal interests and other individual differences can be well catered for. Nevertheless, it is to be expected that the effectiveness of this method will actually depend upon the skills of the individual tutor and subjective reports confirm this.

The obvious limitation of the tutorial method is the very high staff-student ratios it requires. At Oxford and Cambridge it is maintained with ratios of 1:8 and a high calibre of academic staff. However, outside Oxford and Cambridge, the growth of academic institutions and the very rapid increase in student numbers has made such an individual student service impossible to maintain. In the USA, the average staff-student ratio is 1:16; over half the adult population has at some time experienced post-secondary education; and many of the courses provided do not place an emphasis upon individual depth of thought. Thus, the needs and resources of modern post-secondary education are different from those of the past. Yet, throughout this book, I have repeatedly urged the need to teach skills. Should they, then, only be taught to an elite? In many countries such an ethos would be socially unacceptable. Here lies a conflict between the needs of society and what it is willing to accept, unless other more economic methods can be found.

(b) Student counselling
It has been a recurring theme in this book that post-secondary education should be a social activity. Consequently, it is not only an intellectual, but an emotional experience. High student motivation can compensate for bad teaching. Good teaching cannot compensate for bad student motivation. Consequently, a teacher's responsibility for the emotional welfare of his students towards his subject is more crucial than attention to their intellectual welfare. Both are important; motivation is essential.

There are many different kinds of counselling requiring different kinds of specialist knowledge. Broadly, what is being considered here is educational counselling. Educational counselling is *not* a service only required by students in difficulty or potential failures. Nevertheless, it cannot be sharply distinguished from student health services, particularly the psychiatric aspects of a clinician's work, because there is no sharp distinction between health and illness. Careers Advisory Services may use a counselling approach; but counselling is not giving advice. Some universities provide services concerned with student housing, nursery schools for students' children, study methods and other student welfare services.

Counselling in North America is on a larger scale than anywhere else. Some universities employ over 50 professional staff and have budgets of over a quarter of a million dollars. A ratio of one counsellor per thousand students is normal. In many other countries there is no recognition of any need for student counselling. In Australia, a ratio of one counsellor to 3,000 students is common but 1 : 2,000 is generally regarded as satisfactory. In some countries student counsellors are part-time non-specialists with other academic duties with which their counselling role conflicts both in the time they can afford and their impartiality as counsellors.

Counsellors also vary in their theoretical orientation. Psychoanalytic theories have had a wide influence, but behaviourism has been less important. Carl Roger's "Client-Centred Therapy" is popular where his writings are available. Many counsellors would regard themselves as eclectic or having derivative theories, but most would see themselves as performing a practical task without the basis of any elaborate theory. In effect, all theories have emphasised the importance of maturity, personal adjustment and a genuine wish to help the student. Counsellors need to be non-threatening, trusting, dependable, accepting, and empathic. Clearly no one technique succeeds with students.

Figure 5.17 lists some of the well-established repertoire of activities performed by counselling services (Frederick, 1972). Frederick distinguishes between preventive and casualty services and thinks that more investment should be made in preventing student crises than is common in most post-secondary educational institutions at the present time.

There is little doubt that counsellors require some training but too much training can desensitise counsellors in precisely those characteristics of warmth and empathy which are so important. Nelson-Jones (1972) has said that counsellors need to be skilled in assessment and diagnosis by psychotherapy, group therapy, behaviour therapy, systematic training methods, role play techniques, occupational counselling and other methods, in addition to having a knowledge of psychology, the ability to assess research evidence and practical experience.

It is particularly in the early weeks of a student's life at university that he requires reassurance. The reassurance required may appear to be about different things, such as whether he has chosen the right course, whether he will be socially accepted and whether he has adequate academic ability. The demands upon students to adjust to their new environment vary widely but the need for self-confidence is basic to most of them.

Figure 5.17: Activities Performed by Counselling Services (Frederick, 1972)

1. Counselling proper (both individual and group): informational, vocational, academic, study skills, supportive, brief therapy, medium and long-term therapy;
   in relation to therapeutic counselling, some major nodes are: behaviour therapy and modification, analytically- and insight-based therapy, reality therapy, rational-emotive therapy, gestalt therapy, bio-energetic and neo-Reichian therapy, Rogerian and non-directive therapy, IPR therapy, communication therapy, transactional analysis, psychodrama.
2. Crisis intervention: walk-in service, night and weekend service, 24 hour phone; Nightline-type satellites, Crash pad, machinery for drug and medical emergencies; financial aid (both long-term and emergency).
3. Developmental activities (i.e. aimed at growth rather than therapy): career exploration groups; growth groups, encounter groups; sensitivity training, social skills groups; minority support groups (e.g. overseas students, homosexuals, mature age students), life-planning workshops, relaxation training, assertion training.
4. Outreach activities (preventive and practical projects): schools liaison, intending student advisory service, orientation for freshmen; campus assistance office, information centre, satellite counselling offices in union and halls; liaison with parents, research and action in relation to needs of special groups (such as commuter students, married students with children, part-timers), extension of services to non-students (such as students' spouses and local community residents).
5. Consultation: acting as a formal or informal consultant to faculties, departments, administrators, specialist committees, student groups, selection boards, discipline boards, halls of residence, other welfare services, schools and community organisations.
6. Training and Teaching: graduate intern counsellors, under-graduate and postgraduate students; courses for non-professionals, inservice training for a variety of groups, work with volunteer students (such as "Nightline" staff); work with local school counsellors and advisers, clergy and with outside organisations such as CABs.
7. Research and Innovation: domestic self-evaluation; socio/educational and demographic studies of the institution; development, evaluation and refinement of counselling methods; pure academic research.

In England, Ryle has suggested that 2% of students experience severe psychiatric illness requiring hospital admission; 10 - 20% at some time during their course have emotional or psychological problems requiring some treatment and a further 20% experience temporary psychological or psychosomatic symptoms. These figures should be compared with the 10 - 15% of the population in the student age range who report with neuroses to general medical practitioners. The rate for women is up to twice as great as that for men.

It should be remembered that in most cultures women experience role conflicts not experienced by men. Too often their parent culture does not encourage career ambitions. There is some experimental evidence that women students who easily identify themselves with warm motherly roles perform less well in academic examinations.

Ryle writes, "the students' survival in an institution is dependent upon how far he can perceive the institution as providing an experience which is both relevant to his goals and consistent with his personal integrity".

At the University of Melbourne, Priestly (1957) calculated that 16% of students reporting to the Student Health Centre had problems requiring psychiatric attention. 6% were incapacitating and 10% were less serious. Nearly half (48%) reported educational worries or difficulties and the remainder had other minor problems including financial difficulties. In the study by Lipset and Altbach (1966) 74% of students reported for educational stress. In New York, Watson (1963) found a larger proportion suffered from maturational stresses (25%), family problems (16%), and depression (10% in men and 18% in women).

Is counselling effective? We have found little evidence. This is partly because counselling is so varied that no one criterion is appropriate in more than a small number of cases. At the University of Minnesota, Campbell (1965) found that counselled students had a 25% higher graduation rate than a control group. At the Scottish University of Aberdeen, the introduction of a counselling service halted the increasing rate of student dropout. Such studies seem to suggest that counselling is effective and important. Yet tests of statistical significance carry little weight when the problems are concerned with people's feelings. Even in economic terms if a counsellor only increases the number of highly qualified students who enter the labour market by two or three per year, he is performing a useful service. Once again solutions to the criterion problem raise value questions.

(c) Student-to-student counselling

Student-to-student counselling has not been widely used outside the USA, but there it has developed very rapidly, particularly in the last ten years. Its strongest advocate has been William F. Brown (1972) who has argued that the American increase in student numbers from 1.5 million in 1940 to 7.4 million in 1970 and possibly 11.4 million in 1980 has rendered traditional college counselling facilities hopelessly inadequate, particularly when students first arrive at college. Even the provision of freshmen orientation programmes has proved too expensive with doubtful benefit. Indeed, Brown quotes extensive evidence to show that orientation courses lasting a short time with little extensive follow up, and courses at which attendance is compulsory, appear to have little or no effect upon academic grades subsequently received. Only where orientation courses are voluntary are the effects demonstrably beneficial. Brown argues that the use of students as counsellors is cheap, voluntary, overcomes the generation credibility gap, fosters co-operative learning and is a valuable educational activity in itself.

Students are selected as counsellors on the basis of their previous experience as leaders, the recommendation of tutors in their hall of residence, college grades, acceptance by fellow students and recommendations by academic staff. Although larger educational institutions in the USA are generally better provided with professional counsellors and use students as counsellors less than smaller colleges, they spend significantly more time training students for this role. This may be because the need for counselling is greater in larger, and possibly impersonal, institutions.

From the results of his own research Brown concluded that student-to-student counselling improved the study skills and academic attitudes of counselled freshmen. They performed better in first year examinations and students' reactions were generally favourable. Although men and women student counsellors were equally effective with students of their own sex, female counsellors were significantly less effective with male students than any other sex combinations. Women students made better use of the advice they were given than men. Tests of study skills suggested that professional and academic counsellors were equally effective but freshmen reacted more favourably to their fellow students as counsellors than to professionals. Freshmen who received counselling obtained better grades and were more likely to complete their courses successfully.

Brown's work sounds like a success story, but he would be the first to state several reservations. Evaluations of orientation courses for freshmen before they come to colleges show little or no evidence of their effectiveness. Indeed, there is even some evidence of dis-orientation by such courses (Foxley, 1969). However, it seems that Brown does not distinguish sufficiently between counselling given to individual students and that given to small groups. It is clear that the latter is less likely to cater for individual needs and is less likely to be diagnostic of genuine difficulties. Consequently, we may conclude that individual counselling by students may be worth extensive experimentation in all countries attempting a rapid expansion of post-secondary education.

IV Practicals and simulations

Although practical classes have been held for a long time, and simulation is commonly regarded as a new technique, neither is a teaching method. They are both principles of teaching and both have been applied for centuries. Presentation and discussion methods use language and illustrations to depict reality. Simulation involves the use of a model which is a simplified version of reality. Practicals involve learning by doing. Practicals and simulations are more direct methods of learning than presentations and discussions.

These principles may be applied in such a wide variety of situations that it is difficult to make any generalisations about them. It is probably for this reason too that very few investigations have been conducted to study their effectiveness. Consequently, although individual teachers may claim that they know a great deal about methods using these principles, a review of the educational literature suggests there is a lack of established generalisable knowledge on these subjects.

(1) Practical teaching

Nowhere is this lack of knowledge more striking than in the understanding of the effectiveness of giving students "practical experience". This includes (a) demonstrations, (b) laboratory experience, (c) clinical practice, (d) microteaching and (e) educational excursions such as geological fieldwork.

(a) Demonstrations
Although demonstrations are practical techniques for those who demonstrate, for others they are a presentation method. Consequently, if there is no follow-up activity by the students, they will gain little more than information. Students will need to apply this information in practice if they are to learn practical skills. When learning a manual technique in medicine, this follow-up activity could consist of repeating and practising the skill. Where the purpose is to teach the interpretation of experimental results, mere repetition of the experiment is unhelpful. It may consolidate the learning of information but it will not make a student think about it. Interpretation is a kind of thinking. Where demonstrations are used to give information they will need to be related to theoretical aspects of a course and are therefore more likely to occur during lectures than practical laboratory classes.

Thus although Cunningham (1946) has surveyed 37 American experiments comparing demonstrations and laboratory classes and found little difference between them, the differences, if any, probably lie in their purpose and the criteria of effectiveness consequently used. If used in isolation, demonstrations probably teach little more than information. If used in combination, the effect of the demonstration is unclear. This has probably restricted the number of empirical investigations of the effectiveness of demonstrations.

In spite of the shortage of controlled studies Henderson (1969) recommends a number of precepts for giving demonstrations:
Explain each stage step by step stressing the key points and explaining briefly why certain things are done or not done.
Keep student groups as small as possible and frequently gather

them into small groups in front of a blackboard or around a bench or machine for demonstrations or discussions rather than use mass demonstrations.
Question the groups to ensure that the procedure at each stage is understood by all.
Allow one or two students to repeat what has been taught.
Let some students practise what has been taught.
Always make sure that all students can see properly.
Ensure that apparatus is in perfect working order.
Remember to link demonstrations with other aspects of the course.

(b) Laboratory work
From experimental evidence it seems possible that laboratory work teaches manual skills and some powers of experimental interpretation. In other respects there is little evidence to justify the time, space, equipment, money and personnel lavished upon it.

However, the amount of experimental evidence is small, and the criterion tests have been very restricted. Watson (in Gage, 1963) has complained that most of the few empirical investigations that have been conducted employ dubious designs, inadequate statistical treatments and tests of undetermined reliability. He seems to say that scientists are unscientific when investigating science teaching.

The most extensive series of experiments has been conducted by Kruglak (1951, 1952, 1953, 1954, 1955a, 1955b, 1958 and Kruglak and Goodwin, 1955). He used paper and pencil tests and measures of laboratory behaviour to see whether experience of physics at school had any effect upon students' performance in the same subject at college. His studies may be interpreted as showing that competence in the laboratory and knowledge of the subject are independent abilities. Students with laboratory experience at school were better at handling apparatus than those who did not study the subject and those who studied it without laboratory experience. Those who had studied the subject without laboratory work did no worse in college examinations than those who had laboratory experience; but they both did better than students who had not previously studied it. Men were better at laboratory work than women and, even when initial differences were controlled, they learned laboratory skills at college more quickly than women.

Kruglak's experiments cast some doubt upon the central role usually claimed for laboratory experience in science teaching. Yet vast expenditures of money, time and equipment are justified on the basis of this claim. Yager, Englen and Snider (1969) gave one group of students laboratory experience, gave a demonstration to a second group and permitted no experiments or demonstrations for a discussion group. On subsequent tests the laboratory group was superior in manual laboratory skills but no group showed other measurable advantages. Similar results have been obtained by other experimenters (e.g. Pella and Sherman, 1969; Chester, 1938; Coulter, 1966; Cunningham, 1946; Goldstein, 1937; Mallinson, 1947).

However the evidence available does not prove that laboratory work is entirely useless. It is possible that the findings cited may reflect the design of questions in the tests used rather than any quality of the teaching being tested. Grozier (1969) was unable to demonstrate that students with laboratory experience had distinctive scientific attitudes, but they were better able to interpret scientific data. Lahti (1956) found that a problem solving technique in the laboratory was superior to the description of a case history, a thematic discussion with questions and answers and a fact finding approach. But the differences did not reach the normal level of statistical significance; nor were there differences in the effectiveness of the method at different times of the day.

These two experiments hardly represent a convincing demonstration of the value of laboratory work. In view of the time required to make scientific discoveries, it is doubtful whether a heuristic approach can ever be completely genuine unless it is trivial. It seems as if interpretation of data, experimental design, the application of statistical techniques, selection and recognition of equipment and graphic description of data can all be learned equally effectively by traditional classroom methods or private study. But it is hard to see how some techniques of observation and recording could be learned other than in a laboratory.

At the present time we must conclude that "the laboratory ideal" is neither vindicated nor disproved. Throughout this century scientists have enjoyed great success and prestige. They have not been obliged to justify their teaching methods. But the disenchantment with science and a tougher economic climate will soon bring a time of reckoning. More investigations need to be conducted. So great is our commitment to "the laboratory ideal" that scientists flinch from rejecting it.

At a more subjective level writers on this subject are almost unanimous that the organisation of laboratory teaching is crucial and various methods have been described, but, to my knowledge, they have never been compared experimentally. Other writers emphasise the importance of careful planning, the choice of stimulating and useful problems for investigation and the precise objectives to be achieved. Henderson (1969) recommends using many small scale experiments rather than one large one, because they provide a much needed intermediate stage between a demonstration on the one hand, and heuristic teaching and full scale research on the other. If manual and interpretative skills are all that can be taught from laboratory classes he is probably right. In an experiment by Henshaw and others (1933) short periods of practice at manual skills were as effective as longer ones; and presumably many small experiments will give more practice at interpretation than a single large one. Beard (1972) emphasises the clarity of instructions to be given and, although programmed learning may have limited use in other aspects of post-secondary education, an algorithmic approach results in clear and very thorough teaching (Macdonald Ross, 1971).

Parakh (1968) observed that school teachers only talk half the time in laboratory classes, compared with three quarters in others. The contrast may be greater in post-secondary education. Hurd and Rowe

(1966) found that students' place of residence influenced their group dynamics in the laboratory. It would be foolish to generalise this finding to other institutions, but it shows that science teachers may need to take many commonly neglected factors into account when planning laboratory teaching.

(c) Clinical teaching

Whether clinical teaching is required is not usually a difficult decision for teachers. Any training for clinical work will include it. The more difficult decisions, and the ones on which there is little direct evidence, are concerned with how a student's background knowledge is to be related to his clinical experience, how interpersonal skills should be taught, the way to assess clinical performance during teaching and how to handle the triangular relationship between the patient, student and teacher without undermining mutual confidence.

On the traditional medical curriculum, as we saw in Chapter 4, students were expected to absorb vast blocks of information before entering the clinical situation in which they were already expected to have learned how to apply the information. Because all students could not be given the same clinical tasks, the knowledge they had acquired was often inappropriate to the situations they faced. Curricula centred upon clinical problems to teach students to work out solutions to problem situations which have not been described by their teachers. Since this is a situation in which most medical staff work, the approach is practical and realistic. The clinical performance of students at McMaster University is a testimony to the success of problem-centred curricula.

When using demonstrations and laboratory experiments in the physical sciences it is frequently assumed that students are capable of observing what takes place. The cost of poor observation in clinical situations is frequently so great that clinical teachers have realised long ago that powers of observation need to be meticulously trained. The use of audio-visual aids, role play and micro-teaching techniques before students enter the clinical situation are too often neglected.

Henderson (1969) says that a clinical teacher needs "the ability to express facts clearly and concisely; to encourage students to link theoretical knowledge to practical work; to teach them to observe; to reason out suitable practical treatments and later to evaluate their results; to ensure that answers are clearly given; to use accurate scientific terminology and possess a good vocabulary; to possess a directness and confidence which enables him to check students' performances accurately". No doubt these things are true but I know of no evidence on their relative importance, nor or whether other important factors are omitted.

The same is true of clinical performance itself. Little work has been conducted on differences in clinical style, but when I used the Flanders Technique (Flanders, 1970) to compare the relationships and patterns of interaction between patients and a number of psychotherapists I found widely contrasting yet acceptable differences in style. Until more techniques of this kind are developed clinical teaching will remain unscientific and amateurish.

(d) Micro-teaching

Microteaching illustrates an extraordinary success story in the field of educational research. It was initiated by Dwight Allen and his colleagues at the beginning of the 1960s and by the end of the decade 55% of American teacher training institutions reported using the technique.

The technique consists of three stages: teach, evaluate feedback and re-teach. In the first stage a trainee teacher may teach for 5 or 10 minutes to achieve previously specified objectives. The process is video-recorded. At the end the pupils usually complete a questionnaire which is used in conjunction with a supervisor's notes and comments when showing the trainee the recording of his performance. This second stage normally follows at once. The third stage, which consists of a repeat of the first two, follows after the trainee has had a chance to revise his preparation.

Certain features of the technique may be noted. It consists of genuine teaching, though reduced in time, content and pupil numbers. Hence it is classified here as exemplifying the principle of practice rather than simulation and it is described as "micro". It is also "micro" in the sense that very small teaching techniques may be evaluated and trained, whereas delayed general comments on a full teaching period are often too global. These techniques may include pausing after asking a question, the use of eye contact, prompting, clarification of pupils' ideas and the use of praise. Theoretically the alternation of teaching and evaluative feedback may be continued until some specified level of performance is reached.

There is little doubt that as a method of training teachers in specific skills microteaching is highly effective. In one of the earliest investigations trainees who spent 10 hours a week for 8 weeks were judged superior to controls who spent 20 - 25 hours a week with traditional instruction and practice. Furthermore microteaching grades appeared to give a better prediction of grades at the end of the course (Allen and Fortune, 1967). Even when using fellow trainees as "pupils" Emmer and Miller (1968) were able to demonstrate superior ability to motivate, to judge class readiness and to use questions and their answers. Perrott (in press) has demonstrated the training of teaching skills such as, handling incorrect pupil responses, calling on non-volunteers to answer questions, giving prompts, seeking clarification of responses given and skills in asking questions which either require a set of related facts or higher order thinking. In most cases, the statistical values of these changes were highly significant. A long series of studies by Borg et al (1970) shows an even longer list of changes in teachers' behaviour when teaching widely differing pupils and subjects. Furthermore, they showed that the effects scarcely diminished after four months; indeed some skills continued to improve.

Where there may be doubt is not in the effectiveness of microteaching but in the value assumptions that underlie it. It is not obvious that school teachers should always be willing to give prompts to pupils who do not know the answer to questions, that asking questions is always a good teaching technique, or that pupils who rarely answer questions should always be called on to do so; nor is it obvious that repeating one's own question or repeating a pupil's answer is always an undesirable technique. If these things are not always true, it does not follow that the highly significant changes in teaching style are necessarily improvements. As in other fields of scientific discovery, whenever man invents a powerful tool his responsibility in using it is all the greater.

In other words, researchers in microteaching have so far underestimated the subtlety of teaching techniques. On the other hand, the fact that significant changes in teaching style can be achieved may itself become a powerful research technique when changes in style are compared with teaching effectiveness using other objective criteria. This point is well recognised by Allen and Ryan in their book "Microteaching" which will probably remain standard reading on the subject for a long time.

(e) Fieldwork

It is arguable that in geography, geology and biological subjects fieldwork is as intrinsic to the discipline as clinical practice is in medicine. Indeed, educational visits are used in the teaching of many subjects; yet I know of no controlled empirical study of their effectiveness.

Nevertheless, Henderson (1969) claims there are five stages in the effective handling of field excursions. First, students should obtain the factual background and technical skills required to understand the specific purpose of the excursion. The study of igneous intrusions in the field, including the effect of heat and fusion on the chemical composition and physical structure of sedimentary rocks, will need to begin in the classroom many months before the excursion. According to Henderson, students too often "fail to see the implications of all that is available to them on field trips because of an inadequate preliminary knowledge of their subject".

The second stage involves specific preparation and orientation prior to each sortie. It includes a brief outline of the nature and purpose of the fieldwork. In spite of his complaint that students are often given insufficiently detailed preparation, Henderson recommends leaving some surprises and posing some problems, possibly in written form, during the fieldwork itself.

The third stage is the sortie. Detailed planning is important and a recent visit by the teacher is essential. Students frequently need guidance on clothing and study materials to take with them.

Henderson recommends that the fourth stage, the follow-up, should be held the next day, or very soon afterwards, but not the same day. A lapse of time is necessary to allow some consolidation of learning. The purpose of the follow-up is to make the learning permanent and this often involves relating the students' observations to various aspects of the discipline. For example, understanding of a geological process may only be achieved by relating students' observations made at widely separated times. A common difficulty with follow-up sessions is that they lack spontaneity. The use of visual material not previously shown can add some novelty, while the drudgery of writing descriptive reports is to be avoided.

Henderson's fifth stage is to assimilate students' observations to later learning. He recommends frequent subsequent reference to the fieldwork in lectures and other work. In short, fieldwork differs from a pleasure cruise in that it is fully integrated with the rest of a student's course.

(2) Projects

The major characteristic of the project method is that students produce a thesis, a plan, a model, a written or oral report, or some other piece of work. Although this product is the ostensible objective when using the method, the real objectives are in terms of the learning required to produce it. Thus, the project method features prominently in the subject-centred and student-centred curricula described in Chapter 4.

The processes of doing a project obviously vary, but they commonly have four overlapping phases, each with many parts. In the first phase the student gradually selects a problem, theme, or issue to investigate. At first, he may only have an interest in a general subject area but, as he finds available sources of information, a typical student needs to narrow down his field of enquiry. Having selected his problem, the student may decide his procedure to solve it. This may include defining what is relevant, designing an experiment or some other process of observation and anticipating likely solutions. The second phase will include the interpretation of data and the formulation of arguments based upon that data. Consequently, it may continue beyond the third phase, which may include fieldwork, experiments, surveys and other methods of collecting data. Only when the solution has been selected and developed in the student's mind can the student plan the organisation and presentation of his product. A good problem can normally be stated in simple, clear and precise terms stating relationships between variables. It is limited in scope and testable within the time available. Its hypothesised solution should be consistent with most known facts.

In the project method the problem is often set by the student himself. The procedure for its solution is frequently initiated by the student or group of students. Projects may last from a few hours to several years. The teacher's role is indirect and non-authoritarian.

In an important new book, Adderley et al (1976) claim a large number of advantages for the project method. Students are responsible for their own learning. Projects oblige students to look deeply into a subject and to combine disciplines. Students gain commitment and satisfaction from producing their work, partly because it may have a permanent value. Students gain experience in research techniques by searching, selecting, collecting and presenting information. Team projects may break down the isolation of undergraduate study yet be sufficiently flexible that students may work at different speeds. Adderley et al admit however that the project method is not clearly defined, students are relatively difficult to control and, whether the projects are produced by individuals or a team, they are difficult to grade and students complain that their contribution to their total assessment is not always clear.

It is claimed (Adderley et al, 1976) that projects, especially team projects, can achieve objectives insufficiently considered when using other methods. They provide considerable enjoyment; they train students not only for independent work, but for group work by requiring co-operation with others, tact and diplomacy, leadership, decision making and chairing of a discussion. Most of all, students begin to learn the techniques of research by using its methods, calculating its costs and recognising its constraints.

Although there has not been a great deal of empirical research into the effectiveness of project methods, comparisons suggest that it is as effective as other methods for teaching factual information. Timmel (1954) found no difference between projects and lectures. Novak (1958) reported that students, particularly average students, receiving traditional teaching, learned more information but those doing projects made significant gains on an attitude test. Morris (1930) also found lectures to be more effective than projects when using course grades as the criterion. When compared with laboratory classes Goldstein (1956) found no advantage in projects. However, research studies of this kind carry little weight since we have seen that projects are not used to teach factual information.

(3) Simulation techniques

Simulation normally involves the construction of an operational model of a real situation. Military strategists have long used such models to work out the most advantageous moves in battle. More recently astronauts have learned to adapt to the lunar landscape in simulated conditions on earth. Both used simulations for learning about complex situations. Simulated models are usually simplified and students may learn from their operation, evaluation and sometimes from constructing them.

A great deal of intellectual energy has been spent producing basic definitions of simulation, gaming, role play and other terms of this genre. In my view this is a waste of time. The important questions are, how effective are these methods and how should they be used? The first cannot be definitively answered because every one is different and the second cannot be answered in objective terms for the same reason. There can be little doubt subjectively that their effect upon students is sometimes remarkable, but this is rarely appreciated by a non-participant observer. I shall classify simulation techniques here into gaming and role play, but it should be appreciated that not all simulations fit these two categories easily.

(a) Games

One of the earliest users of games for teaching purposes was Guetzkow at the Department of International Relations in the North-Western University of Illinois. Over a period of several days graduate and under-graduate students played the roles of international diplomats in specified international situations. In this way they learned to feel the emotions of nations other than their own and to gain a first-hand understanding of political behaviour unavailable from the dispassionate study of history. Similar simulations have been devised and used in several British universities to experience the Arab-Israel conflict.

In the Esso Students' Business Game groups of students represent members of companies, each of which should plan their production and marketing strategy systematically. The game is played as a competition between the companies. As in real life, chance factors are introduced, information may be available to some companies and not others and the economic health of a company depends upon a complex interaction of factors. As part of the learning process the complexity may be increased as the game proceeds. New rules may be introduced either at the discretion of the teacher who acts as 'game controller' or after suggestions and discussion by the students.

There are many other games describing urban economic and educational processes. For example, students may play the roles of government officials, welfare agencies and individual citizens where there is a shortage of housing. There has been a recent increase in catalogues of games in use and available for purchase.

Games have many uses. We have seen that they can teach empathy. They show the dynamics of systems, particularly social systems at work. They can condense the time perspective of real situations. They teach students to express themselves clearly and show them the penalties for not doing so. They can teach critical thinking, anticipation and self awareness. Students may understand how other people think and appreciate the role of chance in real life. Many of these are objectives not easily taught by other methods.

Rex Walford (BBC, 1972) has given very clear instructions to teachers intending to use games. They should first ask whether gaming is the appropriate method and whether the proposed game is a reasonable representation of reality. Since the use of games requires some managerial expertise, does the teacher know enough about the game to organise it? It is essential that the teacher should first have experience of playing the game. He should not spend a long time giving explanations or a long sheet of rules. It is better to have a trial run and sort out the consequent problems. Participants should not be forced to join in.

The most important precept of all is to discuss the game thoroughly afterwards. Some games can be discussed while they are in progress, and, if so, this allows the full benefit to be obtained before incidents are forgotten. In any case, it is often useful to stop a game and discuss its progress or whether the rules should be developed before proceeding.

(b) Role play

The element of competition in games can have undesirable effects if not carefully managed. Role play eliminates this element. The method was first used systematically by Morena as "psychodrama", a clinical technique; but it does not assume a particular psychological theory.

Role play is normally used to teach interpersonal and practical skills by asking students to act roles to which they are unaccustomed. Because this requires students to identify themselves with the behaviour of another by changing participants' perception, it may change attitudes towards the tolerance for which I argued in Chapter 1.

A good role play exercise has a number of requirements: a clearly defined, though not necessarily explicit, purpose; a situation which is fairly realistic to the participants; a number of students willing to act; a fairly non-authoritarian approach by the teacher; and adequate time.

Usually, the teacher first describes the purpose of the exercise and then describes the roles to be played. To allow maximum participation and interpretation by the participants, the roles should not be detailed. The roles often involve a conflict situation. Participants may be given conflicting information, or some information may be withheld from certain participants or the audience (if any). It is frequently useful if the role playing can be recorded, since there are frequently disagreements about what actually took place and one purpose of role play is to objectify interpersonal perceptions.

When empathy is the objective it is common practice to reverse or change the roles if time allows for a second exercise. If time is short, it is debatable whether participants should be given roles which conflict with their natural disposition or are consonant with it. In staff training courses it is sometimes salutory for authoritarian senior members of a company to be interviewed by their junior staff, but the teacher could encounter difficulties if the role conflict is so great that it elicits hostility from his class. This does not often happen, provided the members are willing participants; and there is accumulating evidence that this method can produce marked shifts in attitudes in a shorter time than other methods.

V Conclusion

This chapter considers a large number of teaching methods. Inevitably many have been excluded and others have been treated superficially. The major decision with which the chapter is concerned is the choice of teaching method. For this reason the chapter has concentrated upon the objectives that each may achieve.

CHAPTER 6: The Management of a Course Some Analytic Models

Introduction

Conclusion

CHAPTER 6: The Management of a Course. Some Analytic Models.

Introduction

A simple model was given in the opening chapter to illustrate some of the key decisions in mounting a course. The model also related to the plan of this book. This chapter addresses itself to that part of the model labelled "administration". In British universities "the administration" refers to a group of people quite separate from the academics, as though the academics delegated all administration to specialist hand-maidens. However in a quite normal sense of the word, academics are managers, although it is a word seldom used in discussing their work. As the opening sentence of this book says: "Teaching consists of taking and acting upon decisions". A teacher in higher education is an important decision maker for his decisions have immediate and far reaching effects on his students. In the long term they also influence the general social culture of a country. In an important sense, teachers decide what is to be taught to the next generation of influential people. In part they select those people at the stages of admission and examination. They decide on teaching methods, and allocate considerable financial and human resources.

Yet there is no tradition of analysing and commenting on a teacher's work either in terms of management or in terms of organisational development. Consequently this chapter cannot proceed from an established approach, not even a commonly accepted language. Still less are there published volumes on accepted practices in course management, although in very recent years beginnings have been made.

Making decisions and acting on them can be described as a process. One general description of that process might contain the following steps:

Sizing up the situation
Deciding on some action
Carrying out the action
Evaluating the action.

This chapter will concentrate largely on the first step of this process. That is it will present some examples of models designed to help the teacher size up situations. The reason for this emphasis is not only that descriptions of good practice (ways of carrying out the action) are scarce. There is a more powerful reason. A good manager is adaptable, and able to cope with new situations. A concentration on good practice, although it might widen the repertoire of a teacher, still ultimately leaves him working by recipe, that is following prescriptions worked out in past and possibly differing situations. Only by having ways of perceiving a current situation and systematically analysing it can a teacher respond creatively. Thus although the building of a repertoire of actions is necessary, and indeed the acquisition of evaluation techniques also, they are together insufficient to equip a teacher to react effectively to new events or developing conditions. And it is in the nature of organisations that they develop and change and it is in the nature of teaching that we must react quickly to the unforeseen.

This chapter, then, offers eleven models. They are only by way of illustration. The practising teacher needs many more and will need to adapt those presented here in those aspects he finds inappropriate. Each model is introduced by way of a pertinent question. They are:

Model 1 Can we get an overall view of the management decisions needed?

Model 2 Which objectives take priority?

Model 3 Should the university accept the course?

Model 4 How much time do we need to prepare? Which committees are involved?

Model 5 How can we set out our objectives and relate them to teaching and assessment methods?

Model 6 How much latitude have we in timetabling?

Model 7 Can course designing be shared out?

Model 8 Can teaching costs be reduced?

Model 9 Who should do what in a teaching department?

Model 10 What are the characteristics of the department's organisation?

Model 11 Is the department organised to make policy decisions?

I Model 1. Can we get an overall view of the management decisions needed?

A teacher might start by compiling some kind of a 'map' designed to bring order to the matters that he has to make decisions about. An example of such a map is presented in Figure 6.1. It consists of three columns, representing respectively the students, the staff, and the teaching institution. In order for a course to be effective it might be assumed on logical grounds that students must have the ability, opportunity, and incentive to learn. Teaching might be analysed in terms of how it affects those three aspects of student learning. For instance counselling on study skills would be a way of increasing the students' ability to learn. Presenting the student with clear course objectives and a well organised programme of study, as has been noted earlier in this book, increases the opportunity a student has for applying himself effeciently to the task of learning. Lively presentations, variation in teaching method, personal contact with staff and examinations may each provide incentive or disincentive for students to work. So far the 'map' can be seen as providing a check list of questions to ask: even the plan for a particular class can be checked over for how it will influence the ability, opportunity and incentive of the learners. This check list is the beginnings too of a systematic evaluation of teaching because it reminds one to look for a purpose in every aspect of teaching and indicates where to look for the manifest effects of those features of teaching adopted to achieve a purpose.

The map, however, does more. It can reveal the need for policy decisions. We might, for instance, be able to establish as a fact that the students' ability to learn is enhanced by exercises which increase their speed of reading. However it is one thing to demonstrate that student learning may be advanced by this method - it is quite another to agree that it should be. We may argue (some do) that it is no part of a university lecturer's business to help students to learn how to read; they should have learned that at school and should not have been selected if they had failed to do so. Perhaps the example seems trite (even though few university courses teach study skills despite the evidence of their efficacy): but other examples are more familiar and problematic.

Figure 6.1: Decision Areas in Course Planning

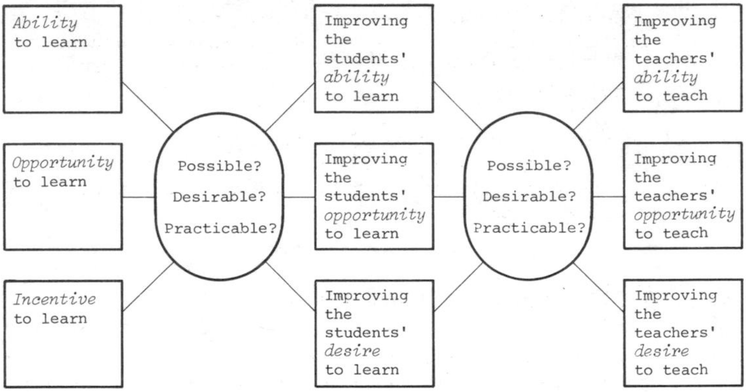

Ability to learn

Opportunity to learn

Incentive to learn

Possible? Desirable? Practicable?

Improving the students' *ability* to learn

Improving the students' *opportunity* to learn

Improving the students' *desire* to learn

Possible? Desirable? Practicable?

Improving the teachers' *ability* to teach

Improving the teachers' *opportunity* to teach

Improving the teachers' *desire* to teach

Each connection between boxes, three on the left of the diagram, none on the right, raises three kinds of question:

1 Is it theoretically possible to make improvements? Has the effect been demonstrated?
2 Is it desirable to make the improvement by the possible method at the probable cost?
3 Are there sufficient resources and the organisational means of accomplishing what is required?

In Chapter 5 it is argued that personalised systems of instruction are very effective and popular with students, particularly on courses involving both practical and theoretical work. Why then are they not more common? Aside from the general ignorance of the method among university staff it might be supposed that the initial time and effort involved in producing the necessary course materials, the rigour of the course analysis involved, and the adjustments to the normal college administration needed to accommodate the system all tell against it. In other words teaching methods are adopted or rejected not only on the grounds of the soundness from an educational viewpoint but also on whether or not they are administratively convenient, emotionally acceptable, and financially viable.

It is doubtful whether many decisions in course planning are systematically identified and then made on a basis of an overt analysis of their social and political acceptability, administrative convenience and cost. Perhaps successful managers in education work more intuitively, but some illative sense ensures that their judgements are nearer the workable balance of soundness, acceptability and feasibility than those of their less successful colleagues. Any claim for the value of this kind of map rests on the supposition that some display which notes and relates decisions and their effects enhances illation. It is a reasonable but not proven supposition which applies to all the models in this chapter.

If the left-hand side of the 'map' allows for exploration of the relationship between teacher and taught then the right-hand side sets out the grounds upon which teacher and institution interact. The institution in turn may influence the ability, opportunity, and incentive of the teacher to teach. Thus the institution may improve a teacher's *ability* in all three aspects of teaching by the introduction of a staff training scheme. It may affect his *opportunity* of teaching by such matters as timetables, facilities and work load. Incentives are provided by pay, benefits, and promotion prospects.

Each connection between the columns 1) highlights matters of policy and thus allows the teacher/manager to enquire what, if any, policy exists, 2) points to the need for policy, and 3) provides one context in which policy decisions may be made.

II Model 2. Which objectives take priority?

The first chapter of this book puts a logical argument for the use of educational objectives. The teacher/manager has to make a choice of objectives. Although as part of his duty as a teacher of a subject he will have to decide what objectives are appropriate, he will by no means be free to base a course on his personal preferences, even though he is an expert in his academic field. In practice a course must always meet the objectives of several groups of people whose interests coincide enough for them to share an investment in the course, without necessarily being identical. To assign priorities between these partially competing claims the teacher/manager needs another model - one which identifies and relates the sources of course objectives.

Figure 6.2 identifies three major sources from which objectives may arise:

(1) The subject matter of a course and the interests and perceptions of the staff who teach it;

(2) The requirements of the profession or the attributes of the social role for which a student is being prepared;

(3) The wishes and abilities of the students, and their previous experience and education.

Figure 6.2: Three sources of educational objectives

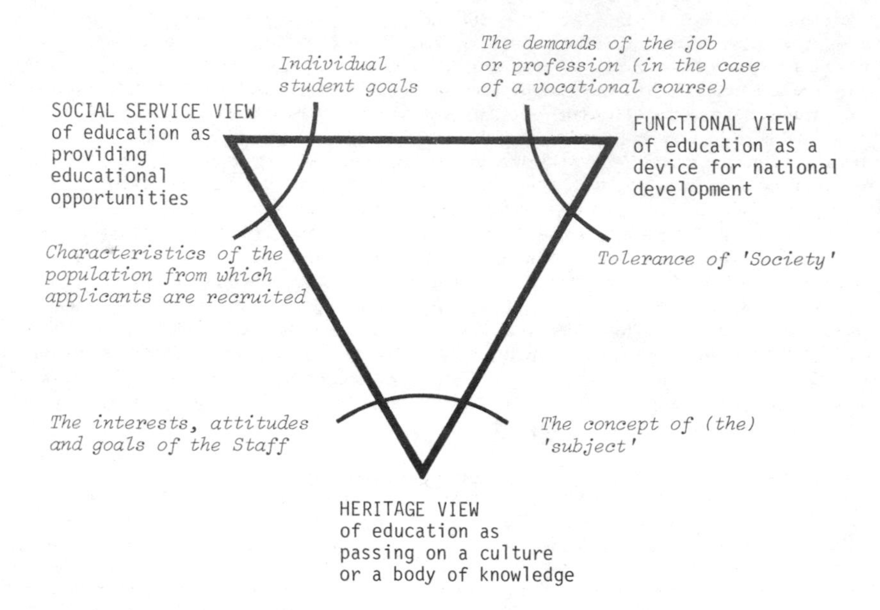

This list accords with three purposes of an education system:
(1) to pass on the future, the heritage, or a body of knowledge from one generation to the next;
(2) to produce the qualified manpower to benefit a future society or as an instrument of national development;
(3) to advance individuals either socially or in terms of their personal development.

For convenience these three purposes may be labelled the cultural purpose, the functional purpose, the social purpose. Although it is possible for an educational system, perhaps even an educational institution, to serve all three purposes well, it is doubtful whether a course can do so. The academic study of a subject does not provide a professional training; a literature course may fulfil a cultural purpose well, but its functional value may be low. A student-based course which encourages students to develop their own curriculum may do much to advance the maturity of the individual whilst making him positively disruptive of society and involve such liberties with subject matter that pure minded academic dismiss the course as of little educational value.

This is not to say that a course can serve only one purpose. Indeed it must meet some of the students' objectives or none are likely to be recruited. It must be thought to serve society in some way, or at least have some social approval, if it is to be supported from public funds. And if it is to have teachers and a subject matter, it must accommodate the former's interests and the latter's internal logic.

It is to say, however, that on a particular course the three masters cannot be served equally because there will almost certainly be some matters over which their demands conflict. On such occasions priorities must be given. Thus it is imperative that those responsible for a course, the teacher/managers, have a policy on the matter and then apply it consistently. Courses exist in which the selection criteria owe more to the standards of the students offering themselves than to the demands of the course, the course content rests firmly on academic tradition, while the examinations purport to indicate a graduate's suitability for a profession. Such inconsistency within one course can only lead to confusion, wasted resources and loss of morale. That is not creative tension, it is destructive muddle-headedness.

This model may not only help a teacher/manager to describe the nature of a policy decision which faces him, but also to illustrate to his colleagues that there is a policy decision to be made and therefore the need to adopt a means of making it.

III Model 3. Should the University accept the course?

While the teacher/manager decides with his departmental colleagues what type of course they wish to design, the committee which represents the institution as a whole will have to decide whether or not to admit the course to the prospectus. On what basis is the Senate to discharge its duty to offer a defensible combination of courses at reasonable cost and to uphold academic standards? Hywel Jones has reported a checklist adopted by one university (in Fielden J. and Lockwood G., 1973)

(1) Background - What are the factors which prompt the initiators to make the particular proposal? (eg student demand, national criteria, new academic field of importance etc.)

(2) Context - How and where would it fit into the existing framework of studies?

(3) Students involved - How many students will take it? What kinds of students?

(4) Methods of teaching - What pattern and sequence of teaching methods will be used? What is the rationale?

(5) Method of assessment - This should involve the question of course assessment, as well as examinations, showing the relationship to the objectives which have to be achieved.

(6) Teaching manpower - Who will teach it? What staff teaching resources will be involved? A supporting statement should be included from the relevant head of department on the viability of the proposal in this respect.

(7) What other costs?

(a) Library and other (eg audio-visual) materials (supporting statement to be obtained from librarian)
(b) Computer
(c) Laboratory or other facilities
(d) Technical support services
(e) Equipment and materials
(f) Secretarial services
(g) Travel
(h) Administrative services

In assessing these costs, it is necessary to take into account the cost of providing support for the research interests of any new academic staff appointed. These are likely to be high if they are outside the existing major areas of research activity in the university.

(8) Space implications

(9) Effect, if any, on professional recognition of degree

(10) Timing of introduction - When would it be introduced?

It is interesting to note that this list concerns itself strictly with matters of management. The academic quality of the course is not mentioned. In practice it may be that a university controls its academic standards almost entirely by its appointments and promotion procedure. Once an academic is given responsibility his colleagues very seldom assess and comment on the quality of his academic work openly. It would indeed be difficult for a Senate to uphold academic standards by scrutiny and judgement of work in an esoteric field, although it might be possible to make some kind of evaluation of the intellectual level of work involved and some of the academic values implied. In practice any scrutiny of academic content is undertaken at departmental and faculty levels where committees may examine course plans. However, as a course plan can be no guarantee of academic excellence in teaching, responsibility for quality will remain with the department and often with an individual. It may seldom or ever be reviewed or reassessed.

On the management matters listed above, Senate members can be provided with data by the administration. Much of it will be predictive and thus may vary considerably in its quality

IV Model 4. How much time do we need to prepare?

To change existing courses takes time. To set up new courses takes even longer. Some specimen 'lead times' have been collected by Fielden and Lockwood (1973). Three examples suffice to illustrate the range.

Topic	Start time	Final decision after
Minor changes to course options	October	8 months
Introduction of a Masters Course	October	22 months
Changes in methods of examining in undergraduate Finals	May	28 months

These times have been established empirically and will doubtless vary from one university to another. Once they have been identified and published a good administration might set about the task of shortening the time.

Within that working time there may be a great deal of planning and committee work to be done. Some plan of operations may be necessary, perhaps a simple bar chart, or something as complicated as a critical path analysis. Figure 6.3 is an operational plan (produced by the University of Aston) for organising an academic course. A model of this kind not only helps a teacher/manager keep on time, it is also a very useful document for a college administration to give to an academic preparing a course for the first time.

Figure 6.3: Operation of decision making machinery
Approval of new undergraduate course

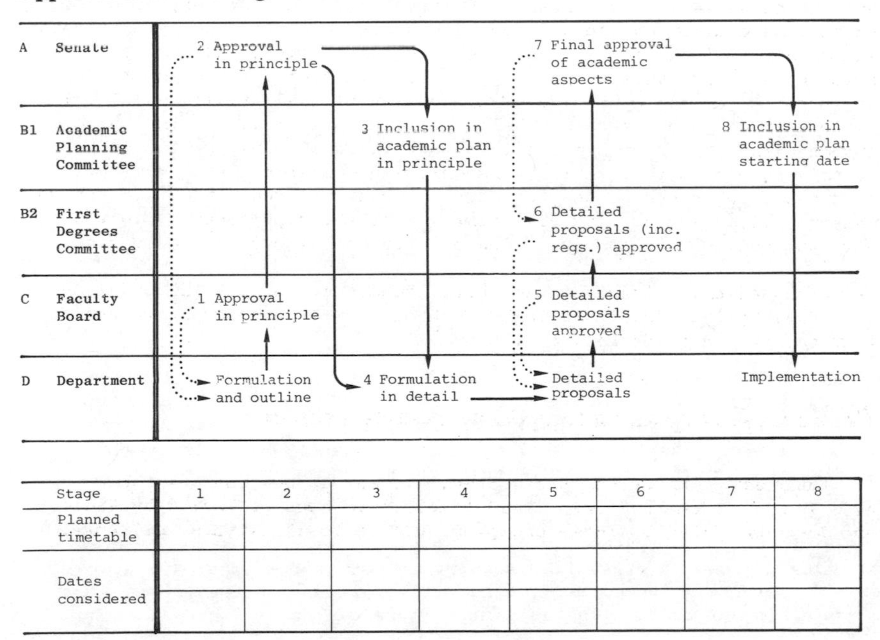

Stage	1	2	3	4	5	6	7	8
Planned timetable								
Dates considered								

The diagram shows that at the University in question the normal procedure is for a course plan to pass through the scrutiny procedure twice; once as an outline then as a detailed proposal. The department submits an outline to the relevant faculty board. The outline is organised under a series of headings similar to those given in Model 3. The board may refer the plan back to the department but if they approve it, it is passed directly to Senate which is asked to agree to such a course in principle. On such an occasion the Senate might consider parts (1), (2), (3), (9) and (10) of Model 3. That is, background, context, students involved, professional recognition and timing. They might go so far as to set constraints under items (6), (7) and (8): manpower, costs and space.

The plan will then go back to the department. If the Senate agrees in principle the matter will also be referred to the academic planning committee who will appraise the department and inform it of matters of administration it needs to take into account.

The department then prepares a detailed proposal which first goes to the Faculty board for discussion of academic content then to the First Degrees Committee who will concern themselves with formal regulations. Senate is then asked for final approval. They may refer the matter back if they are not satisfied but if the course is acceptable it is passed to the academic planning committee who ensures that all necessary administrative decisions are made at university level. Thereafter the department may give the course.

V Model 5. How can we set out our objectives and relate them to teaching and assessment methods?

A course usually has too many objectives to hold in the mind. In any case they require such careful wording that a record is necessary. Is a simple list sufficient? The problem is that essentially objectives need to be classified according to at least two quite different schemes. The first is in accordance with the internal logic of the subject. Ask any academic to outline his subject matter for a course and he will give, not a list of topics in random order, but a *structured* exposition showing here a progression, there a section with subsections. He may even produce a diagrammatic representation rather than a list.

This same material needs to be classified again if it is to be the basis of rational planning for a course. This second classification seeks to arrange the material according to the kind of learning task it involves for the student. Thus this second classification system is based on some conception of the psychology of the learner. It makes distinctions such as between knowledge, skills, and attitudes. Knowledge might be subdivided to differentiate "learning to-recognise-an-event-or-condition-when-it-occurs" from "learning to-describe-the-event-or-condition-even-in-its-absence". Why make such distinctions? Basically there are only two reasons, either the distinction leads to different teaching methods (a skill like surgery is not learned from a lecture) or a difference in assessment method (recognition and recall require quite different modes of assessment. There can be an incidental, but

Figure 6.4: A suggested Analysis Scheme for the Work of Training and Educating Graduate Biologists intending to enter the Teaching Profession.

ASPECTS	INTEGRATION AND ADMINISTRATION
ASSUMPTIONS 01	Content and method must be synthesised Judgement by peers is an effective learning situation
LEARNING OBJECTIVES i) Each End of a Continuum of ATTITUDES AND VALUES (02)	Away from: - overemphasis on factual acquisition - assessing traditionally - regarding content as self-justifying - having no concept of cost/benefit Towards: - Adopting appropriate methods of achieving objectives - Continual evaluation of efficienty a) of teacher b) of pupils' achievement - Evaluating alternatives in terms of cost/benefit
ii) Knowledge (03)	A conceptual model to assess priorities Of lesson analysis, curriculum analysis Of a variety of forms of assessment Of a variety of procedures of formal assessment. PRY Methods of application of time/money costs/benefit analysis.
iii) Skills (04)	In matching objectives with methods In improving own performance In determining achievements of pupils Efficient coordination of all procedures
METHODS OF TEACHING AND LEARNING SITUATIONS (05)	Lesson analysis Criticism by self and peers Criticise, construct and use procedures for pupil assessment Criticise standard scheme of assessment Assist in school examinations Criticise simulation schemes in cost/benefit terms
WHAT IS TO BE ASSESSED	Checking analysis sheets by student and tutor Checklist of special situations Effectiveness of selection of assessment Awareness of time/cost/benefit criteria
METHODS OF ASSESSMENT	By teachers, tutor, self and peers on teaching practice By theoretical and/or practical assessment Further Work usually needed in PRY Not assessed on course - long term objective

valuable benefit in addition: this second classification often suggests aspects of a learning objective which might otherwise have been overlooked.

All planning grids for courses involve this double classification. Figure 1.2 on page 10 shows the essential elements of such a grid. It should be remembered that classifications like this involve many distinctions which are close to being arbitrary and are essentially descriptive, reflecting the individual's conception of his subject. Some may be more useful than others when it comes to suggesting teaching and assessment methods but no two people's analysis is likely to be the same and neither need be wrong.

Once the analysis of objectives is complete a planning grid can be extended to show the first step in creating a course to suit them. The course is not derived by some inevitable logic from the objectives but suitable methods of teaching and assessment may be noted opposite each objective. 'Suitability' in this context must include the techncial soundness of the method ("Do people actually learn 'a' from teaching method 'x'?"; "Is success in learning 'a' actually measured by assessment method 'y'?" and its acceptability and cost. Not all these things may be known and so a great deal of judgement and guess-work is involved. At a later date decisions may be changed in the light of experience, but in order to change them, the judgements and the guesses may have to have been recorded. Thus the planning chart may be extended to display a good deal of information about the decisions taken during the initial planning. The chart also serves the purpose of revealing to the planner some decisions he does have to make which might not otherwise have occurred to him.

Elaborations in the simple chart presented in Figure 1.2 may be conjoured to fit the needs of the moment and the temperament of the planner. All such models conceal as much as they reveal and so their limitations must be borne in mind by all users. A rather baroque example may be found in Warren Piper et al (1977) a sample of which is reproduced in Figure 6.4.

VI Model 6. How much latitude do we have in timetabling?

Part of Chapter 4 was about the sequencing of learning activities. Courses typically are made up of many sequences, not necessarily related one to another, which may overlap. Not all items will be part of a sequence. Many could equally well be taught near the beginning, as near the end of a course. The result is that when it comes to planning a timetable it is helpful to know how much freedom there is for the timing of any single item. Figure 6:5 is part of a diagram designed to fill such a purpose. It appears in UTMU (1976).

The diagram was used in planning a course in architectual design. The numbers in each box refer to a list of course objectives. The general chronological sequence is from the top of the page downwards; the main teaching sequence is the projects, each of which can begin only after that preceding it has finished. On the left of that main

Figure 6.5: Architectural Association School Plan 1st year course 1970-1971

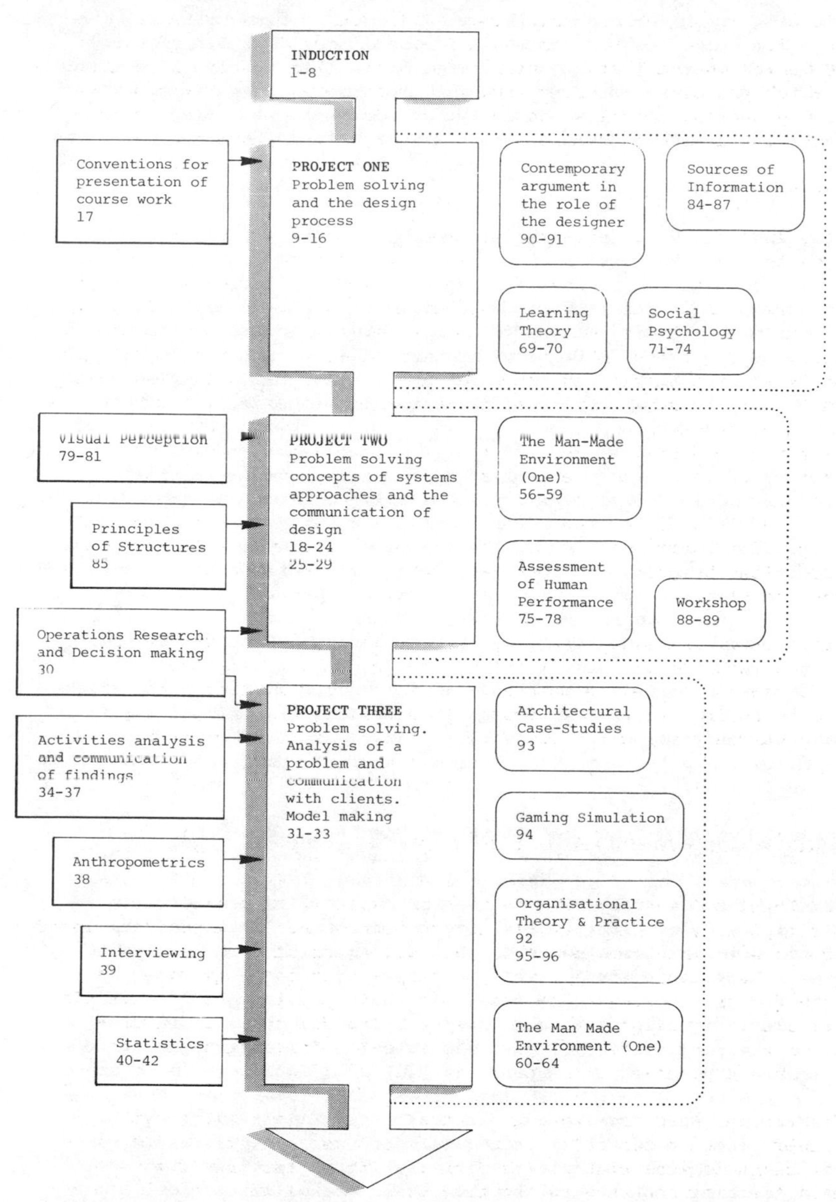

Numbers in boxes refer to specific learning objectives

sequence are supporting classes whose content is to be directly related to the project work. Those objectives represented on the right of the diagram are to be pursued in activities not intimately related to the project work (eg in lectures, and seminars). The lines indicate where the objectives come in the overall sequence of events. For example, objectives 56-59 are not to be attempted until 9-16 have been completed, but it does not matter whether they come before or after objectives 18-29, 75-81 and 88-89. In this way the course planner is given a clear indication of the amount of freedom he has in designing the timetable.

VII Model 7. Can course designing be shared?

Earlier chapters have described the process of moving from preparing objectives to designing assessment and teaching methods. In the last section objectives were related to planning the timetable. Should all these stages in planning be undertaken by the same individual or team, or should some be delegated? The first is the most usual, but it is not the only possibility.

A number of strategies are open to a course leader. Here are four possible variations. The reader will be able to think of others.

(1) The course leader or a committee decide on teaching and assessment methods working from a syllabus. They then assign *activities* to individual staff according to a timetable (eg six lectures on Beowulf; four laboratory classes to complete a set list of experiments). Exams may be set jointly or by individual teachers.

(2) The course leader or a committee decide upon the criteria by which the achievement of certain objectives will be measured then specify deadlines for objectives and allot some course time. The individual teachers are left to devise their own teaching programme within the time allotted.

(3) There could be a practice similar to the last except that the responsibility for devising the criteria of success is also delegated to teachers. The effect here is of individual teachers (or small teams) being entirely responsible for a part of a course which they can conduct with little reference to other parts once the 'grand plan' has been adopted. This gives teachers considerable freedom. What is its price?

(4) The course staff confine themselves to producing and administering tests, leaving the students responsible for devising their own learning programme. The staff may publish clearly written course objectives to guide the students. Also to a greater or lesser degree, the staff can make working materials and reading matter available to students (as in the Keller Plan), or provide lectures which students may voluntarily attend. This gives the students greater responsibility in planning their course activities than in the previous strategies.

VIII Model 8. Can teaching costs be reduced?

In an industrially developed country the per capita cost of education is almost certain to rise. That is because productivity in general is related much more to investment in technology and machinery than it is to the employment of more people. So the productivity per person goes up, and with it, the standard of living reflected in a large pay packet. In education 'productivity' - (the number of students and the quality of education offered) is related more to the number of teachers employed than advances in educational technology. The teachers pay goes up to keep in line with industrial workers but the number of teachers employed per student does not drop in compensation. So the cost of education rises.

Even in most developing countries, where the majority of people are involved in labour-intensive agriculture in which increased productivity involves a proportionate increase in farm workers, post-secondary teachers tend to be in that part of the community whose living standards are rising. So it follows that even in these circumstances the cost of education usually rises.

We might expect, as in Britain at the moment, that the pressure to teach efficiently will be more than a passing phenomenon. Having a target staff:student ratio may be sufficient as a guideline for staffing institutions and possibly even its larger departments, but it can become costly if applied at the level of staffing each course, at least as far as the cost of teaching concerned. Say an institution works on a ratio of x students to one member of staff. In a certain year x additional students join the course, the department takes on a new member of staff. However it is the tradition in most universities (although not all post-school educational establishments) that only a proportion of the lecturers' time is put over to teaching. So unless the department gets full value for money from his other activities such as research and administration, the teaching will carry the extra burden. The system assumes a more or less static ratio of a teacher's time spent on teaching and other activities. This is often enshrined in the terms of employment but even when it is not, it forms part of a conservative tradition. It further assumes that the ratio will continue to fit a department as it grows. However the chances that the man-hours required by teaching, research, and administration will remain constant in a growing (or shrinking) department must be remote.

What are the alternatives to taking on academic staff in proportion to student numbers? Hywel Jones (op.cit.) has listed some:

(1) Varying the amount of teaching per member of staff

(2) Changing the combination of teaching methods so as to effect a difference in overall staff:student ratio (eg more lectures and fewer tutorials, or introduce PSI)

(3) Enlarge all teaching groups such as lecture and tutorial classes

(4) Change the mixture of subjects taught to increase those that use fewer staff

(5) Reduce the number of course options

(6) Require all staff to spend a greater proportion of time teaching

(7) Deploy staff to specialise in various forms of teaching to get best value from them (eg high-priced professors give main lectures and prepare self-instructional material, juniors supervise the use of self-instructional material)

(8) Give teaching staff short-term contracts, because the longer they stay, the more they tend to be paid

(9) Employ more part-time sessionally paid staff

(10) Employ post-graduate students at lower rates of pay

(11) Introduce more peer-teaching systems.

Many of the arrangements listed above run counter to the British tradition and would meet resistance from the teachers' unions. Other countries' traditions differ, but any university may lack the flexibility to keep changing these arrangements to meet the circumstances of the moment.

IX Model 9. Who should do what in a teaching department?

This model (adapted from an idea by A.N. Oppenheim at the London School of Economics) allows the teacher/manager to check whether the actual distribution of work among departmental staff accords with an ideal.

The staff of most departments share between them a number of duties such as undergraduate teaching, graduate supervision, research and administration. These can be subdividied. For example, undergraduate teaching can be given to students of one's own department or service teaching in another department. Administration can be within the department of sitting on collegiate and university committees. How should these different forms of work be shared out between the staff? A number of different arrangements have been suggested.

(1) Seniority arrangement - tasks are arranged on an implicit value scale and are organised according to seniority. Frequently this takes the form of senior staff doing least teaching and most administration.

(2) Specialisation arrangement - each member tends to take on the type of work he is good at or likes

(3) Haphazard arrangement - through no deliberate policy some

staff just do more of everything

(4) Compensatory arrangement - staff with heavy duties of one type are relieved of others

(5) Equal shares arrangement - all types of work and responsibilities are distributed to give approximately equal loads

(6) Development arrangement - staff are assigned work to form a progression of increasing complexity and responsibility so as to develop individuals' capacities in all aspects of departmental and university work.

These possible arrangements may be discussed at a full meeting of academic staff and some agreement reached on which arrangement is the one to be aimed for. Such a discussion implies some measure or criterion of load in each type of work.

In order to check the preferred arrangement against reality the number of duties of each type undertaken by each member of staff (in, say a term of a year) is totalled. It is probably sufficient for this exercise to take raw figures giving no weightings to distinguish between, say, re-delivering a long-prepared lecture and giving a new one, or the work involved in belonging to different committees. However, it

Example

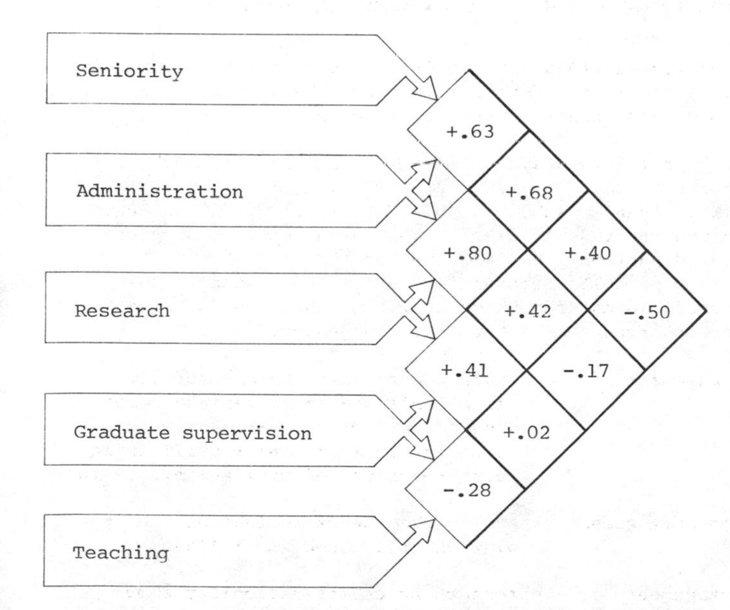

may be worth giving double weighting for convening a committee as distinct from serving on it. A correlation matrix of the type illustrated below may be constructed. (This is simply a way of comparing each factor with each of the others. In this diagram +1.0 would mean a perfect positive correlation; -1.0 would mean a perfect negative correlation). In the example given, seniority correlates highly with research, but negatively with teaching load. Also those who take a high administrative load tend to take a high research load. (With such crude data a rank correlation is probably least distortive.)

The example suggests a department fitting the seniority arrangement: the more senior a staff member is, the less teaching and the more research, administration and graduate supervision he is likely to undertake. It is a very common arrangement.

In a compensatory arrangement one might expect to find negative correlations between teaching and research, and in a specialisation arrangement one might find, for example, a high positive correlation between teaching and graduate supervision (the gifted teacher). In a department which specialises in research, one might expect research seniority to correlate negatively wtih administration and teaching, and to have no correlation with seniority.

X Model 10. What are the characteristics of the department's organisation?

One way of looking at organisations in general, and academic departments in particular is to consider four parameters: personal power, institutionalised power, achievement, and affiliation. Every organisation facilitates all four to some extent. It is the relative emphases placed upon them which is of interest.

(1) Personal power organisations

Irrespective of its original purpose, this kind of organisation exists to carry out the will of its boss. Characteristically its members are organised into an implicit or explicit power hierarchy. People are often grouped functionally and contact is mostly by word of mouth rather than written in memos. Staff who are successful empathise with the boss. Meetings of the department, or whatever the organisation is, are not committees but tend to be occasions for giving instructions or briefing a team. Contributions by members other than the boss tend to be reporting or explaining their actions. In this sense they are retrospective rather than decision making. The climate is authoritarian rather than consultative.

(2) Institutionalised power-ascendant organisations

The major purpose of institutionalised power-ascendant organisations is the exertion and containment of power. Work responsibilites between people in these organisations are clearly drawn and well observed so that roles tend to be formalised. The organisation is hierarchical and high status individuals are frequently unavailable or inaccessible to those of lower rank. The written word holds precedence over the spoken word and is frequently a point of reference. For example the Statutes and Ordinances of Senate, the decisions recorded in minutes of a previous committee meeting or written edicts from a Head of Department are regarded as rules and regulations members are obliged to obey rather than general principles for guidance. Channels and forms of communication are controlled centrally and tend to be about procedures rather than purposes. Procedures become institutionalised often outliving their original purpose. Control is legalistic. Because responsibilities are clearly defined, blame can be apportioned and is often passed on down the hierarchy.

Committees often exhibit the principle of collective responsibility. They legitimise decisions including some that have already been taken. They may adjudicate between two or more points of view and groups of people.

(3) Achievement-ascendant organisations

Organisations that are achievement-ascendant are primarily concerned with some task. Procedures are adaptable to fit the purposes of the moment. People may be organised in different ways for different purposes, sometimes concurrently. Thus the organisation is less rigidly hierarchic than with personal power and institutionalised power-ascendant organisations. Communications move more easily up and down the levels of the organisation and there is more communication between those on the same level in different departments. A large proportion of the communications are about goals, progress and productivity. Goals tend to be formulated by the Head of Department or some other dominant person, perhaps in collaboration with others in the organisation. The reward system is linked to the achievement of these goals. For example a head of department in a university may decide that his department will be research oriented and reward his academic staff with promotion who best achieve these goals as evidenced by the number of their publications. Committees are concerned with the production and formulation of ideas perhaps by the collation of information from different sources such as the various committee members. When the size of a committee, or some other factor, prevents the production of ideas, an achievement-ascendant organisation characteristically forms working parties or other sub-groups to produce them.

(4) Affiliation-ascendant organisations

Affiliation-ascendant organisations are dominated by the need to accommodate their individual members. All members of the group, including the leaders, are easily accessible. There are frequent informal contacts; jokes and other apparently irrelevant activities are tolerated and even encouraged. Responsibilities are widely shared and are often not well defined. Individuals, including senior members, are sensitive to the social climate of the group and readily identify with it.

Because these organisations depend upon the inter-personal contact their characteristics are difficult to maintain when they are large. Many of their characteristics typify small informal groups such as pressure groups within a larger organisation.

Meetings of departments which are affiliation-ascendant contain more expression of feeling and opportunities to let off steam and have one's say. This is necessary if members are eventually to agree, and identify with, a course of action, a cause, or a body of people such as an institution. This in turn is necessary if the department or organisation is to engage in concerted activity with all members playing their part.

(5) Combinations of these characteristics

Organisations may be seen as taking their character from the combination of these factors. Organisations which are high on personal or institutional power and low on achievement tend to become stultified, and staff morale is usually low. Organisations high on achievement but low on power and affiliation tend to be unstable and ephemeral. Those high on affiliation may be congenial for a while, but only some personality types stay for long if achievement is low. There is a tendency for high affiliation to conflict with high personal or institutional power except where individuals are willing to subordinate their own desires; and this is rare in academic institutions because they tend to encourage independence of mind.

Similar conflicts appear in academic committees. For example a university Senate may have difficulty in waiving its rules of procedure to permit the free expression of the emotions of its members.

XI Model 11. Is the department organised to make policy decisions?

Figure 1.1 identifies seven headings under which course management decisions have to be made. Such a model can be used as a basis for a revealing exercise in checking how well institutional and departmental organisation is fitted to making these decisions. In principle the exercise is simple. First the teacher/manager, perhaps with the involvement of his colleagues, draws a diagram similar to that shown in Figure 1.1. Figure 6.6. shows a diagram produced by one department of an English local authority college. The lines on the diagram link decisions which directly affect each other: if one is changed the other will require adjustment.

Once the diagram has been constructed then a number of questions may be asked: "who makes each of the decisions?", "Is any one person or committee of people specifically responsible for any set of the decisions,", "In what order are the decisions made,", "At the time that they are made, is relevant information concerning related decisions available to the decision makers,". An enquiry of this kind can do a number of things.

Figure 6.6: Decision Areas in Course Planning

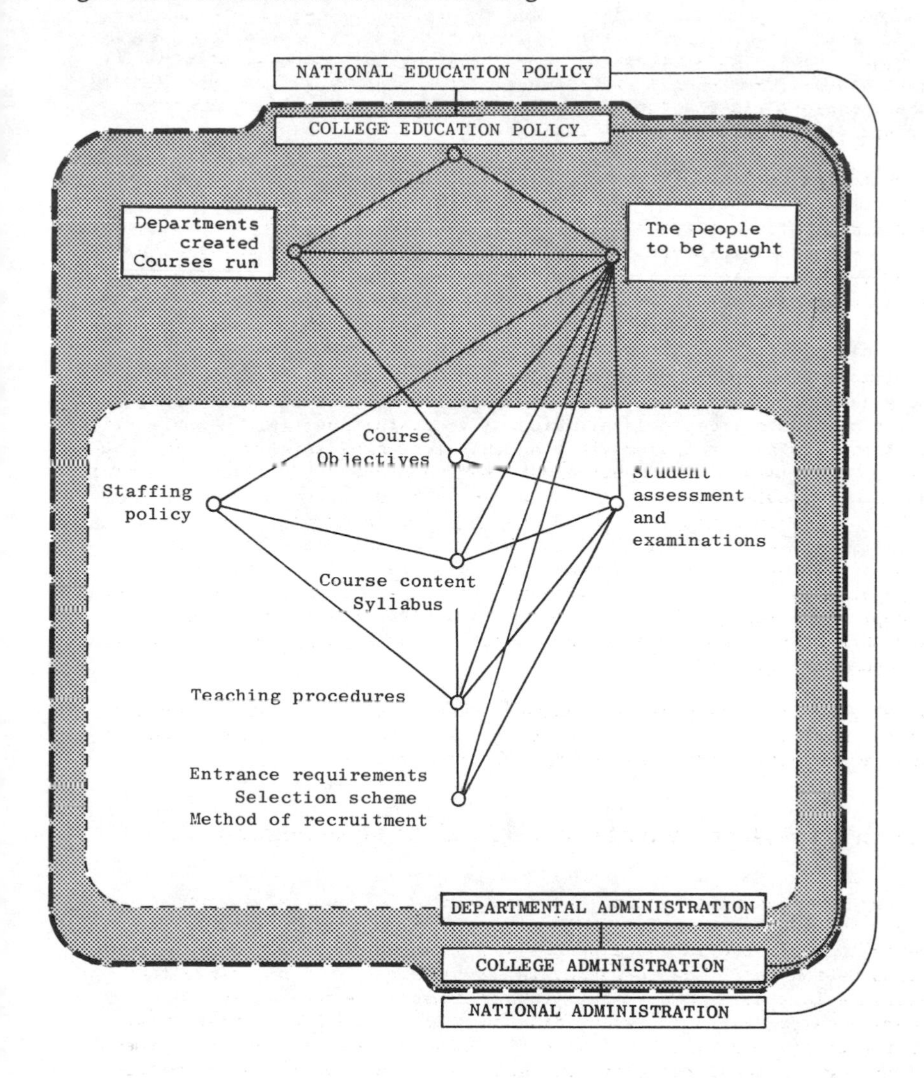

It can reveal decisions which in the past have gone by default. It can suggest procedures that might be adopted to ensure that decisions get made in the right order. It may suggest modifications to the actual organisation of a department so as to ensure that responsibilities are divided sensibly amongst the members of the department and that relevant committees or individuals have access to relevant information.

Conclusion

The models and checklists presented are only examples of ways in which ideas can be organised. If they are good models they will allow the teacher/manager to organise more information than he can hold in his head at any one time. They will reveal decisions that need making and indicate some of the relationships between issues. Some models suggest ways of recording decisions that have been made.
Many more such models could be suggested. The first edition of this book included a model for considering student recruitment and selection. Two other rich sources of this kind of modelling are Fielden and Lockwood, (1973) and Warren Piper and Glatter, (1977).

CHAPTER 7: Evaluation and the Development of Teaching

I. Evaluation of courses

II. Some Paradigms in Evaluation

IV. The Training of Post-Secondary Teachers

V. Conclusion

Chapter 7: Evaluation and the Development of Teaching

I Evaluation of courses

There is no one way to evaluate a course. A course consists of a sequence of many decisions, actions or events. The number of events makes it impossible to evaluate every part. In any case, different types of event require different evaluation methods. For example evaluation of student learning may require a test; student attendance, a register; and teacher style, some means of classifying behaviour recorded on videotape. Furthermore events interact so much that attempts to evaluate one effect of a course will often interfere with others. There is an observer effect. Evaluation is always selective and relies a good deal on intelligent guesswork and inference. This means that evaluators require skills to interpret information they collect, and should always be ready to say when they cannot do so.

(1) Five elements in decisions

In a sense, most of this book has been about evaluation of certain decisions in the design of courses. There are five elements in each of these decisions: (a) aims, (b) general principles, (c) perception of specific circumstances, (d) a choice, and (e) implementation.

(a) The teacher's *aims and objectives for the course* imply a set of values. They may be expressed as 'wants', 'intentions', 'desires', 'oughts' or in any other value words. They can only be justified or evaluated with reference to a general philosophy of education. This subject is beyond the scope of this book, but was introduced briefly in Chapter I.

(b) There are *general principles* to implement these aims. They have the form:

> if you want to achieve X in circumstances Y
> then it is usually best to do Z

In effect this can be re-expressed:

> if you do Z, in circumstances Y,
> X will usually result. (see fig.7.1)

Such generalisations should be based upon evidence or upon ideas that can be justified. It is evidence to support generalisations that most teachers lack and that most of this book seeks to provide. In particular the chapters on assessment, student selection and teaching methods attempt to condense a large body of evidence from which teachers can derive their own general principles. The chapters on course content and administration attempt to suggest ideas from which the reader may also form his own principles

(c) General principles can only be successfully applied in relevant circumstances, and have to be perceived as relevant by the teacher. Principles apply in a context. The particular context imposes constraints.

Figure 7.1: A Dynamic Decision Model

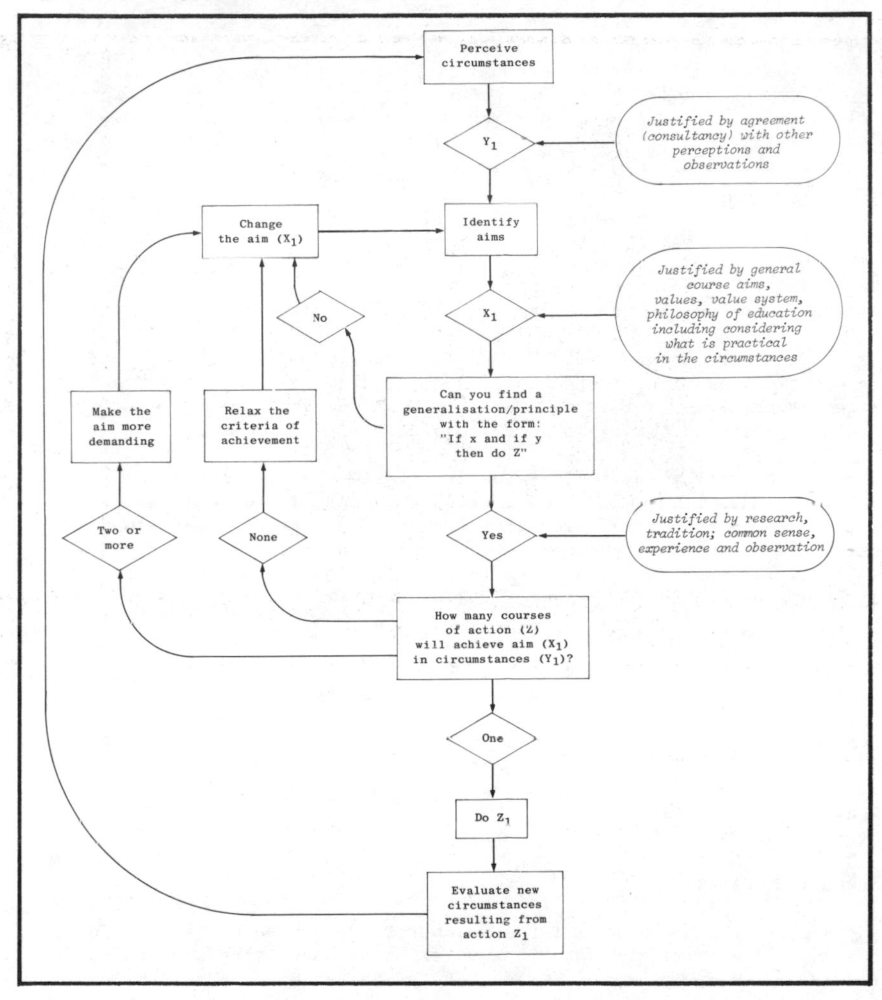

Decision tasks are boxed in rectangles; decisions taken are in diamonds; and their justification is in clouds.

X_1, Y_1 and Z_1 stand for particular instances of aims (X), set of circumstances (Y) and courses of action (Z) respectively.

Y may include the students' knowledge, the resources available, the teacher's preferences, the student's assessment etc.

When, in the circumstances, no generalisation can be applied, the teacher does not have to abandon his aim (X_1), he may aim (X_2) to change the circumstances in which he has to work. He may only change his immediate aim.

The assessment of the situation requires *perceptual skill* to recognise what is, and what is not, likely to be effective. It is possible to evaluate a teacher's perceptual skill against other observations.

Section I(4) in this chapter describes some of the methods that have been used by evaluators. It appreciates the social and environmental context in which courses are managed. (Figures 7.7, 7.3, 7.5 and 7.8)

(d) Given that a number of general principles could be perceived as relevant in a particular course, the teacher must make *a choice*. Such choices are not necessarily either right or wrong. They may be more a matter of consistency or preference. Nonetheless a teacher's ability to choose appropriate action can be evaluated.

(e) So, too, can the *implementation* of his decision. Evaluation of how decisions are implemented boils down to studying the teacher's styles, techniques, skills and sub-skills at an ever more detailed level according to how far one wants to go.

Actually the implementation of a decision often requires applying rather more specific principles to even more specific circumstances. So in teaching there is a hierarchy from the very general decisions mostly considered when the course is first discussed and planned, down to the highly specific intentions in the classroom when a teacher corrects a misconception, chooses coloured chalk, praises a weak student, pauses for a moment, and so on. All these involve decisions that can be evaluated. The multitude of small decisions could in theory be evaluated separately, but it is easier to group them together and regard them as constituting the teacher's style.

Each decision has its aim, general principle, perception of specific circumstances, choice and implementations. In principle any of these could be evaluated. Any could fall short of the standards the teacher might wish to attain.

(2) Evaluating aims

It can sometimes be helpful for a teacher to recognise his aims more clearly. It is all too easy to lose sight of underlying aims in the pressure of everyday work. Consequently evaluation of a teacher's aims often has to be done by an independent evaluator. It would require a teacher to have a very detached mind to make a balanced evaluation of his own values. He could normally only do this by comparing them with those of others or with some ideal.

In practice, most independent evaluators would not wish to judge a teacher against values imposed by them. They are more concerned to describe, than to judge. Nonetheless they may, and in my opinion should, try to find out how a teacher justifies his values and moral principles. An independent evaluator may use several different methods. They all share the basic difficulty that a teacher's values are internal and private to him. The evaluator must elicit them.

(a) Written statements
Values may be elicited simply by asking the teacher to write them down. For example, in Britain, the Council for National Academic Awards expects teachers seeking validation of their courses to set out their objectives in this way. Of course, the considered words a teacher may write to impress the evaluation committee may be vague on some points and omit others.

(b) Exploration by interview
The use of an interview technique may go deeper and exact more clarity and precision. Points omitted can be raised.

These two methods may be used to evaluate the teacher's intentions, irrespective of whether he has so far carried them out. In other words they may be used in "formative evaluation" (which helps to formulate decisions yet to be implemented) or in "summative evaluation" (which is retrospective).

(c) Inferences from behaviour
Another approach is to ignore what a teacher says he intends, and try to infer his values from what he does. This approach can only be retrospective. The critical incident technique, in which the evaluator considers what the teacher did on a particular occasion can be helpful provided the incident was not exceptional. This technique usually needs to be combined with an interview or some other consultative method.

(d) Underlying values used in justificiation
An evaluator may work with a teacher to make underlying values explicit. This can be done by seeking their justification. A teacher's aims usually form a hierarchy from the broad aims of a course design to the intentions behind minute details of teaching behaviour. Each aim can be justified by the next most general aim in the hierarchy combined with some factual information. For example, a lecturer may want his students to know something of the forces at work in the Zambian economy, because he wants them to understand the interaction of economic forces in the Third World, because he wants them to be able to apply the principles of economic interaction in other contexts, because.....

One difficulty in eliciting higher order aims is that when asked to justify values most people only give factual support: "the Zambian economy illustrates the interaction of the forces in the Third World", "the principles of interaction in the Third World can be applied in other contexts" and so on. Evaluators require dispassionate understanding, and skill in questioning combined with some philosophical ability to overcome difficulties of this kind.

(e) Clarification and resolution of conflicts
It can be helpful for an evaluator to make conflicting aims explicit. In practice we cannot avoid conflicting values. No-one has discovered the perfect philosophy of life. In post-secondary education there are some well known conflicts. Do we educate for depth or breadth of knowledge? How far should our courses be vocational or liberal? Should they focus upon the discipline of the subject or the needs of

the students? What is the best distribution of expenditure between different courses?

The aims a teacher chooses to disclose are not always the most dominant or important, and independent evaluators need a sympathetic understanding of this point. For many teachers, prestige, social advancement and acceptance by colleagues are the most important aims. A teacher may also be forced to adopt conflicting aims if he must satisfy a head of department or Faculty Board with aims different from his own.

Most evaluators seek to work within the value system of those they seek to assist. They need educational empathy. Of course an evaluator will have his own aims, but it is no help to a teacher to be given recommendations alien to his thinking. Hence evaluation of aims usually involves clarifications rather than recommendations.

Yet this empathy, and evaluation itself, assumes certain values. An evaluation could aim to improve efficiency, teaching effectiveness, academic standards, the breadth of choice open to the teacher, acceptance by colleagues and professional accountability. These aims are not necessarily in conflict, but they may require different methods.

(3) Evaluating general principles used

We all take decisions on the basis of general principles. This is not an empirical truth; if the decisions are rational, it is a logical necessity. Neither the decisions, nor their underlying principles, are necessarily conscious or explicit. It is sometimes the role of an evaluator to make them so.

Decisions are taken in a general context of ideas and information. Information reduces uncertainty. It can be used to explain decisions made. Insofar as there are no reasons for preferring one choice to another, decisions are arbitrary, random and irrational.

It should be noticed that because educational decisions involve choices, much of the most important information is comparative. It compares the outcomes of possible courses of action or factors influencing those outcomes.

One difficulty in justifying educational decisions is that their general principles are almost always based on partial information. Consequently general principles are never absolutely certain. They are always probabilistic. This is because the circumstances upon which they are based can never be exactly the same as those in which they are applied. The question in education is always whether a decision is *reasonable* in the light of information available; not whether it is certain.

The problem of generalisability lies at the centre of many controversies in the field of educational evaluation. How can generalisations be obtained? Answers to this question are controversial and the following six methods are not exhaustive.

(a) Tradition and ritual.
In practice the generalisations that most of us use in education are based on nothing more than tradition and ritual. The pressures for conformity and against innovation are too great.

(b) Common sense
Many educational generalisations are derived from common sense. For example, it is common sense that television can teach a larger number of students at any one time than some other methods. Yet we should remember that the history of education is littered with fallacious concepts once deemed to be 'common sense'.

(c) Experience
Other generalisations are obtained from experience. For example teachers who observe the consequences of their decision may reflect on possible causes. This requires thinking back through their own experience, searching available data and seeking other information. This is sometimes called "causal comparative" or "ex-post facto" reasoning. The selection and interpretation of experience is obviously open to subjective error. The method also requires teachers to be constantly thinking about their teaching and reflecting on it; but the pace of work usually prevents this.

The fact that a general principle expresses a relationship,

if ..... in circumstances Y, then .....,

means that any attempt to evaluate that generalisation requires studying both sides of the relation. Similarly, insofar as generalisations are comparative, evaluation of them requires looking at both sides of the comparison. This is more complex than verifying the truth of a simple fact and the range of methods is correspondingly restricted.

(d) The traditional experimental paradigm
In the 1960s it was often assumed that the traditional experimental paradigm could produce generalisations as valid as those in psychology. It has also been assumed by too many critics of this view that every experimenter adopts a hypothesis testing approach. There are several standard criticisms of the traditional hypothesis testing paradigm when borrowed from the physical sciences and applied to education.

(i) Replication
The first is that any set of experimental conditions can never be exactly replicated. There are always differences in time, space, subject matter or the people involved.

(ii) Control
When possibly influential interactions between these variables are taken into account, absolute experimental control is impossible. It is also impossible because people in educational situations are unpredictable.

(iii) Restricted hypotheses
Experimental methods usually necessitate hypotheses that are too narrow

in that the decision maker must relate them to other hypotheses as well as specific circumstances before they can be applied. A given experiment can usually only test a limited number of hypotheses.

(iv) Manipulation
The belief that experimental designs require people to be pre-programmed has contributed to an almost emotional reaction against experimental methods in the 1970s. This is sometimes connected with popular views about free will, control and determinism.

(v) Explanatory value
Since there could always be many explanations of an experimental result, no experiment will prove one explanation to be true. According to the scientific experimental paradigm, progress is made when a hypothesis or explanation is shown to be false. But in education, because experimental conditions cannot be well controlled, it is always difficult to be sure that an explanation is false. However, it may be replied that the fact that a hypothesis can never be finally proved true or false does not rule out successive approximation towards one or the other. In education, as in applied science, we take decisions upon the information we have. The immediate task is to take a decision and experimental observations, even if only partially controlled, are better than incidental observations and no control at all. Obtaining the ultimate truth is probably impossible.

(vi) Generalisability
The lack of perfect control can lead to apparently contradictory results.

(e) Correlational analyses
Correlational analyses can be informative in the context of gradually building up a picture. The causal mechanism is unimportant except insofar as it may inform a decision maker of the limits of a generalisation.

(f) Descriptive surveys
Descriptive surveys also provide important opportunities towards generalisations in education provided sufficient data is gathered. Descriptive surveys may use many techniques to gather the data including questionnaire or interview methods. The difficulty is that most descriptions are too specific to form the basis of generalisation. In practice they are more usually used to show the limitations of applying generalisations. Consequently descriptive methods are more important to evaluate teachers' perceptions of these constraints.

(4) Evaluation of a teacher's perceptions of course constraints

It is clear that course decisions could be inappropriate because the circumstances were not what the teacher supposed. Specific circumstances can be unpredictable. They can create constraints which prevent the successful application of general principles. The teacher's perception of them might be in error. For example the students might not have the background knowledge he assumed. The equipment for the laboratory session might not have arrived as early as expected. The size of the class may have been unusually great. Regulations may not have been what he thought. Recent changes or discoveries may have necessitated last minute changes in the syllabus. The timetable may have been very inconvenient. Some personality or chance event may have soured personal relationships and administrative confusion may have got the course off to a bad start.

There could be any number of such specific circumstances which a teacher did not, or could not, have perceived when first planning the course. Similarly when teaching a class there could be all manner of student reactions, difficulties in the subject matter or administrative hindrances which the teacher did not perceive.

It is obviously impossible to evaluate every conceivable misperception of the specific circumstances in which a teacher works. The list could be extended indefinitely and the act of evaluation would seriously interfere with what was being evaluated.

Some diagnostic procedure is required. It is a question of recognising the constraints of specific circumstances. The evaluator has at least four groups of questions to check the teacher's perceptions. These are the questions attempted by the methods listed in Figures 7.2, 7.3, 7.5, and 7.8. There is no suggestion that the Figures are complete. The number of questions that could be asked is infinite.

(a) What are the consequences of the course and why?
The first and most obvious diagnostic test is to ask how far objectives have been achieved. Related questions might include "What do the students learn?", "Which, of two or more procedures, result in the greatest achievement?", "How do student dropout and absenteeism compare with other courses?", "How do students change and develop during the course?" and "What are its long term effects?". Some answers to these questions could be obtained by studying examination results and course work, conducting experimental comparisons on teaching methods, collecting data on dropout and absenteeism, comparing a large sample of students across different years of study, and repeatedly testing the students to plot their long term development.

However, these answers are limited in their usefulness. Insofar as objectives have not been achieved, something is unsatisfactory; but the converse is not necessarily true. Objectives can be achieved in spite of defects in a course. For example, when teaching in one subject is poor, students often compensate by devoting extra private study time to that subject.

Another objection is that the methods proposed concentrate on the most easily measured objectives and neglect those, like attitudes and interpersonal relationships, which are important but not so easily quantified.

It may also be objected that the consequences evaluated by examination results, student dropout and so on, may be too global; but they need not be. The difficulty when considering global consequences is that in most cases, it is not possible to say what aspects of a course are most influential. A teacher can only guess from some correspondence between his doing one thing and the occurrence of another. Global

Figure 7.2:
Methods to study the consequences of course decisions

METHOD	EXAMPLES	PURPOSE OF EXAMPLE	ADVANTAGES	DISADVANTAGES
Examination results and Tests of Learning	Standardised scholastic Attainment Tests in USA	To evaluate course achievement	A direct measure of achievement when criterion referenced tests are used	Course evaluation confounded with student assessment
Course work	As in Contingency Management Courses (see page	To find out difficulties and assess learning	Minimum observer effects	
Longitudinal development	Bennington Study To observe changes in students' open-mindedness during a course (Feldman & Newcomb 1973.)	To observe change over a long period	Individual variables controlled in before, after and delayed observations. Observes general effects	Unique sample? Lengthy and costly. Delayed results can't influence or be generalised. Requires long cooperation - observer effects
Cross-sectional study	To observe differences between year groups of students (Feldman & Newcomb 1973.)	To infer changes during the years of a student's course	Data obtained at one time	Assumes comparability between year groups
Statistical tests upon course data	To correlate course attendance with course performance, or place of residence with hours of work	To find associations between variables influencing achievement of course objectives	Quantitative Relative objectivity. Distinguishes significant differences from chance variations	Statistical expertise needed Suitability of test
Experiments	Comparison of two ways of sequencing course content	To compare the effects of two or more teaching conditions (sets of circumstances)	Maximum practical control of irrelevant factors Relatively rigorous	Artificial data and conditions Perfect control impossible Evaluator requires training
Quazi Experimental Designs	Compare the performance of students with one, and more than one, major subject	To find the relative difficulty of single and combined honours degrees	Minimal artificiality	Variables uncontrolled
Description of Behaviour/ Performance	Plot time of dropout	To find out extent and nature of any course dissatisfactions	Behaviour not artificially contrived	Observer effect

consequences are usually too imprecise to claim, without some artificiality, that there is a correlation, still less a causal connection, between one event and another.

However the methods suggested in Figure 7.2 on page 234 are more appropriate when an evaluator does not attempt to evaluate a whole course, but only one small part of it in detail. The detail includes plotting the interaction of all the factors which might possibly influence the part being considered. If the part is not small enough, the detail will soon be too great. The teacher may feel that such an evaluation will only tell him something of little consequence; but this is better than telling him nothing through attempting evaluations of great consequence.

We may conclude that achievement tests and similar measures of the consequences of a course are important because they may indicate the urgency and seriousness of course defects; but they do not rule out the need for further enquiry nor demonstrate where the defects occur. These methods are rather like taking a patient's temperature; it is a sensible first step, but it is insufficient for diagnosis. One can be ill with a normal temperature. Further specific and more detailed tests are necessary. But how are these to be chosen?

(b) Seeking feelings and opinions

To narrow the choice in medicine, it is a natural next step to question the patient, beginning with how he feels and then working towards more detailed questions. In the same way, the use of consultations with staff, questionnaires and interviews with students, or enquiries amongst others involved in the course, are amongst the natural next steps to narrow the field when evaluating courses. But even this assumes the enquiry has been narrowed to certain hypotheses or to knowledge of what questions to ask. In practice there is usually no difficulty because teachers seeking an evaluation are usually willing to state an area of interest. Similarly, if students are asked to state what, in their view, are the best and worst features of a course, general agreement about weak features can assist the direction of enquiry.

Thus, as in any research, there is a gradual narrowing and focussing upon specifiable problems. Yet if we are to ensure that attention is eventually focussed on the most important issues, it is necessary to begin by considering a wide range of possible misperceptions. For this reason the evaluator will begin by using unstructured interviews and open-ended questionnaires. Only later will he use rating scales, sharply focussed questions and evaluation methods used for specific problems. An evaluator may begin with very non-directive questions and finish with an instrument as specific as a course component dependency table (see Figure 7.4). In between he may use fairly structured interviews or questionnaires to find out subjective information from the students, for example "What are their objectives in taking the course?", "What is the intellectual challenge of the course?", "How is it structured?", "Why did they apply to this university?", "What were their expectations?" and so on. The technique of asking staff and students to rank the importance of certain objectives (previously obtained from pilot interviews) is a way of studying the compatibility of staff and student objectives (see Table 7.3).

Figure 7.3: Methods seeking feelings and opinions

METHOD	EXAMPLES	PURPOSE OF EXAMPLE	ADVANTAGES	DISADVANTAGES
Free response opinionnaires	to obtain students' reactions to proposed course changes	To gather personal opinions and answers to general questions	Wide coverage of topics Easy to administer Large samples	Vague questions Unsystematic answers Difficult to interpret and generalise responses Partial response
Restricted response question-naires and Rating scales	a) College environment questionnaires (see page 72)	To compare college norms, values, life styles	as below	as below
	b) Students' judgements of a course	To obtain relative judgements	Easy to administer Quick to complete Wide range of judgements obtainable Can compare group responses Quantifies judgements	Doubtful validity Questionnaire designs often poor Selectivity of questions Individuals' standards vary Quantification easily abused and misinterpreted
Compatibility of student and teacher preferences	Compare student and teacher objectives	Diagnose conflicts eg in goals and motives	Legitimises student aims Conflicts explicit Co-operation possible	Restricted to paired preferences
Course component dependency table	See *Figure 7.4*	What parts of the course depend upon what other parts	Obtain students' views	Ignores logic of the subjects Data slow to obtain
Structured interviews	a) Students obtain views for "Alternative Prospectus" b) Public opinion of universities	To obtain answers to questions important to the interviewer	Random sample Spontaneous response Anonimity Independent evaluator	
Unstructured interview	Informed discussion with teachers or students about a course, method or incident	To obtain perceptions To learn what is important to others	Individual non-quantifiable subjective data obtained	Skill required Small sample time Content validity untestable
Colleague feedback	Study Methods Counsellor informs teacher of students' anxieties	To inform teacher's perceptions of students	Use of intermediary Trusted colleagues can convey sensitive information	Creates ambiguous colleague relationships
Teachers' subjective judgement	Impressionistic mid-term course evaluation	To decide whether to invite independent evaluation	No observer effect Synthesise and interpret impressions unspecifiable in advance Unique participant observer	Biased observer

Subject Given Help (made easier)

Figure 7.4

Subject Giving Help	1470-1750-	1750-1940	Harmony and Counter-point	Analysis	Mini Recital	Mean Rating of help given
Music 1470-1750		3.4	3.4	3.5	2.6	3.2
Music 1750-1940	2.6		3.9	4.0	3.3	3.4
Musical Technique Harmony and Counterpoint	3.8	3.9		4.1	2.1	3.5
Analysis	3.6	4.4	3.7		2.2	3.5
Mini Recital	2.4	2.8	2.4	2.2		2.4
Mean Rating of help given by other subjects	3.1	3.6	3.3	3.4	2.5	

Students were asked how far their preparation for the row examination helped their preparation for the column examination.
Ratings are on a 5-point scale.

(c) What happens?
A third way to assess the validity of the perceptions which influence a teacher's decisions, is to obtain independent observations of what actually happens on a course. Just as the doctor may seek a description of how an accident occurred, how the disease has developed and whether the pain has got worse, so the educational evaluator may seek descriptions of what actually happens on a course. These descriptions gradually build up a picture when related to general principles, common sense, the evaluator's experience and research findings. They eliminate some explanations of what has happened as much as suggesting others.

Just as the doctor will increasingly supplement the patient's account with his own specialised techniques of observation, the educational evaluator will do the same. The specialised technique varies with what is to be observed.

For example an evaluator may compare a teacher's weekly record of a course - the subjects taught, work set, received, marked and returned - with published syllabuses, student diaries (see Figure 7.6) and the timing of a course using a course mapping technique (see Figure 7.7). Similarly the expected pattern of a teacher's duties as specified in a job description could be compared with an analysis of his day to day workload obtained from his diary and compared with general observations. Some indication of the nature of a course from the student's point of view can be obtained from time costing the literature he must read and the assignments he must carry out against the time available. Particularly in large departments, course defects occur when necessary information is not passed on or disseminated. Very little research has been done on how course information is disseminated. Most students discover

Figure 7.5: Methods to study what happens on a course

METHOD	EXAMPLES	PURPOSE OF EXAMPLE	ADVANTAGES	DISADVANTAGES
Diaries	a) UK Committee of Vice-Chancellors' Report ( ) b) Student diaries to find out how long students work	To record and classify what a person does	Relatively private and detailed information obtained	Dubious accuracy of records Classification Co-operation/ motivation of person required
Workload analysis	Compare job description and work diary	Obtain data to assist planning Compare with other students, teachers and professions	Some objectivity Comparisons possible	Selectivity of data Time and cost of observation and data collection
Case Study (of one example in detail)	Nuffield Newsletters Nos. 1 - 7 (1973-75)	To stimulate ideas and/or illustrate them Exploration	Easily compiled useful background information	How typical? Subjective bias Often voluminous, irrelevant and timewasting
Case Analysis (of many examples)	Marton on Study Methods	Exploration	Generalisations possible without selective data collection	Evaluator imposes assumption How analyse/extract common elements Laborious
Census	Student data	To compare this year's students with previous years' or national figures	Adjust teaching to students	Low predictive validity in most subjects Records don't include suitable data Non-quantitative records time consuming to compare
Critical Incident Technique	Investigation of a) a student's suicide b) selection of a course tutor	In depth study to show the complex interactions in specific circumstances	Considers detail	Generalisability from one incident How was it critical?
Literature analysis	a) List technical vocabulary students must learn b) Library searches c) Page counts	To assess course literature	Public data Considers subject matter	Cross disciplinary comparisons difficult Subjective interpretation
Teacher's records	Records of subjects taught, attendance, marks obtained, difficulties experienced, unexpected events, constraints etc.	To view a complete account of selected aspects of a course	Observations: made at the time throughout a course interfere little	Is the information relevant, too selective and meticulously collected?

METHOD	EXAMPLES	PURPOSE OF EXAMPLE	ADVANTAGES	DISADVANTAGES
Operational research	Plot information flows between both teachers and students	To study the procedure of planning and implementing a course	Clarity Makes procedures and assumptions explicit Testable	Inferences from data limited
Special instruments	a) Flanders interaction b) VTR c) Audiotapes	Observation and/ or measurement of student-teacher interaction	Relative objectivity Detail and analysis possible	Experts often required Restricted application
Library records	a) List of books borrowed b) Records of library attendance (see *Figure 7.11*)	To find out how and why students use the library	Quantitative a) topic specific b) time specific	Time consuming Students may use other sources for books
Record of selected events	a) Wish to change courses Contact between staff and students b) Lateness in handing in course work c) Types of tutorial contribution	Quantify occurrence of specific events/ incidents	Focuses on one type of event	Interpretation Selected sample of events may be unrepresentative
Documentary analysis	Headteacher's reports (Entwistle & Wilson 1972) Letters of application Committee membership Calendar Regulations	To evaluate non-quantifiable data To assess values, conceptions of education To assess who controls the course	Wide variety of information considered. Categories of data not necessarily assumed before collection	Not quantitative Interpretive skill required Subjective
Action research	A teacher's day to day self-evaluation	a) To develop skills b) To observe actions and their consequences to suggest solutions to problems	Deals with non-classifiable data Considers participants' perspectives	Objectivity validity and selectivity of observations doubtful
Course mapping	Plot on a date planner objectives to be achieved during a course	Students monitor own practice Shows connections of inter-disciplinary courses	Overview of course Easy to carry out	
Participant observation/ Description	Students give feedback on teaching style	Teacher self-awareness	Not over selective data. Observer effect low. Insider's experience. Non-verbal and non-quantitative data possible.	Subjective impressionistic

Figure 7.6: A specimen sheet from a student diary (Bligh, 1977)

17/11/76

Name ....

This page is dividied according to the hours of the day. Please record what you did during each particular hour. You may subdivide for short activities if you wish, or block off sections where appropriate (e.g. sleep). Please complete this form each day; do not wait to do several days at a time. Please answer frankly. This questionnaire is confidential between you and the Director of Teaching Services. You should hand it to him when you meet on .... at a.m./p.m.

DAY Hour	15	30	45	Hour
M'night				
1		SLEEP		
2				
3				
4				
5				
6				
7	Listening (Radio 3)			
8	Breakfast		Reading	
9	Reading			
10	READING			
11				to Queen's Building.
12	20th CENTURY	GERMAN	LITERATURE	LECTURE.
13	LUNCH		Correspondence	
14	Laundry			
15		to Music Department	Instrumental	practice
16	Instrumental practice			
17	TEA		Listening	
18	Reading			
19	Reading		to Great Hall	CHAMBER ORCHESTRA REHEARSAL
20	SYMPHONY	ORCHESTRA	REHEARSAL	
21	"	"	"	
22	back to Birks	Conversation		
23	Conversation			And so to bed. M'night

It is usually possible to classify the diary entries under headings like these adapted for particular subjects.

- F Formal teaching in music including lectures, seminars, tutorials and instrumental teaching.
- C Formal class teaching in non-music subjects. (Combined honours and additional music students)
- W Music work. Independent study in music.
- O Other work. Independent study in non-music subjects. (Combined honours and additional music students).
- X Extra-departmental musical activities, including practice and performances with the orchestra, choral society, operatic societies, and instrumental groups.
- R Informal recreation including having coffee with friends, visiting another's residence, "chatting with friends" and informal discussion.
- R̲ Formal recreation not included in X. Includes visits to the theatre, cinema, poetry readings, church and other organised activities.
- T Travel, including journey to work, walking between departments (combined honours). Journeys to Dartington and travel for shopping purposes.
- D Domestic. including getting dressed, having a bath, cooking, eating, cleaning, and any other activity essential to everyday life not classified elsewhere.
- S Sleep. Rest during the day was also counted as sleep.
- M Miscellaneous, including the introduction to the enquiry given by the Director of Teaching Services.

that the most valuable information does not appear in syllabuses and notice boards but is passed on by senior students, derived from past examination papers, detected from hints in tutorials and so on.

It is obviously impossible to observe everything that happens on a course. Some sampling techniques are required, but sampling assumes that the evaluator has already narrowed his field of enquiry. For example the critical incident technique attempts to describe an incident in detail and then ascribe causes and consequences to it; but part of this task has been done when deciding that the incident is critical. Marton (1976) has used detailed analysis of interviews on study methods to describe what happens when students read a text on economics, but an analysis of the tape recordings and categorising what was said assumes hypotheses of what categories are relevant. The same is true of any attempt to record selected events such as smiles and eye contact between teachers and students, requests to change courses, lateness in submitting work, absenteeism and so on.

There are always limitations to the inferences that can be placed upon sampled observations; but this does not render them useless. There is no absolute proof in educational evaluation. It is always

Figure 7.7: Evaluation in Course Design.

In the picture above the author is using a course mapping technique to assist a professor design the sequence of topics within a one-year postgraduate course in population studies. Every topic is described on cards - one card for every hour of teaching. The professor's initial proposals have been stuck on the wall display. A complete duplicate set of cards is laid out on a line of tables in front of the display. The duplicate set can be rearranged to try out new ideas for sequencing the course, while the wall display remains undisturbed for comparison. The author is seen noting problems in what has been proposed, possible solutions and the professor's reasoning as he modifies the original sequence.

Each vertical column represents a week. Each contributor (i.e. tutor) to the course is represented with a different coloured card. Notice, the needs of the students and the logic of the subject do not require tutors to teach at regular weekly intervals throughout the course. Notice the two-week orientation module on the left, and that there are self-paced weeks with no teaching when students can catch-up if necessary, go on fieldwork, complete assignments or read around the subject. The last six weeks are mostly project work.

impressionistic. For example if recommended textbooks are rarely borrowed from the library, it does not follow that students do not read the recommended books. They may possess their own copies or read library editions without borrowing them. In one study at Exeter it was found that students preferred to use the City Library for some purposes. This brings us to a brief consideration of resources.

(d) What are the teacher's resources?
Resources are major course constraints. A teacher's perception and evaluation of his resources, and how they can be used, limits the decisions he can take. His options are restricted to what he thinks is possible. An evaluator may wish to check these perceptions independently.

Constraints on resources may be physical or human. Physical resources include the provision of libraries, staff workrooms, computers, recreational facilities, facilities for research, student accommodation, laboratories, buildings and finance. Human resources include the imagination and intellectual skills of the teacher himself, the social climate in which he works, the support of his head of department, the number and quality of students, the opportunity to further his knowledge by teaching, study, scholarship or research, the degree of teamwork between staff, the support of technical, illustrative, secretarial and maintenance staff, and the structure and academic organisation of the institution.

What are the teacher's resources?

Relevant Methods listed in Figure 7.2, 7.3 & 7.5 (e.g. Survey methods) are not repeated here

Figure 7.8

METHOD	EXAMPLES	PURPOSE OF EXAMPLE	ADVANTAGES	DISADVANTAGES
Inventory	How many books	To find out quantity	Quantitative Replication possible	Time-consuming Data limited use
Simulation	Trial leasing of word processor	To see whether resource can and will be used	Practical	How similar?
Modelling	Model committee structure	To ensure the optimum use of resources	Theoretical tryout before implementation	The assumptions of models are always questionable
Accountancy	Calculation of costs of new teaching method	To compare with cost of previous method		
Specialist opinion	Advice on the best computer to buy	To judge the quality of resources	Informed judgement	Experts disagree Academics delegate their freedom and responsibility

Evaluation of each of these things typically involves consideration of their quantity, quality, use and cost. Let us take library provision as an example. The amount of provision may be partly judged by an inventory counting the number of books relevant to a particular course, noting of which texts there are multiple copies, estimating the student: book ratio, and interpreting the balance between books and journals.

However the inventory carries little weight without a value judgement on the quality of the resources. Are the books up to date? Are various schools of thought in the subject fairly represented? Are the texts appropriate to the course? These value judgements do not supersede those implied by the aims of the course (see page 228); the aims are their context.

Evaluation of the use of resources has two facets: *can* they be used, and are they? For example, 'Does the location of the library hinder its use?', 'When is it open in non-timetable hours?', 'Are books openly accessible?', 'What systems of loan, reserve and reference exist?', 'Can recommended books be easily found?', and 'Are library staff welcoming and helpful?'. These are questions primarily about how far a library can be used. But, as we saw on page 141, opportunities are not always used. To evaluate this facet of his course a teacher may want to find out how far students read recommended books, how often they visit the library, at what times reading spaces and study accommodation are used (see for example Figure 7.11) and how many books the average student borrows per year, and which ones.

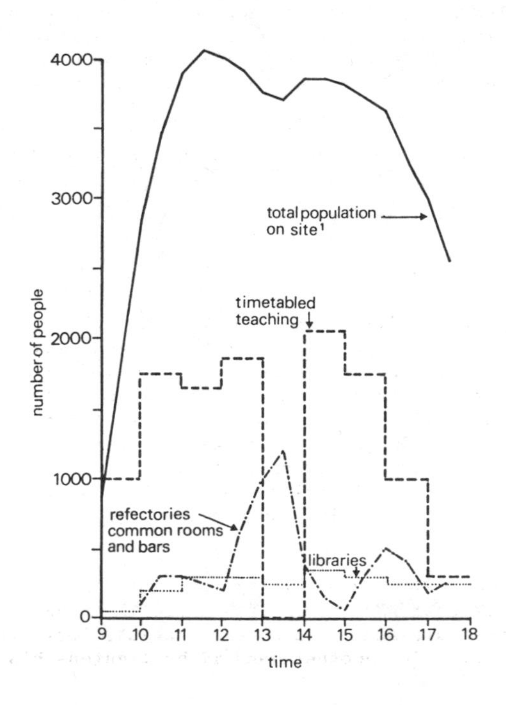

Figure 7.9: A day's activities at University College, London

(This was part of a study carried out at University College, London, giving some indication of the day time use of space during the College, including use of the library.)

1. Total population on site includes students, academic, administrative and support staff.

Some idea of the costs of resources may be obtained from simple accounting procedures, but the economics of teaching is outside the scope of this book. Questions of cost-benefit are difficult to answer and the answers have obvious limitations. The benefits are often uncertain and intangible. Only indirect approaches are possible. Nonetheless they can open avenues of enquiry for an evaluator. What is the cost of library services per credit obtained? (See O'Neill, 1971). How do courses compare in their ratio of costs to usage? Are there alternative methods of providing reading material, for example, a folder of essential reading selected and produced for a particular course?

When evaluating any resources, or when recommending changes in their use, the choice of resource, its quantity, quality, use and cost are interacting factors. This is particularly true of human resources. One factor omitted from consideration is the unit of production; but Baumol and Bowen (1972) have commented that teaching is one of the performing arts. It is as nonsensical to expect increasing production when increasing costs as to expect a Beethoven quartet to be played in half the time if you double the musicians' pay. The analogy is questionable but as Bowen and Douglass (1971) have remarked, cost-effectiveness in teaching is normally made not by increasing production, but by modifying resources in one or more of nine ways. High cost employees may be replaced by cheaper labour, for example most college teachers do some work which might be done just as well by secretaries or assistant teachers. Staff may be used more intensively. Students may be required to take more responsibility for their own learning. Capital may be substituted for labour, for example by using mechanical teaching aids in place of lectures. There could be more intensive use of capital, particularly buildings and equipment. The teacher may have to accept cheap equipment. Expensive components of the curriculum could be phased out and overhead costs could either be reduced or, by increasing student numbers, spread more thinly.

One conclusion will be clear from the methods of evaluation listed in Figures 7.2, 7.3, 7.5 and 7.8 it is always impossible to evaluate every part of a course. Evaluation is always partial.

(5) Evaluating the teacher's choice of actions

In practice a knowledge of general principles and the particular circumstances in which they must be applied to achieve an objective, may not be enough. More than one general principle may be applicable in a particular set of circumstances, or none at all. The teacher needs to choose one. For example, imagine that a teacher *aims* to teach certain information. He *generalises* from the research literature that he may do so by one of three methods: lecturing, prescribed reading and television. He *perceives* that his television facilities are poor. So he must choose between lecturing and recommending specific readings. (see Fig. 7.1 page 226).

This choice can be evaluated. It is made by tightening the aims or criteria. For example the teacher may say that he wants to teach the information as cheaply as possible and, as a generalisation, lecturing is cheaper with large classes. On the other hand if he tightens his aim by wanting students to be able to solve certain problems as well as acquiring information, he may prefer recommending reading because he can usually add some problem solving tasks. In this example aims are tightened, that is they are made more demanding, because more than one general principle seems applicable. When there is no general way of achieving what a teacher wants, his aim must be slackened until one, and only one, general principle can be applied. (see Fig. 7.1 page 226)

Thus a teacher is continually selecting one, and only one, action by modifying his aims in the light of methodological generalisations and the constraints he perceives in a particular case. In everyday life he makes these choices with great rapidity without consciously specifying aims, generalisations and constraints. For this reason, as we have seen, choices may be evaluated under these three headings, but there is a fourth.

Choices of action can be evaluated on the basis of their rationality. The choice between lecturing and recommending further reading could be made quite irrationally, in the sense that it is inconsistent with other decisions already taken. For example, if a teacher had previously taken a decision on the grounds that his students were not capable of long hours of work, it might be inconsistent to recommend long hours of reading and problem solving now. Similarly another teacher might accept or reject a course of action as a result of prejudice or emotional factors. Most commonly there is insufficient educational evidence to justify a firm generalisation and teachers have to act in the way that is most reasonable and consistent with those generalisations which can be more firmly established. Hence choosing a course of action requires rational judgement. Similarly, when teaching, circumstances are never the same from one occasion to the next. Teachers have to make reasonable guesses at the best thing to do.

However, we could say that a decision was wrong but reasonable. If we say the consequences of an action were disastrous but the teacher could not have known, we draw a sharp distinction between our evaluation of the choice and our judgement of the teacher. We might say that he should know next time, and in this way a teacher's observation of the consequences of his act should be continually modifying his generalisations and his perceptions of specific circumstances. Hence the model shown in Figure 7.1 (see page 226) is a dynamic model. A teacher's aims and knowledge are progressively modified with every action he takes and the manner in which he carries it out. Both decisions themselves and their manner of implementation, change the circumstances in which the teacher works. This leads us to methods to evaluate teaching styles.

(6) Evaluation of teaching styles and techniques

(a) The importance of teaching styles

The way a teaching decision is implemented is a matter of style or technique. A teacher's style is composed of the teaching techniques or skills which he generally uses. Clearly a teacher may use many valuable techniques but still be a poor teacher because of one vitiating fault. Teaching is such a complex interaction of many skills that the use of a few valued techniques does not turn a poor teacher into a good one. The effectiveness of the teacher therefore depends on the combination of techniques he employs to implement his decision. In other words it depends upon his teaching style. Many combinations of teaching techniques may be equally effective, although others may be less so. Thus in the evaluation and development of teaching, although some styles should be discouraged, there is no one style which is better than all the rest. There is no one correct way of teaching which is the embodiment of perfection.

Furthermore the skills of teaching are not only diverse, but conflicting, so that no-one could possess more than a few of them. The extrovert qualities that make one man a good lecturer may make him an insensitive personal tutor. Consequently it is logical nonsense to attempt to describe a teacher's style on a linear scale. A profile system is necessary. This was shown in a small scale study (Simpkins et al, 1972) when evaluations of teaching made by arts students showed that teachers esteemed on one dimension may be poorly regarded on another. Even though there were signs of a 'halo' effect, these students recognised that different teachers had different talents.

This leads us to a very important principle in the evaluation and development of teaching. Teaching requires us to use and develop the talents we have, not to try to be what we are not. Again we shall see that far from there being one right way to teach, some styles are effective precisely because they are different from those usually or recently experienced by students. Too often teachers try to model themselves on someone whose natural abilities may have been quite different.

The principle of teachers' individuality places a responsibility on each individual teacher. If a teacher is to practise his own individual style, a high degree of self-understanding is necessary. For this a gradual process of self-assessment is required together with acceptable educational aims, a knowledge of general principles and evidence such as that described in this book, and the perceptual skill to assess college environments and the social contexts of his work. It should be an integral part of each course that students and colleagues should help each individual teacher discharge this responsibility, but too often the necessary spirit of cooperation is lacking.

Methods of self-assessment are also important for much more fundamental reasons. A teacher who does not know his good and bad techniques cannot choose appropriate teaching methods, he will not know which skills need to be improved and he will not know what objectives he can achieve. Furthermore, he will be unable to teach students how to learn from his particular teaching style. It is fairly obvious that if different teachers have different styles, students will need to adopt different learning strategies with different teachers. With some teachers it is best to take detailed notes, with others to ask questions, with others to read sections of a certain textbook before hearing the teacher on the same topics, with others to think of examples which apply the principles described by the teachers, and so on. Yet most teachers in post-secondary education give students no guidance on what they expect them to do during their teaching. They leave students to find this out for themselves by a painfully inefficient process of trial and error. Many students never do.

All this raises the question 'How can teaching styles be evaluated?', 'What are the important techniques influencing the effectiveness of teaching styles?' and 'What teaching styles are most effective?'

There are two broad methods of evaluating teaching style: by classifying observations and obtaining the subjective opinions and judgements by students and other observers. It cannot be said too strongly that the research method used largely controls the teaching characteristics described, because research methods control the choice of data for consideration. This point has been insufficiently appreciated by those committed solely to rating methods, particularly those who only consider students' ratings. There need to be many more studies using classified observations of teachers' behaviour.

(b) Classified observations of teaching

Explicit and repeatable observations of teachers' behaviour are probably more valid than subjective student ratings. Ryans (1967) made a very large number of observations and identified three basic teaching styles: the friendly, understanding, sympathetic person; the responsible, business-like, systematic style; and the stimulating imaginative teacher. These differences should be seen against the ethos of particular subjects. Part of the purpose of teaching literary subjects is to stimulate the students' imaginations; consequently it is hardly surprising that teachers of these subjects aim to be stimulating and imaginative teachers rather than business-like and systematic. A teacher of accountancy is more likely to be 'responsible, business-like and systematic' while a teacher of social work will wish to be understanding and sympathetic.

Cantrell (1971) analysed the lecturing styles of 30 visiting lecturers at Makere University on 16 parameters including the use of visual aids, the state of the audience, voice qualities, feedback from the audience, thought patterns, inspirational effects and certain personal qualities. The most important quality was the pattern of thought in the lectures, while voice production was the least important. The clarity of the pattern of thought seems to result from careful preparation keeping the fallibility of the audience in mind. Cantrell concluded that the most common faults in lecturing can be put right by training and a more scientific approach to teaching problems. However, since there was only one observer, it is difficult to know how far the results reflect his perceptions or the behaviour of the lecturers.

These two studies only ask 'What differences are there in teachers' styles? They partly reflect the way teaching decisions are implemented and partly the decisions themselves. They don't ask 'What styles are most effective?' Two factors seem to be particularly important stylistic correlates of effective teaching; the ability to explain and some factor involving personal acceptability.

The ability to explain has been investigated by Gage and his colleagues

(1968) at the University of Stanford not by observing differences in style and then looking to see if they were different in effectiveness, but the other way round. They looked for differences in style between periods of teaching known to contrast in effectiveness. They recorded a very large number of lectures on the same subjects, obtaining measures of students' comprehension and ratings by both students and trained judges on a very large number of scales. They also obtained objective measures of lecture style including linguistic usage, the use of gestures, speed of delivery and a host of other variables. Gage found that ratings of explaining effectiveness correlated highly with comprehension scores, but Unruh could not find any single factor that was consistently significantly related. However in addition to the importance of gesture and movement, Rosenshine found two factors important in effective explanation. The first was the frequency with which objects, events and principles were related, particularly by words such as "because", questions asking "why", and statements giving cause and effect or comparisons. He also found that teachers who presented a rule followed by examples and finished by a restatement of the rule, obtained higher comprehension scores from their students. Linguistic categories, such as word length, the length of clauses, the structure of sentences and the use of prepositional phrases, discriminated effective from ineffective teachers. The use of visual teaching, the speed of delivery and pauses were also related to teaching success. Dell and Hiller (1971) showed that successful explanations often involved a task orientation for the students, used words which stated problems clearly, used a high proportion of proper nouns and stated relationships between elements of the subject. Conversely, they discovered many phrases which produced vagueness. These included ambiguous designations such as "all of this", "somewhere" and "and things"; negative intensifiers such as "not all", "not many", "not very"; approximations such as "about as" and "almost"; indeterminate quantifications such as "a few" and "some"; expressions of possibility or probability such as "may", "might", "the chances are", "probably", "sometimes" and "frequently"; and vague expressions of multiplicity such as "aspects", "sort of" and "kind of".

The importance of the studies by Gage and his associates lies in their thorough analysis of great detail and of the use of objective measures on a very large number of teachers teaching precisely the same topics. In this way many variables were carefully controlled without prejudicing individual styles.

In an interesting experiment Mastin (1963) instructed 20 teachers to teach one topic with an "indifferent" attitude and another topic the following week "enthusiastically". The characteristics of "indifference" and "enthusiasm" were vetted by a board of "experts". 19 out of 20 classes did better on multiple choice tests after enthusiastic teaching; teachers were rated higher and influenced students' attitudes more when they were apparently enthusiastic and the degree to which students were affected by enthusiasm was unrelated to their intelligence. The importance of an enthusiastic style has been confirmed by Coats and Smidchens (1966) who found that 36% of the variation in tests of audience recall were attributable to the 'dynamism' of the speaker as measured by techniques such as eye contact and variation in pitch and volume of the voice.

So far the study of teaching styles has received insufficient attention so that standard methods of classifying observations have not been developed. One important exception to this is the Flanders Interaction Technique. Insofar as personal acceptability depends upon personal interaction, the styles of teaching resulting in the personal acceptability of teachers may be judged by using a modification of this technique (Bligh, 1971, 1972c).

In the Flanders Interaction Technique utterances are classified at regular intervals, for example every three seconds, into one of a number of categories such as those shown in Figure 7.10. Although at the end of a period of teaching, the totals in each category may be interesting, totals do not measure interaction. This may be done by recording each utterance in relation to the previous one, to which it is a reaction, on a matrix with each category represented in each direction. Each cell will then correspond to a pair of utterances such that the first number of any pair designates the row, and the second number designates the column in the matrix. The interpretation of this technique should be essentially comparative. It is possible to calculate the proportions of time teachers and students spend talking. The proportion of utterances of a particular kind may also be studied. For example, if the majority of student contributions are answering questions the style of teaching is likely to be very different from when most of their utterances are either asking them or expressing ideas of their own. More important, a teacher's style may be judged by the kind of utterance with which he characteristically reacts to student utterances. Patterns of interaction can be worked out. The instrument is highly reliable and can discriminate between different teaching styles with considerable subtlety. By observing a few simple rules (Bligh 1971) teachers may modify the instrument to their own purposes.

(c) Parameters of style based upon subjective judgements

(i) Students' ratings

The most commonly used method of evaluating teaching styles is the use of students' opinions expressed on rating scales in questionnaires.

The difficult task is to decide on what characteristics a teacher's style should be rated. Presumably the characteristics should be important and related to teaching effectiveness; but very few relationships of this kind have been definitely established. Those that have, such as audibility, are so obvious that students' opinions are hardly necessary to identify them.

A further difficulty lies in the degree of generality of the charactistic. If it is too specific it will not be useful because no comparisons or generalisations can be made from it. Consequently, the information obtained cannot easily be used. If the characteristic is too general, different students judge upon different criteria, and their judgements tend to be influenced by irrelevant factors (the "halo" effect).

Too many studies have overemphasised expository techniques in lecturing and other presentation methods. On the basis of students' ratings Hall and Schein (1967) concluded that intellectual competence, skill in communications, commitment to teaching, and personal influence were the

Figure 7.10 Flanders' Interaction Analysis (Modified)

Teacher Talk	Response	1. Accepts feeling. Accepts and clarifies an attitude or the feeling tone of a student in a non-threatening manner. Feelings may be positive or negative. Predicting and recalling feelings are included. 2. Praises or encourages. Praises or encourages student action or behaviour. Jokes that release tensions, but not at the expense of another individual; nodding head, or saying "Uh hm?' or 'go on' are included. 3. Accepts or uses ideas of students. Clarifying building or developing ideas suggested by a student. Teacher extensions of student ideas are included, but as the teacher brings more of his own ideas into play, shift to category 5. Answer questions.
	Questions	4. Asks questions. Asking a question about content or procedure, based on teacher ideas, with the intent that a student will answer.
	Initiation	5. Giving facts or opinions about content or procedures, lecturing, expressing his own ideas, giving his own explanation, or citing an authority other than a student. 6. Giving directions. Directions, commands, or orders to which a student is expected to comply.
Student Talk	Response	7. Student talk - response. Talk by pupils in response to teacher. Teacher initiates the contact or solicits student statement or structures the situation. Freedom to express his own ideas is limited.
	Questions	8. Student questions. Questions concerning content or procedure that are directed to the teacher.
	Initiation	9. Student talk - initiation. Talk by students which they initiate. Expressing own ideas; initiating a new topic, freedom to develop opinions and a line of thought going beyond the existing structure.
Silence		10. Silence or confusion. Pauses, short periods of silence and periods of confusion in which communication cannot be understood by the observer.

(The Flanders' Categories have been modified to include 'student questions' (8) and omit teacher 'criticizing and justifying authority' (7). Flanders' category (8) is therefore written as (7) here.

major characteristics of a good teacher. Australian students in New South Wales rated clear speaking and knowledge of how to interest students as important characteristics. They rated scholarship and social and personal characteristics less highly (Magin, 1973). Only 4% of teachers were judged to present opposing views on their subject and to encourage students to make up their own minds, yet such independence of mind is an avowed objective to many university teachers.

Enquiries without this exposity emphasis place more weight on friendly relationships with students. In a small survey Mayberry (1973) concluded there are four major skills in teaching dentistry: "dental communication skills", "interpersonal skills", "instructor student rapport" and "availability".

Gibb (1955) compared teachers with other leaders and adduced four major factors: "friendly democratic behaviour", "communication skills", "systematic organisation", and "academic emphasis". Using a standardised questionnaire, Leonard (1972) found that sociology students' conception of their ideal teacher was one who allowed students some self-direction, revised a course with the examinations in mind, gave direct answers to questions, made attendance voluntary, gave lectures which supplemented standard reading material, allowed time for student participation, gave slightly lower than average grades, and strove for personal relationships with his students. A survey by Eble (1969) in California emphasised the teacher's dynamism, clarity of explanation, interesting style, enjoyment of teaching, friendly interest in students, encouragement of discussion and consideration of other views than his own.

Like other researchers Hildebrand (1973) has found that students prefer teachers who contrast the implications of various theories, who present facts and concepts from related fields, who are excellent public speakers, who explain clearly, who make difficult topics easy to understand and who show interest and concern in the quality of their teaching. Where Hildebrand's study is interesting in that it relates students' preferences to their social goals and the kind of teaching they receive. For example students who were interested in self knowledge and self preparation for graduate or professional training prefer teachers with a good command of their subject. Organisation and clarity are favoured by those who seek upward social mobility.

Interestingly students with humanistic values who were seeking self development and self knowledge favoured dynamic and enthusiastic teachers. Not surprisingly students who learned predominantly from seminars and small group discussion emphasised the teacher's rapport and skill in controlling groups of students.

A very large number of studies of student evaluation of teaching have been published in the last fifteen years. Those mentioned here are a random selection to show the diversity of teaching techniques and characteristics which investigators have thought worth considering. To obtain some knowledge of common teaching styles it is necessary to know what characteristics and technqiues are commonly found in the same individual. In other words we need to know how they are commonly clustered; and to do this a relatively new statistical technique known as "cluster analysis" is necessary. In spite of the large number of investigations, to the best of my knowledge no-one has ever used this statistical technique on ratings of teacher's techniques.

Factor analysis to demonstrate common factors in techniques and characteristics rated has been used by several researchers, but it seems likely that the common factors obtained reflect the characteristics of the student raters rather than the teachers being rated.

Using factor analysis Greenwood et al (1973) derived eight factors from specific items of behaviour - facilitation of learning, obsolescence of presentation, commitment to teaching, evaluation, voice communication, openness, currency of knowledge and rapport. Students and their teachers tended to react in a similar way when identifying teaching behaviours except that students were more extreme. Isaacson and his colleagues (1963, 1964) have identified six factors using factor analysis: skill, student-teacher rapport and group interaction. Factor analyses by Holmes (1971) and Spencer and Aleamoni (1970) produced student stimulation and attention as an important factor, but their other factors were too general to be useful in the present context. Indeed the vagueness and generality of derived factors is so great that they are virtually useless as guides to the teacher who wants to assess his own teaching.

Some attempts have been made to obtain factors by combining data from a number of different studies using student assessment of teaching. In the study by Riley, Ryan and Lifshitz (1950, 1969) for example, students were asked to rate their teachers using a four point scale on ten characteristics derived from an extensive survey of earlier work. These were: organisation of subject matter, speaking ability, ability to explain, encouragement to think, attitude to students, knowledge of their subject, attitude to their subject, fairness in assessment, tolerance of disagreements, and being "human". Although the study was carefully carried out, we see, once again, the distinction between evaluation of teaching and teachers being blurred.

There is some doubt as to how far knowledge of students' ratings leads to improvement in teaching, but it probably helps to remove teachers' illusions. Centra (1972) has shown that teachers who regarded themselves more favourably than their students did, tended to be less self-satisfied some time later. Like other researchers, Centra found differences in the way different subjects were taught, general agreement between students' and teachers' ratings of teachers' profiles, and little difference in the esteem with which experienced and inexperienced teachers were held. On the whole women in this study were more favourably rated than men.

(ii) Ratings by colleagues, supervisors and others with teaching experience

What aspects of teaching style are noticed by observers with teaching experience? An interesting enquiry by Cartmell (1971) related the subjective course mark for teaching awarded by supervisors of 60 trainee teachers in the British Air Force to specific teaching techniques. The best 30% according to the supervisory grading were more task oriented and structured their teaching material more carefully in that they took slightly longer to state objectives, they used more recapitulation sessions, their questions were better posed, they needed to repeat, rephrase or otherwise clarify fewer questions, they had fewer questions incorrectly answered, they repeated more of the students' answers in toto, they used a wider variety of visual aids and focused the attention of students on them more frequently. So far as the emotional climate of the classroom was concerned successful teachers made more jokes, they allowed more laughter in the classroom, and they gave students reinforcement more frequently either verbally or by smiling. Distracting mannerisms were also less frequent with successful teachers. When all the grades for the trainee teachers were considered, there was a linear relationship between a high grade and their task orientation, but on measures of the emotional climate, trainees in the middle 40% were inferior to the top and bottom 30% who were similar. Cartmell interprets these findings by saying that a good teacher needs a balance between task and emotional orientations. Those in the lowest 30% had an imbalance while those in the middle 40% were task oriented but introverted.

It might be thought that the perceptions of teaching style by those with teaching experience will differ from students' perceptions because they will empathise more readily, they will be aware of the teacher's problems and they will be more acutely aware of specific teaching techniques. However research does not confirm this. Indeed it is not the opinions of students, but the opinions of supervisors, which seem to differ from those of other people. Webb and Nolan (1955) obtained ratings of various characteristics of teachers' styles including interest in the subject, sympathetic attitude to students, the presentation of subject matter, a sense of proportion and humour, self-reliance and confidence, personal peculiarities, and appearance. The views of students and the teachers themselves correlated highly, but there was little relation between these and the way supervisors perceived the teaching. Supervisors' ratings were not significantly related to intelligence, experience, level of schooling or enthusiasm of the teachers.

However, although they were in a minority, judgements of supervisors may have been more valid. The teachers in this enquiry were not highly experienced; Unruh (1968) has found that the judgements of experts are significantly better than chance; and although Maslow and Zimmerman (1965) confirmed that students and teachers agree on who the good teachers are, their conceptions of a good teacher were quite different. Both students and colleagues find difficulty in disentangling their conceptions of good teaching techniques and styles from their memories of teachers they judge to have been good or bad.

Crawford and Bradshaw (1968) have also shown considerable agreement amongst university students, teachers and administrators on the characteristics of "effective teaching" with others with the same status and sex. However percipients of different status and sex differed markedly in their opinions.

Such differences reflect the doubtful validity of subjective judgements and point again to the importance of choosing a valid method of enquiry. Indeed, the very paradigms of enquiry are currently in question and we will now digress briefly from the main themes of this chapter to consider a selection of views.

II Some Paradigms in Evaluation

Evaluation is currently an area of controversy in education. Even though advocates of the various schools of thought will probably classify the model presented in this chapter with others emphasising decision making, it is an attempt to relate each school and to show how its methods focus upon some aspects of evaluation and neglect others.

It has been argued that different, although overlapping, methods are required to evaluate values, general principles, specific circumstances, decisions and their style of implementation. Each of these has paradigms of its own and forms part of the wider paradigm of educational evaluation. For example, the experimental paradigm which dominates the study of chemistry, only contributes to generalisations in education. Experiments contribute little to the justification of values or decisions and experimentalists have seldom claimed that they do. For this reason it was considered earlier. Paradigms with wider claims are considered here, although some may be equally restricted in practice.

The major dimension is the subjectivity-objectivity of the methods used. Subjectivists are more likely to evaluate widely, using many criteria, because when the criteria conflict, they can happily choose between them subjectively. Objectivists are less willing to resolve conflicts in this way, regarding it as error-prone and arbitrary; they prefer to evaluate more narrowly.

(1) Evaluation as art criticism

(a) The approach

At the subjectivist end are all those who justify their evaluative judgements on the basis of their expertise and experience. Eisner (1975) believed educational evaluation should be like art criticism, a matter for connoisseurs and experts. This view emphasises that judgements of courses and teaching occur in a culture of rules, traditions and symbols and can only be understood in this context. Educational criticism, like the writings of critics in the arts, should enable the reader to appreciate the strengths, weaknesses and difficulties of what is criticised. In this sense it is itself educational and an art form. It does not apply a fixed standard, but generates reflection. Behind this lies an image of man (see Eisner, 1969) and a view of education. On Eisner's view, education is not an industrial process with superintendents, raw materials and product specifications - nor is it a change in behaviour or a biological process of growth. It is an encounter with work, problems and tasks. Its objectives are expressive and evocative, not prescriptive. It seeks diversity, not homogeneous goals.

(b) Limitations of the approach

(i) Critics disagree

One difficulty of evaluation as art criticism is that critics disagree. One can agree to disagree in art, because little of consequence need follow an expression of preference; but in education decisions require choices which may change the lives of other people. Evaluation as art criticism is "summative" and retrospective. It ignores the decision making aspect of the model in Figure 7.1.

(ii) Is might right?
If there is no objective indication of whose criticism is best, the subjective judgement of the stronger person will prevail. Authority, power and tradition are likely to be cemented. The opinions of the junior teachers are less considered. Hence the critics become a conservative force.

(iii) How can authority be justified?
How is the authority of the critic validated? - surely not the same way as other academic authority, by the publication of research which could be replicated, because Eisner's argument claims a diversity in which replication is impossible. How is the experience, and hence the expertise, of the critic related, relevant or similar to the case he is evaluating? This implies an analysis to match the particular case and the critic's experience. (In this way, a challenge to the subjective judgement of a critic is likely to be perceived as a personal criticism and a threat to his prestige.)

(2) Evaluation by committee

(a) The approach
Accreditation committees evaluate, but they avoid some of the objections of the "art critic". Being a group, experience is wider. More perspectives are available. Discussion makes perceptions explicit. Disagreements can be resolved by majority opinion. Consequently they can, and do, make recommendations and take decisions.

(b) Its limitations
But committees are equally conservative. They often contain hidden vested interests, such as those teachers of the corresponding courses in a neighbouring college which recruits students from the same catchment area. They tend to evaluate courses as they appear on paper, rather than what actually happens. In the classroom a single observer can dramatically affect the way students and teachers behave; a committee certainly would.

(3) Evaluation as illumination

(a) The approach
A subjective approach of growing popularity in Britain is "illuminative evaluation". Parlett and Hamilton (1972) model their paradigm on the methods of social anthropology. "It's primary concern is with description and interpretation rather than measurement and prediction." It aims to study courses: how they operate, the influences upon them, what those directly concerned regard as their merits and de-merits and what it is like to be a participant. The "instructional system" (which is the formalised teaching plans and arrangements, pedagogic assumptions,

the syllabus, techniques and equipment) is distinguished from "the learning milieu" (which is "the social-psychological and material environment in which students and teachers work together").

Its method has three overlapping stages: observation, further enquiry and explanation. At the observation stage "common incidents, recurring trends and issues frequently raised" are noted. At the second, observation and enquiry become progressively more directive, systematic and selective. The explanatory stage includes "spotting patterns of cause and effect" and "weighing alternative interpretations". Data is collected by "observation, interviews, questionnaires and tests, and documentary and background sources".

(b) Its limitations
In terms of the model presented at the beginning of this chapter, illuminative evaluation concentrates upon information gathering about particular circumstances of courses and teaching. It describes what happens. Most of its difficulties derive from this limitation.

(i) Not decision making, only information collection
It *contributes* to decision making, but does not itself include decision making or recommendations. Social anthropology is not a decision making activitiy.

(ii) No attempt to justify values
It might also be said that a social anthropologist does not pass value judgements upon the societies he observes. He seeks only to describe and interpret.

Illuminative evaluators are here fired upon by critics from two directions. One critic will say, "How can you describe and interpret an educational process without using values or words which have value connotations? 'Education' itself is a value laden concept. Particularly when observing something within your own culture which has inevitable associations with your past experiences and emotions, how can you divorce your values from your descriptions and interpretations?"

If the illuminative evaluator still insists that his observations are value free, a second critic will say "In as much as you apply no values, you are not evaluating at all. No amount of information or illumination alone will make an evaluation. Evaluation implies the use of values. It implies criteria and standards."

If the illuminative evaluator does not use any values he will avoid having to justify them and any biases they imply. Following Scriven's (1972) "Goal Free Evaluation" some illuminative evaluators say they want to avoid being biased by knowing the values and goals of the course. They should describe and interpret all the effects of a course without having their minds clouded by knowing what the effects are intended to be. This knowledge might bias their perception.

(iii) Covertly applies generalisations
The insistence upon the distinctiveness of every particular case makes proponents of illuminative evaluation sceptical about the truth or relevance of generalisations in any particular evaluation.

But interpretations, explanations and even descriptions cannot be given without applying generalisations. Consequently illuminative evaluators need to explain where such generalisations come from and how they can be justified. This is difficult if they maintain not only that all "instructional systems" and "learning milieux" are distinctively different, but, when criticising experimental approaches, that these differences are multiplied by their complex interactions and cannot easily be disentangled.

In practice we all anticipate, interpret and explain everyday experience by using generalisations. Admittedly the generalisations may have varied validity, but we cannot avoid using them. We can only try to improve them and make them explicit. Consequently, while rightly emphasising the uniqueness of each teaching situation, illuminative evaluators are tempted to hide their own generalisations. Indeed even the belief that some other paradigms have over emphasised the "instructional system" at the expense of the "learning milieux" seems to be an observation or interpretation derived from an unstated generalisation.

(iv) Inadequate justification
Parlett and Hamilton can fend off many a critic by showing that they are eclectically open to data from any method or source. The price is to explain how conflicting evidence from different sources is reconciled, and how evidence is weighed. These difficulties are not clearly resolved. Indeed, the details of the paradigm are vague (and this may be a difficulty in social anthropology too!). In particular the third stage, giving explanations, is critical to illuminative evaluation, but it is not clear how the explanations are arrived at, how they are justified and how one is preferred to another. In other words, explanations are not justified except impressionistically by the subjective opinion of the evaluator.

(v) Double subjectivity
Parlett and Hamilton recognise that subjectivity is a problem. They rightly point out that any evaluation, and indeed any academic enquiry, involves judgement in handling information, but in illuminative evaluation great credence is placed in the evaluator's subjective interpretations of other people's subjective impressions. With every interview question and every response there is a selection and interpretation each compounding the next. Yet illuminative evaluation commonly assumes the validity of interviews to exclude vast areas of data by successive narrowing of the enquiry. It is not clear how this process is justified. How, for example, are defence mechanisms allowed for? Similarly, the use of students' or teachers' opinions may be diplomatic and provide pointers towards useful hard data, but the validity (as distinct from consistency) of opinions for the evaluation is, as we shall see later, sometimes questionable.

(vi) Possible selective use of data.
Although traditional evaluations are criticised as over-selective in their use of information, inevitably illuminative evaluation will also be open to the charge of mis-selection. Although illuminative evaluation has enjoyed initial popularity as a reaction against the practical and theoretical difficulties of the scientific paradigm, it is popular

amongst evaluators because it offers them considerable freedom in the selection of methods and data. For example in their emphasis upon the "instructional system" and "learning milieu", and in their reaction against the specification of objectives, Parlett and Hamilton omit to mention whether students'learning may be relevant to the evaluation of courses and teaching.

No evaluator can collect all possible data without serious interference with the course he is evaluating. What is required is a standard procedure and a checklist of methods to ensure that the selection is made wisely. In this respect illuminative evaluation has a useful role at the beginning of an evaluation. Although it is not a strictly diagnostic approach (and what could be?) it can direct attention to unnoticed facts and ill-considered issues. In practice this may be all that is necessary to stimulate course improvements. If so, although illuminative information will have been given, evaluations will have been made by others.

Illuminative evaluation is not an all purpose paradigm but it is a useful first step in focussing upon the specific circumstances of a course. As Eraut (1976) remarks, it is "hypothesis-seeking" not "hypothesis-testing".

(4) Evaluation as informing decisions

(a) The approach
In an important book Stufflebeam et al (1971) say that evaluation is a process with three stages: *delineating* what information is useful for judging a decision, *obtaining* it, and *providing* it. There is a cycle of *evaluating, decision making, action* and *evaluation* in which evaluating the performance of the last decision may inform the next.

This, in a nutshell, is Stufflebeam's paradigm. He goes on to present and apply a complex model of evaluation relating different types of evaluation, decision and decision setting.

He says there are four types of evaluation. There are those that give information about the *context* of a decision - its objectives and the particular circumstances in which it will be taken and acted upon, such as the presence of certain resources, unmet needs, opportunities not taken and problems or difficulties unresolved. Secondly, compared with context evaluation, which is on a large scale, *input* evaluation is ad hoc and consists of obtaining much smaller items of information for day to day decisions on how best to use resources, what teaching strategy to use and how to implement bigger decisions already taken. Thirdly, *process* evaluation is to provide continuous feedback to teachers or others who implement decisions. Finally, *product* evaluation measures or interprets attainment.

There are also four types of decision. *Planning* decisions specify the major changes or objectives to be achieved. *Structuring* decisions give the means to achieve them. *Implementing* decisions refine, control and carry through the plan of action. And *recycling* decisions maintain quality control. Decisions to recycle may be taken at any time, they ascertain achievement, and they determine whether to continue, terminate, develop or radically change the action.

Stufflebeam points out that we only take decisions when we want to change something. We may want big or little changes, and our decisions may be well or poorly informed. This gives four theoretical possibilities, but in practice it would be very difficult to have a lot of information about all aspects of large scale changes (*metamorphic* changes). Hence there are three *decision settings* about which an evaluator could give information

(i) Homeostatic settings.
When the changes required are small (homeostatic settings) we are more likely to be able to find out much of what we need to know. For example when we are trying to maintain the status quo, or do what we have always done before, we probably know many of the relevant facts. Hence homeostatic decisions are preferred by people afraid of uncertainty, who do not like big changes.

The need for evaluation is greatest when our knowledge of the effects of decisions is least.

(ii) Neomobilistic settings
Political developments and technological innovations could stimulate large changes without us having much knowledge about them. For example it would be difficult to foresee all the consequences of using a new examination system. Stufflebeam called these neomobilistic decision settings.

(iii) Incremental settings
When there is little information available it is much more common to attempt only small changes (incremental settings). Developmental activity usually consists of a series of incremental improvements, based more upon personal experience than hard data.

Stufflebeam et al argued that decisions in these different settings require very differing types of evaluation. For example in Britain the Council for National Academic Awards (CNAA) lays heavy emphasis upon context evaluation when a College which has no courses previously approved by the Council submits an application. The College is invited to submit a description of its present academic work; an analysis of its current enrolment; its academic and administrative structure; the means employed to maintain standards; its human, physical and financial resources including its libraries, staff workrooms, residential and communal accommodation; its policy for research and staff development; its student services; its proposals for academic and other developments in the next five years; the aims and intentions of the proposed course, how they are to be achieved, and the quality and experience of the staff involved.

Stufflebeam's model can be used to draw attention to the kinds of evaluation required. For example when a college is seeking renewal of CNAA validation for one of its courses, it is a homeostatic decision setting which should not require expensive use of time and money on context evaluation while process and product evaluations would be much more pertinent. (In practice these evaluations by the CNAA still have a heavy emphasis upon context evaluation.)

(b) Its limitations

(i) Values are ignored

Stufflebeam's definition of evaluation is purely in terms of information and ignores values, while his initial argument led him to the conclusion that evaluation is the "process of ascertaining relative values of competing alternatives". Consequently he does not judge decisions or prescribe what decision ought to have been taken.

(ii) Methods of evaluation are unclear

He does not tell us how to evaluate; he is more concerned with how evaluations are used.

(iii) Overlooks the justification of knowledge

He neglects epistemological questions (e.g. "What can we know about the teaching on this course?") in favour of a pragmatic approach (e.g. "What action will achieve what is wanted?" and "Is the teaching on this course effective?"). But doesn't a pragmatic approach beg epistemological questions?

(iv) All evaluations are formative

The cycle - evaluation, decision, action - makes virtually all evaluation formative. On this view summative evaluation has no value unless it is also formative. (See page 56 for definitions of "formative" and "summative"

The model presented in this chapter is, perhaps, nearer to Stufflebeam's paradigm than any other. It avoids some of these difficulties, but has weaknesses of its own. For example the extension of the word "decision" to include behaviour which is not intentional may offend some philosophers. There is also an uncomfortable boundary between decisions and style. How small does a decision have to be before it is more convenient to subsume it under "style"? Stufflebeam's model works rather better with decisions of contrasting size. Both Stufflebeam's model and my own imply, on the one hand, a chronological succession of decisions in which evaluation of one creates the conditions of the next, and, on the other, a logistic hierarchy of decisions each entailing successively smaller ones. These relationships are difficult to disentangle; yet they are too simple. In reality there is always a network of interdependent decisions. Educational matters are inevitably complex. Simplicity is a virtue provided nothing crucial is excluded and in this respect Stufflebeam's approach is more complete than others.

(5) Evaluation as assessment of objectives achieved

(a) The approach

This approach was originally advocated by Tyler (1949) and later expounded by Popham (1972). Something of its rationale was described in Chapter 1. Briefly, it is that education is a rational activity. Teaching and learning are pursued for a purpose; they are means to some ends. The purpose of evaluation is to find out how far those ends have been accomplished.

(b) Its limitations
Objections to this approach have focused on evaluating only achievement of objectives. The points that follow lean heavily upon those listed by MacDonald-Ross (1973).

(i) Disregards the value of objectives
To assess only the achievement of objectives takes no account of whether the objectives are worthwhile. A course could achieve all its objectives and still be a bad course.

(ii) Judgement is necessary, but not sufficient
Students could achieve all their course objectives in spite of bad teaching, not because of it. Students sometimes work harder when they recognise that the teaching is poor than when it is mediocre.

(iii) Cannot assess all objectives achieved
No list of objectives in terms of students' behaviour can ever be sufficient; and if it were, it would be impossible to test them all. It may be replied that all evaluations involve sampling and that carefully worded objectives usually give guidance on how to select the sample.

(iv) Inevitable ambiguity
However, MacDonald-Ross points out that one can never make objectives absolutely clear. They are always ambiguous.

(v) The validity of tests
One can never be completely sure what a test is testing. There could be any number of reasons why a student answered a question in the way he did. He could reach the answers by one of many possible routes and since these may vary with the way the subject was taught, an evaluator would need to observe the process of teaching as well as the learning it produces.

(vi) Diversity of objectives cannot be tested
In courses where the aim is diversity, rather than homogeneity, in what students learn to do, it would never be possible to specify the test precisely.

(vii) Pre-specficiation of objectives impossible.
In courses which are "voyages of exploration" the methods of evaluation could not be decided until afterwards.

However it is important to see that these difficulties are not objections. They boil down to saying that evaluation of objectives achieved is not easy and not sufficient. They do not destroy the value of the approach, indeed an approach that does not look at outcomes is scarcely plausible; yet in the fervour of reaction against the objectives approach in recent years some evaluators have thrown the baby away with the bath water.

(6) Other paradigms

It is not suggested that the paradigms dealt with in this section form a complete list. In particular there is a variety of systems approaches which generally assume that teaching, motivation, time, money and/or other resources are put into the system where there is a process producing some output which may be assessed in quantity or quality. Systems approaches are commonly, but not necessarily, comparative. They commonly ask questions such as "Which method results in most learning?", "Could the course be run more economically?", "What changes could occur if the influence of a certain variable in the system is reduced?" and so on.

Good et al (1980) argued that a systems approach is able to accommodate long sequences of cause and effect, recognises that both the student and the educational system change after a period of time, make it easier to provide critical analyses of evaluation research, permit integration of studies of varying types and make communication about evaluation more precise. They present a model in which it is not the output which is assessed, but the level of knowledge in a student at any given time. The output corresponds to what a student forgets; input to what he learns.

The limitations of systems approaches will obviously vary with the system. While they may make a better attempt to take account of all the complexities of teaching and learning, they inevitably simplify by being selective.

The model presented at the beginning of this chapter could be regarded as being a system of a kind. As with most educational systems, no claim is made that it is the only framework in which to understand what a teacher does. Assessment of what teachers are, and what they might be, are entirely different questions and it is to these that we will now turn.

Figure 7.11: Students in Library at four times of day during Spring Term

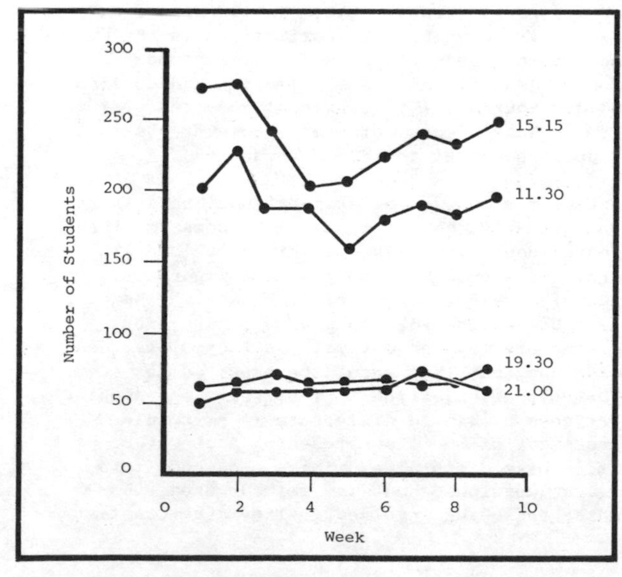

III Methods of Assessing Teachers in Post-Secondary Education

It makes no sense to talk of assessing a person unless it is known what he is to be assessed for. The purpose of an assessment controls the relevance of the criteria to be used. Surprisingly this obvious point has frequently been forgotten by precisely those theorists who in other contexts emphasise the importance of objectives. In the previous section we discussed the assessment of teaching styles, rather than the assessment of persons, so that teachers may use them to improve their teaching. However when promotions are considered it is a person who is assessed, because it is a person who is promoted not his course or teaching style.

In these cases the assessment is made with reference to a particular decision which has to be taken. Thus it is frequently not the merit, but the appropriateness of a teacher's skills that should be judged. When such decisions are unfavourable there need be no implied condemnation of the teacher.

Not unnaturally teachers are highly sensitive to any form of assessment of their work. This sensitivity can be eased if these points are recognised. Nevertheless, whether they like it or not, teachers are assessed. They do seek promotion and they do apply for new jobs. The question is not whether teachers in post-secondary education should be assessed but 'how and when, and what for?' If teaching is a major function of post-secondary teachers it seems reasonable to suppose that the effectiveness of their courses should be a major consideration of promotion boards. The difficult with this suggestion is that the assessment of teaching proficiency then becomes obscured by other assessments most of which are equally intangible. In 1966 Astin and Lee surveyed 1,110 post-secondary educational institutions in the USA and found that 96% of the persons consulted considered classroom teaching a major criterion for salary increase, promotion and confirmation of tenure, while personal attributes (57%), length of service (47%) and research (47%) appeared to be less highly esteemed. However there appears to be a conflict between esteem and common practice.

In this section I shall argue for the use of self-evaluations. There tends to be an assumption that a teacher is assessed by someone other than himself. I should have thought that assessment of one's own teaching in order to improve it should be both the most important and the most frequent kind of assessment. I see no reason why such assessments should not also be considered, along with others, for promotion purposes. The teachers may use any methods they please, and they ought to use more than one, but they should be expected to justify their choice. The obvious objection is that self assessment will be biased; but there need be little difference in principle between these and the assessment of one's own research that may be part of doctoral dissertations. Like doctoral examiners and moderators, promotion committees can ask questions about the methods used, the validity of evidence and the reasoning involved. They can then form their own judgement in the light of their knowledge and experience. This method has been accepted for assessment of doctoral theses for centuries. It has scarcely ever been considered for assessment of teaching. However I have used a method like it. A college invited me to select three teachers for promotion on the basis of their teaching. 86 lecturers accepted an invitation to submit evidence of any kind of their teaching competence. Their submissions included lists of objectives, course plans, visual aids, publications, samples of students' references, testimonials from students and colleagues, evaluations by student questionnaire and a very wide range of other material. Testimonials were available from their Heads of Department and a shortlist of candidates was prepared. Each shortlisted candidates was allowed a certain amount of time with me as external consultant. They could plan to use this time in any way they wished. They could let me observe their teaching, meet their students, ask them questions and so on. Finally, there was a formal interview with the College Promotions Board. Although many of the candidates were excellent, the salient characteristic of those who were successful was their flair and originality in teaching.

This begs the question of what weight should be given to different factors and the various evaluation methods by promotion boards. Lester (1974) argued that in academic life there cannot be regular formulae as there are in some industries. Many of the principles applying to promotion in industry are inapplicable in higher education because a department may wish to seek out a unique individual who happens to possess the right qualifications for a position. According to Kelly and Hart (1969) both students and their parents think that teaching is more important than research. From the work of Halsey and Trow (1971) it seems unlikely that university teachers would believe this so strongly. The professors in Kelly and Hart's sample also conceived the purpose of their teaching differently from students in that they saw themselves as having a character-building role.

(1) Current practice

What is current practice? We might expect that it varies from one part of the globe to another; but responses to our albeit small scale enquiry suggest that variations are as great within a single country, as between countries. In most universities there is no formal method by which teaching is assessed. Many departments replied that the head of department assesses teaching, sometimes after consultation with colleagues, but usually on his own. If much of his time is confined to his office and no method is found to breach the traditional privacy of the classroom, it is hard to see how such inevitably subjective judgements could be well-informed; and in this case, they are open to prejudice.

Second to the private opinions of heads of departments or faculites, the use of students' opinions is the most widely used method. Outside communist countries there does not appear to be any geographical or cultural association with this method. It is used in every continent, and with the exception of North America, it does not seem to be more favoured in one than another. Students' opinions are sometimes consulted informally, while in other places formal rating methods are used. In one Danish department of biochemistry a special staff-student committee was appointed for the purpose.

In their survey in the USA Astin and Lee (1966) found that teaching was evaluated by heads of departments in 85% of them, by other senior personnel in 82%, by other teachers in 49% and by informal student opinions in 41%. Observations of scholarly research and publications were used in 44%, but direct observation of teaching was taboo in 40%. Presumably the value attached to research will vary greatly from one type of post-secondary educational institution to another, and in any case it is always difficult to know the trustworthiness of this kind of data collected by questionnaire methods.

(2) The use of students' opinions

Dwyer (1972) has reviewed 62 studies on the characteristics and relationships of criteria for evaluating teaching effectiveness. He has concluded that the reliability of students' ratings is a function of the number of raters, and that they have more reliability than validity. Ratings are not significantly related in length of teaching experience, the age of the teacher, class size, sex of the teacher or student, the severity of the teacher's grading of students, or the maturity of the rater. Students give low ratings to teachers who are authoritarian, who do not prepare their lectures, who use sarcasm, or who "dwell on the obvious". The teacher's academic knowledge and knowledge of teaching techniques are not directly related to students' ratings. Although ratings of teaching appear to be unrelated to the quantity of research and publications by the teachers, those holding higher degrees tended to receive higher ratings on course organisation.

In spite of the steady flow of research articles in the USA advocating consideration of student opinions, surveys by Gustad (1967), Astin and Lee (1966) and Perry (1969) give a clear indication of their declining use. Our survey suggested that elsewhere their use is irregular, reflecting the enthusiasms of individuals, but increasing. Probably less than 12% of American colleges now use student opinion systematically. In a more restricted survey, Bryan (1968) found that 49% of American colleges had a plan for student assessment of teaching, 38% had never systematically obtained student ratings of teaching, and 13% had discontinued it.

It should not, however, be thought that students are always critical. Analysis of essays by students in a dental school on their best and worst teachers showed that students were more often appreciative than critical and that they consistently valued well organised lectures and the teacher's approachability (Flood Page 1972)

If my earlier argument that different teachers have different talents is valid, we should expect that different teachers will be good at teaching different things. Hoyt (1973) has attempted to assess teaching effectiveness by combining teachers' ratings of the relative importance of certain objectives with students' ratings of teacher behaviour and their progress on the objectives. He concluded that students' ratings of their progress were reliable but subject to a 'halo effect'. Teachers' judgments of the relative importance of objectives were consistent and there was some evidence that students' judgments of their own progress had some validity. Different items differentiated 'successful' and 'unsuccessful' teachers on different objectives, and virtually every item did so on one or more objectives. The size of the class appeared to be strongly related to whether or not a given item discriminated progress on a given objective; but it should not be inferred from this that size of class has a direct causal relationship with objectives achieved.

The difficulty of using ratings by students or other observers is that they are likely to reflect the personalities or needs of the raters. Hogan (1973) has found students' ratings of the same instructor during two different semesters were quite consistent. Correlations between ratings of the same teacher on different courses were surprisingly low. Correlations for different instructors teaching on the same course correlated highly on some factors but poorly on others. These findings seem to imply that some of the variation in students' ratings of teachers is related to differences in the course being taught rather than the teachers themselves.

Although the consistency of students' judgments is normally regarded as something in their favour, it could be because students quickly get fixed ideas about what teachers should do. Kohlan (1973) used factor analysis and identified eleven factors accounting for 68% of the variation in student ratings at the beginning and late in a course on business administration. Kohlan concluded that students' opinions of their teacher crystalised very early in a course and that teachers should think very carefully about the early impressions they make upon students.

Smithers (1970) has shown that different students expect different things from their lecturers. Consequently no lecturer can please them all. For example students who scored highly on a test of dogmatism wanted their teachers to set clear objectives, to set attainable standards, to keep to the point, to prepare thoroughly, to use appropriate visual aids, to give summary handouts, to have clear blackboard organisation, and to link their subject with other work. In short they wanted their teachers to tell them precisely what they had to learn and to save them the trouble of thinking for themselves.

In contrast to arts and social science students, engineers were like the dogmatists. They wanted the lecturer to go slow enough for them to take full notes. They did not want him only to talk around brief notes and to provide only the essentials as a framework; nor did they wish him to take a distinctive line on unresolved problems. In the same way anxious introverts were less willing to explore ideas not in the textbooks, to exercise their imaginations, or to prefer a lecturer who takes a distinctive line on controverial issues. They preferred lecturers who read out notes relevant to the examinations. Falk and Lee Dow (1971) have quoted markedly contrasting judgments by students which corresponded with their subsequent performance. No cause and effect can be inferred from this correspondence; but, since they were all judging the same thing, it is difficult to claim that the differences lay in what they were judging. It seems more likely that the differences lay in the students who were judging.

Another apsect of the subjectivity of student ratings on questionnaires has been demonstrated by Follman et al (1974) who showed that students' ratings could vary significantly with the design of the questionnaire.

The most common method is to ask students to rate a characteristic of a teacher's performance on a 5 point scale. The use of a 4 point or 6 point scale prevents them from always choosing the mid point, but this does not occur very often. Gauvain (1970) recommends the use of a 3 point scale and claims that its power of discrimination is just as good. Simple statements with which students or other observers are asked to agree or disagree have been widely used and permit wide aspects of teaching to be considered. Observers may also be asked to select adjectives from a list or from a pair thought to describe teaching or teachers' opinions of colleagues and experts.

If students' judgemnts of teachers are highly reliable but probably invalid owing to their subjective nature, it does not follow that students' judgments should not be used. It does imply that they should be interpreted with considerable care and that the use of subjective measures alone is inadvisable. If a teacher is genuinely trying to help his students, he would be foolish never to ask them how far he is succeeding; but this is to use students' opinions to improve teaching not to assess the teacher. This distinction is of crucial importance when considering the use of students' opinions.

(3) Observations by colleagues and experts

Bayley (1967) has argued that teaching can only be assessed by fellow teachers' observations. He dismisses students' opinions as unacceptable to the staff, and self evaluation as biased. Yet classroom observation suffers from an uncertainty principle. The observer may affect what he observes. Consequently, this kind of observation requires considerable skill, experience and tact. Even experienced teachers have a tendency to think that others should teach in the same way as they do. There is no general evidence that if an observer has himself experience of teaching, his judgments of other teachers are any more reliable or valid. For example Gromish et al (1972) compared the ratings by students and heads of departments of 24 university teachers and found no significant correlation. The heads of departments also awarded an overall grade in addition to 38 detailed ratings of each teacher; but there were poor correlations between them. Gromisch argues the case for a more detailed analysis when using rating methods.

The use of observation checklists can at least provide some consistency in what is being judged. Evidence from students' judgments of teachers suggests that this is where unreliability occurs. Once they judge the same thing they agree upon what takes place. As we have seen, their diffences seem to stem from different values and different ideas about what is effective and important.

In his review of research, Dwyer (1972) has shown that students and teachers tend to agree in their ratings of other teachers; but in colleges where new teaching staff have supervisors, the ratings by supervisors do not correlate highly with those by students and they tend to be more generous the longer they have known the new teacher. This suggests that even professional raters make subjective errors in their judgements. Thus they may be professional, but not expert. This is consistent with the views of Hildebrand (1972, 1973) who also considered many objections to the use of student evaluation of teaching and concluded that each campus should have a centre to provide the organisation and processing of evaluations, but not for interpreting them or establishing their associated policy. He thought the entire academic community should take part and norms should be calculated so that individuals may make private comparisons.

(4) Research publications

There is a belief that good researchers are also good teachers. It is particularly common amongst the teachers themselves (Maslow and Zimmerman, 1956). Yet I know of no evidence for this. They appear to be independent abilities and this is confirmed by systematic observations (Stallings and Singhal, 1970). Bourgeois (1967) examined available literature related to the characteristics of college teachers in the U.S.A. and concluded that a doctoral qualification is a sign of a good researcher but not a good teacher. Postgraduate colleges train researchers, not teachers, but half of them in the U.S.A. eventually take employment as teachers. In any one year, only 30% of the teaching staff engaged in research and 90% of published research was produced by 10% of the teachers. This seems to suggest a mismatch between courses for postgraduates and their subsequent careers. Accordingly Bourgeois thinks that some training of college teachers is necessary.

In many countries the number of publications is thought to be the major criterion for promotion. Yet publications are not necessarily research publications and Heywood has shown that researchers do not always publish. Heywood (1967) found that 29% of teachers in Colleges of Advanced Technology in England had a teacher training qualification, the majority had first class or upper second class degrees, 70% had experience in industry, 80% were undertaking research projects but only 11% had published results.

Promotiom boards with lists of candidates' publications may judge the quantity, but can they judge the quality in specialised aspects of a subject? Using the number of times an article was cited by other authors as a measure of quality, Cole and Cole (1967) concluded that there was a high correlation between the quality and quantity of articles published by physicists. Nevertheless some academics produced a large number of low quality articles and others a few of high quality. Quality appeared to be more strongly related to awards received than quantity. Cole and Cole thought that the reward system encourages good quality researchers to publish extensively, and to channel the efforts of poor researchers into other activities such as teaching. There was also a strong relationship between departmental membership and the quantity and quality of publications produced. This raises another question of justice.

(5) Institutional background

How far does an academic's promotion depend upon his own merit or upon the prestige of the institution he happened to attend? Hargens and Hagström (1968) tried to investigate this by controlling for 'academic productivity' and they found that the prestige of the institution at which an academic took his doctoral qualification did have an effect upon their reputation, although it diminished in time and with higher occupational status. This seemed to imply that mobility between institutions of different repute might be restricted. In a later study (1969) Hargens concluded that mobility of academics between institutions of different standing and geographic location was greater than his earlier results had led him to suppose.

(6) Productivity

With growing financial strains, student unrest and the development of management techniques, governments in Europe and North America are beginning to seek tangible rewards for their investments. Cost benefit analyses are becoming more popular and the number of graduates qualifying and entering the national labour force seems to be one measure of productivity. If institutions and departments are judged upon this kind of criterion it may be a short step to attempt judgments of the productivity of the individual teacher! This conception of education requires no further comment here.

Dahllöf and Patriksson at the University of Göteborg have argued that pass rates of university degrees are irrelevant as a measure of efficiency. Many students have no intention of taking a degree and only aim at taking some limited number of courses. Consequently it is impossible to look at a university as a closed system if one tries to evaluate its 'productivity' The whole area of higher education has to be included because there is a continuous flow of students from one type of institution to another. Students who transfer from one course to another that suits them better should be regarded as successes not dropouts. This error arises, they say, from considering a college as a 'closed system'. (SRHE 1973).

Elton (1975) has suggested that a teacher can be assessed from inspection of students' course work including projects, his willingness to experiment and innovate, the extent to which he is involved in curriculum reforms, his use of student feedback for improvement, his attendance at educational meetings, his knowledge of new developments and an examination of his prepared teaching materials. The Nuffield Group for Research and Innovation in Higher Education has recommended consideration of a teacher's materials which should be publicly available, contributions to inter-university teaching projects, publications on teaching and educational conferences, and supervision of theses. They also suggest consulting external referees on teaching.

(7) Sex

Are teachers assessed for promotion on the basis of their sex? Although academics pride themselves on their tolerance and their liberal attitude, there is mounting evidence in academic life of discrimination against women. For example Dinerman has reviewed a number of investigations conducted in American universities and colleges. Even when allowing for factors such as the smaller number of women who enter higher education, disproportionately fewer women enter academic life in relation to their qualifications, they enter at lower levels and are less readily promoted. Material presented for publication is less readily accepted when the author's name if female, yet we have seen that publications are one path to promotion. Women are asked to teach 'stable' parts of the curriculum in which little research and controversy is possible. Consequently their teaching and research topics are not mutually supportive. Unconnected topics divide attention. The benfits of teaching one's research interests are unavailable. Innovation and contributions to academic life are restricted by the unconscious exclusion of women from informal networks of communication. Students are conditioned to expect women to play subordinate rather than innovative roles. Where women compensate by outstanding teaching performance, the inability to assess it properly militates against its consideration for promotion.

In contrast to the United States, Tessa Blackstone and Oliver Fulton (1974) have found that in Britain women teach less than men except in the social sciences. In both countries women academics are concentrated in certain subject areas, particularly the humanities, and are virtually absent from the applied sciences. In all subjects their numbers are small. Women publish less than their men colleagues. Although this difference is less marked in social and applied sciences, it is more noticeable in the United States.

(8) Motivation

The focus and strength of a teacher's motivation may be one factor that should affect their promotion; but what motives do they have? Lofthouse (1973) has noted that although salaries and promotion appear to be related to number of publications and unrelated to teaching, there is no corresponding relation to academics' expressed interests, nor to how they spend their time. He therefore points out that academics are not dominated by a single motive aspiring for promotion.

The average British academic works 50½ hours per week for a mean of 47 weeks per year. More senior academics work longer hours than their junior colleagues. 37% of this time was spent with undergraduates, 5% with graduate course work, 6% with graduate research, 24% on personal research, 11% on professional work outside the university and 18% was unclassifiable university work. (Committee of Vice-Chancellors and Principals, 1972.)

Marsh and Stafford (1967) found that, compared with similarly qualified professional and technical staffs outside the academic professions, academics in the U.S.A. are prepared to sacrifice monetary rewards for job satisfaction obtained from intellectual stimulus.

Goodwin (1969) compared the occupational goals of business executives with those of college professors and students. Those in the business world were more concerned with monetary gain, while those in the academic world showed more concern for others and society in general. Professors had more in common with each other than with others outside the academic world, professors of engineering being least like their fellows. The goals of students in different subjects tended to reflect those of their professors. The similarity was greatest with able students, while the least able students bore greatest similarity with businessmen. Both businessmen and professors were strongly concerned with their own self development.

Although motivation should probably be a major criterion in any promotion system, there is little controlled evidence on the motivation of teachers in post-secondary education. Nevertheless it is likely that this is one of the factors that affects the opinions of promotion committees.

(9) Other possible methods

Because justice must always be done, methods and criteria for teachers' promotions can never be a ripe field for innovation and experiment. Nevertheless, in the long run, this may be what is required.

Miller (1974) has suggested new methods including the use of student achievement on standardised tests, inspection of teaching materials and detailed consideration of special incidents. Since special incidents may be atypical, the last of these may be more suitable as a staff training technique than a method of assessment. Such innovations and experiments are more acceptable if they are self administered. In this way their publicity may be controlled by those whose careers may be threatened.

(10) Conclusions

The assessment of teachers is troubled by two recurring problems. There is no accepted criterion because of the wide variations in their work. There is usually a conflict between individual circumstances and general codes intended to ensure justice between individuals.

IV The Training of Post-Secondary Teachers

(1) The changing scene

A book published by the International Association of University Professors and Lecturers in 1967 entitled "The Recruitment and Training of University Teachers" (Hacquaert, 1967) makes virtually no reference whatsoever to training in teaching techniques. Under the heading "training facilities" Hacquaert begins "whatever the importance attached to teacher training, the fact remains that preparation for the university teaching profession is mostly directed towards scholarship". The rest of the discussion, and indeed the whole book, is devoted to the teacher's acquisition of knowledge of his speciality and his engagement in research. In a world-wide survey he was unable to find more than two institutions where a training was given, and even one of these he assumes "is more professional than pedagogic".

Thirteen years later the world picture had changed. The 1970's have seen the widespread introduction of courses on teaching for university teachers. These have sometimes been organised by a resources or media centre, sometimes by an enthusiast, but more frequently by a committee officially established for the purpose. In some colleges the Education Department has been charged with special responsibility for training their colleagues, with obvious consequent conflicts in inter-faculty relationships. Now financial cutbacks have halted the impetus.

The fate of staff development units now presents a varied picture. In Australia they have been recommended by the Williams Report and the Committee of Vice-Chancellors has matched its official encouragement with financial support so that nearly every university has agreed to appoint someone to help new teachers. In the U.S.A. many colleges made such appointments long before they were considered elsewhere; but provision is still patchy. In Sweden, Canada and the United Kingdom a number of centres have been established and the respective Committees of Vice-Chancellors have established research posts to monitor and encourage their development. So far there appear to be only isolated developments of this kind in Eastern Europe, and South America, but there are signs of growing interest on the continents of Africa and Asia, while closures have begun in Europe and North America.

(2) Some common assumptions

(a) An academic emphasis
Having recognised the need for some sort of training of teachers in post-secondary education, the responses of academics have been predictable. To provide a training it is assumed that one must provide a course and the course itself should be academic. It is of course true that academics should require academic justification for what they do; but it is an assumption to suppose that the training itself should necessarily be academic. The assumption is made because this is what academics

themselves do. Yet much of the skill of teaching lies in interpersonal relationships which no amount of intellectualising can produce without other personal qualities.

Nevertheless Cantrell (1972) has suggested five reasons why improvement in university teaching could be made by courses. Many teachers lacked a knowledge of subjects relevant to their educational work. In his survey he found wide variability in teachers' ideas, objectives and teaching methods; and while he abhors uniformity he considers some cross fertilisation of ideas would be fruitful. Thirdly, he found signs of isolationism amongst university teachers, who were so deeply involved in their own research or teaching, that they had little interest in the wider university educational communities. Cantrell also reported an atmosphere of amateurism which he thought could be profitably reduced by professional courses. And finally, many university teachers were genuinely anxious to learn more about teaching with their colleagues.

(b) Short courses

The courses provided have typically been one or two weeks during a vacation. It is assumed that the intellectual knowledge acquired at these times will be accurately stored in teachers' memories and faithfully applied in the heat of a teaching situation. Again the assumption is not surprising because it is made by most vocational courses in post-secondary education. The limitation of one or two week courses becomes apparent when it is remembered that new teachers continue to develop their individual styles for three to five years. Having then established certain techniques and confidence, they frequently feel more free to innovate during their second five years of teaching. Thus the counselling required is of a long-term nature. This has not always been appreciated even by authorities in this field.

(c) Didactic tone

It is sometimes asserted by teachers who object to such courses, that no-one could tell them how to teach their subject. They assume that the courses are didactic in tone. Paradoxically it is frequently teachers who would never make that assumption about their own teaching, who assume it in others. For example, teachers of arts subjects who value independence of thought and want students to develop their own opinions, assume that courses on teaching will not, or cannot, encourage individual approaches in teachers.

Recommendations suitable for one teacher are not necessarily suitable for others. Yet apart from the fact that teachers' different objectives will require different techniques, we have already seen that different teachers have different talents which need to be developed in different ways. For this reason the very word "training" is often regarded as inappropriate because it suggests a single end product. Learning to teach is a process of self development. New teachers need to acquire attitudes to students, their subject and their work which may be very individual.. For this reason group discussion and individual counselling are important methods for helping teachers' personal needs.

(d) Available qualified counsellors

It is also frequently assumed that there are seers capable of providing the necessary wisdom; yet although the study of teaching methods has begun, the study of teaching techniques which form those methods is hardly distinguished. It is the acquisition of teaching eechniques that is important when learning to be an effective teacher. These are far more subtle than knowledge of teaching methods. They include the inflection of a voice, a smiling glance, the raising of an eyebrow, the arrangement of chairs, the preparation of a punch line, the use of an 'explaining link' and so on.

(e) The problem of fear
The basic problem in the training of post-secondary teachers is fear. Teaching involves personal relationships and we are afraid of learning about ourselves. This is a normal fear for any individual, but academics are particularly sensitive about their self esteem. Acceptance by others depends upon reputation. Independence of mind depends upon confidence.

(f) The problem of authority
A related issue is the problem of authority. Academic staff see themselves as authorities within their particular area. Their perception of their professionalism, social prestige and academic freedom depends upon their sense of their own authority. In so far as the training of teachers implies that there are trainers, there will be a fear that the trainers have authority in at least some aspects of each teacher's personal role. In this respect the trainer of in-service teachers in higher education stands in an ambivalent relationship to his trainees. He is an authority on some aspects of their personal relationships, yet also an equal, and possibly junior, colleague.

(g) Indirect approaches to staff development
There are more methods of training which attempt to avoid the problems of fear and authority. They are necessarily indirect. They include the use of study leave, job exchanges, encouragement to attend conferences, the circulation of publications and in house newsletters about teaching, the provision of information services, co-operation in the provision to students of, for example, study counselling and participation on working parties to redesign curricula. All these indirect approaches require institutional supporting policies.

(h) The problem of departmentalism
In practice, while lip service may be paid to the importance of good teaching and staff development, the support is usually lacking. Promotion is more for publications than teaching. Heads of departments who gained their own promotion that way do not feel able to assess the teaching performance of their staff. Time for staff development is not made available. Money is not set aside for this purpose. Departments protect themselves from staff developers and other outside influences. They carry out no regular review of their courses unless obliged to do so by non-departmental forces such as college regulations, validating bodies or professional institutions.

Apart from these methods there are two broad groups of training activities which take contrasting approaches to the problems of fear self-esteem and authority. Firstly the trainer can see himself as a counsellor, a consultant an equal colleague a listener who helps teachers to clarify and solve their own problems. Secondly there is the trainer who runs courses, particularly workshops where the emphasis is as much upon the teaching skills as upon the provision of knowledge.

We will consider each of these direct approaches to staff-development in the next two sections.

(3) The need for counsellors

The rapidity with which the demand for training courses has sprung up has caught post-secondary educational institutions unawares. There is both a lack of knowledge and a shortage of personnel competent to undertake such training. Even when there has been financial provision to make senior appointments, some Australian universities, for example, have had difficulty in finding suitable applicants. In any case it is not teaching that is required but a consultation service. This needs to be a continuing activity through the academic year; not only available for one or two weeks during the vacations. Nor is the availability of research information sufficient. Intrinsic to the notion of a consultation service is consultation with fellow teachers with the same problems, not only 'experts'.

A crucial step in this development is the reduction of the traditional privacy of a teacher in his classroom. As soon as we accept that different teachers should develop different teaching styles, any "training" which does not take this into account is inadequate. It cannot be taken into account if no-one but the students ever sees the teacher teach. Marital relationships have traditionally been private. Yet few would not benefit from a little confidential counselling or discussion with others who are married. Many of the same principles apply to teaching. The teaching counsellor requires similar professional ethics to the marriage guidance counsellor. The same bonds of friendship and confidence are required between colleagues as within marital discussion groups. The counsellor's role is sometimes compared to that of a doctor; but there is no suggestion that teachers seeking guidance have something wrong with them. The analogy of a social worker and client is better than doctor and patient.

There is reason to think that services in teaching techniques are best provided by more than one person in any post-secondary educational institution. Although I have been employed full-time in this kind of work for over half my professional life I still make many errors of judgment which soon become apparent. How many I make which never become apparent can only be speculated. Since I suspect that my fallibility is not unique, the provision of a second opinion is usually valuable. It is also very unlikely that a counsellor's personality will be congenial to every potential colleague. Nor is the range of one man's academic understanding always sufficient. An alternative source of counsel is therefore an advantage.

While approachability is more important than seniority, teaching counsellors need to be recruited from those with wide academic and wide teaching experience. Persons with such experience will not seek junior posts. Consequently the provision of junior posts for this purpose is inappropriate and a false economy.

Many of the qualifications required by counsellors are obvious and need not be elaborated here. They must be the intellectual equals of the colleagues they wish to help. They need to be able to avoid the pitfalls of academic politics. Although it is usually appreciated that they need wide, rather than lengthy, experience of teaching; it is less appreciated that they need to be the kind of people who have considered their own teaching in a self-conscious way at the time they were developing their own teaching skills. Similarly the importance of empathy is usually well understood; but what I call "cognipathy" is not. Empathy is the ability to understand how others are feeling; "cognipathy" is the ability to understand how others are thinking. A counsellor well trained in one academic discipline sometimes has difficulty in understanding that teachers trained in another may use very different patterns of reasoning on educational matters. Cognipathy therefore requires flexibility in conceptual frameworks and in ways of relating them.

Owing to the lack of knowledge and the uncertainty of many authorities beginning to be concerned with the 'training' of teachers in higher education, too many people have spent time surveying what is required and what other people are doing, and too few have been doing it. The present need is for many more investigations into techniques of teaching, and building a pool of counselling experience.

(4) Courses for teachers in post-secondary education

(a) Relatively common needs and objectives

This leads us to consider the nature of courses for teachers in post-secondary education in those countries that provide them. So far I have argued that the assumed traditional emphasis upon formal courses is misplaced in this kind of teaching, partly because its objectives are often highly specific to individual teachers, and partly because personal contact is the most appropriate method to achieve many of the interpersonal objectives appropriate in teacher "training".

This is not to say that there are no objectives in common and none that can be achieved by formal courses. Harding (1974a) has listed 71 objectives of training university teachers which might be derived from general aims. Some are based upon evident staff needs such as "confidence in public aspects of speaking", "the ability to create and maintain student interest", and "deciding how much material to include in a course".

King (1973) has shown that three new university teachers in every four in the U.K. have more anxiety about lecturing than anything else. They worry about the size of the class, the problem of maintaining interest, how much information to include, the lack of feedback and difficulties in the manner of presentation. Anxieties about discussion techniques were concentrated upon their organisation and control in relation to personality factors.

After reviewing the work of the Association of American Colleges on the assessment of college teaching, Korn (1972) has concluded that teachers' most pressing needs are to know how to plan students' learning, and to make the methods of planning more public by publications in journals, awards for good teaching, and a system of grants, visiting professorships and sabbatical leave. He sees the role of the Promotions Committee as crucial. Harding also sees course design as a common need. He says the teacher will need "to convert general aims of a course into detailed objectives", "to prepare materials and design learning experiences which relate to specified objectives" and "to suggest alternatives", "to relate test items to objectives", "to inform students of the aims and objectives of their courses" and "to be willing to seek creative comment from colleagues and students on the nature of their objectives". Harding believes there are some objectives of training teachers in post-secondary education which relate to their professional roles. They need to be able to identify role conflicts and ambiguities in their work, to see when they should act as 'givers' and when 'facilitators' and to examine aspects of their authority and justify its use. There are numerous teaching skills which range from adequate preparation to the ability to find out students' interests and motives. Harding also attaches importance to a new teacher's motivation. Will he contribute to an institutional value system which places emphasis upon the teaching role? Will he be receptive to innovation - constructive but critical? How far will he find pleasure in teaching and be willing to test and experiment with it?

From experience in Zimbabwe, Gregory and Hammar (1974) concluded that such courses required prior consultation between planners and participants, plenty of activity and teaching practice with prompt feedback and verbalisation of what has been learned by the participants, early and obvious benefits for the participants' efforts, and opportunity for participants to assess the course. Cantrell's research (1972) also led to some firm recommendations. The training, if offered, must be given by very good teachers. The content must be practical, have scientific credibility, and be fairly concentrared. While providing an impeccable organisation, individual needs should be catered for, and for this purpose local courses were better than national or regional ones. The word "training" was regarded as objectionable, and "staff development" is worse. The concept of a "working group" was regarded more favourably.

(b) The content of post-secondary "teacher-training" courses

The content of such courses appears to be extremely varied. In Canada, Australia and the United Kingdom the contents of courses for university teachers was investigated by research officers appointed by their respective Committees of Vice-Chancellors. The contents of courses for polytechnic teachers in the United Kingdom has been described by Harding (1974b). No one topic was considered in more than half of them. The topics considered most frequently were the applications of audio visual aids, the teacher's role, the specification of objectives, the function of student assessment, the psychology of learning, lesson planning, programmed instruction and the educational system. Many included some introduction to the educational institution and most contained some practical teaching which was very often video-recorded for further discussion using micro-teaching techniques.

Reviewing the literature on video-playback in Teacher Education, Fuller and Manning (1973) say there is little empirical evidence that seeing one's own teaching performance on television improves teaching effectiveness. But subjective ratings are almost universally favourable.

It is clear that self-confrontation by video tape arouses interest and motivation in teachers. Estimates by student teachers of their own behaviour are very inaccurate but the bulk of the evidence seems to indicate that video playback can improve their realism. However, video playback does not increase their realism in perceiving others. The first reaction of many teachers is over concentration on their own body, either in overall judgments such as "I look awful", or by specific concentration on physical cues, such as the position of the arms or posture.

Video feedback does not appear to help teachers to recall personal, professional or perceptual problems. Nor does it help to reduce dogmatism as measured by the Rokeach Scale. But on the whole it seems to increase receptivity and this is important. Micro-teaching was used over a two year period at the University of Tel Aviv with teachers of dentistry. Attitude scales showed a highly significant improvement particularly in those who attended regularly; of course the persistence of such changes is always difficult to determine. (Perlberg et al, 1972.)

There are signs that video playback can be threatening and induce a stress reaction. Perlberg and O'Bryant (1968) say that the anxiety of faculty members can be alleviated by assuring them that there would be no administrative use of the video tapes, but this ignores the fact that the stress more often lies in *self* confrontation not confrontation by others. Such stress can inhibit learning. The stress inherent in self confrontation may be affected by dogmatism and related constructs such as close mindedness and authoritarianism. Yet of 12 studies considering self esteem, four found increases and eight found no difference. The increases do not appear to persist. On the opposite side, there is some evidence that students become more aggressive towards their teachers after seeing playback and the same tendency has been observed in university teachers who do not know the videotaped teacher. Time is required to absorb the impact of playback. Although the first viewing of the self appears to have the most impact, group cooperation appears to decrease following videotape replay.

The Clinic to Improve University Teaching at the University of Massachusetts was staffed by senior students who were to help teachers to identify their particular strengths, to recognise problems and to develop techniques to solve these problems by consultation with the senior students in the light of the teacher's objectives, video-recordings of his teaching, and student ratings on 47 questions. Repetition of this process amounts to a mirco-teaching approach.

The course organiser and leaders of micro-teaching sessions need to take great care to set a constructive and sympathetic tone. The literature on micro-teaching almost unanimously supports the view that some kind of focus is necessary. The more precisely the micro-teaching goal is specified, the more effective the effort appears to be, but there is a danger that it sometimes has a homogenising effect. Although micro-teaching works just as well on as off the campus, the presence of students and teaching supervisors has improved its effectiveness.

(c) Evaluation of courses for teachers
It is extremely difficult to investigate the effectiveness of short courses given to academics on teaching. What is learned becomes a small part of their total knowledge and psychological makeup. Consequently large scale effects on their teaching behaviour should not be expected. Yet this is galling for course organisers who will advocate that participants should assess the effects of their teaching since they cannot easily demonstrate the effectiveness of their own.

In one medical school (Anderson et al 1972) pre-tests, post-tests and delayed tests nine months later showed that although attitudes had not changed to the extent that might be wished, over half the participants in a small workshop course had obtained direct benefit from it.

In another small scale investigation (Miller 1973) a programme designed to increase teachers' capacities to be emphatic, genuine and respecting improved their performance in student counselling situations, but did not benefit their classroom teaching.

There is reason to think from follow-up surveys that participants at short courses on teaching methods are more willing to experiment with new methods; but since attendance at such courses is usually voluntary, potential innovators may be more likely to attend. Indirect evidence is available from Evans and Leppman (1968) who invesitgated the resistance of university teachers to the introduction of instructional television using a case history approach in one university and a survey method in nine others. They concluded that the majority of academics are opposed to innovations of this kind, and that would-be counsellors and innovators need a far sighted psychological approach if they are to be successful.

It is possible that attitudes to teaching innovations are consolidated by faculty group pressures, are related to personal security, and change little throughout a teacher's career. When investigating the attitudes of teachers in a south-western American state university, Peters (1974) found little difference in attitudes to innovations in teaching between teachers of different rank; but teachers of mathematics and chemistry preferred more formal methods while lecturers in education and psychology showed a preference for informal teaching techniques.

It may be unreasonable to expect large measurable differences between teachers who attend courses and those who do not. Courses are only one short part of the intellectual climate in which teachers move. Doing the job itself influences their subsequent job behaviour more than role play and discussion.

Formal courses are one way towards creating a profession informed about teaching in addition to specialist disciplines. The written word is probably more effective.

There is also a need to recognise the important role students may play and to enlist their support. They may not be able to give an objective or valid evaluation of a teacher or a total course, but they usually have constructive suggestions when suitably approached. Too often it is assumed that students are like children, their teachers know what is good for them, they must do as they are told and play no constructive part in the design of their own courses. Students need to feel they control their own lives. Motivation cannot be imposed, yet we have seen it is crucial.

V Conclusion

The first section of this chapter is concerned with the evaluation of teaching, where "teaching" is conceived as creating the conditions in which learning can take place. If an evaluation discovers something wrong with the conditions for learning, and of course, those conditions can never be perfect, improvements can probably be made by changing an earlier decision, namely one of those considered in the previous six chapters. For example an evaluation could reveal that the objectives are wrong, that unsuitable students are enrolled for the course, that the content of the course is inappropriate, that the teaching methods are ineffective or that any other decision is at fault.

However it is also possible that the assumptions behind the evaluation itself are wrong. Accordingly the second section of this chapter looked at some of the assumptions behind ways to evaluate teaching.

Another possibility is that, while the decisions are correct, the teachers do not have the necessary skills to carry them out. For this reason the third section dealt briefly with the evaluation and assessment of teachers.

There is no point in evaluating teachers if there are no means to improve their teaching. The last section therefore first raises how teacher training is perceived and then considers two broad approaches to carrying it out. However it is not a detailed review of the training of post-secondary teachers. This book is about seven decisions when teaching students, not decisions when teaching academics.

In this book we started with a very simple model with selected emphases of the interdependence of decisions when teachers design a course. The main purpose of the book has been to present information which may influence these decisions. Most teachers continually modify their methods according to student response.

Consequently the cyclical path followed by a teacher on this model may be extremely complex. We have not pretended that the model can fully represent the teacher's situation, but as a simple teaching device capable of infinite variation it provides one useful way for post-secondary teachers to conceive their job.

BIBLIOGRAPHY

Page Reference

186 Abercrombie, M.L.J. 1965 The anatomy of judgement. London. Hutchinson.

74 Abercrombie, M.L.J. 1966 Perception and communication in teaching methods in university departments of science and medicine. Report of a conference held at the University of London Institute of Education.

31 Abrams, H.K., and Byrd, A.R. 1971 Survey of grading procedures of American and Associated Medical Colleges. Journal of Medical Education. Vol.46 316-339.

75 Acland, H., and Hatch, S. 1968 Three aspects of student residence: Recruitment, participation and academic performance. Dept. Higher Education, University of London Institute of Education, P.14.

199,200 Adderley, K.W., Ashwin, C., Bradbury, P., Freeman, J., Goodlad, S., Greene, J., Jenkins, D.E.P., Rae, J., and Uren, O. 1975 Project methods in higher education. Society for Research into Higher Education, London.

153 Agar, 1962 Instruction of industrial workers by tape recorder. Affarsekonomi No.10.

117 Aiken, E.G., Thomas, G.S., and Shennum, W.W. 1975 Memory for a lecture: effect of notes, lecture rate, and informational density. Journal of Educational Psychology, 67, 439-44.

75 Albrow, M.C. 1965 The influence of accommodation on 64 Reading University students, (Mimeo). Cited by Miller, G.W. in Success, failure and wastage in higher education. Harrap Co. Ltd., London.

195 Allen, D.W. and Fortune, J.C. 1967 An analysis of micro-teaching: A new procedure in teacher education. Cited by Peck, R.F. and Tucker, J.W. in Travers, R.M.W. (ed) Second handbook of research on teaching 1974. 940-978.

197 Allen, D. and Ryan, K. 1969 Micro-teaching. Published by Addison Wesley.

77 Altman, E. 1968 The mature student teacher. New Society No.274, 930-932.

280 Anderson, J., Day, J.,., Freeling, P., and McKerron, G.C. 1972 The workshop as a learning system in medical teacher education. British Journal of Medical Education No.6, 296-300.

75 Anderson, D.S. and Priestley, R.R. 1960 Notes on the Study of failure in Australian Universities, (Mimeo). University of Melbourne. Cited by Miller, G.W., in Success, failure and wastage in higher education. Harrap, London.

149 André, R. 1973 Distribution of Higher Education in Economics and English. Research Register into Higher Education in Western Europe. Society for Research into Higher Education.

71 Anstey, E., and Mercer, E.O. 1956 Interviewing for the selection of staff. Allen and Unwin.

139 Appleton, W.S. 1969 The struggle to concentrate. American Journal of Psychiatry. Vol.126, No.2, 256-259. Psychological Abstracts (1970) April Vol.14, No.4, Abstract No.5629.

76 Armstrong, H.G. 1967 Wastage of ability amongst the intellectually gifted. British Journal of Educational Psychology. Vol.37, No.2, 257-259.

117 Aronson, E., Turner, J.A., and Carlsmith, J.M. 1963 Communicator credibility and communication discrepancy as determinants of opinion change. Journal of Abnormal and Social Psychology. Vol.67, 31-36.

73 Astin, A.W. 1963 Differential college effects on the motivation of talented students to obtain the Ph.D. Journal of Educational Psychology, Vol.54, 63-71.

73 Astin, A.W. 1964(a) Distribution of students among Higher Educational Institutions. Journal of Educational Psychology, Vol.55, 276-287.

73 Astin, A.W. 1964(b) Personal and environmental factors associated with college dropouts among high aptitude students. Journal of Educational Psychology, Vol.55, 219-227.

73 Astin, A.W. 1965 Classroom environment in different fields of study. Journal of Educational Psychology, Vol.56, 275-282.

73 Astin, A.W. 1967 The Conference on the Cluster College Concept: Students Journal of Higher Education, Vol.38, 396-397.

53 Astin, A.W. 1968 Undergraduate achievement and institutional excellence. Journal of Science, Vol.161, (3842) 661-668.

264 Astin, A.W. and Lee, C.B.T. 1966 Current practices in the evaluation and training of college teachers. The Educational Record, Vol.47, 361-365.

24 Atkinson, J.T., and Litwin, G. 1960 The achievement, motive and test-anxiety conceived as motive to approach success and motive to avoid failure. Journal of Abnormal and Social Psychology, Vol.60, No.1.

187,188 Back, K.W. 1973 Beyond words. Pelican Books.

157 Bacquet, R., Chaudagne, H., Larcebeau, J., and Leon, A. 1954 An experiment on information with classes of children in the last year at Elementary School. (Une experience d'information dans les classes de fin d'etudes primaires). Bulletin de L'Institut National D'Orientation Professionelle, janvier-fevrier, 1954, 1, 3-27.

186 Barnett, S.A. 1958 An experiment with 'Free-group Discussions'. Universities Quarterly, Vol.12, 175-180.

154 Banathy, B.H., and Jordan, B. 1969 A classroom laboratory instructional system (CLIS). Foreign Language Annals, Vol.2, 466-473.

24 Barzun, J. 1946 Teacher in America. Boston, Little, Brown and Company.

114 Bassey, M. 1968 Learning methods in tertiary education. Nottingham Regional College of Technology, internal paper.

41 Bassey, M. 1971 The assessment of students by formal assignments. Research Office for the Study of Higher Education, New Zealand University Students Association. 22pp.

10 Baume, A.D., and Jones, B. 1974 Education by objectives Curricular Study 1. Nelpress, North-East London Polytechnic, 67pp.

245 Baumol, W., and Bowen, W. 1966 Performing Arts: the economic dilemma. The Twentieth Century Fund, New York.

78 Bay, C. 1967 Political and Apolitical students: Facts in search for theory. Journal of Social Issues, Vol.23, No.3, 76-91.

268 Bayley, D.H. 1967 Making college teaching a profession. Improving College and University Teaching. 15, 115-119.

170 Beach, L.R. 1974 Self-directed student groups and college learning. Higher Education, Vol.3, No.2, 187-200.

195 Beard, R.M. 1972 Teaching and Learning in Higher Education. 2nd Edition. Penguin. 253pp.

122-127 Beard, R.M., and Bligh, D.A. 1972 Research into Teaching Methods in Higher Education. 3rd Edition. Society for Research into Higher Education.

27 Beard, R.M., and Pole, K. 1971 Content and purpose of biochemistry examinations. British Journal of Medical Education, Vol.5, 13-21.

154 Beckman, E.G. 1970 'Professor Stevens, The Class is Ready'. Audio-Visual Instruction, Vol.5, No.3, 74-75 and 123.

151 Belson, W.A. 1952 An enquiry into the comprehensibility of 'To for tonight'. BBC Audience Research Dept., Report No. LR/5 1080, 56pp.

163 Belson, W.A. 1956 A technique for studying the effects of a television broadcast. Applied Statistics, Vol.5, No.3, 195-202.

163 Belson, W.A. 1959 The effects of television upon the interests and the initiative of adult viewers. BBC, 11pp.

187 Benne, K.D., and Sheats, P. 1948 Functional Roles of Group Members. Journal of Social Issues Vol.4, No.2, 41-49.

94 Berger, G. 1972 "Opinions and Facts" in Interdisciplinar OECD.

90 Berman, L. 1968 New priorities in the curriculum.

86,91 Bernstein, B. 1971 "On the classification and framing of educational knowledge" in M.F.D. Young; Knowledge and Control. Collier MacMillan.

145 Berry, R. 1965 Rapid reading reconsidered. Education. 596.

115 Betts, D.S., and Walton, A.J. 1970 A lecture match or anything you can do I can do better'. Physics Education, Vol.5, No.6, 321.325.

133 Bigelow, G.S., and Egbert, R.L. 1968 Personality factors and independent study. Journal of Educational Research, Vol.62, No.1, 37-39.

50 Biggs, D.A., and Tinsley, D.J. 1970 Student made academi predictions. The Journal of Educational Research, Vol.63, No.5, 195-197.

44 Biggs, J.B. 1973 Study behaviour and performance in objective and essay formats. Australian Journal of Education, Vol.17, No.2, 157-167.

136 Biggs, J.B. 1978 Individual and Group Differences in Study Processes. British Journal of Educational Psychology Vol.48, 266-279.

124 Biran, L.A. 1966 A comparison of a scrambled and sequential presentation of a branching programme. Research Report on Programmed Learning No.9, National Council for Programmed Learning, University of Birmingham, England.

124 Biran, L.A., and Pickering, E. 1968 Unscrambling a herringbone: an experimental evaluation of branching programme. British Journal of Medical Education, Vol.2, 213-219.

26 Black, P.J. 1968 University examinations. Physics Education, Vol.3, No.2, 93-99.

269-271 Blackburn, R.T., and Trowbridge, K.W. 1973 Faculty accountability and faculty workload: a preliminary cost analysis of their relationship as revealed by Ph.D productivity. Research into Higher Education, Vol.1, No.1, 1-12.

271 Blackstone, T., and Fulton, O. 1974 Men and women academics: an Anglo-American comparison of subject choices and research activity. Higher Education, Vol.3, No.2, 119-140.

152 Bligh, D.A. 1970 A pilot experiment to test the relative effectiveness of three kinds of teaching method. Research in Librarianship, Vol.3, No.15, 88-93.

173,252 Bligh, D.A. 1971 Teaching students in groups. University Teaching Methods Unit, London. 44pp.

113,114,115, 118 Bligh, D.A. 1972(a) What's the use of lectures? 3rd edition. Penguin, 254pp.

1-8, 45-46 Bligh, D.A. 1972(b) Education technology - an approach to educational decisions. Overseas Universities, No.19, 8-12.

252 Bligh, D.A. 1972(c) Evaluation of teaching in groups by interaction analysis, in Varieties of Group Discussion in University Teaching, University Teaching Methods Unit, London, 82-94.

24-28,66, 185 Bligh, D.A. 1973(a) Teaching and learning in higher education. Seven broadcasts, BBC, London.

140 Bligh, D.A. (ed) 1973(b) Introductory course for lecturers II background papers. University Teaching Methods Unit, London. 74pp.

107,114,117, 152,249 Bligh, D.A. 1974 Are varied teaching methods more effective? Ph.D Thesis of the University of London. 639pp.

250 Bligh, D.A., Jaques, D., and Piper, D.W. 1980 New methods and techniques in post-secondary education. Educational Studies and documents No.31, UNESCO.

97 Bloom, B.S. 1956 Taxonomy of educational objectives cognitive domain. Longmans.

66 Bloom, B.S., and Peters, F.R. 1961 Academic prediction scales. New York, Free Press.

39 Bojsen-Møller, F. 1973 Test reliability in macroscopic anatomy and special embriology, in Register of Research into Higher Education in Western Europe 1973. Society for Research into Higher Education p.144.

197 Borg, W.R., Kelly, M.L., Langer, P., and Gall, M. 1970 The Minicourse: A micro-teaching approach to teacher education. Beverley Hills California. Cited by Peck, R.F., and Tucker, J.A., in Travers, R.M.W. (ed) Second handbook of research on teaching. 1974 Rand McNally 940-978.

269 Bourgeois, D.P. 1967 A study of faculty opinion concerning selected factors related to excellence in teaching at the University of South-western Louisiana. Unpublished M.A. thesis quoted by Miller, R.I. 1972. Evaluating faculty performance. Jossey Bass, P.217.

245 Bowen, H.R., and Douglass, G.K. 1971 Efficiency in liberal education. McGraw Hill.

72 Boyer, E.L., and Michael, W.B. 1965 Outcomes of college in Review of Educational Research, Vol.55, No.4, 277-291.

139 Bradley, R.M., and Hindmarsh, I. 1968 Research students: Time wasters? New Society, No.322, 802-803.

134 Bray, J.H., Maxwell, S.E., and Schmeck, R.R. 1980 A Psychometric Investigation of the Survey of Study Habits and Attitudes. Applied Psychological Measurement, Spring Volume 4, No.II 195-201.

162 British Broadcasting Corporation. 1958 Audience research report. Your life in their hands. VR/58/598. BBC, 58pp.

200-201 British Broadcasting Corporation. 1972 Games and simulations. 40pp.

48 British Medical Association Report. 1948 The training of a doctor. Butterworth, London.

166 Brody, H.A., Lucaccini, L.F., Kamp, M., and Ruzen, R. 1973 Mount Zion Hospital and Medical Center, San Francisco. Computer based simulated patient for teaching history-taking. Journal of Dental Education, Vol.37, No.8, 27-31.

74,75 Brothers, J., and Hatch, S. 1971 Residence and student life. Tavistock Press. 364pp.

69 Brown, B.R. 1967 Student stress and institutional environment. Journal of Social Issues, Vol.23, No.3, 92-107.

154 Brown, G.H. 1968 Providing communication experiences in programmed foreign language instruction. Professional Paper, 35-68 Alexandria, Virginia: George Washington University, Human Resources Research Office.

65 Brown, R.D. 1968 The intellectual and academic aspects of college life. Journal of Educational Research, Vol.61, No.10, 439-441.

134 Brown, W.F., and Holtzman, W.H. 1955 A Study - Attitudes questionnaire for predicting academic success, Journal of Educational Psychology, Vol.46, 75-84.

134 Brown, W.F., and Holtzman, W.H. 1966 Manual of the survey of study habits and attitudes. The Psychological Corporation, New York.

191 Brown, W.F. 1972 Student-to-student counselling, an approach to motivating academic achievement. University of Texas Press.

90,93 Bruner, J. 1977 The process of education. Harvard University Press.

268 Bryan, R.C. 1968 Student ratings of teachers. Improving college and university teaching. Vol.16, 200-202.

33,37 Bull, G.M. 1956 An examination of the final examination in medicine. Lancet, Vol.2, 368-372.

31 Burke, R.J. 1968 Student reactions to course grades. Journal of Experimental Education, Vol.36, No.4, 11-13.

50 Burke, R.J. 1969 Some preliminary data on the use of self evaluations and peer ratings in assigning university course grades. Journal of Educational Research, Vol.62, No.10, 444-448.

68 Butcher, H.J. 1969 An Investigation of the 'Swing to Science'. Research in Education, Vol.1, 38-57.

122 Bunyard, J.K. 1968 Programmed instruction in Northern Nigeria. Paper presented to the Third Annual Conference of the Association for Programmed Learning and Educational Technology.

117 Buzan, T. 1974 Use your head. BBC Publications, London.

191 Campbell, D.P. 1965 Results of counselling 25 years later. Philadelphia and London, Saunders.

76 Campbell, R., and Siegal, B.S. 1967 The demand for higher education in the United States 1919-1964. American Economic Review, Vol.57, No.3, 482-494.

248 Cantrell, E.G. 1971 (Department of Medicine Southampton University). Thirty lectures. British Journal of Medical Education, 5, 309-319.

277 Cantrell, E.G. 1972 Attitudes of junior medical school staff towards a proposed course in teaching. Report to The Social Science Research Council. Mimeo 64pp.

143 Carmichael, L., and Dearborn, W.G. 1948 Reading and visual fatigue. Harrap.

253 Cartmell, Sq.Ldr.,A.E. 1971 The use of C.C.T.V. in the assessment of teaching effectiveness. Programmed Learning in Educational Technology, Vol.8, No.3, 173-185.

127 Castle, W., and Davidson, L. 1969 An evaluation of programmed instruction in a new Medical Faculty. British Journal of Medical Education, Vol.3, No.9, 359-361.

123 Cavanagh, P., Morgan, R.G.T., and Thornton, C. 1963 The British European Airways Study. Occupational Psychology Vol.37, 76-84.

253 Centra, J.A. 1972 The utility of student ratings for instructional improvement. Educational Testing Service, New Jersey, 74pp.

32 Chase, C.I. 1968 The impact of some obvious variables on essay test records. Journal of Education Measurement Vol.5, No.4 Winter 315-388.

64 Chauncey, H., and Hilton, T.L. 1965 Are aptitude tests valid for the highly able? Science, Vol.148, No.3675, 1297-1304.

194 Chester, W. 1938 Laboratory by demonstration. Journal of Higher Education, Vol.9, 32-36.

73 Chickering, A.W. 1967 Curriculum, teaching and evaluation - implications for student mental health development and counselling. NASPA, Vol.5 (October), 167-174.

138 Child, D. 1970(a) Some aspects of study habits in higher education. International Journal of Educational Science, Vol.4, No.1, 11-20.

138 Child, D. 1970(b) Some reference groups of university students. Educational Research, Vol.12, No.2, 145-149.

154 Chomei, T., and Houlihan, R. 1968-1969 An experimental study of the effectiveness of a newly devised short-delay playback system in a language laboratory. Audio-Visual Language Journal, Vol.6, 59-72.

162 Chu, G.H., and Schram, W. 1967 Learning from television: what the research says. Stanford Institution for Communication Research.

62 Cleary, T.A. 1968 Test bias: Prediction of grades of negro and white students in integrated colleges. Journal of Educational Measurement Vol.5 No.2, 115-124.

77 Cleugh, M.F. 1972 Stresses of mature students. British Journal of Educational Studies. Vol.20, No.1, 76-90.

160 Cline, D.W., and Garrard, J.N. 1973 Evaluation of the SAID teaching programme. The American Journal of Psychiatry, Vol.130, 582-585.

133,140 Clift, J.C., and Thomas, I.D. 1973 Student workloads. Higher Education, Vol.2, 44-460.

132 Clossick, M. 1968 Student residence: A new approach at the University of Essex. Research into Higher Education Monographs. 63pp.

249 Coats, W.D., and Smidchens, U. 1966 Audience recall as a function of speaker dynamics. Journal of Educational Psychology, Vol.57, No.4, 189-191.

140 Cohen, L. 1970 Linking university studies and industrial training. An assessment of the thick-sandwich course by civil engineering students and their industry-based supervisors. Vocational Aspects of Education, Vol.2, 57-61.

52 Cohen, L., and Child, D. 1969 Some sociological and psychological factors in university failure. Durham Research Review, Vol.5, No.22 365-372.

269 Cole, S., and Cole, J.R. 1967 Scientific output and recognition: A study in the operation of the reward system in science. American Sociological Review, Vol.32, No.3, 377-390.

32,48 Colton, T., and Peterson, O.L. 1967 An Assay of medical students' abilities by oral examination. Journal of Medical Education, Vol.42, 1005.

271 Committee of Vice-Chancellors and Principals of the Universities of the United Kingdom 1972 Report of an enquiry into the use of academic staff time. Published by Committee of Vice-Chancellors London, 36pp.

69 Coombs, R.H., and Davis, V. 1967 Socio-Psychological adjustment in collegiate scholastic success. Journal of Educational Research, Vol.61, No.4, 168-188.

44 Cooper, B., and Foy, J.M. 1967 Guessing in multiple choice tests. British Journal of Medical Education, Vol.1, 212.

47 Cortis, G.A. 1968 Predicting student performance in colleges of education. British Journal of Educational Psychology, NO.38, Vol.2, 115-122.

124 Coulson, J.E., and Silberman, H.F. 1960 Effects of three variables on a teaching machine. Journal of Educational Psychology, Vol.51, 135-143.

194 Coulter, J.C. 1966 The effectiveness of inductive laboratory, inductive demonstration and deductive laboratory in biology. Journal of Research in Science Teaching, Vol.4, 185-186.

117,151,152, 157 Council for Cultural Co-operation 1966 European Research in Audio-Visual Aids. Part ii Abstracts, published by Council for Europe.

77 Couper, M., and Harris, C. 1970 Cat to University: The changing student intake. Educational Research, Vol.12, No.2, 113-120.

30,40,51, 69 Cox, R.J. 1974 Students and student assessment: A study of different perceptions and patterns of response to varied forms of assessment in the University of Essex. Ph.D thesis University of Essex, England, unpublished.

33 Cox, R.J. 1967 Examinations and higher education: A surv of the literature. Universities Quarterley, June.

254 Crawford, P.L., and Bradshaw, H.L. 1968 Perception of characteristics of effective university teachers: A scaling analysis. Education and Psychological Measurement, Vol.28, 1079-1085.

47 Crocker, A.C. 1968 Predicting teaching success. Education for Teaching, Vol.76, 49-52.

77 Crotty, W.J. 1967 Democratic and consensual norms and the college student. Sociology of Education, Vol.40, No.3, 200-218.

23 Crouzet, Y., and Ferenczi, M.V. 1973 Development of tests for the linguistic guidance of students learning French or needing French to pursue their studies. In Register of Research into Higher Education in Western Europe 1973. Society for Research into Higher Education, p.55.

127 Croxton, P.C.L., and Martin, L.H. 1968 Progressive evaluation and the control of programmed classes in degree courses in Tobin, M. (ed) Problems and methods in programmed learning, proceedings of the 1967 Association for Programmed Learning and the National Centre for Programmed Learning, Birmingham Conference, Vol.3, 83.

193,194 Cunningham, H. 1946 Lecture demonstration versus individual laboratory method - An analysis of 37 research studies: Science Education, March, Vol.30, 70-82.

155 Cutler, R.L., McKeachie, W.J., and McNeil, E.B. 1958 Teaching psychology by telephone. American Psychologist, Vol.13, 551-552.

163 Daines, J.W., and Neilson, J.B. 1963 Report of an investigation into the Associated Television series 'Theatres and Temples of the Greeks'. University of Nottingham, Institute of Education.

33 Dale, R.R. 1959 University Standards. Universities Quarterly, Vol.13.

54 Davis, T.N., and Satterly, D.J. 1969 Personality profiles of student teachers. British Journal of Educational Psychology, Vol.39, 183-187.

59 De Vittorelli, I. 1972 Les depenses des etudiants etrangers inscrits a Louvain au premier semestre, 1970/71 (The expenses of foreign students in their first term at Louvain, 1970/71), Louvain, Secteur Social et Culturel, 3 Krakenstraat, 100pp.

59 Delfosse, F. 1972 (in preparation) Le budget des etudiants a Louvain, enquete aupres des etudiants celibataires dans les premiers et deuxiemes cycles a l'UCL en 70/71 (Student budgets at Louvain: an enquiry conducted among unmarried students in the first two cycles at the Catholic University of Louvain in 1970/71) Dossiers No.17, Louvain, Secteur Social et Culturel, 3 Krakenstraat, 150pp.

249 Dell, D., and Hiller, J.E. 1971 Computer analysis of teachers' explanations. In Westbury, I., and Bellack, A. (eds) Research into classroom processes, pp209-217 Teachers College Press, New York.

160 DSIR Working Party (Chairman Francis, W.L.) 1963 The film in scientific research. Department of Scientific and Industrial Research, 67pp.

126 Dick, W. 1963 The tension as a function of paired and individual use of programmed instruction. Journal of Programmed Instruction, Vol.2, No.3, 17-23.

271 Dinerman, B. 1971 Sex discrimination in academia. Journal of Higher Education, Vol.42, No.4.

163 Divo, F. 1961 Jugend und Fernsehen (Young people and television). Frankfurt, Main, 25pp.

55 Doty, B.A. 1967 Some academic characteristics of mature women students. Journal of Educational Research. Vol.61, No.4, 163-165.

47 Doty, B.A. 1970 Predictions of teaching effectiveness of women who begin teaching after the age of 35. The Journal of Teacher Education, Vol.21, No.4.

94 Doyal, L. 1974 Inter-disciplinary studies in higher education. Universities Quarterley, Vol.28, No.4, 480-487.

163 Dubin, R., and Hedley, R.A. 1969 The medium may be related to the message: College instruction by TV. Eugene, University of Oregon Press.

107 Dubin, R., and Taveggia, T.C. 1968 The teaching learning paradox.

164 Dumazedier, J. 1956 The impact of television programmes on rural audiences. Press, Film and Radio in The World Today, UNESCO, Paris.

164 Dumazedier, J., and Sylwan, B. nd Experiment in using kinescopes for adult audiences. Reports and papers on mass communication, No.26, UNESCO, Paris.

167 Dupont, M., and Servais, P. 1973 Study of the social-psychological conditions of an "authentic studentship" at the university. Entry in Register of Research into Higher Education in Western Europe. Society for Research into Higher Education, P.155.

149 Durey, P. 1967 A survey of student library-use at the University of Keele. Research in Librarianship, Vol.2, No.7, 3-8.

120 Dwyer, F.M. (Jnr) 1971 (The Pennsylvania State University, Philadelphia) An experimental evaluation of the instructional effectiveness of black and white and colored illustrations. Didakta Medica.

266,269 Dwyer, F.M. 1972 Selected criteria for evaluating teacher effectiveness. Improving College and University Teaching, Vol.21, No.1, 51-52.

49 Easton, R.E. 1968 Differences between oral examination grades given by doctor-nurse pairs. British Journal of Medical Education, Vol.2, 301-302.

252 Eble, K.E. 1969 Teaching, research and professing. Toledo, Ohio: Centre for Study of Higher Education, University of Toledo.

255 Eisner, E.W. 1969 Instructional and expressive educational objectives: their formulation and use in the curriculum, in "Instructional objectives" ed. Popham,W.J. Chicago AERA Monograph series.

122 Elley, E.W.B. 1966 The role of errors in learning with feedback. British Journal of Educational Psychology, Vol.36, 296-300.

120 Elwood, W.K., and Haley, J.V. 1974 (University of Kentucky) Effective learning by slide-guide method: Evaluation of a course in micro-anatomy. Journal of Dental Education, Vol.38, No.3, 161-167.

41 Elton, L.R.B. 1968 The assessment of students - A new approach. Universities Quarterley, Vol.22, No.3, 291-301.

271 Elton, L.R.B. 1975 Paper read to the "Conference on the Evaluation of Teaching in Higher Education", University Teaching Methods Unit, London.

156 Engel, C.E., Irvine, E., and Wakeford, R.E. 1972 Dept. Audio Visual Communication. British Medical Association Report on the transferability of an individual learning system. British Journal of Medical Education, 6, 311-316.

197 Emmer, E.T., and Miller, G.B. 1968 An assessment of terminal performance in a teaching laboratory: A pilot study. University of Texas Research and Development Center for Teacher Education. Cited by Peck, R.F., and Tucker, J.A., in Travers, Second handbook of research on teaching, 1974, pp 940-978.

134 Entwistle, N.J., and Entwistle, D. 1970 The relationship between personality, study methods and academic performance. British Journal of Educational Psychology. Vol.40, 132-143.

132 Entwistle, N.J. 1972 Students and their academic performance in different types of institutions, in Butcher, H.J., and Rudd, E., Contemporary problems in higher education, McGraw Hill.

135,136 Entwistle, N.J. 1974 Sylbs, sylfs and ambiverts: labelling and libelling students. Inaugural lecture, University of Lancaster.

135 Entwistle, N.J., and Brennan, T. 1971 The academic performance of students II, types of successful students. British Journal of Educational Psychology, Vol.41, 268-276.

31,51 Entwistle, N.J., and Percy, K.A. 1973 Critical thinking or conformity? An investigation of the aims and outcomes of higher education. Paper read to the Society for Research into Higher Education 9th Annual Conference.

51 Entwistle, N.J., and Wilson, J.D. 1970 Personality, study methods and academic performance. Universities Quarterley, Vol.24, No.2, 147-155.

124 Evans, J.L., Glaser, R., and Hommes, L.E. 1962 An investigation of 'Teaching Machine' variables using learning programmes in symbolic logic. Journal of Educational Research, Vol.55, No.9, 433.

48 Evans, L.R., Ingersol, R.W., and Smith, E.J. 1966 The reliability, validity and taxanomic structure of the oral examination. Journal of Medical Education, Vol.41, 651-657.

279 Evans, R.I., and Leppmann, P. 1968 Resistance to Innovation in Higher Education. Jossey-Bass Inc., San Francisco, 198pp.

55 Evans, K.M. 1967 Teacher training courses and students' personal qualities. Educational Research, Vol.10, No.2, 72-77.

267 Falk, B., and Lee Dow, K. 1971 The assessment of university teaching. Society for Research into Higher Education, London. 47pp.

267 Falk, B., and Lee Dow, K. 1971 University teaching: reality and change. Quarterley Review of Australian Education. Vol.4, No.4.

54 Faunce, P.S. 1968 Personality characteristics and vocational interests related to the college persistence of academically gifted women. Journal of Counselling Psychology, Col.15, No.1, 31-40.

40 Feldhusen, J.F. 1961 An evaluation of college students' reaction to the Open Book examination. Educational and Psychological Measurement, Vol.21, No.3, 637-646.

230 Feldman K.A, and Newcomb T.M., 1973 The impact of college on students, Vols 1 and 2. Jossey Bass

43 Ferguson, A., Wright, M.A., and McNichol, G.P. 1971 Appraisal of student performance: Multiple choice questions, essays and short notes. British Journal of Medical Education, Vol.5, 147-151.

209,210, 224 Fielden, J., and Lockwood, G. 1973 Planning and management in universities. Chatto and Windus, London.

54 Fischer, E.H., Wells, C.F., and Cohen, S.L. 1968 Birth order and expressed interest in becoming a college professor. College of Counselling Psychology, Vol.15, No.2, 111-116.

62 Fishman, J.A., and Pasanella, A.K. 1960 Colleges admission - selection studies. Review of Educational Research, Vol.30, No.4, 298-310.

196 Flanders, N.A. 1970 Interaction analysis. Addison Wesl

25,39 Flood Page, C 1967 Worrying about examinations. Cambridge Institute Education Bulletin, Vol.3, No.6, 2-7.

266 Flood Page, C. 1971 Students' reactions to teaching methods. Universities Quarterley, Vol.25, No.4, 418-434.

268 Follman, J., Lucoff, M., Small, L., and Powor, F. 1974 Kinds of keys of student ratings of faculty teaching effectiveness. Research in Higher Education Vol.2, No.2, 173-179.

124 Foote, B.L. 1973 A case study: design factors for instruction with an audio-visual response teaching machine. Journal of Engineering Education, Vol.63, No.6, 421.

120 Foster, J. 1969 A note on the visibility of black-on-white and white-on-black photographic slides. British Psychological Society Bulletin, Vol.21, p.72.

192 Foxley, C.H. 1969 Orientation or disorientation? Personnel and Guidance Journal, Vol.48, 218-221.

158 Foy, J.M., and McCurrie, J.R. 1973 University of Bradford, Learning from pharmacological films. University Vision No.10, 34-40.

161 Francis, W.L. (Chairman) 1963 Report of a working party. Working party set up by the Department of Scientific and Industrial Research under the chairmanship of Dr. W. L. Francis, H.M.S.O. 67pp.

152 Frank, R.E., and Lesher, R.E. 1971 An evaluation of the effectiveness of taped lectures in a community college setting. Scientia Paedagogica Experimentalis, Vol.8, No.1, 16-21.

158 Fraisse, P., and Montmollin, G. de 1952 Sur la memoire des films. (On remembering films). Revue Internationale de Filmologie, No.9, 37-68.

189 Frederick, J. 1972 Likely development and change in student counselling in North America and Australia in Student Counselling: Scope and training. Proceedings of the 3rd Annual Conference on Student Counselling. Department of Higher Education, University of London Institute of Education, 17-35.

153 Freedman, E.S. 1969 An investigation into the efficiency of the language laboratory in foreign language teaching. Audio-Visual Language Journal, Vol.7, No.2, 75-95.

78 Freedman, M.B. 1969 The college experience. San Francisco, Jossey-Bass Inc., 202pp.

117 Freyberg, P.S. 1956 The effectiveness of note-taking. Education for Teaching, February, 17-24.

145 Fry, E. 1963(a) Teaching faster reading - a manual. Cambridge University Press.

145 Fry, E. 1963(b) Reading faster. Cambridge University Press.

47 Fuller, J.L. 1972 The effects of training and criterion of models of interjudged reliability. Journal of Dental Education, Vol.36, No.4, 19-22.

278 Fuller, F.F., and Manning, B.A. 1973 Self-confrontation reviewed: A concentralisation for video playback in teacher education. Review of Educational Research, Vol.43, No.4, 469-528.

51 Furneaux, W.D. 1962 The psychologist and the university. Universities Quarterley, Vol.17,No.1, 33-47.

142 Gadzella, B.M., and Goldston, J. 1977 Effects of study guides and classroom discussions on students' perceptions of study habits, Perceptual and Motor Skills, Vol.44, No.3 Part I June, 901-902.

88 Gaff, J.G., and Wilson, R.C. 1971 Faculty cultures and interdisciplinary studies. Journal of Higher Education Vol.42, No.3, 186-201.

248 Gage, N.L., Blegard, M., Dell, D., Hiller, J.E., Rosenshine, B., and Unruh, W.R. 1968 Exploration of the teachers' effectiveness in explaining. Technical Report No.4, Stanford Center for Research in Teaching, School of Education, Stanford University.

194 Gage, N.L. (ed) 1963 Handbook of research on teaching. American Educational Research Association, Rand McNally.

97 Gagne, R. 1965 The conditions of learning. Holt, Rinehart and Winston.

117 Gallagher, J.B. (Jnr.) (Tufts University School of Dental Medicine, Boston, Mass.) 1971 An evaluation of the transfer of information by printed materials without a formal lecture. Journal of Dental Education, Vol.34, No.4, 59-66.

126 Gallegos, A.M. 1968 Experimenter pacing and student pacing of programmed instruction. Journal of Educational Research, Vol.61, 339-342.

135 Gardner, R.W., Holzman, P.S., Klein, G.S., Linton, H.B. and Spence, D.P. 1959 Cognitive Control: A study of individual consistencies in cognitive behaviour. Psychological Issues, monograph 4.

268 Gauvain, S. 1970 Questionnaire techniques in course evaluation. Paper given to symbposium on Automation in Medical and other Higher Education, Multiple Choice Questions and Research.

30 Geertsma, R.H., and Chapman, J.E. 1967 The Evaluation of Medical Students. Journal of Medical Education, Vol.42 p.938.

124 Gessner, F.B. 1974 An experiment in modified self-paced learning. Engineering Education, Vol.64, No.5, 368-370.

252 Gibb, C.A. 1955 Classroom behaviour of the college teacher. Educational and Psychological Measurement, 15, 254-263.

158 Gibb, G. 1970 CCTV: Some guidelines for the future use of video-tapes in professional training. Education for Teaching, 81, 51-56. Technical Education Abstracts (1970) Vol.10, No.4, p.152.

102 Gilbert, T.F. 1962 Mathetics: The technology of education. Journal of Mathetics, Vol.1 reprinted as supplement to Recall, Longman London 1970.

124 Goldbeck, R.A., and Campbell, V.N. 1962 The effects of response made and response difficulty on programmed learning. Journal of Educational Psychology, Vol.53, No.3, 110-118.

165 Goldberg, A., and Suppes, P. 1972 A computer-assisted instruction programme for exercises on finding axioms. Educational Studies in Mathematics, Vol.4, No.4, 429-449.

200 Goldstein, A. 1956 A controlled comparison of the project method with standard laboratory teaching in pharmacology. Journal of Medical Education, Vol.31, 365-375.

194 Goldstein, P. 1937 Student laboratory work versus teacher demonstration as a means of developing laboratory resourcefulness. Science Education, Vol.21, 185-193.

263 Good, H.M., Dowdeswell, W.H., and Harmsen, R. 1980 Modelling and Evaluation. Studies in Higher Education, Vol.5, No.1 p.33

156,159 Goodhue, D. 1969 Tape-recorded lectures with slide synchronisation. A description of the method. Journal of Biological Education, Vol.3, No.4, 311-319.

102 Goodlad, S. 1975 Education and Social Action. Allen and Unwin.

271 Goodwin, L. 1969 The academic world and the business world: a comparison of occupational goals. Sociology of Education, Vol.42, No.2, 170-187.

121 Gordon, H.P., and Morgan, A.F. 1971 (School of Dentistry, University of Washington, Seattle.) A modified approach to the teaching of oral pathology. Journal of Dental Education, 35, 513-516.

54 Gottsdanker, J.S. 1968 Intellectual interest patterns of gifted college students. Educational and Psychological Measurement, Vol.28, 361-366.

65 Gough, H.G., Durflinger, G.W., and Hill, R.E. Predicing performance in students teaching from the California Psychological Inventory. Journal of Educational Psychology, Vol.59, No.2, 119-127.

62 Green, R.L., and Farquhar, W.W. 1965 Negro motivation and scholastic achievement. Journal of Educational Psychology, Vol.56, No.5, 241-243.

163 Greenhill, L.P., Carpenter, C.R., and Ray 1956 Further studies of the use of television for university teaching. Audio-Visual Communication Review, Vol.4, 200-215.

253 Greenwood, G.E., Bridges, C.M. Jnr., Ware, W.B., and McLean, J.E 1973 Student evaluation of college teaching behaviours instrument: factory analysis. Journal of Higher Education, Vol.44, No.8, 596-604.

277 Gregory, I.D., and Hammar, B. 1974 Case study of first course in teaching skills and methods for university medica staff. British Journal of Medical Education, 8, 92-98.

268 Gromisch, D.S., et al 1972 A comparison of student and departmental chairmen evaluations of teaching performance. Journal of Medical Education, 47, 281-284.

145 Groveman, A.M., Richards, C.S., and Capel, R.B. 1977 Effects of study-skills, counselling versus behavioural self-control techniques in the treatment of academic performance. Psychological Report, August, Vol.41,No.1, p.186.

23 Groves, P.D. 1968 Marking and evaluating a class test and examinations by computer. The Computer Journal, Vol.1C No.4, 365-367.

195 Grozier, J.E. 1969 The role of the laboratory in developing positive attitudes towards science in a college general education science course for non-scientists. (Doctoral dissertation East Texas State University, cited i Trent, J.W., and Cohen, A.M., Research on Teaching in higher education, in Travers, R.M.W., Second hanbook of research on teaching, 1974).

40 Gust, T., and Schumacher, D. 1969 Handwriting speed of college students. Journal of Educational Research, Vol.62, No.5, 198-200.

265 Gustad, J.W. 1967 Evaluation of teaching performance: Issues and possibilities in C.B.T. Lee (ed) Improving college teaching, Washington, D.C. American Council on Education, 265-281.

114 Guyot, Y. 1970 Edole Normale Superieure de St. Cloud. Espace pedagogique et relations professeur-etudiants (Teacher location and teacher-student relationships.) International Review of Applied Psychology, Vol.19, No.2, 161-171.

23 Haak, L.A. 1960 A method of measuring individual student progress. The significance of the improvement factor. Journal of Higher Education, May.

273 Hacquaert, A. 1967 The recruitment and training of university teachers. International Association of University Professors and Lecturers. Ghent, Belgium.

113 Hale Report, 1964. University Grants Committee (1964) Report of the Committee on University Teaching Methods (Chairman Sir. E. Hale) H.M.S.O.

32 Hales, L.W., and Rand, L.P. 1973 An investigation of some assumptions and some characteristics of the Pass/Fail grading system. Journal of Educational Research, Vol.67, No.3, 134-136.

25 Hall, D.T. 1969 The impact of peer interaction during an academic role transition. Sociology of Education, Vol.42, No.2, 118-140.

118 Hall, K.R.L. 1950 The effect of names and titles upon the serial reproduction of pictorial and verbal material. British Journal of Psychology, Vol.41, 109-121.

250 Hall, T., and Schein, E.H. 1967 The student image of the teacher. Journal of Applied Behavioural Science, Vol.3, No.3, 305-337.

24 Hallworth, H. 1964 Anxiety and school examinations. Educational Review, Vol.16, No.3.

52 Halpin, G.B. 1968 A predictive failure in veterinary students: A method of selection for counselling. British Journal of Medical Education, Vol.2, 202-203.

265 Halsey, A.H., and Trow, M. 1971 The British Academics. Faber & Faber, 560pp.

74,139 Hammond, S.B. 1957 Draft report of the first year student survey, University of Melbourne (Confidential), cited from Miller, G.W., 1970 Success, failure and wastage in higher education, Harrap 264pp.

276 Harding, A.G. 1974(a) The objectives of training university teachers. Mimeo, 26pp.

277 Harding, A.G. 1974(b) Training of polytechnic teachers. Society for Research into Higher Education, London, 59pp.

270 Hargens, L.L. 1969 Patterns of mobility of new Ph.d's among American academic institutions. Sociology of Education, Vol.42, No.1, 18-37.

270 Hargens, L.L., and Hagstrom, W.O. 1967 Sponsored contest mobility of American academic scientists. Sociology of Education, Vol.14, No.1, 24-38.

162 Harrington, R.W., and Knoblett, J.A. 1968 Instructional closed-circuit television: A case study. Journal of Educational Research, Vol.62, No.1, 40-45.

126 Hartley, J. 1968 Some factors affecting student performance in programmed learning. Programmed Learning and Educational Technology, Vol.6, No.3, 206-218.

117 Hartley, J., and Davies, I.K. 1978 Note-taking: A critical review. Programmed Learning and Educational Technology, Vol.15, No.3 August 207-224.

126 Hartley, J.R. 1968 An experiment showing some student benefits against behavioural costs in using programmed learning. Programmed Learning and Educational Technology, Vol.5, No.3, 219.

34,49 Hartog, Sir P., and Rhodes, E.G. 1935 An examination of examinations. London 1935.

26 Hastings, J. 1961 Tensions in school achievement examinations, in Harris, T., and Schwahn, W. (eds) The learning process. New York.

77 Hatch, S., and Reich, D. 1970 Unsuccessful sandwiches? New Society, 14 May, No.398.

195 Heard, P.D. and Rowe, M.B. 1966 A study of small group dynamics and productivity in the BSCS laboratory block program. Journal of Research Science Teaching, Vol.4, 67-73. Cited by Shulman, L.S., and Tamir, P. in Travers, R.M.W. (ed) 1974, Second handbook of research on teaching. p.1124.

53 Hecker, D.L., and Lezotte, L.W. 1969 Traditional patterns and achievements of transfer students and the technical associate and baccalaureat levels of higher education. The Journal of Educational Research, Vol.63, No.3, 107-110.

37 Heffer, P., Holloway, P.J., Rose, J.S., and Swallow, J.N. 1965 An investigation into dental undergraduate examining techniques. British Dental Journal, Vol.118, 334-358.

96 Heiss, A. 1973 An inventory of academic innovation and reform. The Carnegie Commission on Higher Education, 123pp.

193,195, 196,198 Henderson, N.K. 1969 University teaching, Oxford University Press, 170pp.

195 Henshaw, E.M., Langdon, J., and Howman, P. 1933 Manual dexterity: Effects of training. Industrial Health Research Board, No.67, H.M.S.O. Cited by Beard, R.M. in Teaching and learning in higher education, Penguin, 252pp.

89 Heron, J. 1973 Experiential techniques in higher education. Human Potential Research Project. Centre for Adult Education, University of Surrey, England.

269 Heywood, J. 1967 Qualifications, teaching and industrial experience of some staff in five Colleges of Advanced Technology. International Journal of Electrical Engineering Education, 5, 699-705.

269 Hildebrand, M. 1972 How to recommend promotion for a mediocre teacher without actually trying. Journal of Higher Education, Vol.43, No.1, 44-62.

252,269 Hildebrand, M. 1973 The character and skills of the effective professor. Journal of Higher Education, Vol.44, No.1, 41-50.

34 Hill, B.J. 1973 An investigation into the consistency of marking examinations scripts in B.Sc. Part I in Mechanical Engineering. Higher Education, 221-227.

68 Hind, R.R., and Wirth, T.E. 1969 The effect of university experience on occupational choice among undergraduates. Sociology of Education, Vol.42, No.1, 50-70.

83,87 Hirst, P. 1974 Knowledge and the curriculum. Routledge Kegan Paul.

52 Hoare, D.E., and Yeaman, E.J. 1971 Identifying and interviewing science students at risk of failure. Universities Quarterley, Vol.25, No.4, 471-483.

267 Hogan, T.P. 1973 Similarity of student ratings across instructors, courses, and time. Research in Higher Education, Vol.1, No.2, 149-154.

28 Hohne, H.E. 1955 Success and failure. Scientific Faculties of the University of Melbourne. Australian Council for Educational Research.

74 Holbraad, C. 1962 The accommodation of third year university students and their performance at final examinations (Mimeo, London School of Economics) cited by Miller, G.W. in Success, failure and wastage in higher education, Harrap, London.

29,122 Holland, G., and Skinner, B.F. 1961 The analysis of behaviour, McGraw Hill.

48 Holloway, P.J., Hardwick, J.L., Morris, J., and Start, K.B. 1967 The validity of essays and viva-voce examining techniques. British Dental Journal, Vol.123, 227-232.

48 Holloway, P.J., Collins, C.K., and Start, K.B. 1968 Reliability of viva-voce examinations. British Dental Journal, Vol.125, No.5, 211-214.

253 Holmes, D.S. The teaching assessment blank: A form for the student assessment of college instructors. Journal of Experimental Education 1971, 39, 34-38.

130 Homme, L., Csanyi, A., Gonzales, M., and Rechs, J. 1970 How to use contingency contracting in the classroom. Champaign, Illinois: Research Press.

127 Hopper, E., Evans, J., and Littlejohn, G. 1972 Staff attitudes to instructional innovation in higher education. Programmed Learning and Educational Technology, Vol.11, No.3, 140-155.

47 Houpt, M.I., and Kress, G. 1973 Accuracy of measurement of clinical performance in dentistry. Journal of Dental Education, Vol.7, No.7, 34-46.

116 Howe, M.J.A. 1970 Using students' notes to examine the role of the individual learner in acquiring meaningful subject matter. Journal of Educational Research, Vol.64, 61-63.

74 Howell, D.A. 1962 A study of the 1955 Entry to British Universities - Evidence to Robbins Committee on Higher Education, (Mimeo) cited by Miller, G.W. in Success, failure and wastage in higher education, Harrap, London.

25 Hoyt, D.P. 1965 The relationship between college grades and adult achievement. ACT Research Report No.7, September. American College Testing Programme, Iowa, U.S.A.

266 Hoyt, D.P. 1973 Measurement of instructional effectiveness. Research in Higher Education Vol.1, No.4, 367-378.

64 Hudson, L. 1960 Degree class and attainment in scientific research. British Journal of Psychology 51.

31 Hudson, L. 1963 The relation of academic test scores to academic bias. British Journal of Educational Psychology, Vol.33.

135 Hudson, L. 1966 Contrary imaginations. Methuen, Penguin (1967).

135 Hudson, L. 1968 Frames of mind. Penguin.

159 Hughes, W.H., Collard, P., and Cardew, P.N. 1953 The 'How-to-do-it' Teaching Film: An experiment in its use. The Lancet, Vol.CCLXV, 1953, 484-485.

61 Humphries, L.G. 1968 The fleeting nature of the prediction of college academic success. Journal of Educational Psychology, Vol.59, No.5, 375-380.

196 Hurd, P.D., and Rowe, M.B. 1966 A study of small group dynamics and productivity in the BSCS laboratory block program. Journal of Research Science Teaching Vol.4.

273 International Association of University Professors and Lecturers, 1967. Recruitment and Training of University Teachers.

253 Isaacson, R.L., McKeachie, W.J., and Milholland, J.E. Correlation of teacher personality variables and student ratings. Journal of Educational Psychology 1963, 54, 110-117.

32 James, A.W. 1927 The effect of handwriting on grading. English Journal, Vol.16, 180-205.

126 James, P.E. 1970 A comparison of the efficiency of programmed video-tape and the instruction booklet in learning to operate a desk calculator. Programmed Learning and Educational Technology, Vol.7, No.2, 134-139.

185 James, D.W., Johnson, M.L., and Venning, P. 1956 Testing for learnt skill in observing and evaluation of evidence. The Lancet, 1956, No.2 379-383.

78 Jansen, D.G., Winhorne, B., and Martinson, W.D. 1968 Characteristics associated with campus social-political action leadership. Journal of Counselling Psychology, Vol.15, No.6, 552-562.

78 Jansen, H.L., and Hallworth, H.J. 1973 Demographic and biographic predictors of writing ability. The Journal of Experimental Education, Vol.41, No.4, 43-53.

25 Jehu, D., Pickton, C.J., and Futcher, S. 1970 The use of notes in examinations. British Journal of Educational Psychology, Vol.40, 335-337.

32 Jessee, W.F., and Simon, H.J. 1971 Time utilisation by medical students, on a pass/fail evaluation system. Journal of Medical Education, Vol.46, 275-280.

31 Johnson, P.C., and Abrahamson, S. 1968 The effects of grades and examinations on self-directed learning. Journal of Medical Education, Vol.43, No.3, 360-366.

113 Jones, H.E. 1923 Experimental studies of college teaching. Archives of Psychology, Vol.68.

66 Jones, C.L., Mackintosh, H., and McPherson, A. 1973 Dictating failure: A comment on national differences in pedagogy and achievement. University of Edinburgh Centre for Sociology (Mimeo).

113 Johnson, P.E. 1967 Some psychological aspects of subject matter structure. Journal of Educational Psychology, Vol.58, No.2, 75-83.

40 Kalish, R.A. 1958 An experimental evaluation of the Open Book Examination. Journal of Educational Psychology, Vol.49, No.4, 200-204.

32 Kandel, I. 1936 Examinations and their substitutes in the United States. Carnegie Foundation for the Advancement of Teaching, Bulletin 28, New York.

160 Kanner, J.H. 1968 The instructional effectiveness of colour in television: A review of the evidence. ERIC Clearing House on Educational Media and Technology, Stanford University, California.

54,61 Kapur, R.L. 1972 Student wastage at Edinburgh University Factors related to failure and dropout. Universities Quarterley, Vol.26, No.3, 353-377.

124 Kaufman, R.A. 1964 The systems approach to programming, in Ofiesh, G.D., and Meierhenry, W.C. (eds), Trends in programmed instruction. Papers from the National Society for Programmed Instruction and Department of Audio-Visual Instruction Conference, 1963.

154 Keating, R.F. 1963 A study of the effectiveness of language laboratories, New York. Institute of Administrati Research, Teachers' College, Columbia University.

129 Keller, F.S. 1968 'Goodbye teachers ....' Journal of Applied Behaviour Analysis, 78-89.

37 Kelley, A.C., and Zarembka, P. 1968 Normalisation of student test scores: An experimental justification, Journal of Educational Research, Vol.62, No.4, 160-164.

48 Kelley, P.R., Matthews, J.H., and Schumacher, C.F. 1971 Analysis of the oral examination of the American Board of Anaesthesiology. Journal of Medical Education, Vol.46, 982-988.

71 Kelly, E.L. 1957 Journal of Medical Education, Vol.32, p.78.

265 Kelly, R., and Hart, B.D. 1969 Professor role preference of entering college students and their parents. The Journa of Educational Research, Vol.63, No.4, 150-151.

127 Kent, T.H., Dax Taylor, D., and Buckwalter, J.A. 1972 University of Iowa College of Medicine. Field test of programmed texts for teaching general pathology. Journal of Medical Education, 47, 873-878.

123 Kennedy, W.A., and Willcutt, H.C. 1964 Praise and blame as incentives. Psychology Bulletin, Vol.62, 323-332.

276 King, M. 1973 The anxieties of university teachers. Universities Quarterly, Vol.28, No.1, 69-83.

76 King, E.J., Moor, C.H., and Mundy, J. 1973 Post-compulsory secondary education: A new analysis in Western Europe. London, Sage Publications, 450pp.

77 Kipnis, D. 1968 Social immaturity, intellectual ability and adjusted behaviour in college. Journal of Applied Psychology, Vol.52, No.1, 71-80.

269 Klapper, H.L. 1969 The young college faculty member - a new breed? Sociology of Education, Vol.42, No.1, 38-49.

24 Klug, B. 1971 Student profiles. Butterworth Press.

125 Knight, M.A.G. 1963 The Royal Air Force Study. Occupational Psychology, Vol.37, No.1, 68-75.

267 Kohlan, R.G. 1973 A comparison of faculty evaluations early and late in the course. Journal of Higher Education, Vol.44, No.8, 587-595.

122 Komoski, P.K. 1962 An immodest proposal concerning the use of programmed instruction in emerging nations. New York Center for Programmed Instruction.

27 Kondas, O. 1967 Reduction of examination anxiety and 'stage fright' by group desensitisation and relaxation. Behaviour Research and Therapy, Vol.5, No.4, 275-282.

276 Korn, J.H. 1972 Promoting good teaching. The Journal of Higher Education, Vol.3, No.2, 123-132.

40 Krarup, N., and Olsen, C. 1969 Open book tests in a university course. Higher Education, Vol.3, No.2, (April, 1974).

97 Krathwohl, D.R., Bloom, B.S., and Masia, B.B. 1964 Taxonomy of educational objectives. A classification of educational goals, Handbook II: Affective domain. Longmans, 195pp.

194 Kruglak, H. 1951 Some behaviour objectives for laboratory instruction. American Journal of Physics, Vol.19, 223-225.

194 Kruglak, H. 1952 Experimental outcomes of laboratory instruction in elementary college physics. American Journal of Physics, Vol.20, 136-141.

194 Kruglak, H. 1953 Achievement of physics students with and without laboratory work. American Journal of Physics, Vol.21, 14-16.

194 Kruglak, H. 1954 The measurement of laboratory achievement. American Journal of Physics, Vol.22, 442-462.

194 Kruglak, H. 1955(a) Measurement of laboratory achievement. American Journal of Physics, Vol.23, 82-87.

SDTS-U

194 Kruglak, H. 1955(b) The effect of high school physics and college laboratory instruction on achievement in college physics. Science Education, Vol.39, 219-222.

194 Kruglak, H. 1958 Evaluating laboratory instruction by use of objective type tests. American Journal of Physics, Vol.26, 31-32.

194 Kruglak, H., and Goodwin, R.A. 1955 Laboratory achieveme in relation to the number of partners. American Journal of Physics, Vol.23, 257-264.

195 Lahti, M. 1956 The inductive-deductive method and the physical science laboratory. Journal of Experimental Education, Vol.24, 149-163.

68 Laitos, K. 1973 The first year of study in university as a predictor of later achievement (A follow up). In Research Register into Higher Education in Western Europe 1973, Society for Research into Higher Education, 228pp.

160 Lajeunesse, L., and Rossi, R. 1960 Influence de certain modifications de la structure des films sur l'integration des contenus cinematographiques per des enfants d'age scolaire. (The influence of certain modifications in the structure of films in the integration of the cinematograph content by school children). Revue Internationale de Filmologie, Vol.10, 32-33, janvier-juin, 1960, 90-100.

160 Laner, S. 1954 The impact of visual aid displays showin a manipulative task. The Quarterley Journal of Experiment Psychology, Vol.6, Part 3, 95-106.

119 Laner, S. 1956 An experimental study of pictorial metho of instruction. Thesis for Ph.D degree, University of Reading.

160 Laner, S. 1960 Training made easier. Problems of progr in Industry, No.6. Dept. Scientific and Industrial Resear H.M.S.O. London, 50pp.

120 Laner, S., and Sell, R.E. 1960 Occupational Psychology, Vol.24, 153-167.

144 Larkin, J.H., and Reif, F. 1976 Analysis and Teaching of a general skill for studying scientific text. Journal of Educational Psychology, August Vol.68, No.4, 431-440.

67 Last, J.M., and Stanley, G.R. 1968 Career preferences of young British doctors. British Journal of Medical Education, Vol.2, 137-155.

137 Laurillard, D. 1978 A study of the relationship bet some of the cognitive and contextual factors in student learning. (Unpublished Ph.D Thesis, University of Surrey)

152 Lavach, J.F. 1973 (College of William and Mary). The effect of arousal on a short and long-term memory. The Journal of Educational Research, Vol.67, No.3, 131-133.

122 Lawless, C.J. 1969 Programmed learning in the developing countries of Africa. Programmed Learning and Educational Technology. Vol.6, 189-196.

162 Layard, R. 1973 London School of Economics. The new media and higher education. Minerva, Vol.11, No.2, 211-227.

166 Layard, R. 1974 The cost-effectiveness of the new media in higher education. Chapter 7 in Lumsden, K.G. (ed), Efficiency in universities: The La Paz Papers. Elsevier Scientific Publishing Company, 149-174.

65 Leeds, C.H. 1969 Predictive validity of the Minnesota teacher attitude inventory. Journal of Teacher Education, Vol.20, No.1, 51-56.

122 Leith, G.O.M. 1966 Research in Programmed Learning. Special Education, Vol.55, No.2.

125 Leith, G.O.M., and Wildbore, J.F. 1968 Schedules of responding. Research Report No.23 of School of Education, University of Birmingham.

123 Leith, G.O.M. 1968 Learning and personality. Paper read at the National Programmed Learning Conference, Glasgow.

126 Leith, G.O.M. 1969 Programmed learning in higher education. In Media and methods edited by Unwin, D., McGraw Hill, 68-87.

125 Leith, G.O.M., and Buckle, C.F. 1965 Mode of response and non-specific background knowledge. Interim Technical Report, National Centre for Programmed Learning, School of Education, Birmingham.

123 Leith, G.O.M., and Davis, T.N. 1969 The influence of social reinforcement on achievement. Educational Research, Vol.11,No.2, 132-137.

44 Lennox, B. 1967 Multiple choice examinations. British Journal of Medical Education, Vol.1, 203.

252 Leonard, W.M. 1972 Student preferences for what makes a good college teacher. Improving College and University Teaching, Vol.21, No.1, 10-13.

265 Lester, R.A. 1974 Anti-bias regulation of universities. Carnegie Commission on Higher Education. McGraw Hill, 168pp.

165 Levien, R.E. (ed) 1972 The merging technology: Instructional uses of the computer in higher education. A Carnegie Commission on Higher Education and Rand Corporation Study. McGraw Hill Book Co., 585pp.

135 Levine, F.J. 1976 Influence of field-dependence and study habits on academic performance of black students in 'predominantly white university'. Perpetual and Motor Skill Vol.42 June (3 pt.2)

30 Levine, H.G., and McGuire, C.H. 1971 Use of profile system for scoring and reporting certifying examinations in orthopaedic surgery. Journal of Medical Education, Vol.46, 78-85.

28 Levine, H.G., and McGuire, C.H. 1971 Rating habitual performances in graduate medical education. Journal of Medical Education, Vol.46, 306-311.

7 Lewis, B.N. 1971 Course production at the Open Universit (a) Some basic problems. British Journal of Educational Technology, Vol.2, 4-13.

157 Lewis, E., and Steinberg, H. 1951 An experiment in the teaching value of a scientific film. British Medical Journal, Vol.21, p.465.

129 Lewis, E.J., and Wolf, W.A. 1973 Implementation of self-paced learning: Keller Method in a first year course. Journal of Chemical Education, Vol.50, No.1, 51-56.

91 Lewis, R.W. 1972 Course content in structured knowledge areas. Improving College and University Teaching, Vol.20, p.131.

53,191 Lipset, S.M., and Altbach, P. 1966 US Campus alienation. New Society, September 8th.

43 Lipton, A., and Huxham, G.J. 1970 Comparison of multiple-choice and essay testing in pre-clinical physiology. British Journal of Medical Education, Vol.4, 228-238.

113 Lloyd, D.H. 1968 A concept of improvement of learning response in the taught lesson. Visual Education, October, 23-25.

139 Lloyd, K.E. 1971 Contingency management in university courses. Educational Technology, Vol.11, No.4, 18-23.

271 Lofthouse, S. 1974 Thoughts on 'publish or perish'. Higher Education, Vol.3, No.1, 59-80.

53 Lohle-Tart-Esser, M. 1973 Success and failure among university freshmen, in Register of Research into Higher Education in Western Europe, 1973. Society for Research into Higher Education, p.161.

64 Lysaught, P. 1970 Selection testing for learning programmers. Bulletin of the Clearing House for Self Instruction Materials for Health Care Facilities. Universi of Rochester, NY, Vol.4, No.1.

166 Lumsden, K.G. (ed) 1974 Efficiency in universities: The La Pas Papers. Elsevier Scientific Publishing Company, 278pp.

62 Lunneborg, C.E., and Lunneborg, P.W. 1970 Relations between aptitude changes and academic success during college. Journal of Educational Psychology, Vol.61, 169-173.

123 MacDonald-Ross, M. 1967 Advances in programming technique in problems and methods in programmed learning. National Centre for Programmed Learning, Birmingham.

262 MacDonald-Ross, M. 1973 Behavioural objectives: A critical review. Instructional Science Vol.2, No.1.

195 MacDonald-Ross, M. 1971 Practical work in science, a talk given at the University of Birmingham, cited by Beard, R.M. in Teaching and learning in higher education, 1972, Penguin, 250pp.

160 Mackintosh, D.M. 1947 A comparison of the efficiency of sound and silent films as teaching aids. Scottish Educational Film Association, Research Publication No.3, 1947, 20pp.

145 MacMillan, M. 1965 Efficiency in reading. English-Teaching Information Centre, Occasional Paper No.6.

115,182 McCarthy, W.H. 1970 Improving classroom instruction: A programmed teaching method. Journal of Medical Education, 46, 605-609.

65 McClain, E.W. 1968 16PF scores and success in student teaching. Journal of Teacher Education, Vol.19, No.1, 25-32.

64 McComisky, J.G., and Freeman, J. 1967 Concept attainment and type of education - the comparative study. International Journal of Educational Sciences, Vol.2, No.1, 47-50.

117 McDougall, I.R., Gray, H.W., and McNicol, G.P. 1972 The effect of timing of distribution of handouts on improvement of student performance. British Journal of Medical Education, Vol.6, 155-157.

27 McGuire, C.H. 1963 A process approach to the construction and analysis of medical examinations. Journal of Medical Education, Vol.38, p.556.

28 McGuire, C., and Solomon, L. 1973 Materials for the evaluation of performance in medicine. Centre for Educational Development, University of Illinois College of Medicine. Mimeo.

155 McKeachie, W.J. 1969 Teaching tips. A guidebook for the beginning college teacher. D.C. Heath & Co., Lexington Massachusetts.

73 McLeish, J. 1970 Student attitudes and college environments. Cambridge Institute of Education, 251pp.

67 McPherson, A.F., and Jones, C.L. 1973 Varieties of consumer demand for Scottish tertiary education in Flood Page, C. and Gibson, J. (eds) Motivation: Non; cognitive aspects of student performance - papers presented at the Society for Research into Higher Education 8th Annual Conference.

252 Magin, D. 1973 Evaluating the role performance of university lecturers. Universities Quarterly, Vol.28, No.1, 69-83.

24 Malleson, N. 1959 Evading failure by university students. The Listener, March 5th.

51,53 Malleson, N. 1967 Students leaving mechanical engineering courses. Universities Quarterly, Vol.22, No.1.

194 Mallinson, G.G. 1947 The individual laboratory method compared with the lecture demonstration method in teaching general biology. Science Education, Vol.31, 175-179.

271 Marsh, J.F., and Stafford F.P. 1967 The effects of values on pecuniary behaviour: the case of academicians. American Sociological Review, Vol.32, No.5, 740-754.

122 Martin, H. 1965 L'enseignement programme au Dahomey. Education Dahomeeme, No.5.

254,269 Maslow, A.H., and Zimmerman, W. 1956 College teaching ability, Scholarly activity and personality, Journal of Educational Psychology, 47, 185-189.

249 Mastin, E. 1963 Teacher enthusiasm. Journal of Educational Research, Vol.56, No.7, 385-386.

137 Marton, F. 1975 What does it take to learn? in Entwistle, N.J., and Hounsell, D.J. (eds) How students learn. Institute for Research and Development in Post Compulsory Education, University of Lancashire.

252 Mayberry, W.E. 1973 Some dimensions in clinical teaching. Journal of Dental Education, Vol.37, No.7, 8-12.

152 Menne, J.W., Hunnum, T.E., Clingen-Smith, J.E., and Nord, D. 1969 Use of taped lectures to replace class attendance Audio-Visual Communication Review, Vol.17, 42-46.

155 Meyer, T.C., Hansen, R.H., Ragatz, R.T., and Mulvihill, B. 1970 Providing medical information to physicians by telephone tapes. Journal of Medical Education, Vol.45, 1060-1065.

124 Middleton, R.G. 1964 The effects of size of step on programmed learning using a spelling programme. Educational Review, Vol.16, No.2, February.

49 Miller, G. (ed) 1962 Teaching and learning in medical school. Harvard University Press.

279 Miller, J.P. 1973 The effects of human relations training on teacher interpersonal skills. The Alberta Journal of Educational Research, Vol.19,No.1,37.

130 Miller, L.K. 1970 Token economy for the university classroom. Paper presented at the 1970 American Psychological Association Conference. Reported in Goldschmid, B., and Goldschmid, M.L., Individualising instruction in higher education, A review.

272 Miller, R.I. 1974 Developing programmes for faculty evaluation. Jossey Bass, 248pp.

51 Miller, C.M.L., and Parlett, M. Up to the mark: A study of the examination game. Society for Research into Higher Education, London. 128pp.

140 Milton, O. 1974 Accent on learning: P.S.I. or the Keller Plan. Teaching-Learning Issues No.25, Learning Research Centre, University of Tenessee.

126 Moore, D. 1967 Group teaching by programmed instruction. Programmed Learning and Educational Technology, Vol.4, No.1, 37-46.

147 Moore, M.G. 1973 Toward a theory of independent learning and teaching. Journal of Higher Education, Vol.44, No.9, 661-679.

69 Morea, P.C. 1969 Interests in relation to student success. Occupational Psychology, Vol.43, 145-150.

122 Morgan, T. 1965 A study of the social and psychological aspects of team teaching. National Centre for Programmed Learning, Birmingham.

67 Morris, R.N. 1969 The sixth form and college entrance. Routledge and Kegan Paul, 223pp.

200 Morris, V. 1930 Quantitative measurements in institutions of higher learning. Yearbook NO.18 of the National Society of College Teachers of Education. University of Chicago Press, p.114.

55 Morrison, A., and McIntyre, D. 1967 Changes in opinion about education during the first year of teaching. British Journal of Social and Clinical Psychology, Vol.6, No.3, 161-163.

37 Mowbray, R.M., and Davies, B.M. 1967 Short note and essay examinations compared. British Journal of Medical Education, Vol.1, 356-358.

132 Muggen, G. 1972 Een instrument voor studietijdmetingen An instrument for measuring study times (Summary in English) Wageningen, Bureau Onderzoek van Onderwijs, Landbouwhogescho 50pp.

31 Mumma, R.B., Silvera, R.S., and Carpenter, N.J. 1971 Pass/Not pass as a system of grading in dental education. Journal of Dental Education, Vol.35, No.5, 325-329.

164 Mundy, P.G. 1962 A comparison of the use of television (BBC) Programmes for Schools and sound films as a teaching aid. Thesis for M.A. degree, University of London.

70 Musgrove, F. 1967(a) Social class and level of aspiration in a Technological University. Sociological Review 1967, Vol.15, No.3, 311-322.

52,53,75 Musgrove, F. 1967(b) University freshmen and their parents' attitudes. Educational Research, Vol.10, No.1, 78-80.

34 Natkin, E., and Guild, R.E. 1967 Evaluation of preclinic laboratory performance. Journal of Dental Education, Vol.31.

50 Nealey, S.M. 1969 Student-Instructor agreement in scorin an essay examination. The Journal of Educational Research, Vol.63, No.3, 111-115.

159 Nelson, K.G., and Ozgentas, I. 1961 Istanbul physics film experiment - technical report. Research and Measureme Bureau, Ankara, 41pp.

189 Nelson-Jones, R. 1972 Counsellor training in Britain - a one-year course in student counselling: Scope and training. Proceedings of the 3rd Conference on Student Counselling. Department of Higher Education, London.

55 Newcomb, T.B., Koenig, K.E., Flacks, R., and Warwick, D.P. 1967 Persistence and the change: Bennington College and its students after 25 years. John Wiley & Sons, London and New York. 292pp.

191 Nisbet, J., and Welsh, J. 1966 Predicting student performance. Universities Quarterly, Vol.20, 468-480.

91 Northedge, A. 1976 Implicit analogies. Programmed Learning in Educational Technology, Vol.13, No.4.

200 Novak, J.D. 1958 An experimental comparison of a conventional and a project centred method of teaching a college botany course. Journal of Experimental Education, Vol.26, 217-230.

131 Novak, J.D. 1970 Relevant research on audio-tutorial methods. School Science and Mathematics, Vol.70, No.4, 457-464.

42 Nuffield Group for Research into Higher Education. Newsletters 1, 2, 3, 4, and 5. Nuffield Foundation 1973/74.

122 Okunrotifa, P.O. 1968 A comparison of the responses of Niger peoples to two sets of programmed materials in geography. Programmed Learning and Educational Technology, Vol.5, No.4.

118 Oleron, G. 1953 Etude sur l'efficacite de l'ecoute a la radio. (Study of effectiveness of listening to radio). Cahiers d'etudes de radio-television, I. 39-75.

117 Oleron, P. 1959 Sur l'ambiguite des effets de prestige. (The ambiguity of prestige effects). Cahiers d'etudes de radio-television, 24, 388-392.

121 Ollerenshaw, R. 1962 Design for projection: A study of legibility. 13th Renwick Memorial Lecture. The Photographic Journal, 41-52.

245 O'Neill, J. 1971 Resource use in higher education. Carnegie Foundation for the Advancement of Teaching.

125 Owen, S.G., Hall, R., Anderson, J., and Smart, G.A. 1965 A comparison of programmed learning instruction and lectures in the teaching of electrocardiography. Programmed Learning, Vol.2, 2-14.

119 Oztilmen, N. 1963 Overt and covert response modes with pictorial and non-pictorial stimuli in learning Turkish words. Indiana University.

72 Pace, C.R. 1962 Methods of describing college cultures. Teachers' College Record, Vol.63, 267-277.

72 Pace, C.R. 1963 College and university environment scales (CUES): Preliminary technical manual. Educational Testing Service, Princeton, N.J.

72 Pace, C.R. 1969 CUES technical manual 2nd edition, Educational Testing Service, Princeton, N.J.

161 Packham, D., Cleary, A., and Mayes, T. 1971 Aspects of Educational Psychology V. Isaac Pitman, London.

195 Parakh, J.S. 1968 A study of teacher-pupil intereaction in BSCS yellow version biology classes. American Biology Teacher. Vol.30, 841-848. Cited by Shulman, L.S., and Tamir, P. in Travers, R.M.W. (ed) 1974 Second handbook of Research on Teaching, p.1124.

93,98 Parker, J.C., and Rubin, L.J. 1966 Process as content. Rand McNally.

135 Parlett, M.R. 1969 Undergraduate teaching observed. Nature, Vol.223, 5211.

256 Parlett, M.,and Hamilton, D. 1972 Evaluation as illumination: A new approach to the study of innovatory programmes. Occasional paper 9. Centre for Research in Education Sciences, University of Edinburgh.

121 Parnell, R. 1951 British Journal of Ophthalmology, Vol.35, p.467.

138 Pask, G. 1975 Conversation, cognition and learning. Elsevier Scientific Publishing Company, Amsterdam.

155 Paul, J., and Ogilvie, J.C. 1955 Mass media and attention. Explorations, Col.4, 120-123.

158 Paulsen, K. 1957 Was Bleibt? Kinder besinnen sich auf einen film. (What remains? Children reflect on a film). Film Bild Ton, VII, 7, Munchen, 7pp.

199 Pella, M.O., and Sherman, J. 1969 A comparison of two methods of utilising laboratory activities in teaching the course IPS. School Science and Mathematics Vol.69, 303-314. Cited by Shulman, L.S., and Tamir, P., 1972 Second Handbook of Research on Teaching, edited by Travers, R.M.W.

278 Perlberg, A., and O'Bryant, D.C. 1968 Video-recording and micro-teaching techniques to improve engineering instruction. Internal paper, University of Illinois, Urbana, Mimeo.

278 Perlberg, A., Peri, J.N., Weinreb, M., Nitzane, E., and Shimron, J. 1972 Micro-teaching and video tape recordings: A new approach to improving teaching. Journal of Medical Education, 47, 43-50.

197 Perrott, E. In press. Micro-teaching. Society for Research into Higher Education.

98 Perry, W.G. 1970 Intellectual and ethical development. Holt, Rinehart & Winston, U.S.A.

266 Perry, R.R. 1969 Evaluation of teaching behaviour seeks to measure effectiveness. College and University Business 47, 18. Quoted in Miller, R.I., 1972 Evaluating faculty performance. Jossey Bass, 145pp.

144 Perry, W.G.Jnr., and Whitlock, C.P. 1955 Harvard University reading course instructor's manual. Cambridge: Harvard University Press, 8-9.

53 Pervin, N.A., and Rubin, B.B. 1967 Student dissatisfaction with college and the college dropout: A transactional approach. Journal of Social Psychology, Vol.72, 285-295.

279 Peters, D.S. 1974 The link is equitability. Research in Higher Education, Vol.2, No.1, 57-64.

120 Peters, J.M.L., and Scheffer, M.C.J. 1961 Onderzoek naar het gebruik van audio-visuele hulpmiddelen big het technisch onderwijs. (Research into the use of audio-visual aids in technical education). Den Haag.

59 Peterson, A.D.C. 1971 The International Baccalaureat, BACIE Journal, Vol.25, No.1, 4-8.

83 Phenix, P.H. 1964 Realms of Meaning. McGraw Hill Series in Education.

31 Philbrick, J.L., and O'Donnell, P.I. 1968 Precision in grading practices - Panacea or problem? Journal of Educational Research, Vol.62, No.4, 173-176.

62 Phillips, C. 1968 Subject choice and university entry. New Society, No.284, 347-348.

33,49 Pieron, H. 1963 Examens et Docimologie Paris. Cited in Cox, R.J. 1967 Examinations and higher education. Universities Quarterly, June, 292-340.

37,39,40 Pilliner, A., and Siann, G. 1973 A survey of Scottish undergraduate assessment as the University of Edinburgh. Scottish Educational Studies, Vol.5, No.1, 25-45.

214,224 Piper, D.W. (ed) 1972 Readings in art and design education Vol.1. After Coldstream, published by Davis Poynter, London.

22 Platz, A., McClintock, C., and Katz, D. 1959 Undergraduate grades and the Miller Analogies Test as predictors of graduate success. The American Psychologist, 1959, 14.

152 Popham, W. 1961 Tape-recorded lectures in the college classroom. Audio-visual Communication Review, 9, 109-118.

152 Popham, W. 1962 Tape-recorded lectures in the college classroom - II. Audio-visual Communication Review, 10, 94-101.

261 Popham, W.J. 1972 Must all objectives be behavioural? Educational Leadership, 29, No.7, p.53.

47 Poppleton, P.K. 1969 The assessment of teaching practice. Higher Education Journal, Vol.17, No.3, 15-19.

131 Postlethwait, S.N., Novak, J., and Murray, H.T. 1964 An integrated experience approach to learning. Minneapolis: Burgess.

131 Postlethwait, S.N. 1970 The audio-tutorial system. American Biology Teacher, Vol.32, 31-33.

131 Postlethwait, S.N., Novak, J., and Murray, H.T. 1972 Audio-tutorial approach to learning, 3rd edition. Minneapolis: Burgess Publishing ompany.

144,145 Poulton, E.C. 1961 British courses for adults in effective reading. British Journal of Educational Psychology, Vol.33, 128-137.

111 Pressey, S.L. 1926 Automatic tutoring by intrinsic programming. In Lumsdaine, A.A., and Glaser, R. (eds) 1960, Teaching machines and programmed learning: A source book. Washington, DC, National Education Association, 286-298.

191 Priestley, R.R. 1957 The mental health of university students, in French, E.L. (ed). Melbourne Studies in Education.

156 Pullon, P.A., and Miller, A.S. 1972 School of dentistry, Temple University, Philadelphia. Evaluation of method of self-teaching laboratory portion of pathology. Journal of Dental Education, Vol.36, No.11, 20-22.

75 Punch, M. 1967 The student ritual. New Society, No.271, 811-813.

22 Pym, D. 1969 Education and the employment opportunities of engineers. British Journal of Industrial Relations, Vol.7, No.1, 42-51.

148 Raberg, A. 1971 Systematiserad Decentraliserad Universitetsbildning: Elevernas kursvarderingar och attityder till utbildningen. (Systematised and decentralised university education: students' evaluation of courses and attitudes to this education). Umea, Pedagogiska Mono. No.7.

62 Rechter, B. 1970 Admission to tertiary studies: An account of an experimental test battery and a proposal for its use. Australian Council for Educational Research, 60pp.

69 Reed, H.B. 1968 College students' motivations related to voluntary dropout and under-over achievement. Journal of Educational Research, Vol.61, No.9, 412-416.

156 Reich, P.R. 1972 Harvard Medical School, Programmed Instruction, in Haematology using a new audio-visual system. Journal of Medical Education, 47, 491-493.

139 Reid, J. 1970 Survey throws light on lectures - and lecturers. The Times Educational Supplement, No.2861, page 13.

32 Reiner, J.R., and Jung, L.B. 1972 Enrolment patterns and academic performance as a function of registration under a pass/fail grading system. Interchange, Vol.3, No.1, 53-62.

160 Rey, A. 1954 La perception d'un ensemble de deplacements. (Perception of a series of displacements). Revue International de Filmologie, No.17, avril-juin, 75-92.

65 Richards, J.N., and Lutz, S.W. 1968 Predicting student accomplishment in college from the ACT assessment. Journal of Educational Measurement, Vol.5, No.1, 17-28.

253 Riley, J.W. (Jnr.), Ryan, B.F., and Lifshitz, M. 1950, 1969 The student looks at his teacher. Rutgers University Press reissued 1969, Port Washington NY, Kennikat Press. Quoted by Flood Page, C. (1974), Student evaluation of teaching - the American experience. Society for Research into Higher Education.

155 Ristenbatt, M.P. 1968 A tutorial communication system - Blackboard-by-wire-picturephone. Unpublished paper, University of Michigan. Reported in McKeachie, W.J., 1969 Teaching tips. D.C. Heath & Co.

144 Robyack, J.E., and Downey, R.J. 1978 Effectiveness of a study skills course for students of different academic achievement levels and personality types. Journal of Counselling Psychology, November Vol.25, No.6, 544-550.

143 Robinson, F.P. 1861 Effective study. Harper and Brothers, New York.

189 Rogers, C.R. 1969 Freedom to learn. Mervill, Columbus, Ohio.

52 Rossman, J.E., and Kirk, B.A. 1970 Factors related to persistence and withdrawal among the university students. Journal of Counselling Psychology, Vol.17, No.1, 56-62.

115 Roth, C.H. 1973 Continuing effectiveness of personalised self-paced instruction in digital systems engineering. Journal of Engineering Education, Vol.63, No.6, 447-449.

44 Rothman, A.I. 1969 Confidence testing, an extension of multiple choice testing. British Journal of Medical Education, Vol.3, 237-239.

102 Rowntree, D. 1974 Educational Technology and curriculum development. Harper and Row.

25 Rubin, K.H., and Tierney, N.C. 1973 Students' self selection of examination dates: A preliminary investigation. Alberta Journal of Educational Research, Vol.19, No.2, 85-89.

139 Rudd, E. 1968 Students in solitary. New Society, No.290.

248 Ryans, D.C. 1967 Teacher behaviour can be evaluated. The Evaluation of Teaching. Washington, D.C. Pi Lambda Thet

24 Ryle, A., and Lunghi, N. 1968 A psychometric study of academic difficulty and psychiatric illness in students. British Journal of Psychiatry, Vol.114, No.506, 57-62.

151 Schneider, W. 1954 Horerlebnis und akutstische Anschauun (Listening and auditory attention). Film Bild Ton, IV, Munchen, 5pp.

75 Schonell, Sir F.J. 1963 Student adaption and its bearing on academic achievement. The Australian University, Vol.1, No.1.

122 Schramm, W. 1962 Learning from instructional television. Review of Educational Research, Vol.132, 156-167.

122 Schramm, W. 1964 A note on programmed instruction, in Comiski and Green, Programmed instruction in Africa and the Arab States. A report on two training workshops, UNESCO, Paris. Educational Studies and Documents No.52, H.

124 Senter, R.J. et al. 1966 An experimental comparison of a intrinsically programmed text and a narrative test. Final Report, No. AMRL-TR-65-227. Aerospace Medical Research Lab Wright-Patterson AFB, Ohio, USA.

127 Severtsev, V. 1974 Case study on the development of higher education in the USSR. UNESCO, 67pp.

76 Sewell, W.H., and Shah, V.P. 1967 Socio-Economic status, intelligence and attainment of higher education. Sociology of Education, Vol.40, No.1, 1-23.

120 Seymour, W.D. 1937 An experiment showing the superiority of a light coloured 'blackboard'. British Journal of Educational Psychology, Vol.7, 259-268.

64 Shatin, L., and Opdyke, D. 1967 A critical thinking appraisal and its correlates. Journal of Medical Education, Vol.42, No.8, 789-792.

61 Sherwin, E., and Child, D. 1970 Predicting the performance of undergraduate chemists. Education in Chemistry, Vol.7, No.4, 156-158.

32 Sheppard, E.M. 1929 The effect of quality of penmanship on grades. Journal of Educational Research, Vol.19, 102-105.

37,39,40 Siann, G., and Pilliner, A. 1974 Students questionnaire on assessment. Committee on Teaching, Learning and Assessment, University of Edinburgh, Publication No.1, 37pp.

246 Simpkins, W.S., Browne, R.K., and Field, T.W. 1972 Teacher differences as perceived by students. Improving College and University Teaching, Vol.21, No.1, 64-66.

111 Skinner, B.F. 1958 Teaching machines. Science, Vol.128, 969-977.

65 Smith, L. 1971 A five year follow up study of high ability achieving and non-achieving freshmen. Journal of Educational Research, Vol.64, No.5, 220-222.

154 Smith, P.D. 1970 A comparison of the cognitive and audio-lingual approaches to foreign language instruction: The Pennsylvanian Foreign Language Project. Philadelphia, Pennsylvania, Chilton Center for Curriculum Development.

127 Smith, R.N. 1971 (Dept. Pharmacology & Therapeutics, Sheffield University). Assessment of a programmed instructional text in clinical pharmacology. British Journal of Medical Education, 5, 325-327.

267 Smithers, A. 1970 What do students expect of lectures? Universities Quarterly, No.3, 330-336.

69,267 Smithers, A.G., and Batcock, A. 1970 Success and failure among social scientists and health scientists at a technological university. British Journal of Educational Psychology, Vol.40, 144-153.

84 Snyder, B.R. 1970 The hidden curriculum. MIT Press.

152 Snyder, W.V., Greer, A.M., and Snyder, J. 1968 An experiment with radio instruction in an introductory psychology course. Journal of Educational Research, Vol.61, No.7, 291-296.

165 Sokolow, S., and Solberg, W. 1971 (University of California School of Dentistry, Los Angeles.) Computer Assisted Instruction in dental diagnosis, a product development. Journal of Dental Education, 35, 249-355.

76 Spady, W.G. 1967 Educational mobility and access growth and paradoxes. American Journal of Sociology, Vol.73, No.3, 273-286.

253 Spencer, R.E., and Aleomoni, L.M. 1970 A student course evaluation questionnaire. Journal of Educational Measurement, 7, 209-210.

68 Spindler, D. 1968 Empirische Untersuchung uber den Studienbetrieb und seine Wisenschaftliche Ergiebigkeit in der Meinung von Studenten der Pedagogischen Hoschschul Oldenburg. (An empirical investigation of the teaching and its value in the opinion of the students of the Teachers' College in Oldenburg.)

61 Spurgin, C.G. 1967 What earns the marks? Physics Education, Vol.2, No.6, 306-310.

31 Stallings, W.M., and Leslie, E.K. 1970 Student attitudes towards grades and grading. Improving College and University Teaching, Vol.18, No.1, 66-68.

269 Stallings, W.M., and Singhal, S. 1970 Some observations on the relationship between research productivity and student evaluations of courses and teaching. American Sociologist, 5, (May), 141-143.

113 Stansfield, J.M. 1971 (Dryburn Hospital, Durham). From a Postgraduate Centre, multiple choice examinations tests on postgraduate lectures. British Journal of Medical Education, 5, 307-308.

62 Stanley, J.C., and Porter, A.C. 1967 Correlation of scholastic attitude test score with college grades for negros versus whites. Journal of Educational Measurement, Vol.4, No.4, 199-218.

39 Starr, J.W. 1968 Final examination versus cumulative assessment in a postgraduate education course: A comparative study. The Durham Research Review, Vol.5, No.20, 239-243.

127 Stavert, G.W. 1969 Programmed learning in action. Bacie Journal, Vol.23, No.1, 16-20.

127 Stavert, G.S., and Wingate, T.H. 1966 Nelson's Navy needed none but ....! Tutor Age, Vol.17, 2-7.

72 Stern, G.G. 1963 Characteristics of the intellectual climate in the college environment. Harvard Educational Review, Vol.33, 5-41.

72 Stern, G.G. 1962 Environments for learning. In Sandford, No. (ed) The American College. John Wiley, NY., 690-730.

24,27 Still, R.J. 1963 Psychological illness among students in the examination period. Dept. of Student Health, Leeds (Mimeo).

154 Stock, H. 1966 Students' opinions of the language laboratory. Bavel, Melbourne, Vol.2, No.3, 24-27.

125 Stones, E. 1966 The effects of different conditions of working on student performance and attitudes. Programmed Learning, Vol.3, No.3, 135-145.

124 Stones, E. 1967 Strategies and tactics in programmed instruction. In Tobin, M.J. (ed), Problems and Methods in programmed learning. The proceedings of the 1967 Association for Programmed Learning and National Centre for Programmed Learning. Birmingham Conference, p.62.

182 Stones, E. 1970 Students' attitudes to the size of teaching group. Educational Review, Vol.21, No.2, 98-108.

76 Stout, R.T. 1967 Blue collar participation in college-going decisions. Administrators' Notebook 1967, Vol.16, No.1, 1-4.

125 Stretton, T.B., Hall, R., and Owen, S.G. 1967 Programmed learning in medical education. Comparison of teaching machine and programmed textbook. British Journal of Medical Education, Vol.1, No.3, 165-168.

62 Stricker, G., and Huber, A.T. 1967 The graduate record examination and undergraduate grades as predictors of success in graduate schools. Journal of Educational Research, Vol.60, No.10, 466-468.

71 Stringer, P., and Tyson, M. 1968 University selection interviewers' ratings related to interviewee's self-image. Occupational Psychology, Vol.42, No.1, p.49.

159 Stuckrath, F., and Schottmayer, C. 1955 Psychologie des filmerlebens in kindheit und Jugend. (Psychology of film viewing in childhood and youth). Schropp'scher Lehrmittel-Verlag, Hamburg, 172pp.

259 Stufflebeam, D.L. 1971 Educational evaluation and decision making. Peacock Publishers.

111 Sturwold, V.G. 1973 Dept. Health, Education and Welfare, San Francisco. Use of audio-visual materials in teaching of periodontics. Journal of Dental Education, Vol.37, No.1, 33-38.

74 Suddarth, B.M. 1957 Factors influencing the successful graduation of freshmen who enrol at Purdue University (Mimeo, Purdue University), cited by Miller, G.W. in Success, failure and wastage in higher education.

164 Suess, J.F. 1973 University of Mississipi School of Medicine. Teaching psycho-diagnosis and observation by self-instructional programmed video-tapes. Journal of Medical Education, 48, 676-683.

23 Sullivan, R. 1971 Continuous assessment. Industrial Training International, Vol.6, No.6, 170-172.

126 Szekely, L. 1950 Productive processes in learning and thinking, in Actor Psychologica, Vol.7, 388-407.

270 S.R.H.E. 1973 Register of Research into higher education in Western Europe, 227pp.

115 Taplin, G. 1969 The Cosford Cube: A simplified form of student feedback. Industrial Training International, Vol.4, No.5, 218-219.

159 Tardy, M. 1960 Etude de la contribution d'un film historique compose a partir de metrages d'actualities a l'ensignement de l'histoire dans le second degre. (Study of the contribution of an historical film made of documentary shots for teaching history in the secondary school). Centre Audio-Visuel de l'Ecole Normale Superieur de Saint-Cloud, Section Recherches No. R.10, 33pp.

164 Tardy, M. 1963 La television directe et ses implications pedagogiques. (Live television and its pedagogical implications). Ecole Normale Superieure de Sant-Cloud, these de 3eme cycle, 356pp.

140 Taylor, R.G. 1968 Tutorial services and academic success. Journal of Educational Research, Vol.62, No.5, 195-197.

74 Thistlethwaite, D.L. 1962 Rival hypotheses explaining the effects of different learning environments. Journal of Educational Psychology, Vol.53.

72 Thistlethwaite, D.L. 1962 Fields of study and development of motivation to seek advanced training. Journal of Educational Psychology, Vol.53.

24,132 Thoday, D. 1957 How undergraduates work. Universities Quarterly, Vol.11, 172-181.

113 Thomas, E.J. 1972 (University of Bristol). The variation of memory with time information appearing during a lecture. Studies in Adult Education, 1, 57-62.

200 Timmel, G.B. 1954 A study of the relationship between a method of teaching a college course in mental hygiene and change in student adjustment status. Unpublished doctoral dissertation, Cornell University Dissertation Abstracts, 1955, Vol.15, No.90.

127 Tobias, S. 1968 Dimensions of teachers' attitudes towards instructional media. American Educational Research Journal, Vol.5, No.1, 91-98.

127 Tobias, S. 1969 Effects of attitudes to programmed instruction and other media on achievement from programmed materials. Audio-Visual Communication Review, Vol.17, 299-306.

124 Tobin, M.J. 1968 Technical education and industrial training. Educational Technology, Vol.10, No.11, 442-444.

49,54 Tomlinson, R.W.S., Pettingale, K.W., McKerron, C., and Anderson, J. 1973 A report of the final MB examination of London University. British Journal of Medical Education, Vol.7, 7-9.

79 Trent, J.W., and Craise, J.L. 1967 Commitment and conformity in the college. Journal of Social Issues, Vol.23, No.3, 34-51.

49 Trimble, O.C. 1934 The oral examination, its validity and reliability. School and Society, Vol.39, cited by Cox, R.C. 1967 Examinations and Higher Education: A survey of the literature. Universities Quarterly, June 1967, 292-340.

261 Tyler, R.W. 1949 Basic principles of curriculum instruction, Chicago.

254 Unruh, W.R. 1971 The modality and validity of cues to lecture effectiveness, in Westbury, I., and Bellack,A. (eds) Research into classroom processes, Teachers' College Press.

172 Uren, O. 1968 The use of texts in language skill development - some problems, in Innovations and Experiments in University Teaching Methods, University Teaching Methods Research Unit, University of London, 50-55.

162 Vaizey, J., Newton, E., and Morris, K. 1971 The costs of new educational technologies, Lisbon, Portugal, Centro de Economia e Financas, Gulbenkian Institute of Science, Gulbenkian Foundation.

158 Van Det Voorde, H.W., and Fraleigh, C.M. 1971 Evaluation by comparison of two methods of teaching dental students oral physiotherapy techniques. Journal of Dental Education, 35, 549-550.

117 Vernon, M.D. 1946 Learning from graphical material. British Journal of Psychology, Vol.36, Part 3, 145-158.

119 Vernon, M.D. 1951 Learning and understanding. Quarterly Journal of Experimental Psychology, Vol.3, 19-23.

119 Vernon, M.D. 1952 The use and value of graphical methods of presenting quantitative data. Occupational Psychology, Vol.26, 22-24, and 96-100.

119 Vernon, M.D. 1953 The value of pictorial illustration. British Journal of Educational Psychology, Vol.23, 180-187.

119 Vernon, M.D. 1954 The instruction of children by pictorial illustration. British Journal of Educational Psychology, Vol.24, 171-179.

119 Vernon, M.D. 1954 The value of graphical material. Medical and Biological Illustration, Vol.4, No.4,203-212.

71,151 Vernon, P.E., and Parry, J.B. 1949 Personnel selection in the British Forces. University of London Press.

133 Verreck, W.A. 1971 Aanullende Gegens op het T.H. Report WE 71-12. (Supplement to TH Report WE-71-12) Mimeo, Eindhoven, Technological University.

Verstraeten, A. 1967 New orientation in higher education. Social Action, Vol.17, No.5, 365-375.

169 Vinacke, W.E. 1957 Some variables in buzz sessions. Journal of Social Psychology, Vol.45, 25-33.

152 Wakeford, R.E. 1972 (British Medical Association). Preparing audio-tape recordings for individual study: Notes on the relative acceptability of different speakers. Medical and Biological Illustration, 22, 13-14.

201 Walford, R. 1972 in Games and Simulations, BBC, London.

42 Wallace, W.F.M. 1974 Effects of exemption from a premedical year: A controlled study. British Journal of Medical Education, 8, 131-137.

54 Walton, H.J. 1968 Sex differences in ability and outlook of Senior Medical Students. British Journal of Medical Education, Vol.2, 156-162.

43,51 Walton, H.J., and Drewery, J. 1967 The objective examination in the evaluation of medical students. British Journal of Medical Education, Vol.1, 225.

71 Ware, J.E., Strassman, H.D., and Naftulin, D.H. 1971 University of Southern California School of Medicine, Los Angeles. A negative relationship between understanding interviewing principles and interview performance. Journal of Medical Education, No.46, 620-622.

22 Watley, D.J. 1968 Career progress of merit scholars. National Merit Scholarship Corporation Research Report, Vol.4, No.1, 23pp.

191 Watson, F.G. 1963 Research on science teaching in Gage, N.L. Handbook of research on teaching. American Educational Research Association, Rand McNally, 1031-1059.

122 Watson, G.D. 1964 Projects of promise. An experiment in programmed learning in Northern Nigeria. West African Journal of Education, February.

254 Webb, W.B., and Nolan, C.Y. Student, supervisor and self-ratings of instructional proficiency. Journal of Educational Psychology, 1955, 46, 42-46.

54 Weinberg, E., and Rooney, J.F. 1973 The academic performance of women students in medical school. Journal of Medical Education, Vol.48, 240-247.

159 Weiss, M.B., Berg, C.R., and Probst, C.O. 1971 (Universi of Illinois College of Dentistry, Medical Center, Chicago). Programmed self instruction of dental techniques: a pilot study. Journal of Dental Education, 35, 455-562.

67,68 Werts, C.E. 1967 Career changes in college. Sociology of Education, Vol.40, No.1, 90-95.

67 Werts, C.E. 1968 Paternal influence on career choice. Journal of Counselling Psychology, Vol.15, No.1, 48-52.

89 Wheeler, D.K. 1967 Curriculum process. Unibooks.

30 Whiteland, J.W.R. 1966 The selection of research students. Universities Quarterley, Vol.21, 44-47.

155 Wilke, W.H. 1934 An experimental comparison of the speech, radio and the printed page as propaganda devices. Archives of Psychology, Vol.25.

34 William, P. 1933 The Northampton Study Composition Scale. Quoted by Cox, R.J. in Examinations in higher education: A survey of the literature. Universities Quarterly, 1967.

61 Wilson, J.D. 1968 Predicting student performance in first year arts and science. Scottish Educational Studies. Glasgow University, Vol.1, No.2, 68-74.

47 Wiseman, S., and Start, K.B. 1965 A follow up of teachers five years after completing their training. British Journal of Educational Psychology, Vol.35, 342-361.

159 Wolker, H. 1955 Das problem der filmwirkung (The problem of the impact of films). Bouvier-Verlag, Bonn, 149pp.

141 Wood, D.N. 1969 Library education for scientists and engineers. Bulletin of Mechanical Engineering Education, Vol.8, No.1, 8-9.

106 World Health Organisation 1972 Aspects of medical education in developing countries. Public Health Paper No.47.

124 Wright, P. 1967 The use of questions in programmed learning. Programmed Learning and Educational Technology, Vol.4, No.2, 103-107.

194 Yager, R.E., Englen, H.B., and Snider, B.C. 1969 Effects of the laboratory and demonstration methods upon outcomes of instruction in secondary biology. Journal of Research in Science Teaching Vol.6, 76-86.

125 Yoakam, G.A. 1955 Basal reading instruction. McGraw Hill, New York.

86 Young, M.F.D.(ed) 1971 Knowledge and control. Collier MacMillan.

49 Young, S., and Gillespie, G. 1972 Experience with the multiple-choice paper in the Primary Fellowship Examination in Glasgow. British Journal of Medical Education, Vol.6, 44-52.

INDEX